The Gospel of John in the Sixteenth Century

The Johannine Exegesis of Wolfgang Musculus

CRAIG S. FARMER

New York   Oxford
OXFORD UNIVERSITY PRESS
1997

Oxford University Press

Oxford   New York
Athens   Auckland   Bangkok   Bogota   Bombay   Buenos Aires
Calcutta   Cape Town   Dar es Salaam   Delhi   Florence   Hong Kong
Istanbul   Karachi   Kuala Lumpur   Madras   Madrid   Melbourne
Mexico City   Nairobi   Paris   Singapore   Taipei   Tokyo   Toronto

and associated companies in
Berlin   Ibadan

Library of Congress Cataloging-in-Publication Data
Farmer, Craig S. (Craig Steven), 1961–
The Gospel of John in the sixteenth century : the Johannine
exegesis of Wolfgang Musculus / Craig S. Farmer.
p.   cm. —(Oxford studies in historical theology)
Includes bibliographical references (p.   ) and index.
ISBN 0-19-509903-6 (cloth)
1. Musculus, Wolfgang, 1497–1563. Commentariorvm in evangelistam
Ioannem.   2. Bible. N.T. John—Criticism, interpretation, etc.—
History—16th century.   I. Title.   II. Series.
BS2615.F35   1997
226.5'06'092—dc20   96-24737

9 8 7 6 5 4 3 2 1

Printed in the United States of America
on acid-free paper

For Richard Luman

Wolfgang Musculus (1497–1563). Courtesy of Bürgerbibliothek Bern.

Preface

In telling the story of the sixteenth-century Protestant Reformation, historians have understandably focused on those figures whose influence was decisive in defining distinct theological traditions. Luther, Melanchthon, Calvin, and Zwingli rightfully hold preeminent place in any attempt to understand the Reformation as a whole because their religious ideas spread far beyond the geographical confines of Wittenberg, Geneva, and Zurich, influencing generations of people throughout Europe and North America. Yet many other lesser-known figures who contributed to the theological legacy of the Reformation period have been left out of the story, figures who were held in high esteem by their contemporaries and whose reformational activities and theological insights were of critical importance in the shaping of the Protestant Reformation.

To a significant degree, this neglect has been addressed in modern scholarship of the last century: the story has been enlarged to include the contributions of figures such as Martin Bucer, Heinrich Bullinger, Johannes Brenz, Balthasar Hubmaier, and Andreas Bodenstein von Karlstadt. Yet in recent years, the momentum to incorporate the contributions of such secondary figures has been slowed somewhat by the focus of social historians who have criticized the preoccupation with personalities and intellectual history as presenting a skewed, top-sided view of the Reformation that fails to take into account its effects on the political, social, and religious life of the masses. This criticism was not completely undeserved, and social historians have made valuable contributions that correct the unbalanced presentation of prior historiography. Nevertheless, no one can rightfully deny that to a great extent the Reformation was indeed about ideas and the personalities who expressed and debated them. The fact that most of these personalities, as churchmen and scholars, occupied a privileged class in sixteenth-century Europe does not belie the influence of their theological protest on popular religion and culture. Just as the story of the Reformation is not exhausted by a recitation of the ideological substance of the protest, so also the Reformation is not understandable in purely socioeconomic terms divorced from the context of the theological debates.

In this book I introduce a figure whose theological writings were widely read and influential in sixteenth-century Europe. His influence, however, is not reflected in modern scholarship; to most students and scholars of the Reformation, Wolfgang Musculus remains a shadowy figure at best. Studies of his life, theology, and political thought have been exceedingly rare, and much work needs to be done in order for us to understand Musculus's contributions as a leading churchman during the turbulent years of the first half of the sixteenth century. I have chosen to introduce Musculus, however, not by writing a critical biography or an overview of his theology but by examining in some detail his interpretation of sacred writ. This might seem to be an odd place to begin when introducing such a little-studied figure as Musculus, but I am convinced that it is a proper place. It was as a commentator on Scripture, after all, that Musculus labored for most of the mature years of his life; his biblical commentaries, judged by their printing history, were exceedingly popular, and in the eyes of his contemporaries Musculus was seen, above all, as a skilled interpreter of the Bible. To examine Musculus as an exegete, therefore, allows us to take him on his own terms and to see him in a role that perhaps defines his central theological contributions to the Reformation era.

This study is defined by a particular method known loosely as the history of exegesis. Fundamentally, this method means that in order for us to understand Musculus as an exegete, we must examine the actual words of his biblical exegesis, and we must do so in context; that is to say, we must study his comments against the sounding board of the antecedent tradition of interpretation. Therefore, in this book I focus on one of Musculus's commentaries, his work on the Gospel of John. I do so by examining his interpretations of the seven miracle stories—the so-called sign passages—in the context of patristic, medieval, and early sixteenth-century exegesis. This approach brings to the fore both the distinctive and the traditional elements in Musculus's work as a biblical commentator. It also allows us to see how Musculus interpreted the fourth gospel in conversation with a host of Johannine interpreters, some of whom addressed different audiences and shared different theological convictions.

Although most of the commentaries I have consulted remain untranslated into English, I have made use of translations when available. Unless noted otherwise, all translations are my own. The following publishers have generously given permission to use extended quotations from copyrighted works: from *The Fathers of the Church*, vol. 33: *Commentary on Saint John the Apostle and Evangelist, Homilies 1–47*, by John Chrysostom, translated by T. A. Goggin, copyright 1957 by The Catholic University of America Press; vol. 78: *Tractates on the Gospel of John 1–10*, by Augustine, translated by John W. Rettig, copyright 1988 by The Catholic University of America Press; vol. 79: *Tractates on the Gospel of John 11–27*, by Augustine, translated by John W. Rettig, copyright 1988 by The Catholic University of America Press; and from *Martini Buceri Opera Latina*, vol. 2: *Enarratio in Evangelion Iohannis*, edited by Irena Backus, copyright 1988 by E. J. Brill.

This book was made possible largely by a generous grant from the Deutscher Akademischer Austauschdienst that enabled me to spend a year in Europe reading medieval and sixteenth-century commentaries on John. I am especially grateful to the helpful staff of the Augsburg Staats- und Stadtbibliothek and to numerous friends at the Gemeinde Christi in Augsburg who provided me and my family with loving support. Several people have read portions of the completed manuscript and offered criticisms that helped me to improve the work significantly: Irena Backus of the Université de Genève, David Steinmetz of Duke University, Lee Magness of Milligan College, and Edwin Tait of Durham, North Carolina. More than anyone, Margaret, my wife of fourteen years, has labored with pen in hand, correcting and editing my prose and challenging me to clarify my thinking and writing. I could not have completed this work without her companionship.

Johnson City, Tennessee   C. S. F.
January 1996

Contents

Introduction   3

ONE
Musculus and the Exegetical Tradition on the Wedding at Cana   11

TWO
Musculus and the Fathers on the Healing of the Ruler's Son   29

THREE
Musculus and the Medieval Commentators on the Feeding
of the Five Thousand   48

FOUR
Musculus and the Humanists on the Miracle at Sea   78

FIVE
Musculus and Sixteenth-Century Catholic Commentators
on the Healing at the Pool of Bethesda   109

SIX
Musculus and the Lutheran Commentators on the Healing
of the Man Born Blind   132

SEVEN
Musculus and the Reformed Commentators
on the Raising of Lazarus   148

Conclusion   178

Notes   183

Selected Bibliography   231

Index   243

The Gospel of John in the Sixteenth Century

Introduction

For over thirty years, Wolfgang Musculus worked as a leader of the religious reformations in the cities of Augsburg and Bern. During that time, he authored a substantial corpus of writings that firmly established his reputation as a first-rate theologian and biblical scholar. One may gain some idea of his popularity as a theologian by examining the printing history of his theological magnum opus, the *Loci communes sacrae theologiae.* First published in 1560, this massive exercise in systematic theology was revised by Musculus for a new edition in 1561. Thereafter printings followed in 1563, 1564, 1567, 1573, and 1599. Furthermore, the work was published in English translation in 1563 and 1578 and in French in 1577, and portions were translated into German in 1618.[1]

In his work as an exegete, Musculus wrote commentaries on Matthew (1544), John (1545), the Psalms (1550), the Decalogue (1553), Genesis (1554), Romans (1555), Isaiah (1557), 1 and 2 Corinthians (1559), Galatians and Ephesians (1561), and Philippians, Colossians, 1 and 2 Thessalonians, and 1 Timothy (1564). All of these works were released in multiple printings, giving evidence of a wide readership that continued long after his death. For example, Musculus's Matthew commentary went through at least nine printings (the last in 1611), and his Psalms commentary was printed at least seven times (the last in 1618) and was translated for an English edition in 1586. His John commentary was similarly successful. The first installment, covering the first seven chapters, was published by the Basel firm of Bartholomäus Westheimer in 1545. The Basel publisher Johann Herwagen then published the entire commentary in 1547 and in the same year released a companion volume to the Westheimer edition containing Musculus's comments on chapters 8–21.[2] Thereafter the book was printed by Herwagen in 1553, 1554, and 1564, by Eusebius Episcopius in 1580, and by Sebastian Henricpetri in 1618.

Through his commentaries, Musculus won fame and honor throughout Europe. He was remembered well into the seventeenth century as a distinguished interpreter

3

of Scripture. The French Oratorian Richard Simon (1638–1712), arguably the great-est biblical scholar of his age, praised Musculus as a scholar who understood the proper way to interpret Scripture.[3] The extent of Musculus's influence as a com-mentator is also attested by his contemporaries. Martin Micron, the Reformed theologian and pastor in Norden, informed Musculus that his commentary on Genesis had been extremely useful to the Protestants in East Frisia. Felix Cruciger, pastor at Secymin and superintendent of the Reformed churches in Little Poland, sent word to Musculus that his "lucubrations on the New Testament" had found a wide and receptive audience among the Protestants there.[4] Musculus's commen-taries seem to have found a similar audience in Scotland, for by 1560 Scottish libraries stocked several of his exegetical works.[5] Guillaume Farel, the Genevan re-former and colleague of John Calvin, wrote from Neufchâtel to Johann Haller in Bern that many people were eager to get their hands on Musculus's new Psalms commentary.[6] Calvin, in the preface to his own Psalms commentary, ranked Musculus's interpretation of the Psalms with Bucer's and noted that Musculus "by his diligence and industry has earned no small praise in the judgment of good men."[7]

Largely on the basis of his reputation as a skilled commentator, Musculus received numerous offers to assume teaching posts throughout Europe. After leaving Augsburg because of the Interim, Musculus received a letter (dated July 17, 1548) from Bernardino Ochino extending an invitation from Thomas Cranmer, arch-bishop of Canterbury, to take a teaching position in London.[8] The invitation was renewed in December of the same year with the added incentives of a generous travel allowance and the opportunity (if Musculus so desired) to lecture at Canterbury. Musculus politely refused because he was expecting to receive an official call from Bern—a call that came in February 1549. Cranmer, however, persistently sought Musculus's services, and in 1551 Musculus received a further invitation to assume the teaching post at Cambridge formerly occupied by Martin Bucer. In the years that followed, Musculus was offered several other honorable positions. The Elector Otto Henry of the Palatinate, to whom Musculus had dedicated the Herwagen edi-tion of his John commentary, wrote Musculus in 1552 offering a teaching position in Neuburg an der Donau. In 1553 Thomas Erastus pleaded with Musculus to join him on the faculty at the University of Heidelberg. Additional calls came from Strasbourg, Augsburg, and Marburg.[9] Persistent rumors also circulated that Musculus was eagerly sought in Poland.[10] Musculus refused all of these calls, usually pleading his age or the ill health of his family, but the evidence clearly indicates that he was recognized throughout Europe for his gifts as a scholar.[11]

REVIEW OF SCHOLARSHIP ON MUSCULUS

Despite his influence and importance in the Reformation period, Musculus has re-ceived little attention in modern scholarship. Only two studies have appeared that focus exclusively on Musculus's thought. In 1933, Paul Josiah Schwab published a condensed version of his Yale dissertation on Musculus's view of religious tolerance. Although the study is narrowly focused, Schwab makes use of a broad spectrum of Musculus's writings, including the commentary literature, theological treatises, letters, and the *Loci communes*, to prove that Musculus expressed a more moderate and tolerant view of religious dissent than most of his fellow reformers.[12] The second work, published in 1959 by Richard Bäumlin, is an article-length study of Musculus's view of natural law. Working primarily from the *Loci communes*, Bäumlin demonstrates that Musculus appropriates thomistic elements in his theory of natural law and that this theory is the key to his distinctive legal justification of magisterial control of the territorial church.[13] In addition to these two studies, a book appeared in 1953 by Helmut Kreßner, who devoted a chapter to Musculus's theoretical justification in the *Loci communes* (chapter 69, "De magistratibus") of the complete political supremacy of civil authority in ecclesiastical affairs. This theory influenced the development of Anglican ecclesiology via John Whitgift and Thomas Erastus.[14]

Tangential investigations of topics from Musculus's *Loci communes* have appeared in other works devoted to the history of dogma.[15] In particular, several studies have noted Musculus's contribution to the development of federal theology.[16] A work on the political thought of Thomas Erastus has argued for his indebtedness to Musculus's notion of the Christian state and presents a summary of Musculus's teaching on the subject.[17] A study on Martin Micron has also pointed to the influence of Musculus's thought.[18] In the history of exegesis, several works have appeared that include Musculus's exegesis in studies of particular biblical passages.[19] His exegesis has also been examined in studies that utilize the history of exegesis to illuminate the thought of John Calvin.[20]

The most important biographical source for Musculus is the work written by his son Abraham Musculus (1434–1591), minister at the Münster in Bern, and published in 1595 by Abraham's son Wolfgang Musculus (1556–1625), minister at Höchstetten.[21] In the nineteenth century two biographical studies of Musculus were published, both heavily dependent on the biography by Abraham Musculus. The first work is a book-length biography by Ludwig Grote, which, for all its shortcomings (including an overly romanticized portrayal and numerous factual errors), still holds the distinction of being the first modern biographical study of Musculus.[22] In his tenth chapter, "Musculus als Dichter," Grote presents all the poems and hymns attributed to Musculus, although he admits that Musculus's authorship cannot be firmly established for many of the hymns.[23] The second work, authored by the Basel professor Wilhelm T. Streuber, is a shorter but more solid treatment of Musculus's life. The work was incomplete at the time of Streuber's death but was edited and completed by Streuber's student Ludwig Lauterburg and published in the Berner Taschenbuch series.[24] Streuber presents a more sober assessment of Musculus than Grote and makes use of other source materials, particularly Musculus's diary of the events leading to the Wittenberg Concord of 1536.[25]

The works of Grote and Streuber remain the standard biographical references for Musculus, but no study on Musculus can now afford to neglect the biographical sketch recently published in 1988 by the Bernese professor Rudolf Dellsperger.[26] Making use of Abraham Musculus's biography, Theodor Beza's literary portrait,[27] numerous letters, and other source materials, Dellsperger presents an excellent critical study of Musculus's career. His copious footnotes alone summarize almost all the work that has been done on Musculus to date.

Aspects of Musculus's career are also treated in the various histories of the Reformation in Augsburg and Bern. The most significant work on Augsburg is Friedrich Roth's magisterial *Augsburgs Reformationsgeschichte*, which gives extensive treatment to Musculus's reformational activities.[28] For Bern, the most important studies are those of Henri Vuilleumier and Kurt Guggisberg.[29] Various aspects of Musculus's career are also treated in biographical studies of other Reformation figures such as Martin Bucer and Caspar Schwenckfeld.[30]

BIOGRAPHICAL SKETCH OF WOLFGANG MUSCULUS

The custom among aspiring scholars in early sixteenth-century Europe was to adopt a latinized form for their name.[31] Wolfgang not only latinized his family name of Meusslin but also adopted the Roman name for Dieuze, the small village in Lorraine where he was born on September 8, 1497; thus, he arrived at the professional name Wolfgang Musculus Dusanus.[32] In his youth, Musculus attended school in Dieuze and in several Alsatian towns before entering a Benedictine monastery in 1512 in the village of Lixheim in Lorraine. As a monk, Musculus eventually acquired ordination and shared in the preaching duties in the monastery and in the neighboring towns until 1527, when he abandoned the religious life.

During his years in the monastery, Musculus had become familiar with the writings of Martin Luther, whose criticisms of ecclesiastical abuses found a receptive audience in the Lixheim cloister. Musculus's sermons took on a decidedly pro-Lutheran tone, so much so that he became known in the region as "the Lutheran monk." Only when the authorities began to clamp down on such dissenting voices did Musculus's position at Lixheim become untenable. With the blessing of his prior, Musculus renounced his religious oaths and headed for Strasbourg with his future bride, Margaretha Barth, the prior's niece.

In Strasbourg Musculus's reputation as a talented preacher won him the attention of Martin Bucer and Bürgermeister Jacob Sturm, who assigned him a preaching office in the neighboring village of Dorlitzheim. On weekdays Musculus worked in Strasbourg as Bucer's personal secretary. After a year, the Strasbourg council placed Musculus on the city payroll as an assistant to Matthäus Zell, preacher at the Münster. During the two years in which Musculus held this position, he attended the theological lectures of Bucer and Wolfgang Capito, began to study Hebrew, and continued to undertake preaching missions in outlying towns.

In early 1531 Musculus moved to the free imperial city of Augsburg, where he assumed a preaching post at the Church of the Holy Cross (Heilig-Kreuz-Kirche). The city was being torn apart by inner conflict among competing religious parties—the Zwinglians, Lutherans, Catholics, and Anabaptists—and the council had appealed to Bucer for preachers who would help to defuse the volatile situation.[33] Musculus quickly rose to a position of prominence among the Augsburg ministers, entering into religious discussions with the Lutherans on the thorny issue of the Lord's Supper and serving as a delegate at the Wittenberg Conference in 1536. He also represented Augsburg at the conferences in Worms (1540) and Regensburg (1541). In 1544 the council sent Musculus to Donauwörth to introduce reform, a task he accomplished in three months. Regarding the Anabaptists, Musculus urged the council toward a more lenient position and initiated a program of prison visitation that resulted in several public recantations. He was less charitable toward the Catholics and urged the council to restrict the celebration of the Mass. In 1537 the council finally forbade all Catholic ceremonies, and much of the Catholic clergy fled the town. Musculus then assumed the preaching post at the cathedral church (Dom), a position he held until he left Augsburg in 1548.

Musculus's departure was prompted by the city council's decision to accept the terms of the Interim. The council had little other choice. The Schmalkald League had been defeated in battle in 1547, imperial troops were in the city, and the Catholic clergy were resuming their ecclesiastical offices by imperial mandate. Musculus fled to Zurich, where he was received by Heinrich Bullinger, and then went to Basel for a meeting with his publisher Johann Herwagen. He was reunited with his family in Constance and then proceeded to St. Gallen, where he remained for several months due to the ill health of his wife and children. In the fall of 1548 Musculus moved his family to Zurich, where he remained until the following spring, when he was appointed to succeed Simon Sulzer as professor of theology in Bern.

Until his death on August 30, 1563, Musculus worked primarily as a scholar, publishing numerous theological and exegetical works and lecturing in the Protestant "Hohe Schule," which had been newly established in 1528 on the model of the Zurich "Prophezey."[34] He served as an ecclesiastical adviser and helped to mediate in the incessant disputes between Calvin and the Bernese clergy. Musculus rarely mounted the pulpit because he never felt comfortable with the local dialect, and he refused the council's offers of a permanent preaching post. Musculus had closed the chapter on his pastoral ministry in Augsburg and was devoted now to a life of scholarship and helping other young men prepare for the ministry. Midway through his commentary on 1 Timothy, Musculus succumbed to a fever and died a few days before his sixty-sixth birthday. He fathered a preaching dynasty in the canton; six of Musculus's sons entered the ministry, and generation after generation of Müslins assumed roles of ecclesiastical leadership well into the nineteenth century.[35]

The primary goal of this study is to characterize Musculus's work as a biblical commentator by examining in detail his commentary on the Gospel of John. To accomplish this goal, I will compare his exegesis of the seven miracle stories—the so-called signs—with the exegesis of his predecessors and contemporaries. By placing his comments in the context of the exegetical tradition, it is possible to establish the distinctive features of his commentary and the extent of his indebtedness to traditional interpretations. This study will show that Musculus was a remarkably thorough and skillful exegete whose commentary reveals a judicious appropriation of patristic and medieval exegetical ideas and methods of interpretation, a critical use of humanist biblical scholarship, and an emphasis on moral and allegorical modes of exposition—an emphasis that distinguishes his exegesis from that of most of his contemporaries.

By selecting the sign passages for exegetical comparison, I am not suggesting that Musculus knew anything of a sign source in the Bultmannian sense. Rather, this group of pericopes serves as a convenient set of passages on which to focus a comparative exegetical study. However, this selection is not purely arbitrary, for it is in the miracle stories that much of the action of John's gospel takes place, and as such the commentator on these passages is often faced with more exegetical questions than the commentator on the purely didactic or discursive sections of the gospel. Each of the sign passages tells a story, and therefore the commentator must explain not only the meaning of Jesus' sayings but also the meaning of his actions. Questions of motivation also arise: Why does Jesus act in this way and not in another? What prompts the behavior and statements of the secondary figures in the stories? How should one characterize these figures? It is the storylike quality of the sign passages that allows more room for imaginative interpretive decisions, yielding a more interesting and diverse spectrum of interpretations in the exegetical tradition.

In selecting commentaries for comparison, I have chosen works that predate Musculus's own commentary. I have included both the works he consulted in composing his commentary (as indicated by his explicit citations) and the works that were available to him in published form. Thus, for example, I have not included Bonaventure's John commentary because it was not published until after Musculus's and because Musculus gives no evidence of having read it. Several of the works consulted here as commentaries did not begin as commentaries at all but rather as homilies (as in the case of Augustine and Chrysostom) or lectures (as in the case of Zwingli and Melanchthon) on the fourth gospel. But because these works provide a continuous interpretation of the entire gospel and because they entered the stream of the exegetical tradition as single works on the gospel, they may rightfully be considered commentaries on John.

This study proceeds as follows. In the first chapter, I compare Musculus's interpretation of the first sign passage with a cross-sectional sampling of the entire antecedent exegetical tradition. In each of the subsequent chapters, I focus on a different sign passage, placing Musculus's exegesis in the context of a different segment of the exegetical tradition: chapter 2, patristic commentators; chapter 3, medieval commentators; chapter 4, humanist commentators; chapter 5, sixteenth-century Roman Catholic commentators; chapter 6, Lutheran commentators; and chapter 7, Reformed commentators. Each of these contexts brings distinctive features of Musculus's exegesis into relief, contributing to a general picture of his work as a biblical commentator.

In adopting this comparative approach to Musculus's John commentary, my primary concern is with the interplay of exegetical ideas and with the similarities and differences of interpretive method. It is not my concern to establish whether or not Musculus actually used each of the commentaries brought to bear on this study. The question of direct influence, however, is not completely ignored. When I can establish Musculus's reliance on another commentator, I do so; but I never assume that the similarity of an idea can serve alone as an adequate criterion for proving dependence. For the purposes of this study, the central question is to what degree Musculus makes use of the methods of his forebears and contemporaries in the exposition of Scripture and to what degree he repeats, rejects, or modifies the traditional interpretations of the Johannine signs.

This study will show that the exegetical tradition exerts a powerful influence on Musculus's commentary and that much of what he says is rooted in the ideas of the past. This point is significant because the exegesis of the Protestant reformers has often been characterized in general terms for its radical discontinuity with the tradition. Take, for example, the statement in a popular introduction to the history of biblical interpretation: "[Catholic exegesis] interprets the Bible by the tradition of the church. Protestant exegesis makes a fresh start, often overturning the accumulated decisions of centuries."[36] While there is an element of truth in this statement, it contributes nevertheless to the general impression that the Protestant commentators worked in an exegetical vacuum. In the case of Musculus, at least, this is demonstrably false.

This study will also show that Musculus makes constructive use of traditional methods of spiritual exegesis. In particular, he shows an extraordinary predilection for moral interpretation, a feature that is so pronounced that it is arguably the distinctive mark of Musculus's exegesis. He also makes liberal use of allegorical exposition, sometimes repeating or modifying traditional allegories and at other times creating his own. This feature, which resonates with the medieval and patristic commentaries, distinguishes his interpretation from most of his contemporaries, who are generally more restrained in their reading of the symbolic meanings of the biblical text. Yet Musculus cannot simply be classified as a medieval commentator because this study also demonstrates that he makes sophisticated use of the critical biblical scholarship of the humanists, particularly in matters relating to translation and textual problems. The complex confluence of forces at work in Musculus's John commentary comes to light in the chapters that follow.

ONE

Musculus and the Exegetical Tradition on the Wedding at Cana

In the course of this study, I will examine Musculus's exegesis in a series of contexts that illuminate the distinctive and traditional elements in his work as a commentator on the fourth gospel. Subsequent chapters will explore his comments against the sounding board of various subgroups within the exegetical tradition. Here, however, I place Musculus's exegesis of the first sign passage (Jn 2:1–11) in the context of a cross-sectional sampling of the entire antecedent exegetical tradition. I want to explain why this is a valuable exercise for our understanding of Musculus and the exegetical tradition.

By examining Musculus's comments against the full stream of Johannine interpretation, we are better able to evaluate the history of exegetical ideas. What may at first glance appear to be an unusual or insightful comment by Musculus may prove to be a commonplace in sixteenth-century exegesis; further investigation may show that this sixteenth-century commonplace is itself a variation on a theme expressed by medieval commentators who, in turn, are dependent on the insights of their ancient forebears. In short, there is a remarkable stability in the exegetical tradition that manifests itself in a contextual study of Musculus's biblical interpretation. By taking into account the entire sweep of this tradition, we are also able to see the development of new concerns and insights in the interpretive history of a given text; that is to say, we are able to discern not only the stability of the tradition but also the evolution of interpretive ideas.

However, to investigate and describe Musculus's exegesis in the context of the entire antecedent tradition poses serious methodological problems in a study that seeks to introduce the interpretive history of considerable portions of the biblical text. The vast amount of exegetical material can easily plunge the historian into an ocean of data that makes coherent and systematic analysis extremely difficult. Therefore, in order to study the interpretive history of a biblical text, historians have usually imposed certain limits on their materials that make it possible to write about the history of exegesis. Frequently, historians have limited the amount of biblical material to be investigated to a single verse, or phrase, or word of the scriptural text. Historians who have studied larger portions of the biblical text have often imposed a different kind of limit; they confine their studies chronologically to a certain period in the history of exegesis. Indeed, the story of the wedding at Cana (Jn 2:1–11) has been thoroughly investigated by historians of exegesis, but all of these studies have focused exclusively on patristic interpretations.[1] No study has attempted in one sweep to survey patristic, medieval, and sixteenth-century exegesis.

In this study I have imposed two limits that make it possible to describe Musculus's exegesis of the story of the wine miracle at Cana in the context of the antecedent tradition. First, I have limited the number of commentaries under investigation to nine of the most influential expositions of the fourth gospel prior to Musculus. From the Church Fathers, I include the interpretations of John Chrysostom (347–407), Augustine of Hippo (354–430), and Cyril of Alexandria (d. 444). From the many medieval John commentaries, I have selected those of Hugh of St. Cher (ca. 1195–1263), Thomas Aquinas (1225–1274), and Denis the Carthusian (1402/3–1471). Finally, from the sixteenth-century commentators on John, I include the interpretations of Desiderius Erasmus (ca. 1466–1536), Philip Melanchthon (1497–1560), and Martin Bucer (1491–1551).

Second, I have not attempted to present an exhaustive study of all of the questions that have troubled interpreters of the Cana pericope. Rather, I have limited my focus to the central exegetical problems identified by Musculus, and I have examined his discussion of these problems in light of the previous commentaries. Musculus's exegesis of the wedding at Cana can be divided into three main topics that provide a framework for the present study. First, he discusses the method Jesus used to perform the miraculous transformation of water into wine. Second, Musculus discusses the troubling problems associated with the encounter between Mary and Jesus in the story. And third, he treats the moral lessons of the story on the subjects of marriage and drunkenness.

None of the topics that Musculus treats are completely new; they all receive attention to greater or lesser degrees by the patristic, medieval, and sixteenth-century commentators who precede him. It is possible, therefore, to demonstrate the relationship of Musculus's comments to the matrix of the exegetical tradition on the Cana pericope and to characterize his understanding of this gospel story in reference to the understanding of his predecessors.

THE METHOD OF THE MIRACLE

Throughout the exegetical tradition, commentators have focused considerable attention on the method Jesus used to produce wine at the wedding feast in Cana. This emphasis is understandable since the gospel text itself carefully highlights the procedure adopted by Jesus in performing his first miraculous sign. In the text Jesus orders the servants to fill six stone urns with water. He then instructs them to draw out some of the liquid and to deliver it to the steward of the banquet. Surely, most commentators argue, Jesus could have used any number of procedures to produce wine; therefore there must be a particular and deliberate rationale for the procedure he chose.

According to Musculus, the ultimate goal of the miracle was to produce faith in the disciples and spectators. In order to facilitate the production of faith, any possible suspicion concerning the authenticity of the miracle had to be minimized. Therefore, Jesus deliberately chose a method that would establish the miraculous nature of the event beyond a doubt. A miracle, Musculus argues, must be unambiguously extraordinary in order to produce astonishment and admiration in the spectators; only then can the miracle be a true sign, something that points to a greater reality. In this case the sign signified that Jesus was endowed with divine power, and thus it produced faith in the disciples.[2]

The water pots have two characteristics that help to make the miracle more obvious. First, since they are related to Jewish ceremonial purification (verse 6), the pots are associated with water, and water only. Musculus argues that "for the proof of the miracle" (*ad evidentiam miraculi*) Jesus deliberately made wine "not in wine vessels, but in those water pots, whose perpetual use was of water."[3] Musculus's explanation here echoes Chrysostom, who notes that the ceremonial function of the water pots would preclude any suspicion that the servants had poured water into containers holding wine dregs and had simply mixed the solution into thin wine.[4] This observation is a standard part of the exegetical tradition and is found, usually with a reference to Chrysostom, in the commentaries of Thomas Aquinas, Hugh of St. Cher, and Erasmus.[5] The second characteristic of the water pots noted by Musculus is their capacity. Although he expresses uncertainty regarding the precise volume indicated by the term *metreta*, he assumes (rightly) that the water pots had a large capacity.[6] The Evangelist intentionally mentions the volume of the pots, Musculus argues, in order "to express the excellence of the miracle." The fact that Jesus ordered all six water pots to be filled to the brim "was evidence of certain and plentiful divine power and also of liberality." The magnitude of the miraculous product would also help to eliminate any suspicion of trickery.[7] Once again, Musculus repeats here a theme expressed by earlier commentators. Thomas, for example, argues that the capacity of the water pots would make it "abundantly clear that the water in such jars could be changed into wine only by divine power."[8] Erasmus argues that it would have been impossible for jars of such size and weight to have been brought in secretly.[9] Like Erasmus, Musculus discusses the difficulties associated with the transportation of such vessels. The number and weight of the jars are evidence, he suggests, that the wedding may have taken place in some kind of civic building, since it would have been too difficult to transport so many heavy objects to a private dwelling.[10]

As the water pots function to verify the miracle, so also the servants and the steward serve as impartial witnesses to the occurrence of the miracle. According to Musculus, Jesus utilized the servants so that they might provide unbiased testimony concerning the source of the miracle. Similarly, since the steward was unaware of the miracle, he provided objective testimony concerning the wine's goodness. At every step of the unfolding of the miracle, "the order had to be preserved by which the miracle would be rendered more conspicuous."[11] Musculus's exegesis is certainly not innovative on this point, for Chrysostom, Thomas, Hugh, and Erasmus offer the same explanation of the roles played by the servants and the steward. However, unlike Musculus, they emphasize the unique prerogative of the steward to judge the wine. For unlike the guests, who had drunk freely and were in no condition to render a sound judgment, it was his duty to remain sober in order to manage the wedding party.[12] Additionally, Erasmus suggests that the steward must have been something of a wine connoisseur; therefore they bring the wine to his judicious palate in order to receive an expert verdict concerning the wine.[13]

Musculus is uneasy with the portrayal of a drunken gathering, and perhaps for that reason he does not emphasize the sobriety of the steward. Instead, Musculus emphasizes the contribution of the steward and servants as indicative of God's "method of operating" (*operandi rationem*) in the world. Although God is certainly able to perform his will without any human assistance, he has graciously allowed human beings to contribute to his purposes. Using an agricultural metaphor, Musculus states: "He arranged it thus that we might plant and water, but he himself adds the growth."[14]

While the use of the water pots, the servants, and the steward all add weight to the veracity of the miracle, there remains one puzzling aspect of Jesus' modus operandi that Musculus addresses. Why did Jesus not create the wine from nothing? Wouldn't the miracle have been more marvelous and more evident if Jesus had created wine without the use of a material medium?[15] This question, first raised by Chrysostom, is a standard component in traditional exegesis of the Cana story. And the solution offered by Chrysostom finds its way into many medieval commentaries on this text. According to Chrysostom, Jesus wisely chose to use a material medium in many of his miracles because creation from nothing, although in his power, would have been too incredible. Jesus "deliberately curtailed the greatness of His miracles so that they might be more readily accepted."[16] However, Chrysostom argues that a second motive was also involved. Jesus wanted to establish the divine origin of created nature in order to refute the Manichaean heresy. Jesus proved that he himself is lord of nature, for "he did in an instant at the wedding what takes place in nature over a long period of time."[17] Thomas and Hugh repeat Chrysostom's explanations, but Thomas adds a third reason: "Christ made the wine from water, and not from nothing, in order to show that he was not laying down an entirely new doctrine and rejecting the old, but was fulfilling the old."[18]

In his discussion of Jesus' reason for using water, Musculus reiterates the solution offered by Chrysostom. If Jesus had simply created wine from nothing, the miracle would not have been believable. Such a miracle would have immediately been vulnerable to the suspicion of magic.[19] However, Musculus argues that another reason is also at work. Certain things, such as the earth, the sea, and the sky, were created by God *ex nihilo*. Wine, however is not produced like these "new creatures" (*nova creatura*) but is the secondary product of another element of creation. Therefore, Jesus created wine from water in order to preserve what Musculus calls the "order of divine working" (*ordo divini opificii*) for, in fact, the conversion of water into wine is a miracle which occurs with regularity in nature.[20] Here Musculus echoes Augustine, who argues that Jesus was merely duplicating in the water pots the same miracle he performs in grape vines every year: "For just as what the attendants put into the water jars was turned into wine by the Lord's effort so also what the clouds pour down is turned into wine by the effort of the same Lord. But that does not amaze us because it happens every year; by its regularity it has lost its wonderment."[21] Likewise, Hugh states that Jesus wanted to demonstrate "that it is he himself who, daily through increments of time, changes water into wine in nature in the middle of the vine."[22] Following the same reasoning, Musculus notes that the conversion of water into wine is not extraordinary in itself since it occurs regularly in nature. What makes the Cana miracle truly miraculous is the speed at which the mutation takes place. Jesus simply accelerates an ordinary process that occurs naturally in the created order.[23]

JESUS AND MARY

In his discussion of the method of Jesus' miracle, Musculus enters into a conversation that takes place, for the most part, in patristic and medieval commentaries. Erasmus briefly discusses a few of the traditional topics, while Melanchthon and Bucer are completely silent concerning this whole sphere of exegetical problems. However, in his treatment of the role of Mary, Musculus deals with a series of problems that are discussed by almost all commentators on the Cana narrative.

The gospel text presents a puzzling drama between Mary and her son that cries out for exegetical explanation. Mary, having noticed the deficiency of wine, reports this problem to Jesus, who seems to reject her with a puzzling reply: "What is it to me and to you, woman? My hour has not yet come."[24] Not dissuaded, Mary patiently instructs the servants to await his command. The problems raised by the text are numerous. Why was Mary at the wedding? What motivated Mary to appeal to Jesus? Why does Jesus reply so rudely (seemingly) to her innocent remark? As Augustine puts it: "Has he come to the wedding for the purpose of teaching the disparagement of mothers?"[25] What does Jesus' enigmatic remark mean? And why, if his hour had not come, does Jesus proceed to remedy the situation? The discussion of these and other questions raises a host of mariological, christological, and theological issues that occupy a significant portion of traditional exegesis on the Cana narrative.

The very presence of Mary at the wedding is the occasion for speculation in medieval exegesis about her relationship to the bride and groom. Hugh and Denis discuss the possibility that John the Evangelist himself was the groom and the nephew of Mary and that Jesus was therefore attending the wedding of his cousin. This explanation, found also in other medieval commentaries, is rooted in a prologue to John's gospel that was traditionally attributed to Jerome.[26] The problem for many medieval expositors is to reconcile this tradition with another seemingly contradictory tradition: namely, that John the Evangelist was a virgin. Hugh argues that Jerome's identification of the groom as John, the nephew of Mary, is not probable because John had committed himself to a life of perpetual virginity.[27] But even if John was the groom, he did not abandon his commitment to virginity. He may have temporarily lost the virginity of mind (a virginity that may be restored by penance) by consenting to marry, but he never lost the virginity of the flesh (a virginity that, once lost, may never be restored).[28] Denis accepts the identification of John as the groom and nephew of Mary and asserts that Jesus came to the wedding on a kind of rescue mission. Before John could consummate the marriage, Jesus persuaded him to enter the religious life.[29]

Sixteenth-century commentaries include little, if any, speculation about the identity of the groom. However, the medieval interpretation is not unknown. Bucer remarks: "It is silly to affirm that John was this groom."[30] All that one can assert, according to Bucer, is that Mary must have known the people at the wedding. Erasmus and Musculus affirm that Mary was related to the groom or bride but offer no speculation regarding the nature of that relationship.[31] According to Musculus, while Mary was invited by virtue of her kinship, Jesus was invited for another reason. His invitation came from Nathanael, whose encounter with Jesus took place immediately before the Cana story (Jn 1:43–51) and whose home town was Cana (Jn 21:2).[32]

Another locus of exegetical discussion centers on the question of Mary's motives in appealing to her son. The harsh reply of Jesus seems to suggest that Mary in some respect erred and therefore deserved correction. Yet most of the commentators are very reluctant to ascribe anything but purity of motivation to Mary's actions. Chrysostom, however, argues that she may have been prompted by human motives that necessitated Jesus' sharp retort. Perhaps, he suggests, she felt that Jesus owed her special obedience since she was his mother. She forgot that her proper place was to revere him as her lord. Thus, Jesus reminds Mary of her station and offers an example of the proper attitude toward parents. In general, parents must be obeyed but not when they stand in the way of a spiritual good.[33]

Most commentators are reluctant to follow Chrysostom down this path. Jesus' reply must be explained, but that explanation should not be sought in a depreciation of Mary's motives.[34] Thomas therefore asserts that Mary's motives flowed out of her kindness and mercy. She simply wanted the trouble to be relieved. In addition, she indicates her reverence for Jesus by the way she makes her request. She does not tell him what to do or how to do it but merely expresses the need for more wine. In this way she sets an example of the proper method of supplication in prayer. Interpreted mystically, Thomas argues that Mary's petition reveals her role as mediatrix: "It is through her intercession that one is joined to Christ through grace."[35] Hugh also ascribes purity of motivation to Mary. Mary knew that it was not necessary to inform Jesus about the situation. However, she wanted to demonstrate two noble things: her compassion and his power. Her entreaty is evidence of her special compassion for the poor, since the failure of the wine indicates the poverty of the families involved.[36] Denis also praises the compassion of Mary, who sympathized with the disgrace of the bride and groom. She, who sinned neither mortally nor venially, had only pure motives. Her behavior is a wonderful example of her intercessory role. Since she ran to the assistance of their corporeal needs without even being asked, even more eagerly will she offer her compassion and assistance to those who invoke her concerning spiritual needs. By using the fewest words possible in her entreaty, she demonstrates her virtue and prudence by simply relinquishing the situation to the will of her son. For Denis, however, she gives an example not of prayer but of monastic obedience: "We are taught to place our situation and need simply and modestly with our superiors, and to relinquish to their power what should be done."[37] According to Erasmus, Mary was compassionate for two reasons. She empathized with the shame and embarrassment of the groom, who had not prepared liberally enough for the banquet. And she was also concerned that this lack of foresight would dampen the merriment of the party. Mary had the right as a mother to seek assistance from her son, and she indicates her reverence for him by the manner of her request.[38] Bucer also wants to exclude the possibility of any baseness of motivation in Mary's petition. She was not looking for an opportunity to become famous from the miracles of her son. On the contrary, one must attribute her behavior "to her love and humanity rather than to an eagerness for vain glory."[39] In addition, the manner of her request is an example not only of faith but also "of praying with few words" (*verbis paucis orantis*). She simply and succinctly states the need, and by doing so she offers a model of the soul praying out of faith.[40]

In his interpretation of Mary's role in the Cana narrative, Musculus follows the general pattern established by the antecedent exegetical tradition. The text could certainly fuel an attack on Catholic mariology, but Musculus strictly limits his polemical remarks. Mary's words and behavior are admirable and establish a model of compassion and faith. While her petition is certainly not regarded as an earthly representation of her heavenly role as mediatrix, it is regarded as a beautiful example of faithful prayer on the part of the believer.

For Musculus, Mary's concern for the troubled circumstances of the banquet reveals her kindness and compassion. She was sincerely troubled by the potential disgrace of the groom. Her concern for his predicament gives an example of the compassion that all Christians should feel for anyone in need. Christian compassion is not mere sentimentalism but expresses itself in a way modeled by the Virgin—namely in the confidence that Christ is willing and able to come to the assistance of those in need. Therefore, Christians should imitate Mary in bringing the needs of others to Christ.[41]

According to Musculus, the simplicity of Mary's request teaches two moral lessons. First, one must not exaggerate the excess or intemperance of those experiencing want. Mary does not come to Jesus as a complainer or accuser; "She does not say: They squandered and intemperately consumed all the wine. But [she says] simply and modestly: They have no wine."[42] The potential disgrace of the groom does not necessarily indicate his culpability in the shortfall of wine. Neither the groom nor the guests, who perhaps drank a little too freely at the beginning of the banquet, should be blamed for the predicament. Rather, just as no one is blamed for the blindness of the man in John 9, so also the lack of wine should be seen merely as an occasion for the revelation of God's glory. Second, Musculus argues that Mary gives an example of how to make needs known to Christ. It is not necessary or fitting to attempt to persuade the Lord with human arguments; in petitioning Christ, one should simply state the need. Mary does not insult Jesus by giving him reasons for heeding her request, but rather she states simply, "They have no wine."

Although Mary's request is praiseworthy, it is her response to Jesus that is emphasized by Musculus. Here is revealed what Musculus terms the "admirable philosophy of the Virgin" (*admirabilis philosophia Virginis*). In this "philosophy" there are three points of emphasis. First, although Mary was treated rather harshly by her son, she did not grieve or answer back but patiently received his "scolding" (*obiurgatio*).[43] Other commentators also eagerly reassure their readers that Mary did not take offense at the words of Jesus. Hugh states that she was "not disturbed or irritated by the response of her son; but rather [she was] confident concerning his power and piety."[44] According to Denis, she continued to believe that Jesus loved and honored her, and she did not receive his words as if said in scolding.[45] Erasmus maintains that Mary was "not offended by the harsh response of her son, nor anxious in the meantime concerning his goodness and power."[46] The theme is repeated by Melanchthon, who praises Mary for her confidence and lack of indignation.[47] Following the general course set by these commentators, Musculus highlights Mary's humble acceptance of the rebuke in order to make a moral application. Mary demonstrates the proper response of those who are reprimanded for sin. When one is admonished concerning sinful behavior, one should not respond with annoyance but should confess the sin and make amends.[48]

The second point in Musculus's "philosophy of the Virgin" deals with the hope and confidence she maintained in the face of seeming rejection. By her attitude she gives an example of the nature of faith exercised in prayer. This point is emphasized by Musculus, Bucer, and Melanchthon and seems to be a special interest of the Protestant commentators. Thomas and Denis make no mention of it, preferring to emphasize Mary's encounter with Jesus as an earthly drama of her role as heavenly mediatrix. Hugh implicitly and briefly makes the prayer analogy in his explanation of Jesus' response to Mary. Jesus' reply shows that God does not always answer prayer immediately.[49] However, all of the Protestant expositors strongly emphasize Mary's persistence and perseverance as illustrative of the proper disposition for prayer. Perhaps they take their cue from Chrysostom, who alludes to this theme, stating: "From this we learn that even if we are unworthy of receiving our request, often we make ourselves worthy by our perseverance to do so."[50]

For the three reformers, Mary's persistence and faith are indicated primarily by her instructions to the servants: "Whatever he says to you, do it" (*Quodcunque dixerit vobis, facite*). She was not put off by Jesus' words, nor did she despair, but she quietly and confidently prepared for the remedy she knew would come. For Bucer, this is a prime example of faith, since faith often perceives the assistance of the Lord even when that assistance is not yet visible.[51] Melanchthon sees in Mary's words "an excellent example of faith which is confirmed in prayer." She trusted only in his mercy and did not rely on her merit. Being committed to his will, and exercising her faith, she expected him to provide what she sought. Mary shows that we must continue to expect Christ's assistance even when he seems to have forsaken us.[52]

According to Musculus, it would have been an entirely natural and understandable reaction if Mary, stung by Jesus' initial rebuff, had instructed the servants to see where they could purchase some wine. But instead, she prepared the servants to await his instructions. She did not know when or how Jesus would remedy the situation, but she knew he would be true to himself and not abandon those experiencing difficulties. Her firm confidence demonstrates the nature of a faith which conquers by petition and perseverance: "This constancy of faith was in the Virgin, which alone penetrates the clouds of an angry God, and which hopes against hope, and by hoping finally conquers."[53]

Thus for Musculus, Mary is a model for the believer in several aspects. Her exemplary manner, however, does not support the superstitious worship and adoration heaped upon her by her admirers. This argument, Musculus's third point in his "philosophy of the Virgin," is the only place where he introduces a polemic against Catholic mariology. Mary does not seek glory for herself; she does not herself give instructions. Rather, "she directs them to Christ, and admonishes them to submit to his words." What is pleasing to her, and to all of the saints in the universe, is obedience to Christ.[54]

While Musculus shows the behavior of Mary in her encounter with Jesus to be admirable and pleasing, Jesus' behavior is not so easily explained. Clearly, he argues,

Jesus was not presenting an example of irreverence toward his mother, since the Bible commands honor for one's parents.[55] What then do Jesus' puzzling words mean? In answering this question, Musculus essentially offers a combination of the interpretations of Augustine and Chrysostom. In fact, nearly all of our commentators repeat the solutions given by these two Fathers. Thomas, Hugh, and Denis summarize the interpretations of both Augustine and Chrysostom and offer them as equally correct understandings of John 2:4.[56] The difficulty of the verse precludes a single reading for these medieval commentators. Thus, two authoritative interpretations are given that, if not mutually exclusive, certainly explain Jesus' words quite differently.[57]

According to Augustine, a proper interpretation of Jesus' statement must be based on an understanding of the distinct spheres of Christ's two natures. His miracle-working capacity belongs properly to his divine nature, which he received from his heavenly father, while his suffering belongs properly to his human nature, which he received from his mother.[58] So when his mother makes her request, Jesus responds by saying in effect: "That in me which does a miracle you did not give birth to, you did not give birth to my divinity; but because you bore my weakness, I shall recognize you then, when that weakness will hang on the cross."[59] Augustine's interpretation is directed against two poles of false exegesis. First, he combats the Manichaean interpretation that finds in Jesus' statement a denial of his fleshly existence. When Jesus called Mary "woman" he was not denying his filial relation to her; rather he was denying her authority in that sphere of operation that pertained to his divinity.[60] Second, Augustine contends against the false interpretation of the astrologers who argue that Jesus was subject to fate. When Jesus says, "My hour has not yet come," he is not declaring his subjection to a fated hour. Rather, he declares that it is not yet the fitting time to undergo the passion; when Jesus suffers, he does it willingly, not by the governance of the stars.[61]

While Augustine understands Jesus' words as a subtle statement concerning christology, Chrysostom sees the words as a strategic maneuver related to the disclosure of the miracle. He argues that Mary, believing herself to have special prerogative by virtue of her motherhood, wanted Jesus to perform the miracle at an inopportune time—that is, before the need for wine was generally known. In order for the miracle to be believed and appreciated, the lack of wine needed to be a public crisis, not a private one.[62] Cyril of Alexandria makes a similar point. By delaying his response, Jesus elicited gratitude for the miracle: "For it behooved Him not to come hastily to action, nor to appear a Worker of miracles as though of His Own accord, but, being called, hardly to come thereto. . . . But the issue of things longed for seems somehow to be even more grateful, when granted not off-hand to those who ask for it, but through a little delay put forth to most lovely hope."[63]

Like Augustine, Chrysostom argues that Jesus was not subject to a fated time; rather, Jesus chose to do everything at the most fitting time. However, while Augustine interprets Jesus' "hour" as the time of Jesus' passion, Chrysostom interprets it as the time of his miracle-working ministry.[64] Therefore, Chrysostom must answer the question: If the hour was not fitting, why then did Jesus proceed to perform the miracle? He did so, Chrysostom responds, precisely in order to demonstrate that he was not subject to any fixed times. Also, Jesus did not want to expose his mother to public shame. Therefore, out of respect for his mother he performed the miracle at a time that was not the most opportune moment.[65] Similarly, Cyril argues that Jesus proceeded with the miracle in order to honor his mother: "Besides, Christ hereby shews that the deepest honor is due to parents, admitting out of reverence to His Mother what He willed not as yet to do."[66]

Unlike the medieval commentators, who present the explanations of Augustine and Chrysostom side by side as two authoritative literal explanations, the sixteenth-century commentators are reluctant to present multiple literal interpretations. They compose their solutions in conformity with one or the other of the two patristic interpretations, or they attempt to blend elements from Augustine and Chrysostom into one explanation. Melanchthon's interpretation follows, in part, the course set by Chrysostom. He argues that Jesus rebuked Mary in order to reject "every prerogative of the flesh" (*omnis praerogativa carnis*). Despite the virtue of her motherhood, Mary was of no more value to Jesus than any other sinful woman. Jesus tells Mary, in effect, to trust only in his mercy and not to rely on any notion of merit.[67] Bucer presents variations on the theme expressed by Augustine. He argues that Jesus rebuked Mary in order to establish his true identity. Everyone knew him to be a man and the son of Mary; but he wanted to declare himself "to be the elected Son of God, from whom they might hope for salvation." Therefore Jesus calls her "woman" and not "mother" in order to shatter their misconceptions.[68]

According to Erasmus, who adopts elements of the themes expressed by both Augustine and Chrysostom, Jesus' rebuke was for the purpose of demonstrating proper spheres of authority. When and how Jesus engaged in the business of the gospel could not be guided by any human authority or feelings but only by the will of the Father. Jesus was not rejecting his mother, or even refusing her request; rather, he was demonstrating that she had no authority in the sphere of his miracle-working. In addition, Jesus did not want to appear as a showman, flaunting a theatrical display of power. Therefore, he deliberately delayed the miracle until the troubled situation was generally known.[69]

Like Erasmus, Musculus incorporates elements of Augustine's and Chrysostom's exegesis into his explanation of Jesus' words. By his words, Jesus teaches that no human authorities should be recognized "in matters of God and faith" (*in rebus dei ac fidei*). In the sphere of the gospel, Jesus did not receive his mother as an authority. Here, Musculus follows Augustine's interpretation. However, in his explanation of the words "my hour has not yet come," Musculus offers an interpretation similar to Chrysostom's. Jesus was not denying his help but rather he was delaying his response until just the right moment. He wanted to time the miracle to best serve the glory of God and the salvation of humankind. The matter of proper timing leads Musculus into a discussion of expectancy in prayer. The timing of God's response to prayer should be left to his prudence. Often God allows people to undergo suffering and evil for a period of time, delaying his response to those who plead for relief. By doing this, God makes them more grateful when they finally experience the benefit of answered prayer.[70]

MORAL LESSONS

Jesus makes two implicit endorsements at the wedding of Cana. First, by his presence at the wedding party, Jesus gives his tacit approval of marriage. This approval is highlighted by the fact that Jesus honors the occasion by performing a miracle. Second, Jesus gives his tacit approval of the celebrating that accompanies such an event, an approval that is highlighted by his provision of a large supply of wine after the guests had apparently consumed all of the wine on hand. Of these two implied endorsements, Musculus wishes to emphasize the first and deny the latter. He stresses the moral application of the story to the subject of marriage but is uneasy with a Jesus who approves of excessive feasting, especially feasting that includes the consumption of large quantities of wine.

In his uneasiness, Musculus follows a line of commentators who are troubled by certain aspects of Jesus' presence at a wedding party. All of the commentators agree that Jesus comes to the wedding to show his approval of marriage, but to some interpreters his participation in the feast seems below his dignity. Cyril emphasizes that Jesus came to the wedding "to work miracles rather than to feast with them."[71] Chrysostom also states that by attending the wedding celebration Jesus "did not consider his own dignity, but our benefit." By attending the party, Jesus demonstrated his humility in associating with sinful people: "He who reclined together with publicans and sinners would, much rather, not refuse to recline with those who were present at the marriage."[72] Similarly, Thomas argues that Jesus decided to attend this wedding in order to give an example of humility. He did not look to his own dignity but rather accepted the form of a servant.[73] In an interesting variation on this theme, Hugh worries that the invitation of Jesus to a wedding banquet might be used to argue against his poverty, for poor people are not normally invited to such feasts. Therefore, Hugh argues that the families of the bride and groom must have been poor, and hence they invited people of their own kind to the wedding celebration.[74]

The mere presence of Jesus at the wedding party does not bother Musculus so much as his provision of additional wine. By accepting the invitation, Jesus demonstrates that his holiness is not jeopardized by association with sinful men and women. Here, Musculus ridicules the monks and nuns who would consider themselves defiled if they had to associate with "seculars" (*secularibus hominibus*) at such an event. Do they think they are holier than Jesus and more chaste than his virgin mother? Although he was not born from a marriage, he came to a wedding and honored it by his presence. For Musculus, this is an example of the divine command to rejoice with those who are rejoicing. Jesus also shows that Christians may accommodate themselves to human custom, with the provision that it is "permissible" (*licitus*) and "honorable" (*honestus*).[75]

It is this provision, however, that makes Jesus' miracle problematic for Musculus. Can Jesus be accused of providing the means for inebriation? Here, Musculus raises an issue that receives little attention in the exegetical tradition on the Cana narrative. The abundance of wine is not problematic for most commentators, who interpret the conversion of water into wine allegorically.[76] Chrysostom sees the conversion as symbolic of the change from a life of luxury and gluttony to a life of abstinence, an interpretation that stands the literal sense on its head.[77] For Augustine, the wine created by Jesus represents the new christological interpretation of the Scriptures. When the Old Testament is read literally, it is tasteless like water. But Jesus changes this water into wine and "what was tasteless acquires taste, what was not intoxicating intoxicates."[78] For Cyril, Erasmus, and Melanchthon, the new wine symbolizes the gospel, which was superseding the Law, represented by the wine, which was running out.[79] The richness of the metaphor of conversion is certainly not lost upon the medieval commentators; Thomas, Hugh, and Denis present multiple spiritual interpretations of the conversion of water into wine.[80]

Bucer and Musculus, however, part with the exegetical tradition in their attempts to explain the significance of the miraculous wine. Rejecting the wealth of symbolic possibilities, they must explain its significance purely on the literal level of interpretation. Why did Jesus create such a large quantity of wine for the wedding party at Cana? While this question is certainly troubling for Musculus, Bucer sees it as an opportunity to portray Jesus as a man who in fact enjoyed celebrations and parties. He contrasts the Jesus who approved of "moderate merriment" (*hilaritatem moderatam*) with the rather prudish morality of the Anabaptists. Jesus was not simply serving necessity in his miracle, for water could have quenched the thirst of the guests. Rather, "and, what you may be amazed at," argues Bucer, "the author of sobriety presented . . . wine to the guests—among whom there were doubtlessly those who drank more than necessity required—and in fact wine of the best quality." Jesus thereby teaches that created things are to be enjoyed and received as gifts of God. Furthermore, God has established for his people times of rejoicing and feasting, as well as times of mourning and fasting. Bucer argues that the dour moralism of the Anabaptists cannot make sense of Jesus' behavior at Cana: "Doubtlessly, the Catabaptists, if they had then been present, would have severely rebuked the Lord, if not even excommunicated him."[81]

While Bucer expresses a cheery delight in the miraculous provision of wine at the party, Musculus expresses a concern that false inferences will be drawn from the story. He opposes "the lovers of wine" (οἱ φιλοίνοι) who seize upon the story to make two false conclusions. First, they argue that inebriation is an ancient and long-cherished custom. Musculus admits that drunkenness is certainly not a recent vice, but he argues that its oldness is no defense of its permissibility. If one defends drunkenness on account of its long history, then one must also defend the ancient vices of lying, jealousy, fornication, and murder. Second, the wine lovers argue that Jesus himself furthered drunkenness in the wedding party at Cana. According to Musculus, this argument falsely assumes that the guests at the party were already drunk before Jesus performed the miracle. The assumption is based on the words of the steward, who says: "Every person serves the good wine first, and when they have become inebriated, then that which is worse."[82] Musculus argues that the steward was speaking in general terms about common custom; he was not referring specifically to the condition of the guests at the Cana wedding party. Furthermore, Musculus finds it unbelievable that the miraculous wine could have been abused for the cause of drunkenness. The wine was simply sampled by the guests in order to verify the occurrence of the miracle. Even if some of the guests had been drunk, Jesus cannot be accused of furthering that vice. Otherwise, Jesus must be blamed for all vices. Christ created iron, but he cannot be blamed for murder. Christ gave language to mankind, but he cannot be blamed for lying and false oaths. Having received so many blessings from God, it is the height of impiety to blame God for the human abuses of those blessings. Thus, Musculus shows the inferences drawn by the wine lovers to be baseless, especially when contrasted with the many places in Scripture that clearly define drunkenness as a vice.[83]

For Musculus, therefore, the Cana narrative offers no implied endorsement of drunkenness or heavy wine consumption. But the story does imply an important moral application. As Musculus states: "This place is usually used for the honoring of marriage for the very reason that Christ was present at this wedding."[84] Nearly every commentator from Augustine to Bucer makes the same argument.[85] Marriage is thus a standard topic of discussion in the exegetical tradition on the Cana narrative. However, while nearly every commentator briefly mentions the honoring of marriage implicit in Jesus' presence at the wedding, most place greater emphasis on the allegorical significance of marriage.

Thus for Cyril and Augustine, the wedding at Cana is a metaphor for the incarnation. As Augustine states: "For the Word was the bridegroom, and human flesh was the bride . . . . That womb of the Virgin Mary . . . was his bridal chamber."[86] In addition to the incarnational metaphor, the wedding at Cana symbolizes for Augustine the marriage between Christ and the Church.[87] These themes are developed further by the medieval commentators; for them, the wedding at Cana becomes more and more an excuse for an extended discussion of the spiritual significance of marriage. Thomas discusses the two themes expressed by Augustine and also interprets marriage as symbolic of the union between Christ and the individual soul.[88]

In the comments of Hugh and Denis, the emphasis on spiritual marriages overshadows the approval of human marriage implicit in Jesus' presence at the wedding. While Hugh mentions the approval of ordinary marriage, his discussion centers on four types of spiritual marriage symbolized by the wedding at Cana: first, the marriage between God and human nature resulting in the incarnation; second, the marriage between Christ and the Church, discussed in the fifth chapter of Ephesians; third, the marriage between God and the soul, which takes place in the sacrament of penance; and fourth, the marriage that takes place between Christ and those who have bound themselves with monastic vows—that is, "between Christ and the religious" (*inter Christum & religiosum*). Hugh discusses each of these marriages extensively and buttresses his comments with numerous biblical statements concerning marriage. He shows remarkable ingenuity in manipulating the details in the Cana wedding story into appropriate symbols for each of the four types of marriage. For example, the temporal reference "on the third day" is for Hugh a symbol of the time of grace, which follows the time before the Law (day one) and the time under the Law (day two). The marriage between God and human nature and the marriage between Christ and the Church both take place in this time of grace. In the marriage between Christ and the human soul, the third day refers to the three moments in the sacrament of penance: contrition, confession, and satisfaction. The same symbol is interpreted in the marriage between Christ and the religious as the three monastic vows of chastity, poverty, and obedience. Hugh shows similar exegetical skill in his interpretation of the water pots, the water, and the wine. It is significant that Hugh's fourth marriage (between Christ and the religious) necessitates a commitment to celibacy and is therefore in tension with Jesus' approval of ordinary marriage.[89]

This tension is more explicit in the comments of Denis on the marriage theme. He argues that although Jesus approves of human marriage, he really intends to call believers into the higher states of spiritual marriage. For Denis, there are two types of spiritual marriage. One is the marriage of the Word with human nature that is celebrated in the womb of the Virgin. The other is the marriage between Christ and the Church which is celebrated in the "bed of the purer conscience" (*in cubili conscientiae purioris*). In addition to these spiritual marriages, Denis argues that there is the "marriage of beatific enjoyment" (*nuptiis beatificae fruitionis*) that is celebrated in the "palace of majesty" (*in palatio majestatis*). While human marriage is legitimate, Jesus' presence at the wedding of Cana also implies a moral exhortation concerning spiritual marriage. Denis states: "Therefore, let us celebrate spiritual marriage in our conscience, by uniting and intimately joining our souls to the Word . . . to the groom of the souls of the saints . . . so that our souls may be fertilized and impregnated by heavenly seed, that is, with the light of abundant grace, in order that they may produce spiritual fruit, that is, virtuous acts." The higher value of spiritual marriage over carnal marriage is emphasized even in Denis's literal exposition. Jesus went to the wedding, he argues, not simply to show his approval of human marriage but, more important, to call the groom back into the higher state of celibacy.[90]

In contrast to the many interpreters who see a wealth of symbols in the marriage theme, Musculus focuses his attention exclusively on ordinary human marriage. This exclusive focus is not characteristic of all sixteenth-century exegesis, for both Erasmus and Melanchthon offer allegorical interpretations of the wedding in their commentaries.[91] Musculus himself, as we shall later see, makes liberal use of allegorical exegesis in his commentary on John. But here Musculus follows the lead of Bucer, his former teacher, in excluding the traditional allegorical interpretations of the Cana pericope. Bucer remarks: "Allegories are weaved out of this, but neither Christ nor the Evangelist said anything allegorically in this. Bare history is that which is related."[92] The traditional allegories must be rejected because they are "uncertain and man-made" (*incerta et conficta ab hominibus*). However, Bucer suggests that marriage is an appropriate topic of discussion in the context of commentary on the wedding at Cana: "Marriage is a commonplace that is usually treated here. . . . The chief point is: 'It is not good for man to be alone' [Gn 2:18]."[93]

Since Musculus, like Bucer, makes no use of the allegorical possibilities of the marriage theme, all that remains for him is the tacit approval of marriage implied by the presence of Jesus at the wedding. However, Musculus magnifies this implication to such proportions that it completely dominates his reading of the story; nearly a third of his comments are devoted to the subject of marriage. He divides his discussion of marriage into six sections with the following titles: "Observations concerning weddings," "What marriage is," "Its source, that is, its author," "How it is honorable," "How it is useful," and finally, "How it is necessary." Musculus is concerned above all to elevate the dignity of the married state over against the Roman priests who, he argues, prefer concubinage and whoremongering to the proper and honorable union of marriage that is established by God.[94]

Although Musculus omits allegory, his treatment of marriage is hardly limited to a simple exposition of the Cana story; in fact, his discussion is completely disengaged from the Scripture text. There is simply not enough scriptural data in the story to fuel the discussion he wishes to pursue. Therefore, Musculus essentially interrupts his running commentary to insert a moral treatise on marriage. In part, Musculus's interest in the subject can be placed in the larger context of the Reformation. The rejection of clerical celibacy by the reformers went hand in hand with an effort to defend the honor and dignity of marriage. More specifically, the defense of marriage was a personal issue for Musculus. His decision to embrace the Reformation was also a decision to break his monastic vows and to marry.

CONCLUSION

The distinctive characteristics of Musculus's interpretation can only be seen when that interpretation is placed in the context of the antecedent exegetical tradition. As the story of the wedding at Cana was interpreted in the patristic and medieval periods, a standard exegetical agenda emerged. This agenda established the interpretive problems facing a commentator, as well as the possible solutions to those problems. This exegetical tradition exerts an influence on Musculus's interpretation; his comments reflect his response not only to the words of the biblical text itself but also to the words of the commentators who precede him. This conversation between Musculus and the exegetical tradition is largely a silent one. That is, Musculus does not himself present to the reader the context that he has assumed. He neither cites nor refers to other commentators in the course of his interpretation. His silence, however, should not be construed as evidence of his independence from the tradition.

The dependence of Musculus on the work of previous commentators can be seen clearly in his discussion of the method of the miracle. The exegetical tradition had established a set of interpretive questions that Musculus assumes in his comments on the story. Why did Jesus use the massive water pots and why did he create so much wine? Why did he make use of the servants and the steward? And why did he not perform a more spectacular miracle by creating wine *ex nihilo*? In addressing these questions, Musculus follows a basic interpretive trajectory established by Chrysostom that reoccurs throughout the medieval tradition—namely, that every detail of Jesus' method was intentionally employed in order to establish beyond doubt the real occurrence of a real miracle.

In interpreting the encounter between Mary and Jesus, we have seen how Musculus follows in the footsteps of previous commentators who express a fundamental sympathy for the virgin mother. Although she is scolded by Christ, Musculus, like most commentators, sees nothing blameworthy in her appeal to Jesus. In fact, her role in the story expresses a beautiful model of patience and faithfulness in prayer. Musculus is also quite conservative in his explanation of Jesus' rebuke, relying, like nearly every commentator, on the explanations of Chrysostom and Augustine.

When Musculus discusses the moral applications of the story to the subjects of drunkenness and marriage, he shows more exegetical independence. In part, he is using the text to express particular concerns of his own age. But his treatment of these subjects is also due to his reluctance to use allegory as a mode of interpretation. If the miraculous wine is not symbolic of a greater spiritual reality, then one is left to explain Jesus' creation of a large quantity of wine and wine only; and clearly that troubles Musculus.

In his discussion of marriage, Musculus takes a standard observation of the traditional exegesis—Jesus' approval of human marriage—and develops it into a full-blown treatise on the subject. While he avoids the traditional allegorizing of the topic, his emphasis on marriage in the context of the story of the wedding at Cana is not new. Earlier commentators had clearly established that marriage is an appropriate topic of discussion for an interpreter of the pericope. Musculus therefore uses the text as a springboard for a thorough treatment of human marriage, a subject of special interest to many of the Protestant reformers. His treatment, however, is certainly not limited to a simple literal exposition of the text at hand. That is, one cannot characterize his exegesis as a simple exposition of the historical or literal meaning of the text in opposition to the uncontrolled speculation of the allegorical interpretations. While his reading may not violate the meaning of the biblical text, it goes well beyond the scope of a simple literal explanation of the narrative. As we shall see, Musculus's tendency to include voluminous moral discussions in the course of his commentary is one of the most characteristic features of his work on John.

TWO

Musculus and the Fathers on the Healing of the Ruler's Son

In Protestant circles, Musculus was considered an authority on the Fathers. He devoted much of his scholarly career to the study of patristic literature, publishing several editions and translations of Greek patristic writings. In almost all of his theological writings, the fruit of this scholarship is evident. Even a cursory reading of Musculus's *Loci communes sacrae theologiae* (1560) reveals an author steeped in the writings of the ancient Church Fathers; patristic references and citations abound throughout this massive work in systematic theology.[1]

It is hardly surprising then that Musculus makes liberal use of patristic exegesis in his work as an interpreter of the Bible. Indeed, in some of his commentaries he makes the evaluation of patristic interpretations an explicit part of his program as commentator. In his Psalms commentary, for example, he makes this purpose clear in the very title of the work: *In Sacrosanctum Davidis Psalterium commentarii, . . . non praetermissis orthodoxorum etiam Patrum sententiis, ita tractantur, ut Christianus lector nihil desiderare amplius possit.* Similarly, in the title of his Genesis commentary, Musculus declares his intention to evaluate the exegetical opinions of "ancient and recent authorities": *In Mosis Genesim plenissimi commentarii, in quibus veterum & recentiorum sententiae diligenter expenduntur.* Although Musculus does not openly declare this intention in his John commentary, he clearly shows his dependence on the patristic exegetical tradition, citing the commentaries of Augustine, Chrysostom, and Cyril throughout.

In this chapter I will consider Musculus's interpretation of John 4:46–54 in the context of patristic commentaries in order to characterize his use of patristic exegesis. While Musculus does not explicitly cite any opinions of the Fathers in his commentary on this short passage, there are definite echoes of patristic exegetical ideas. As a preamble to the exegetical study, I first present an overview of Musculus's educational and scholarly development, focusing on his studies in the Fathers. This survey of his literary, linguistic, and theological education provides an important backdrop for this and the following chapters; it shows the knowledge and tools that Musculus brought to the text as a biblical commentator. Second, I address Musculus's own statements concerning the value of the patristic witness for the Christian in general and for the biblical expositor in particular. His discussion of the relationship of Scripture and tradition is examined in order to assess his estimation of the authority of the Fathers in matters of faith.

MUSCULUS'S EDUCATIONAL FORMATION

A review of Musculus's education begins with the years he spent as a grammar student in Upper Alsace. Very little is known about these years. According to his biographer, Musculus set out as a boy from his hometown of Dieuze in Lorraine and wandered throughout Alsace in search of both patronage and education. He attended in succession the Latin schools in Ribeauvillé (Rappoltsweiler), Colmar, and Sélestat.[2] Although precise information is lacking concerning Musculus's education in these schools, one thing is certain: at Sélestat Musculus received one of the best Latin educations available to a boy in early sixteenth-century Europe.

The Sélestat school, founded in the late fourteenth century, came under the influence of the educational reforms of the Brethren of the Common Life through the rectorship of Ludwig Dringenberg (1441–1477). The fame of the school grew and continued after Dringenberg through the rectorships of three humanistically minded pedagogues: Crato Hofmann (1477–1501), Hieronymus Gebwiler (1501–1509), and Johannes Sapidus (1510–1525). Under the direction of these men, the school produced an outstanding number of scholars, among whom were Jakob Wimpfeling (1450–1528), Martin Bucer (1491–1551), Leo Jud (1482–1542), Paulus Constantinus Phrygio (1485–1543), Beatus Rhenanus (1485–1547), and Hieronymus Gemuseus (1505–1549).[3] This remarkable output of scholars prompted Erasmus to write an encomium in which he states: "That is uniquely yours, that both one and small, you produce so many men distinguished in virtue and in talent."[4]

It was the fame of the Sélestat school that drew Musculus and hundreds of boys from Lorraine, Alsace, and Switzerland. Unfortunately, evidence is lacking to indicate when Musculus arrived in the town. Ludwig Grote argues that Musculus studied there during the rectorship of Hieronymus Gebwiler.[5] Yet Abraham Musculus states that his father remained in Sélestat until his fifteenth year.[6] If his statement is correct, Musculus also studied under Johannes Sapidus, himself a former student at Sélestat, who was appointed rector in December 1510, when Musculus would have been thirteen years old. In any case, both Gebwiler and Sapidus offered essentially the same educational curriculum, inspired by the spirit of the Northern Renaissance.

What books did Musculus read at Sélestat? Although neither Musculus himself nor his son Abraham mention specific works, a glimpse of the daily curriculum at Sélestat is provided by a letter from a student, Boniface Amerbach, written to his father in 1508: "You wrote in your letters that I should write you what our teacher does. As you may know, he expounds Alexander in the morning; at nine o'clock some poems from authors such as Horace, Ovid, etc.; after twelve [we read] in Mantua. On Mondays he adds some poems for us to examine for the meter. At four o'clock we review what we did during the course of the entire day."[7]

This statement indicates that Musculus probably studied Latin using the basic grammar textbook of the Middle Ages, the *Doctrinale puerorum* of Alexander of Villa Dei (b. ca. 1170).[8] The emphasis of the Sélestat school on prosody is reflected by the readings in Horace and Ovid and by the readings in Baptist of Mantua (1447–1516), who, enjoying the reputation of a Christian Virgil, was added to the curriculum as an antidote to the pagan poets.[9] This emphasis is also reflected in Abraham Musculus's description of his father's study in Sélestat: "Later, leaving Colmar he came to Sélestat, and there he gave attention to letters. He was held even at that young age by a love of poetry, and he was very persistent in the reading of the poets."[10] According to Abraham, Musculus's teacher held competitions among the students in reciting poetry from memory, exercises that Musculus found thoroughly enjoyable.[11]

The circumstances that prompted Musculus to leave the Sélestat school and join the Order of St. Benedict are not completely clear. Both religious concerns and financial ones seem to have motivated his decision. The events that led to this sudden change are explained by his biographer as follows. On his way to visit his parents in Dieuze, Musculus stopped to spend the night with his aunt in the village of Lixheim. Being a religious woman, she took the young Wolfgang to the nearby Benedictine monastery for evening prayers. As they joined in the singing of vespers, the monks and the prior were awestruck by the beauty of Musculus's voice. After the service, the prior asked him to enter the monastery, promising to provide for all of his financial needs. Having obtained the consent of his parents, Musculus entered the monastery in Lixheim, where he spent the next fifteen years (1512–1527).[12]

Although we do not know what books were sitting on the shelves of the Lixheim monastery, it is quite possible that Musculus began his reading in the Fathers during these years. According to his biographer, he occupied his time with much study.[13] However, apart from Latin poetry, the Bible, and certain unnamed works of Martin Luther that flowed into the monastery in 1518, we do not know for certain what Musculus read. He was able to continue his reading of the Latin poets because of a fortuitous discovery. In the attic of the monastery, the young monk found a pile of manuscripts that he ordered and pieced together; these turned out to be several works of Cicero and the complete works of Ovid. Musculus was consumed with the reading of these classical authors and after a time began to make his own attempts at versification. He developed this skill to such an extent that he even produced his own shorter version of Ovid's *Metamorphoses*.[14]

Although we know little about Musculus's formal theological training in the monastery, around his twentieth year he began an intensive course of biblical study, following the advice of an "older friend" that a good preacher should be well-versed in the Bible. Musculus soon demonstrated a talent for preaching and was assigned to the office of public preacher. He delivered sermons in the church in Lixheim and in other towns in the vicinity of the monastery. Sometime after 1518, Musculus began to study some of the writings of Luther; these influenced his sermons to such a degree that he became known as the "Lutheran monk."[15]

Although Musculus openly sided with Luther, he remained in the monastery until 1527. In that year he threw aside the cowl, married, and headed for Strasbourg. For three years Musculus lived in that city, working first as a weaver and eventually as a preacher.[16] During his Strasbourg years, Musculus furthered his theological and linguistic education. He attended the lectures of Martin Bucer and Wolfgang Capito and began to study Hebrew.[17] For a time Musculus lived in Bucer's home and worked as his personal secretary, transcribing Bucer's notoriously illegible handwriting into clean copy for the typesetter. Among other works, Musculus transcribed Bucer's commentaries on Zephaniah and the Psalms.[18]

Musculus probably studied in the Fathers during his Strasbourg years; he at least imbibed patristic opinions indirectly through the commentaries of Bucer. It is also likely that he was introduced to the Fathers during the fifteen years he spent in the Lixheim monastery. However, we first hear of his patristic studies after his arrival in the free imperial city of Augsburg. From 1531 to 1537 Musculus worked in Augsburg as preacher at the Heilig-Kreuz-Kirche.[19] During that time he began a private course of study in the Greek language under the tutelage of the Augsburg school rector Xystus Betuleius (Sixt Birk).[20] Musculus was an adept student of languages, and his talent in Greek manifested itself in his work as a translator of Greek patristic literature.[21] The humanistically trained Birk may have suggested this course of study to Musculus as a way to develop proficiency in Greek. In any event, Musculus's translations were deemed worthy of publication, and in 1536 his first work, a translation into Latin of Chrysostom's commentaries on Romans, Ephesians, Philippians, Colossians, and 1 and 2 Thessalonians, appeared in Basel.[22] For the next twenty years, Musculus continued to produce Latin translations of Greek patristic writings, including works from Basil of Caesaria, Cyril of Alexandria, Gregory of Nazianzus, and Athanasius.[23] In addition, he produced a translation in one volume of the Greek ecclesiastical histories.[24] Musculus's work as a translator was not limited to Christian literature, for in 1549 he published a translation of books 6 through 18 of the *Histories* of Polybius.[25]

Musculus's remarkable output as a translator indicates his possession of or access to a significant collection of Greek manuscripts. Due to the efforts of his tutor

Betuleius, Musculus in fact had such access during his tenure in Augsburg. In 1537 the council commissioned Betuleius to make a selection of the best manuscripts and books out of the city monasteries for the purpose of establishing a city library.[26] The council was determined to build a respectable collection and in 1545, at the urging of Betuleius, approved the purchase of 126 Greek manuscripts, mostly works of Church Fathers, for the sum of 742 guilders.[27] Although Musculus's translations of Chrysostom and Basil antedate the purchase, his later translations of Polybius, Cyril, and Gregory of Nazianzus probably utilized the Augsburg manuscript collection.[28]

In his work as a translator, Musculus was not limited to Greek writings, for in 1535, at the urging of Bucer, he produced a German translation of Augustine's letter to the Roman general Bonifacius.[29] This translation, to which Bucer added an introduction and an epilogue, emerged in the context of a political debate concerning the future plans for the Reformation in Augsburg. Bucer and Musculus hoped to create a groundswell of support for a thoroughgoing reformation of the city. By translating the letter in which Augustine justifies governmental intervention in the Donatist controversy, Musculus and Bucer hoped to convince the council likewise to intervene against the Catholic Church in Augsburg.[30] For our purposes, it is important to note Musculus's eagerness to utilize the Fathers in his polemical writings, especially in those directed against Catholicism.

MUSCULUS ON THE AUTHORITY OF THE FATHERS

Although Musculus argues that the patristic writings are potent polemical weapons, he does not limit their value to that arena. In the introduction to his translation of Chrysostom's homilies on Paul, he defends and explains the value of patristic studies, directing his remarks primarily to those who casually dismiss the opinions of the Fathers.[31] Musculus argues that the Fathers, both in their writings and by the example of their holy lives, have permanent worth for the believer.

Musculus condemns the self-assured attitude of those who act and speak as if the Bible was first discovered in the sixteenth century. Pious people of all ages have studied and understood the Word of God. Throughout history, God has illuminated the minds of holy teachers devoted to the Scriptures, especially those who lived shortly after the apostolic age. In fact, Musculus thinks that the Fathers, by "their immense labors, vigils, and studies" (*immensi illorum labores, vigiliae & studia*), far surpass the efforts at biblical scholarship common in his own age. Therefore those who dismiss everything in the Fathers are not only arrogant but also ignorant of history: "They seem to me to err very much, those who are deaf to everything of others, yet adore their own [opinions], as if all knowledge of the truth was completely lacking from the ancients."[32]

Musculus not only recommends a general reading of patristic writings but also specifically names the Fathers he thinks deserve special attention. From the Latin

Fathers, he lists Cyprian, Irenaeus, Jerome, Ambrose, Augustine, and Hilary; from the Greeks, he lists Origen, Eusebius, Cyril, Basil, Gregory, and Chrysostom. These men are the "principal interpreters of the eloquence of God and promoters of the Christian religion." Their writings are "monuments" (*monumenta*) that should not be ignored. Certainly, as human beings, they were able to err, and therefore their writings "should be read attentively and considered with sound judgment." But those who refuse to study the patristic writings never discover the treasure therein: "How will one hold the good, who tests nothing, but despises everything of others? How will one test, who deigns not even to read? How will one read, who hisses at anything he pleases with the highest contempt?"[33] Musculus complains that people too often flatter themselves with their own opinions, not realizing that they are deceived. A judicious reading of the Fathers will help to dislodge these errone-ous opinions. However, the Fathers should not be read indiscriminately or to the exclusion of personal study in the Bible:

> I do not advise that the writings of the Fathers should be examined night and day, superstitiously rather than religiously. For this will divert [us] very much from the reading of the canonical Scriptures, to which the first and better portion of our studies must be dedicated. Let us rather enter by the royal way that the holy men have shown in their writings and by their own example. For as there is the danger that if you indiscriminately embrace everything, you might take hold of a lie instead of the truth, the deception of human opinions instead of certainty of meaning, so too on the other hand it ought to be feared that if you utterly despise [the opinions] of others and admire only your own thoughts, you might reject the very truth expressed in the opinions of others, and instead of that [truth] you might adore the fancies of your own heart. On both sides the danger is quite the same. When the truth has been neglected, what indeed is the difference, whether you are deceived by your own errors or by the errors of others?[34]

While it is possible that the Fathers might lead one astray, deception is more likely to follow from a blind devotion to one's personal opinions. Consequently, those who are wise will suspect their own understanding before condemning the opin-ions of the Fathers.[35]

Musculus suggests that the reading of the Fathers is beneficial in three main ways. First, their writings help one to understand the meaning of difficult passages in the Bible. Before deciding on a particular interpretation of such passages, one should first consult the opinions of previous commentators. Interpreters of the Bible are often deceived because they leap to the first explanation that pleases their own minds; they think their own thoughts "more praiseworthy" (*plausibiliores*) than the thoughts of others. They would do better to listen to "those holy men, whose highest devotion was to remain in the divine Scriptures night and day." In Musculus's opinion, one is more likely to encounter the truth in those ancient expositions than in the interpretations of those who "nowadays" (*hodie*) inspect the passage once or twice and pronounce everything that should be believed.[36]

Second, the reading of the Fathers helps one to recognize the teachings of the ancient heretics. The Fathers should be admired for their zeal and diligence in confuting those errors. But even more, the patristic writings serve as a warning to later generations of the continual threat that the classical heresies pose for the Church. It is the insidious nature of these heresies that they reappear time and again in the history of the Church. For example, Musculus argues, the old battles concerning the Trinity and the divinity of Christ are being fought once more. The diligent study of the Fathers helps one to recognize the "ancient cunning of Satan" and shows one how "the empty phantasms of the heretics must be scattered."[37]

Third, Musculus argues that the reading of the Fathers helps to establish godly living. The patristic writings are full of wise counsel "for planting innocence of life and for correcting the corruption of the Church." This preoccupation with the virtuous life is found above all in the writings of Chrysostom, whom Musculus singles out for praise. When Chrysostom attacks the vices and corruption of his own age, promoting the virtues that the Christian life demands, he in fact speaks timeless wisdom, appropriate to all ages, especially to Musculus's own day.[38]

While Musculus extols Chrysostom in particular and the Fathers in general as an important part of any Christian literary diet, he does not consider patristic authority equal to that of the Bible. The Fathers' opinions have *weight* because of their erudite scholarship and because of the sanctity of their lives, but their views do not have *authority* per se. Musculus emphasizes this point in his discussion of patristic literature in the *Loci communes*, in which he treats the question of the value of this literature in the context of the relationship between Scripture and tradition. The accent of this discussion is quite different from his treatment of the Fathers in the preface to his translation of Chrysostom (*Ad lectorem*). In the *Loci communes* Musculus does not speak to those who have neglected the Fathers. Rather, he addresses the Catholic overemphasis on patristic authority and thus argues that tradition has no authority equal to that of the Bible.[39]

In one area, however, Musculus is willing to allow some authority to tradition—namely, the area of canon formation. Like Luther, he classifies certain books of the New Testament as less authoritative because of the witness of tradition: "Among the books of the New Testament there are some concerning which the opinions of the ancients vary, namely, the latter Epistle of Peter, the two latter epistles of John, the Epistle of Jude, the Epistle to the Hebrews, and the Apocalypse of John, which is not recited among the canonical Scriptures in the Council of Laodicea (chapter 59 and the last); along with these, certain more recent authorities also include that which is attributed to James."[40]

Although Musculus does not exclude these books from the canon, he is willing to ascribe less authority to them on the basis of the opinions of the ancient authorities: "It is not in keeping with my modesty that I should pronounce concerning them. . . . Nevertheless, the judgments of the ancients make me less bound to them than to the rest of the Scriptures—although I do not suggest that anything that is read in them may easily be condemned."[41] Since the canon is now established, it alone is the sole authority for Musculus in matters of faith and doctrine. The voice of tradition can neither add to nor subtract from the voice of Scripture. When the Fathers agree with Scripture, Musculus will listen to them; when they diverge from or go beyond Scripture, he will not. Therefore, the Catholics cannot gain any ground in doctrinal disputes when they argue from the Fathers: "When they bring something against us from the writings of the Fathers, I plainly assert that I refuse to be bound to their authority. For I do not (using the words of Augustine) consider their writings as canonical, but I examine them by the canonical writings. And if anything in them agrees with the authority of the canonical Scriptures, then I accept it; if however it does not agree, then with their permission I reject it."[42]

Musculus presents three arguments for rejecting the Fathers as a locus of authority. First, the Fathers themselves looked only to Scripture as an authority in doctrinal disputes. Therefore, when the Catholics elevate tradition as an authority, they not only disobey the Holy Spirit but also despise "both the examples of the ancient Church, which suppressed heresies by the authority of the sacred Scriptures, and the views of the ancient Fathers."[43] To prove his point, Musculus produces extended citations from Chrysostom, Augustine, and Jerome.[44]

Musculus's second argument sounds the old Abelardian theme concerning the diversity of the patristic witness. The Fathers, with their countless differences of opinions, cannot settle doctrinal disputes. Musculus elaborates this same argument in a letter of 1550 addressed to the Protestant clergy of Hungary.[45] In the letter he states that when the Catholics find a single statement in the Fathers that appears to disagree with Protestant teaching, "they brag" (*iactent*) and judge "our teaching, as if opposing the writings of the Fathers, to be heretical and damnable."[46] They do this, Musculus claims, even when the statements of other Fathers agree perfectly with Protestant teaching. As an example, he discusses the controversy over the proper division of the Decalogue. The Catholics, according to Musculus, argue that the first three commandments should be grouped together on one table and the remaining seven on the other; the Protestants, on the other hand, place the first four commandments on one table and the remaining six on the other.[47] The Catholics claim their division to be an authentic reflection of patristic opinion because of a statement of Augustine that supports the three-seven division, and they accuse the Protestants of introducing new teaching. However, Musculus argues that the Protestants in fact have stronger patristic support since Origen, Athanasius, Chrysostom, Jerome, Ambrose, and Augustine himself (in another place) all support the four-six division. The controversy ultimately shows, Musculus argues, that to make the Fathers the ultimate locus of authority is to resign oneself to endless bickering and debate:[48] "When we cite something from Augustine for the doctrine of grace and justification, there is at hand to [our] adversaries something different to cite from Chrysostom, a thing which I mention by way of example. For from all the Fathers two will not be produced whose writings agree in all things, especially in those which may be cited for our cause."[49]

In the *Loci communes*, Musculus makes a similar argument, but he emphasizes the problem of utilizing the patristic writings as a guide for interpreting the Bible. Those who assert that the patristic witness is needed in order to clarify the obscurities of Scripture have got it backward:

> Who is so stupid, that he thinks that what is clear must be judged by what is obscure, and not rather that which is obscure by what is clear? Whom will they give us from all the Fathers, whose writings we should follow as a light for the illumination of sacred Scripture? If we are willing to follow all those whose writings are extant, it will happen that what is clear in Scripture will be clouded by using their expositions, on account of the diversity of their opinions and expositions. If we should choose only one, there will be no agreement as to who should be chosen; nor will the opinion of one be able to make our consciences certain, when the others have different opinions.[50]

Musculus concedes that certain parts of Scripture are difficult to understand. However, it is not the Fathers but rather the Bible itself that provides the hermeneutical key to unlock the meaning of these passages. Following the famous dictum of Augustine, Musculus argues that the dark places in Scripture are always expressed more clearly in other places in the Bible.[51] The explanations of the Fathers may help to clarify difficult scriptural passages but only when they are read critically against the backdrop of the biblical witness. Quoting Augustine, Musculus states that "no matter how greatly they excel in learning and holiness, I do not therefore consider [what they say] true just because they thought it so, but because they were able to persuade me that it agrees with the truth, either by those canonical authors or by probable reason."[52]

Musculus's third argument for rejecting the authority of the Fathers is based upon his own experiences as a textual critic. There are so many textual variations for every work of the Fathers, he argues, that their original words are obscured in a cloud of uncertainty. A comparison of the different texts shows "how foul a discrepancy is everywhere to be found." How much more, he asks, do the existing texts differ from the originals? Musculus states that if one of the Fathers were alive to see the editions of his works in the sixteenth century, he would probably not even recognize them. Faith cannot be based on the authority of something so uncertain: "The writings of the Fathers have degenerated from their original state with the course of so many ages, partly by the carelessness of antiquarians and partly by the rashness of heretics, that whoever thinks that the consciences of the faithful should be bound by their decisions, is clearly very dimwitted or eagerly malicious toward the Church of God."[53]

Although Musculus rejects tradition as a pole of authority, he gladly uses patristic literature as a polemical weapon. Since the Catholics claim to abide by the judgments of the ancient Fathers, they must yield when the Fathers speak, "not on account of any authority which they deserve, but on account of that authority which they themselves attribute to them."[54] For his own purposes, Musculus claims no need to discover patristic confirmation: "As far as I am concerned, I do not require the testimonies of the Fathers . . . [but am] content with the authority and canon of holy Scripture itself."[55] Nevertheless, he betrays a cheery confidence that the Reformation breathes the spirit of the ancient Church as represented by the patristic writings. Roman Catholicism, according to Musculus, really represents an understanding of Christianity foreign to the minds of the Fathers: "I beseech you, where would the whole Roman see be established, with all those counterfeit bishops, cardinals, prelates, monks, scholastics, sophists, Scotists, Thomists, Occamists, and other such people, who for several centuries now have seized control of the Christian religion by right and wrong, by praying and paying, by force and arms, if they were put to the judgment of the holy Fathers and the ancient canons and councils?"[56] Thus, while Musculus finds no theological justification for the authority of tradition, he claims nonetheless that the Fathers are the theological allies of the Protestants, not of the Catholics.

THE HEALING OF THE RULER'S SON (JN 4:46–54)

In his interpretation of the healing of the ruler's son, Musculus offers no explicit citations of patristic exegesis. Yet by examining his comments in the context of patristic interpretations, it is possible not only to demonstrate a significant indebtedness to the Fathers but also to begin to define the nature of his indebtedness.

Utilizing only those patristic commentaries that were available to Musculus in printed editions, this comparative study is limited to the interpretations of Chrysostom, Cyril of Alexandria, and Augustine and to the metrical paraphrase of Nonnus of Panopolis.[57] These writings also represent the only patristic interpretations of John that Musculus explicitly cites in the course of his own commentary.[58] An examination of his direct citations of these writings does not show a special devotion to or dependence on any one patristic John commentator. Frequently, when encountering a particularly difficult passage, he cites together the opinions of Chrysostom, Cyril, and Augustine. Having cited their opinions, he either sides with one of the three interpretations, rejects them all and offers his own explanation, or affirms all of the interpretations as acceptable exegetical alternatives.[59] All the citations of Nonnus occur in Musculus's comments on the fourth chapter of John. Musculus quotes (in Greek) particular phrases of Nonnus, which he utilizes not to solve exegetical problems but rather to add color to his own comments. Because Nonnus rarely goes beyond the limits of paraphrase, the work sheds little light on a comparative exegetical analysis.[60]

The story of the healing of the ruler's son is loosely patterned on the wine miracle at Cana. Therefore it is not surprising that the two stories raise similar exegetical problems. Both miracles occur at Cana and both involve a petition put to Jesus. In both cases Jesus seems to refuse the petition with words of censure, only thereafter to grant the request. And in both stories the ultimate outcome of the miracle is an increase in faith.[61] Musculus organizes his comments according to this basic pattern, with four main sections entitled "the petition of the ruler" (*petitio reguli*), "the response of Christ" (*responsio Christi*), "the miracle of the boy's healing" (*miraculum sanati pueri*), and "the fruit of the miracle" (*fructus miraculi*).

As an introduction to his analysis of the story, Musculus first explains the meaning of the transitional verse: "He came therefore again to Cana of Galilee where he made the water wine" (Jn 4:46). According to Musculus, the Evangelist purposefully reminds the reader of the first miracle at Cana in order to show why Jesus returned there. Apparently, one miracle alone was not sufficient to establish a firm faith in the people who witnessed it. Therefore, Jesus returned to Cana "that he might irrigate and promote by revisiting with his power and light what he had recently planted by the first of his miracles."[62]

Musculus certainly echoes here the comments of Chrysostom, who argues that Jesus returned to Cana "to make stronger by his presence the faith begotten by the [first] miracle." In addition, by returning to Cana Jesus highlights the superior faith of the Samaritans, who, without the benefit of miracles, believed simply because of Jesus' teaching.[63] Cyril, however, sounds a different note by emphasizing the desire of the people at Cana to advance in faith. Because of their eagerness to advance, Jesus returned in order "to confer an additional benefit on them."[64]

Although Musculus repeats the comments of Chrysostom, he elaborates upon them in order to make a moral application. The fact that Jesus had to return to Cana is, for Musculus, a poignant reminder of the corruption of human nature, which will not retain "the beginnings of heavenly things" (*rerum coelestium principia*) unless they are repeatedly reinforced: "Of all things, they are most easily extinguished." The opposite is true of those evil things that "conform to our depravity" (*pravitati nostrae conformia*); human nature eagerly allows them to take root and grow. By revisiting Cana, Jesus reminds the Christian "to revisit the beginnings of good things" (*revisere bonarum rerum principia*) in order to advance in faith.[65]

The Petition of the Ruler

For many commentators, the identity of the ruler is the first significant exegetical problem. The gospel text states that he was a ruler from Capernaum but is silent concerning his official function.[66] It is also not clear from the text whether he was a Jew or a Gentile. In an effort to answer these questions, many exegetes have concluded that this ruler was the centurion of the synoptic gospels whose son is healed by Jesus (Mt 8:5–13 and Lk 7:1–10).[67]

Among the Fathers, neither Cyril nor Augustine speculate concerning the ruler's official function. Cyril, however, implies that he was a Gentile, while Augustine implies that he was a Jew.[68] Nonnus calls the ruler a "royal man" (βασιλήϊος ανήρ) who was the "commander of an army" (ιθύνων στρατιήν).[69] For Chrysostom, the term "βασιλικός" implies royalty but may be used more loosely: "Either he was actually of royal lineage or he was called royal because there was some other dignity of his office to which the title was attached." Chrysostom rejects an equation of the ruler with the centurion of Matthew because of important differences in the details of the stories. Most important, the centurion exhibits perfect faith, while the ruler's faith is weak and deficient.[70]

Like Chrysostom, Musculus sees no synoptic parallel in his discussion of the ruler's identity. However, he does speculate concerning his official function. The term βασιλικός, he argues, means "royal" (*regius*), but in this story the term is used loosely to refer to an official or prefect of Herod. Musculus argues that this man was probably Herod's prefect for the city of Capernaum. The royal designation, however, has a deeper significance for Musculus. The Evangelist purposely refers to him in this way in order to teach believers to hope for the conversion of their rulers. Although it rarely happens that such rulers believe in Christ, nevertheless it is not impossible, "and therefore one must not despair of such things."[71]

Having established his identity, Musculus turns to the main theme in his analysis of the ruler's petition—namely, the motives and faith that prompt the ruler to come to Christ. In light of Jesus' harsh retort—"Unless you see signs and prodigies you will not believe"—most commentators conclude that something in the man's motivation is faulty or that his faith is deficient. Musculus, however, shows more sympathy with the ruler. Certainly the ruler's faith is weak and in need of support, but the motives that bring the desperate father to Christ are praiseworthy.

According to Musculus, the father is driven by a deep love for his son, a love that causes him to disregard the risks to his professional status in associating with Jesus. Although people come to Jesus for various reasons, many come who are desperate because of their own suffering or because of the suffering of someone they love. Parents who have healthy children often are the most irreligious; they demonstrate no gratitude to God for their children. But this ruler, "desperate for the welfare of his son, finds refuge in Christ."[72]

Unlike Musculus, Augustine sees nothing praiseworthy in the ruler's appearance before Christ. In fact, the ruler simply used his son's illness as a pretext to find out "what sort of person Christ was, who he was, how much he could do."[73] Cyril states nothing concerning the father's motivation, focusing exclusively on the feeble faith of the ruler. Nonnus and Chrysostom, however, like Musculus, show sympathy with the plight of the royal official. Nonnus states that because of his great love, the ruler "was equally scourged by the fire that was afflicting his son, perhaps even more."[74] Similarly, Chrysostom argues that although weak in faith, the ruler is motivated by paternal love: "Fathers are eager, because of their great love, not only to approach physicians in whom they have confidence, but also to address those in whom they have none, wishing to leave nothing untried."[75]

While the Fathers may disagree concerning the motives of the ruler, they show greater consensus in their estimation of his faith. For Augustine, the ruler was either "lukewarm in faith, or even cold, or even of no faith at all." Even though the weakness of his faith is not immediately apparent, it must have been faulty or nonexistent given the stinging rebuke of Jesus: "We do not see the heart of a man lacking faith; but he who both heard his words and looked into his heart declared it."[76]

Cyril also faults the faith of the ruler but offers a more precise diagnosis than Augustine. The ruler's faith is weak because he does not understand who Jesus really is. This lack of understanding is demonstrated by the nature of his petition. In requesting healing for his son, the ruler asks Jesus to do something that only God can do. However, he foolishly supposes that Jesus must be physically present to the sick boy in order to accomplish the healing: "For what need for him to be present to the sick, whom he could easily heal, even absent? . . . But now both thinking and acting most foolishly, he asks power befitting God, and does not think He accomplishes all things as God."[77]

Chrysostom argues that the ruler exhibited a certain amount of faith simply by requesting Jesus' aid. Jesus' rebuke indicates only that the ruler did not believe "fully or soundly." The shallowness and "earthly outlook" of the father's faith is indicated by his words: "Come down before my child dies." These words of desperation show that the father did not believe Jesus was able to heal his son at a distance or that he was able to raise his son from the dead. Therefore, the ruler demonstrates that he believed Jesus to be a prophet, not the son of God.[78]

In his estimation of the ruler's faith, Musculus clearly echoes the comments of Chrysostom, arguing that the ruler believed that if Jesus was able to place his hand on the sick boy, then the illness would be driven away. Hence, he believed Jesus to be a "certain distinguished prophet" (*insigni cuidam prophetae*). Just as Naaman wanted Elisha to cure him by touching his leprosy (2 Kgs 5:1–14), so also the ruler believed it necessary for Jesus to be physically present. However, Musculus does not censure the ruler for the weakness of his faith but rather praises him for using the faith he had. Here, Musculus shows independence from the patristic exegetical tradition. Although the man's faith was "imperfect" (*imperfecta*) and "rough" (*rudis*), Musculus commends him for making use of "the modest beginnings of faith and hope . . . in order to implore for a work of Christ."[79]

According to Musculus, Jesus does not condemn the weak faith of the ruler but promotes and perfects it. Others also believed in Jesus as a prophet, but this faith was never rejected outright.[80] The Samaritan woman, for example, initially believed Jesus to be a distinguished prophet. Yet far from being annoyed with her weak faith, Jesus accepted and perfected it, so that she and her fellow citizens ultimately come to recognize him as the Christ, the savior of the world (Jn 4:42). The ruler from Capernaum also does not understand who Jesus really is. Yet in his mercy Jesus draws him to a fuller understanding and thus strengthens his faith. For Musculus, the beginnings of faith are always graciously accepted, never severely rejected: "A dimly burning wick he does not extinguish on account of his goodness."[81]

The Response of Christ

Since Musculus wants to stress the goodwill of Jesus toward the ruler, the response of Jesus presents something of an exegetical challenge for him. Hearing the request of the desperate father, Jesus answers harshly: "Unless you see signs and wonders you will not believe." When the ruler reiterates his plea—"Lord, come down before my child dies"—Jesus offers him hope with the words: "Go, your son lives." As in the story of the wedding miracle, Jesus' words of censure seem incongruous with his actions. If Jesus is rebuking the ruler for his request, why does he eventually grant it? For Musculus, as for other commentators, the solution lies in understanding whom Jesus is actually addressing. A careful examination of the words shows that Jesus' rebuke is not directed primarily to the ruler at all but to the Jews in general.

Many of the Fathers, however, make no attempt to soften the sting of Jesus' words. Nonnus simply states that Jesus addressed him with his indignant words.[82] Augustine also argues that Jesus' rebuke was directed primarily at the ruler; Jesus looked into his heart and publicly exposed his lack of faith. When he rebuked the ruler, it was as if he said: "'Go, your son lives,' don't be a nuisance to me; 'Unless you see signs and wonders you do not believe.' You want my presence in your home; I can command even with a word. Do not believe from signs. A foreign centurion believed that I could do [the deed] by word and he believed before I did [it]. But you, 'unless you see signs and wonders, you do not believe.'"[83]

Augustine argues, however, that the rebuke was also intended for the Jews, the ruler's "fellow citizens." Unlike the Samaritans, who believed in light of Jesus' teaching, the Jews demand a sign in order to believe. Having witnessed the sign, only a few of the Jews believed, whereas a multitude of Samaritans believed "in light of his word alone." By his rebuke Jesus indirectly praises the faith of the Samaritans, a faith that characterizes the true Christian: "We are like to those Samaritans. We have heard the gospel; we have given assent to the gospel; we have believed in Christ through the gospel. We have seen no signs, we demand none."[84]

For Cyril, the rebuke is directed at the ruler as a representative of those whose minds are still hard. Jesus proclaims that they need miracles in order to penetrate the darkness of their deception. However, he does not reject them because of their lack of understanding but through a miracle he teaches them so "that they may easily be reinstructed unto what is profitable." Jesus shows therefore that he "does not reject our lack of apprehension; but benefiteth even the stumbling."[85]

For Chrysostom, Jesus' words certainly indicate that something was wrong with the ruler's faith. However, he argues that the rebuke was intended primarily to praise the Samaritans who believed without miracles or to upbraid the unbelief of the ruler's hometown, Capernaum. To the extent that Jesus was speaking to the ruler, he was saying in effect: "You have faith that is by no means what it should be, and you are still disposed to believe as if you were listening to a prophet." Jesus indicates therefore that the ruler was no less ill than the sick boy; the ruler's son suffered with a bodily illness, but the ruler himself was ill in "his state of mind." The ruler falsely assumed that miracles were intended primarily for the sake of the body. Jesus challenges this assumption "to show that miracles take place first and foremost for the sake of the soul." Yet a faith that requires no miracles, such as that of the Samaritans, is most pleasing to Jesus.[86]

In his interpretation of Jesus' rebuke, Musculus endeavors more than any of the Fathers to protect the dignity of the ruler. Like Chrysostom, he acknowledges that Jesus' words are partially directed at the ruler. However, he stresses the fact that Jesus uses a plural form of address in his rebuke: "He does not say: Unless you [singular] see, but: unless you people see signs and omens, you [plural] will not believe."[87] Thus, Jesus intends primarily to reproach the Jewish people who will not believe unless they are forced by miraculous signs.

According to Musculus, Jesus also indicates that the Jews were suffering with an illness much more dangerous than the bodily illness of the ruler's boy—namely the "sickness of unbelief" (*diffidentiae morbus*). This sickness is caused by the stubbornness of human reason, which opposes faith until finally convinced either by clear signs or certain arguments. The perversity of human reason infects not only the Jews, who seek signs, but also the Greeks, who seek wisdom (1 Cor 1:22). Neither the Jews nor the Greeks recognize that the things of God must first be believed in order to be understood.[88]

According to Musculus, Jesus' rebuke also has a permanent relevance for all believers. By his admonition, Jesus teaches two important lessons. First, he shows how much he detests unbelief and how he desires an eagerness to believe such as he found among the Samaritans. Echoing the comments of Augustine and Chrysostom, Musculus writes: "What he said here concerning the unbelief of the Jews was certainly done for the praise of the Samaritans." Unlike the Jews, the Samaritans were not moved to faith by signs but, hearing only the teaching of the kingdom of God, confessed: "For we have heard for ourselves, and we know that this is truly the savior of the world" (Jn 4:42). Thus, Jesus teaches the believer to strive for a faith informed by the Word of God, not by the dictates of human reason: "Therefore, let us ask the Lord to give us to believe with a simple and sincere heart the word and the gospel of the kingdom of God, that we should not seek with the Jews signs, nor with the Greeks wisdom of the world, but that with the elect we might captivate our understanding in obedience to faith, whereby we apprehend by a firm and certain faith that Christ the crucified is the power and wisdom of God."[89]

Second, Jesus shows that spiritual illness is always much more dangerous than bodily illness. He makes this truth known not by any specific words but rather by the method in which he deals with the ruler. Before Jesus heals the body of the sick boy, he first addresses the more serious spiritual sickness of the ruler, namely unbelief (*diffidentia*). Musculus argues in fact that the boy was sick "by divine counsel" (*divino consilio*) in order to provide an occasion for the spiritual healing of the ruler and his household.[90]

For Musculus, not only do the words and behavior of Jesus teach eternal truths, but the ruler himself represents truths that have a permanent relevance. First, the ruler represents the "image of paternal love toward children" (*imaginem paterni animi erga liberos*). By nature parents pursue the welfare of their children, a truth children rarely recognize. In all of the gospel stories, one never reads of a son coming to Jesus on behalf of his father; but in several places, parents come to Jesus on behalf of their children.[91]

In addition to the positive image of paternal love, the ruler also represents a negative "image of corrupt love and affection" (*corrupti amoris & affectus imaginem*). This image is indicated by the ruler's neglect of his son's spiritual needs; he seeks only a physical healing.[92] One sees this corruption of paternal love, Musculus argues, throughout the gospels: "What parent ever came to the Lord, who said: 'Lord, my son is not endowed with any fear of God, he is not moved by eagerness for piety, as a result of which I perceive him to be in danger of losing the welfare of his soul. Please, will you help?'"[93] According to Musculus, this distorted paternal love is so deep-rooted in human nature that it continues to influence even Christians. It is a shameful fact that parents rarely solicit the prayers of the Church for the spiritual welfare of their children. Because of the corruption of their love, parents are moved to such piety only when their children are in physical danger.[94]

Thus, not only was the ruler's faith weak according to Musculus, but his love was distorted by worldly values. Insofar as Jesus addresses the ruler, however, he does not rebuke him but rather speaks the words of hope: "Go, your son lives." Jesus never specifically reprimands the weakness of the ruler's faith: "He could have said: 'Don't you believe me able to cure even though absent? What is the need that I should come down with you? Moreover, even if your son should die, don't you believe me able to restore the dead to life?'"[95] Instead, Jesus simply grants the miracle, which heals not only the boy's bodily sickness but also the spiritual sickness of the ruler and his household.

The Miracle of the Boy's Healing

According to Musculus, the miracle of the boy's healing happens in such a way that the ruler and his household might have a sure "experience" (*experientia*) of the miracle. Initially, neither the ruler nor the servants experience the full impact of the miracle. The ruler hears Jesus declare his son well, but he believes that Jesus has seen by prophetic vision the natural recovery of the boy. The servants witness the sudden recovery, but they have no idea how it has happened. Not until the ruler questions his servants concerning the time of the boy's recovery do they have a certain "proof" (*experimentum*) of the power of Jesus' words over sickness and death. Musculus believes that the ruler's boy in fact died and was restored to life since Jesus does not say, "Your son is well," but rather, "Your son lives."[96]

Musculus does not condemn the questioning of the ruler regarding the hour of recovery but rather praises it as a providential validation of the miracle's occurrence: "If the curiosity of the father had not investigated concerning the hour of the healing, the power of Christ manifested in this boy might have been uncertain."[97] Cyril and Chrysostom argue similarly that the ruler's investigation served to prove the miracle's occurrence.[98] Only Augustine condemns the ruler's questioning as evidence of his unwillingness to believe. Like Thomas, the ruler demands certain proof of the miraculous, and thus both men deserved Jesus' reprimand: "The Lord accused him [Thomas] exactly as this royal official. To the latter he said, 'Unless you see signs and wonders, you do not believe.' But to the former he said, 'Because you have seen, you have believed.'"[99] Musculus argues however that Thomas's investigation, like the ruler's, served to make a miraculous event "more manifest and more certain" (*manifestior ac certior*). Such is the nature of God's truth, according to Musculus, that the more it is investigated, the more evident it becomes. Thus, Jesus did not attempt to persuade the ruler of the miracle's occurrence but rather allowed him to experience the truth of the event itself.[100]

The Fruit of the Miracle

For Musculus and the Fathers, the obvious result of the miracle was an increase in faith. Not only the ruler himself but also his whole household ultimately believed. Musculus, like Chrysostom, argues that the ruler initially believed in Jesus "as in a prophet and man of God" (*tamquam prophetae ac viro dei*). Having discovered the power of Jesus' word, however, the ruler no longer believed in him as a prophet, "but as the Christ, the son of God and the savior sent into the world." Therefore, the boy's sickness and death ultimately served as the occasion for the salvation of his father and household.[101]

Musculus and Chrysostom both analyze the mechanism by which the ruler and his household believed. Both argue that the ruler and the servants each possessed information that could not persuade in isolation, but that, taken together, proved the occurrence of the miracle. Regarding the servants, Chrysostom states: "Though they had not been present, nor had they heard Christ speak, nor did they know the time, upon learning from their master that this was the time they held the evidence of His power incontestable, and for this reason they themselves believed in Him."[102] According to Musculus, without the testimony of his servants, the ruler could not believe; without the ruler's own testimony, however, the servants would not have come to faith. God in his wisdom ordered events in such a way that the ruler and his servants would believe by discovering on their own the truth of the miracle.[103]

CONCLUSION

Musculus presents a spirited case for utilizing the writings of the Church Fathers in any attempt to explain the meaning of Scripture. The study of the Bible and the study of the Fathers, he argues, properly go hand in hand. According to Musculus, few scholars have surpassed the erudition and biblical scholarship expressed in the patristic writings, and therefore this body of ancient literature represents an essential resource for the responsible Christian scholar. Certainly, the views of the Fathers do not represent the last word on any topic. A rejection of their authority, however, does not mean we should close our ears. For Musculus, the Fathers deserve our attention not because they speak unanimously or with the voice of ultimate authority but because of their love of God, sanctity of life, and dedication to biblical scholarship.

Musculus demonstrated his own eagerness to learn from the Fathers by a lifetime of tireless patristic scholarship. Indeed, in this arena Musculus had few peers among the Protestant reformers. He cites the Fathers throughout many of his theological works and felt prepared to battle one of the most distinguished Catholic theologians of the early sixteenth century, Johann Cochlaeus, on the basis of the patristic writings.

In his commentary on John, Musculus demonstrates a significant indebtedness to patristic interpretations. His exegesis certainly does not support the caricature of the Protestant scholar who, alone in his study with nothing but the Bible and his own thoughts, pronounces the definitive interpretation, clear to anyone similarly inspired by the Holy Spirit. Musculus not only explicitly cites the interpretations of the Fathers throughout his John commentary but also echoes patristic interpretive ideas in places where he does not acknowledge borrowings. Thus, on the surface Musculus appears to interpret the healing of the ruler's son independently of patristic interpretations. But on a deeper level, a level that can only be seen by a comparison of actual exegesis, Musculus shows a strong reliance on patristic interpretive ideas, in particular the ideas of Chrysostom.

Chrysostom is known for his propensity to discover in the biblical text moral maxims for the Christian life, a propensity that Musculus admires and emulates. In many instances Musculus follows the general outline of Chrysostom's interpretation but adds his own moral application. Thus, in his analysis of Jesus' motives for returning to Cana, Musculus reiterates Chrysostom's idea: Jesus returned to strengthen the faith of the people who witnessed the wedding miracle. But Musculus uses the idea to add his own observation about human nature: because of the corruption of human nature, people easily lose the "beginnings of heavenly things." In addressing the question of the ruler's identity, Musculus follows Chrysostom in arguing that the royal designation is used loosely; the man is royal only insofar as he serves royalty. Again, Musculus elaborates on this observation to make the practical suggestion that Christians should always hope for the conversion of their rulers. In addressing the question of the ruler's motives, Musculus reiterates Chrysostom's emphasis on the fatherly love expressed by the ruler. But Musculus uses Chrysostom's idea as a springboard for an extended discussion of the nature of parental love. Both Musculus and Chrysostom argue that the ruler was no less sick than his son. For Chrysostom, he is sick in "his state of mind," while for Musculus he suffers from the "sickness of unbelief." Again, this observation provides the occasion for an extended discussion by Musculus concerning the nature of human reason, which so often stands in the way of faith.

These examples and others indicate a basic pattern in Musculus's interpretation of the healing of the ruler's son: Musculus accepts and adapts the general lines of Chrysostom's interpretation in order to discuss moral issues of practical importance to all Christians. Musculus's comments echo those of Cyril and Augustine only in instances in which they agree with Chrysostom's exegesis, and in the case of Augustine the points of agreement are infrequent. Certainly Musculus does not reject Augustine in toto, for in his theological writings he cites and refers to Augustine more than any other Father. Yet while Augustine may be the preeminent theologian for Musculus, Chrysostom is the exegete par excellence.

The crucial point is to recognize that Musculus did not work in an exegetical vacuum. He shows himself willing to learn from the masters. While Musculus's hermeneutic assumes the sufficiency of Scripture—*scriptura scripturae interpres*—he does not think interpreters should ignore the comments of others. At the same time, Musculus's commentary is not a mere parroting of the views of others; he does not simply produce a medieval *catena* of patristic opinions. As a sophisticated commentator on Scripture, Musculus takes the middle road: he produces his own understanding of the meaning of Scripture, an understanding that often develops from the insights of others.

THREE

Musculus and the Medieval Commentators on the Feeding of the Five Thousand

The general relation of the Protestant reformers to medieval theological and exegetical traditions is a question that modern scholarship has found difficult to answer. To a large extent, these difficulties arise from a basic impulse of the Reformation itself, an impulse to criticize and judge the past. Often when the Reformers discuss the past, they seem to reject their medieval ecclesiastical and theological heritage in toto. This rejection of the immediate past stems partly from the influence of the Renaissance ideal expressed by the slogan "ad fontes!" The true message of the gospel, they claim, can be uncovered only by jettisoning the accumulations of medieval theology and by returning to the pure biblical and patristic sources. Partly, however, these negative statements concerning the past result from the posturing that emerges in the context of heated debate. The Reformers deride medieval theology because they hold it responsible for producing the worst errors of Catholicism. Therefore, in order to evaluate the influence of medieval theology and exegesis on the Reformers, the historian must cut through the posturing of polemic; the purely negative statements, if read at face value, can blind the historian to the powerful and often positive influences of medieval thinking on the Reformers.

Sweeping statements condemning medieval theology are certainly not lacking in the works of Musculus. Yet a careful reading of his theology and exegesis betrays the influence of medieval theological methods and ideas. The main purpose of this chapter is to characterize Musculus's exegesis vis-à-vis the medieval exegetical tradition by comparing his comments on John 6:1–15 with a sample of medieval interpretations of the pericope. I will show that by setting Musculus's comments against a medieval context, we may gain insight into his exegesis, insight that no other context can provide. I preface this detailed, narrowly focused comparative study by addressing two main questions that are broader in scope. First, what was

Musculus's relationship to medieval theology in general? And second, what was Musculus's attitude toward medieval methods of interpretation—that is, medieval hermeneutics?

MUSCULUS AND MEDIEVAL THEOLOGY

The biographical sources are completely silent concerning the relationship of Musculus to medieval theology. Since he was not educated in a university, it is impossible to point to a particular medieval curriculum that may have exerted influence on his theological development and understanding. However, a reading of Musculus's theological magnum opus, the *Loci communes sacrae theologiae*, shows clearly that he was familiar with many of the primary works of medieval theology. While Musculus usually uses these sources negatively—that is, as a foil for presenting his own positions—he nevertheless demonstrates that he is not willing to ignore medieval theology altogether.

Musculus frequently betrays his impatience with scholastic theology in general. He refers with disdain to the endless disputations and dialectics of the scholastic theologians.[1] His references to scholastic theology are often prefaced with the words "the scholastics say" (*scholastici dicunt*), giving the impression that Musculus has a generalized and vague understanding of medieval scholastic theology.[2] However, in certain places Musculus demonstrates a more sophisticated familiarity with the different scholastic schools and with the questions disputed among them. Thus, at one point he offers a long list of questions that, he argues, are disputed among the Thomists, Scotists, Occamists, and Albertists.[3] In another place he presents an extended summary of the principal theological questions raised by the Scotists concerning the incarnation of the Word.[4] Although Musculus characterizes these questions as "the useless and curious subtleties of the Scholastics and Sophists," he demonstrates a basic understanding of the important issues in medieval scholasticism.[5]

In addition to his general references to scholastic positions, Musculus also cites specific medieval authorities in the *Loci communes*. Most of his citations are from three authors: Peter Lombard, Gabriel Biel, and Bernard of Clairvaux. Like Luther and Calvin, Musculus shows a genuine affection for the works of Bernard. In all ten references, Musculus approves of the ideas expressed by the Cistercian abbot.[6] Musculus's limited use of Biel, however, is entirely negative; in the context of his attack on the Mass, he cites Biel's *Canonis misse expositio* ten times in order to demonstrate the errors of scholastic theology.[7] In a similar fashion, Musculus also cites Lombard's *Sententiae in IV libris distinctae* throughout the *Loci communes* in order to distinguish his own views.[8]

Musculus's use of Lombard, however, often has more than a simply negative function. Frequently, the topics of scholastic theology treated in Lombard's *Sen-*

tences determine the topics, or *loci*, of Musculus's systematic theology. In certain places, therefore, Musculus's work resembles a standard literary genre of scholastic theology—namely, a commentary on Lombard's *Sentences*. Examples of Lombard's influence can be seen in Musculus's treatment of the following topics: "Quae sint partes poenitentiae"; "De meritis erga Deum"; "An non culpa tantum, sed et poena remittatur"; "An post mortem quoque remittantur peccata"; "An voluntatis Dei quaerenda sit causa"; "An voluntas Dei impediri possit"; "Quae sint divinae dilectionis species"; and "De eo quod scholastici dicunt nescire hominem utrum amore vel odio dignus sit."[9] All of these topics are typically medieval, are culled from Lombard's *Sentences* and are thoroughly discussed by Musculus. Under these topic headings, Musculus frequently describes the scholastic solutions as expressed in Lombard and then proceeds to dismantle them, offering his own contrasting views and occasionally using the standard scholastic format of dividing each topic into a *quaestio, objectio,* and *responsio.*[10] However, Musculus occasionally finds Lombard's discussion helpful in a positive sense for framing his own views. For example, in his treatment of God's will, Musculus cites with approval Lombard's assertion that the biblical expressions concerning the will of God may be grouped into two categories: expressions that describe what God's will is in itself, or strictly speaking (*proprie*), and expressions that describe God's will figuratively (*secundum figuram*).[11] Similarly, in his discussion of penance, Musculus adapts the three parts outlined by Lombard—namely, compunction of the heart (*compunctio cordis*), confession of the mouth (*confessio oris*), and works of satisfaction (*satisfactionis opera*)—in order to express his own three moments: sorrow of the heart (*dolor cordis*), changing of the mind (*mutatio mentis*), and conversion to God (*conversio ad deum*).[12] Lombard's *Sentences* is thus an important source for Musculus, not only as a foil but also as a guide to appropriate topics of discussion and to important distinctions within those topics.

MUSCULUS AND MEDIEVAL HERMENEUTICS

In determining Musculus's attitude toward medieval methods of biblical interpretation, we are limited to the few remarks that he makes in the course of his biblical commentaries. Musculus never produced a systematic discussion of his own hermeneutical principles, and even in his long section on the Bible in the *Loci communes,* he does not discuss the rules or methods for discerning the true meaning of Scripture. However, by examining his occasional statements concerning the use of allegory and the spiritual level of interpretation, we can achieve at least a rudimentary understanding of his attitude toward medieval hermeneutics.

The most characteristic feature of medieval exegesis is the attempt to explain the Bible according to different levels of meaning. The assumption of a multiplicity of senses is based on the medieval (and patristic) understanding of the nature of the Bible. As an inspired book, the Bible expresses the words and will of God and thus must consistently edify the Christian reader. Scriptural passages that appear unedifying on the surface must have a higher, spiritual meaning than the meaning expressed by the mere words. Even when the literal meaning is inoffensive, the exegete may appropriately search for the spiritual or allegorical meanings of a text because the Bible, as a book authored by God, is dense in layers of signification.

Medieval hermeneutical theory usually divides the spiritual meaning of the Bible into three main levels: the allegorical, the tropological, and the anagogical; each of these spiritual senses corresponds to a theological virtue. The allegorical meaning, corresponding to faith, shows what one should believe; the tropological meaning, corresponding to love, shows the moral principles that should guide one's life; and the anagogical meaning, corresponding to hope, shows the future or heavenly realities that the believer anxiously awaits. Medieval exegetes utilize, define, and name these spiritual layers differently, and they express differing views concerning the importance of the spiritual meaning versus the literal meaning. Yet all agree that the exegete may legitimately understand certain passages to express spiritual truths that lie hidden under the words of the Bible.

Like many Protestant reformers, Musculus is clearly troubled by what he considers the excesses associated with the spiritual interpretation of Scripture. In his comments on Paul's allegory in Galatians 4:24, Musculus argues that one cannot defend allegorical exegesis on the basis of Paul's example: "that absurd eagerness for allegorizing" (*praeposterum illud allegorizandi studium*) has no defense in an appeal to Paul's interpretation of the Old Testament.[13] Similarly, in his Isaiah commentary, Musculus condemns other expositions he has read in which, "by a contempt for the historical sense, all things are carried directly to the mysteries of the kingdom of Christ."[14] Although the intentions of these commentators are laudable, their method is faulty:

> Their zeal, although hardly reproachable in itself, nevertheless pours out much darkness on the historical simplicity, and opens the doors for transforming the meaning of the Scriptures into a thousand forms in accordance with the cleverness of anybody's intelligence, which to wise persons seems to be more a game than the proper and sincere exposition of the Scriptures. They err especially in the fact that they suppose that by this method the mysteries of Christ the Savior are explained, and his kingdom is illustrated. Thus while they subtly transform everything, they render suspect all exposition of the Scriptures.[15]

Musculus clearly does not reject allegorical interpretation altogether, since he offers allegories in his own exegesis. However, allegorical interpretations should always be circumscribed by a primary devotion to the historical or literal sense. Allegorization is permissible, he argues, only when the historical sense itself clearly suggests the propriety of such an interpretation. Those who readily convert everything into allegories may be condemned because they do so "without the leading of history" (*sine ductu historiae*).[16] The interpreter must always cautiously consider whether the biblical text itself demands a spiritual reading: "One should not lightly flee to allegories in explaining the Scriptures . . . unless evident necessity should compel it."[17]

Unfortunately, Musculus does not clearly express what criteria should be used to determine this "evident necessity." However, he hints at these criteria in his explanation of the meaning of John 5:39: "You search the Scriptures, because you think that in them you have eternal life; and it is these that bear witness of me." Certain parts of Scripture, Musculus argues, require a special "searching" (*scrutatio*) such as that mentioned by Jesus. This searching takes place "whenever the very words of Scripture are inspected more deeply beyond the sense of the letter, so that the sense of the spirit may be drawn out, a thing which should be done in parables, allegories, metaphors, and mystical figures."[18] Here, Musculus argues that a spiritual interpretation is appropriate in places where the literal meaning of a text, by its grammar and context, shows itself in fact to be a spiritual meaning. Yet in addition to these places, Musculus argues that there are "some things in the Scriptures that require a special searching of three kinds." The first kind of searching is a christological reading of the Scriptures: one should examine a biblical text more deeply in order to see how it relates to and reveals Christ. Musculus's second method of searching corresponds to the medieval tropological interpretation of the Bible. Its purpose is "that we might be established in zeal of piety and that we might be prepared for the good works which God has prepared so that we might walk in them." The third searching, corresponding to anagogical interpretation, is the type of exposition mentioned in Romans 15:4—namely, an exposition that nurtures hope.[19]

In his commentaries, Musculus utilizes primarily the moral or tropological method of spiritual exegesis. He suggests, in fact, that the ultimate goal of the commentator should be to expose the moral applications suggested by the biblical text.[20] By the structure of his commentaries, Musculus also highlights the tropological reading of the Bible; to each section of textual "explanatio," he appends a section usually entitled "observatio" or "notanda," in which he discusses the moral maxims that may be derived from the text.[21] Although Musculus occasionally introduces allegorical or anagogical interpretations, his commentaries are dominated by tropological exposition. The interpreter, he argues, must expose this level of meaning because many people who read the Bible "will cling to the shell of it and will not be able to reach the sweetness of the kernel."[22]

THE FEEDING OF THE FIVE THOUSAND (JN 6:1–15)

In order to provide a medieval context for Musculus's interpretation of the fourth gospel, we must select appropriate medieval exegesis for comparison, a selection made difficult by the large number of medieval John commentaries. Even if we limit ourselves to the commentaries that were available to Musculus in printed editions, we find at least fifteen possible candidates for comparison.[23] As indicated by the number of printed editions, two commentaries were very popular in the late fifteenth and early sixteenth centuries: the "postils" of the Franciscan Nicholas of Lyra (d. 1349) and the "enarrationes" of the Bulgarian archbishop Theophylact (ca. 1050–1108).[24] These two commentators are an obvious choice for this study for an even more important reason: they represent the only medieval commentators on John whom Musculus actually cites in the course of his own commentary.[25] In addition to these two, I have chosen the commentaries of the Dominicans Thomas Aquinas (1225–1274) and Hugh of St. Cher (ca. 1195–1263), who, judging by the number of printed editions, followed only Lyra and Theophylact in popularity.[26] I have also chosen the commentary of the Carthusian *doctor ecstaticus*, Denis of Leeuwen (1402/3–1471), which was reissued during the time Musculus was working on his John commentary.[27] Finally, in order to include early medieval exegesis, I have chosen the commentary of the Benedictine monk, Rupert of Deutz (ca. 1075–1129), and the *Glossa ordinaria*, which was compiled in the early twelfth century at the cathedral school in Laon.[28]

This comparative study will take place on two basic levels. First, I compare the literal exegesis of Musculus and the medieval commentators on four basic segments of the miracle story. Second, I compare the way these commentators interpret the story for its spiritual significance on the three main levels defined by medieval hermeneutics: tropology, allegory, and anagogy. The sheer length of Musculus's comments precludes an exhaustive treatment of his exegesis. Stretching to nearly thirty densely printed folio pages, his interpretation of these fifteen verses dwarfs even the most garrulous of the medieval commentators. Therefore I have highlighted the parts of his exegesis that provide the best points of comparison with the medieval interpretations.

The Literal Interpretation

The Setting (Jn 6:1–5a)

John's account of the miracle begins with Jesus crossing the Sea of Galilee sometime around the Passover celebration. Followed by a large number of people who have seen previous signs, Jesus climbs a mountain, where he sits with his disciples. From this vantage point, Jesus notices the crowd of followers who approach.

The primary exegetical problem in John's account of the setting of the miracle is its chronology. For Musculus and for certain medieval commentators, the problem emerges with the first two words of the narrative: "post haec" (after these things). In the previous chapter, Jesus is in Jerusalem during a "feast of the Jews," traditionally understood as Pentecost, and yet the miracle of the feeding of the five thousands takes place around the time of the Passover. Therefore, a considerable amount of time seems to have elapsed between chapters 5 and 6. The phrase "post haec," however, suggests a smooth chronological transition between the events of the two chapters. In traditional exegesis, the problem is compounded by the attempt to harmonize the chronology of the miracle with the synoptic gospels.

While many medieval commentators are uninterested in the chronological problems presented by John's account, Rupert of Deutz and Hugh of St. Cher attempt to resolve these difficulties. Rupert suggests that one must read the words "post haec abiit" (after these things he departed) not as a prepositional phrase but rather as an adverbial construction: "post abiit" (later he departed). Clearly, he argues, Jesus could not have crossed the lake from Jerusalem, where the events of chapter 5 take place. Furthermore, since the Passover is "at hand," nearly a year has elapsed since Jesus was in Jerusalem. To discover what Jesus did in the course of that year, Rupert argues that one must consult the other gospels, in particular the gospel of Matthew.[29]

While Hugh is familiar with the type of solution offered by Rupert, he thinks the chronological difficulty is better solved by an understanding of the miracle of the feeding as a "recapitulation" (*recapitulatio*). He argues that the healing of the paralytic in chapter 5, which took place during Pentecost, must have followed the miracle of the healing in chapter 6, which took place during the time of the Passover. Therefore, according to Hugh, John has interrupted the chronological sequence of events in his gospel in order to recapitulate the story of the feeding of the five thousand.[30]

In his discussion of the chronological problem, Musculus makes no use of Hugh's solution. His comments, however, closely resemble the remarks of Rupert. It is not necessary, he argues, to understand the miracle of the feeding to have occurred immediately after the events of the preceding chapter. Musculus accepts the traditional exegetical assumption that the paralytic was healed during the feast of Pentecost. Therefore, like Rupert, he argues that "approximately the space of a year came in between." The activities of Jesus during that year are passed over by John but are related by the other evangelists. Thus, for Musculus the phrase "post haec" is intended to remind the reader not of the events of the preceding chapter but of the events that John has omitted and that are related in the synoptic gospels. It is impossible to read the transition between chapters 5 and 6 as a continuous narrative, "unless you are willing to take away the authority of truth from the other evangelists."[31]

Musculus continually refers to the other gospels in his exposition of the feeding miracle in order not only to resolve the different accounts but also to provide information and details in his exposition of John's narrative. Thus, in his analysis of Jesus' reasons for crossing the lake, Musculus argues that the evidence from the other gospels demonstrates that several different factors motivated Jesus to make the journey. Musculus's discussion of this traditional exegetical topic closely corresponds to previous medieval exposition, especially the comments of Hugh and Denis, who, like Musculus, present multiple explanations of Jesus' motives.

For Musculus, the first motive behind Jesus' retreat was the need to withdraw from the savagery of Herod, who had just executed John the Baptist. This explanation, which is also offered by Rupert, Hugh, and Denis, emerges from Matthew's account, in which Jesus hears of John's execution and immediately retires to a deserted place (Mt 14:13).[32] Second, from Mark's gospel (6:31), Musculus argues that Jesus also crossed the lake in order to provide a time of rest and quiet for his disciples, who were weary from their efforts in preaching the gospel throughout Galilee. Among the medieval expositors, only Denis joins Musculus in assigning this Markan motive to Jesus' retreat.[33] Third, Musculus argues that Jesus crossed the lake in order to avoid the Passover feast in Jerusalem. Here, Musculus cites the comments of Cyril of Alexandria, who argues that Jesus did not want to provoke the Jews in Jerusalem before the time of his passion. Denis and Lyra also argue that Jesus was avoiding the Jewish leaders in order to forestall his own death. Thomas and Hugh, basing their remarks on the comments of Chrysostom, argue in a similar vein that Jesus was attempting to appease the Jews after infuriating them with his harsh words. Similarly, Theophylact states that Jesus, by withdrawing, was "soothing" (καταπραύνει) their anger.[34] Musculus's fourth and final explanation of Jesus' motives is without medieval counterpart. He argues that Jesus crossed the lake in order to provide the occasion for the future miracle. Musculus emphasizes that the miracle of the feeding did not take place by happenstance. Rather, everything that Jesus did "was carried out by a certain fixed and determined superintendence."[35]

By assigning multiple causes to Jesus' retreat, Musculus engages in a typically medieval exegetical approach. John's narrative offers no explicit explanation of the reasons for Jesus' crossing of the lake. But by consulting the other gospels, the exegetical tradition, and his own theological presuppositions, Musculus provides the reader with a detailed analysis of the various factors that prompted Jesus to cross the Sea of Galilee.

A similar approach is at work in Musculus's analysis of the motives that prompted the multitude of people to follow Jesus. Here, however, John's gospel indicates the reason: they followed Jesus "because they were seeing the signs which he was performing on those who were sick" (Jn 6:2). Although the text seems to suggest a single motivating factor, Musculus follows a general impulse in the medieval commentary tradition to assign various motives to the people who were following Jesus. For Musculus and the medieval commentators, the signs motivated people in different ways to follow Jesus. That is to say, the fact that they all followed because of the signs does not indicate unanimity of purpose. In fact, Rupert argues that some of the people did not follow because of the signs. Otherwise, how would one understand Jesus' statement: "You seek me, not because you saw signs" (Jn 6:26)? Therefore, Rupert states that the multitude of people followed him "with various dispositions" (*diversa mente*).[36] Theophylact concedes that they followed because of the signs, but he argues that "the better" (κρείττονες) are those who follow Jesus on account of his teaching. Similarly, Thomas states that the "less perfect and less perceptive" followed because of seeing the miracles, while the "better disposed" followed Jesus because of his teaching.[37]

Musculus argues that some of the people were indeed following in order to hear Jesus' teaching. These people were affected by the signs, but in a particular way: they saw the signs, concluded that Jesus was sent from God, and therefore followed him in order to hear divine instruction. A second group of people, according to Musculus, were motivated by base curiosity. They saw the signs and followed in order "to observe and hear unusual and new things" (*res insolentes ac novas spectare & audire*). Finally, some people saw the signs and followed Jesus in order to obtain bodily healing, either for themselves or for loved ones. Thus, Musculus argues, the disposition of those who followed Jesus was "varied" (*varius*), even though they all followed because of the signs.[38]

In dividing the multitude of people into three main groups, Musculus may be following the lead of Lyra, who offers precisely the same three divisions: those wanting healing, those desiring instruction, and the curious who simply want to see something new.[39] Hugh and Denis also mention these three groups but add two others: some, such as the Pharisees, followed in order to trap Jesus in his words, and others followed in order to be fed (bodily) by Jesus. Denis adds one further motivating factor: "Because the Lord Jesus was also very handsome according to the body and very eloquent . . . it is very likely that many were following him being delighted by his appearance and eloquence."[40] By dividing the crowd into various groups of people motivated by different factors, Denis, Hugh, and Lyra exhibit a typically medieval approach. Although it is impossible to prove their influence on Musculus's interpretation, it is important to note that his commentary exhibits not only the same medieval *divisio* method of exegesis but also the same exegetical ideas.

Further evidence that Musculus is influenced by Lyra emerges from his discussion of the quality of the signs Jesus was performing. John's gospel states that the people followed because of the signs Jesus was doing "on those who were sick" (Jn 6:2). This description prompts Lyra to discuss the special quality of Jesus' signs compared to spectacles produced by magic. Lyra concedes that "some curious and useless things are indeed produced well by the magical arts, as for example that statues speak and similar such things." However, only the kind of signs that Jesus performed, healings that led people back to God, were produced by divine power.[41]

Like Lyra, Musculus states that John specifies the kind of signs Jesus was performing in order to distinguish them from useless counterfeits. According to Musculus, if one observes in signs nothing but "unusualness and novelty of things" (*insolentiam ac rerum novitatem*), then one may easily be deceived by the signs of false prophets. It is necessary, he argues, to employ sound judgment in order to determine "what kind of signs may be appropriate to mockers and scoffers and what kind may be appropriate to the savior sent from God." The signs of Jesus, he argues, presented "a certain external and visible exemplar of heavenly grace and salvation." They were not done simply in order to produce astonishment but rather to heal the sick and to bring glory to God.[42]

The signs of unclean spirits bear an entirely different stamp, according to Musculus. They serve curiosity and produce amazement but are ultimately unprofitable. In contrast to the authentic signs done by God's power, these counterfeit signs are (like Lyra's talking statues) laughable, a point Musculus drives home with his discussion of the signs attributed to Muhammad. While Jesus healed the sick, cast out demons, and raised the dead, Muhammad "understood the howling of a wolf, heard a shoulder of a sheep on a table telling him that he should not eat it because it contained poison, and . . . split the globe of the moon and then repaired it." The signs of Muhammad and other false prophets are obvious, according to Musculus, because they serve no higher purpose; they simply provoke wonder and astonishment.[43]

When Musculus discusses the quality of Jesus' signs, he reiterates a traditional exegetical observation. Yet he does not simply parrot the views of previous expositors but rather expands and elaborates the topic in order to give his own distinctive analysis. Similarly, in his discussion of the mountain, Musculus is not plowing new exegetical ground. Yet his comments, while assuming the context of previous exposition, offer their own unique insights when seen in that context.

For most medieval commentators, Jesus' ascension of the mountain is significant primarily on an allegorical or mystical level of interpretation. As will be later shown, this level of interpretation also plays an important part in Musculus's own interpretation of the mountain. Literally, however, the mountain is interpreted by medieval commentators as a place suitable for teaching (Lyra, Theophylact, and Denis) or for rest and refreshment (Thomas).[44] While John's gospel simply states that Jesus sat on the mountain with his disciples, the medieval commentators assume that Jesus must have been teaching them, as was his custom. Theophylact states that Jesus wanted to communicate certain mystical teachings to his disciples. Therefore, he argues, it was suitable for Jesus to seek a place free from noise and activity.[45]

According to Musculus, Jesus' main purpose in ascending the mountain was to provide a place of rest and quiet for his disciples. For this purpose, a mountain was well-suited, since it offered shady places against the heat of the hot desert sun. In fact, Musculus argues that Jesus knew of certain hidden caves that would ideally provide his disciples with rest and refreshment. In his wisdom, Jesus foresaw that the desert plains were entirely unsuited to this purpose; if they had settled there, they would have been far too conspicuous and the multitude would have converged on them from every direction. Therefore, Musculus states, Jesus headed for "the recesses of this mountain" (*montis huius recessus*).[46]

While he concedes that John does not indicate what Jesus and the disciples were doing on the mountain, Musculus believes that their activity can be inferred from John's use of the word "sitting." This word, he argues, signifies rest, and therefore one must assume that Jesus was providing "refreshing nourishment" (*alimonia refocillans*) to the disciples. Musculus cites Mark 6:31 to demonstrate that the disciples were in need of bodily nourishment: "For there were many who were coming and going and they did not even have time for eating." Therefore, "if he led them out into the desert so that they might rest and acquire food, who can doubt that they were eating food on the mountain?" Musculus also assumes that Jesus was providing spiritual nourishment for the disciples—that is, "he was renewing their minds and forming them for the future labors of the kingdom of God." While he concedes that gospel text does not explicitly indicate that Jesus was teaching the disciples, Musculus argues that "it is presumed from the nature of Christ, who, according to his custom, always instructed them in the knowledge of the kingdom of God."[47]

Although Musculus treats the topic of the mountain much more thoroughly than most medieval commentators, his comments demonstrate how the observations and questions of medieval exegesis often dictate the basic course of his own interpretation. Similarly, in his discussion of Jesus' apparent avoidance of the Passover celebration, Musculus assumes and expands upon a traditional medieval exegetical topic. Since Jesus is on a remote mountain during the time of the Passover, he seems to violate the law that prescribes attendance of all men in Jerusalem during the celebration. A standard component of the medieval exegetical tradition is the attempt to explain Jesus' violation of the law.

Nearly every medieval commentator solves this problem in the manner expressed succinctly by Denis: "For just as he often observed legal things, in having to show himself a true man under the law, so sometimes he disregarded it, showing himself to be true God and legislator above the law."[48] In addition to this solution, Theophylact, Thomas, and Hugh add a further explanation: Jesus was showing by his avoidance of the Passover that the ceremonies of the law were about to end.[49] Lyra contributes a third solution to the problem, arguing that Jesus was legally excused from Passover attendance since the Jews were seeking to kill him.[50]

Musculus, like the medieval interpreters, argues that Jesus did not entirely disregard the precepts of the law. Jesus had already gone to Jerusalem many times "lest he should appear to despise the law of God" (*ne videretur legem dei contemnere*). In an argument similar to Lyra's, Musculus states that it was proper on this occasion for Jesus to stay away from Jerusalem since the Jewish leaders now wanted to kill him. Jesus did not want to provoke his enemies before the proper time. For Musculus, however, the more troubling question is one that is absent from the medieval commentaries. Why, he asks, did Jesus not encourage the following multitude to return to Jerusalem in order to fulfill *their* obedience to the law? To this question, Musculus offers two solutions. First, since John states clearly that the Passover was "at hand," it is possible that enough time remained for the people to return to Jerusalem for the Passover feast. After the miracle, Jesus may indeed have encouraged them to go. Second, Musculus argues that it would have been improper for Christ, who was the goal and fulfillment of the law, to send the people back to the shadowy figures of the law. The people were in fact fulfilling the true intention of the law by following Jesus: "In what way were they acting against the law of God and not rather fulfilling it, who, having left behind that shadowy and figurative Passover, were following Christ the true Passover?"[51]

The Dialogue between Jesus, Philip, and Andrew (Jn 6:5b-9)

According to John's narrative, after Jesus sees the approaching multitude he "tests" his disciple Philip by asking him: "Where are we to buy bread, that these may eat?" Philip answers that even a large sum of money (two hundred denarii) could not provide enough food to satisfy such a huge crowd. Another disciple, Andrew, then intrudes upon the dialogue with the observation that a certain boy is in possession of five barley loaves and two fish. Yet such meager provisions, Andrew notes, hardly amount to anything for such a large number of people.

The literal interpretation of this dialogue in medieval exegesis may be distilled into its response to two central questions: First, what does it mean for Jesus to "test" someone, and why does he single out Philip for this particular test? And second, what do the statements of Philip and Andrew indicate about their respective dispositions? These same questions are assumed by Musculus in his discussion of the dialogue between Jesus and the disciples. However, Musculus expands and develops both the questions and the answers of medieval exegesis in order to address the themes and issues that are of particular importance to him.

The medieval interpreters agree that Jesus does not test Philip in order to learn something. Indeed, John himself states plainly that Jesus "knew what he was intending to do" (verse 6). Since any limitation of Jesus' knowledge is excluded a priori by the medieval commentators, they assume that the testing of Philip is not for Jesus' benefit but rather for the benefit of others. Thus, in medieval exegesis the test has two primary purposes. First, medieval commentators (Rupert, Theophylact, Hugh, Thomas, Denis) argue that the test was a pedagogical device used by Jesus in order to instruct Philip and the other disciples.[52] Rupert states that Jesus was acting just as a benevolent teacher who sometimes questions a pupil, not because the teacher doubts the pupil's ignorance but because he wants to capture the attention of the pupil, who will then learn more effectively.[53] Some medieval commentators (Theophylact, Hugh, Thomas, Denis) argue that Jesus singled out Philip for the test because he was more in need of instruction than the other disciples. Philip's ignorance is demonstrated, according to these interpreters, by his request of Jesus in John 14:8: "Lord, show us the Father, and it is enough for us."[54] Denis, however, suggests that Jesus also tested Philip because of a special love and friendship that existed between the two.[55] The second purpose of the test in medieval exegesis is Jesus' desire to intensify the impact on the disciples and crowd of the impending miracle. The response of Philip and Andrew has the effect of publicizing the lack of any human means to supply the needed victuals. Therefore, Jesus' miracle would, according to Theophylact, Hugh, and Lyra, appear all the more evident and memorable.[56]

Like the medieval commentators, Musculus is quick to assert that Jesus' test of Philip was not for his own benefit since it would be impious to suggest his ignorance of future contingencies. In Musculus's interpretation, the test was for the benefit of others, serving both to instruct the disciples and to publish the impending miracle. Although Musculus presents the same two purposes of the test that are found in medieval exegesis, he raises more questions, gives more observations, and offers a more detailed analysis than is found in most medieval commentaries.

In his discussion of the pedagogical purpose of Jesus' test, Musculus explains, unlike the medieval commentators, why the instruction was needed. The disciples, he argues, were suffering with the "sickness of unbelief" (*morbum diffidentiae*). By his test Jesus was exposing this sickness and thereby preparing their minds for the future miracle. In addition, the disciples needed to recognize that the situation was quite beyond their ability. Philip, Musculus argues, was no more unbelieving than any of the other disciples. He was simply "appointed by the Lord" (*ordinatum a domino*) to serve as the conduit of Jesus' instruction to all of the disciples: "It must not be supposed that by that testing he had consideration only of Philip. In the one, he tested all, in the one he exercised the souls of all for the future miracle." In fact, says Musculus, Jesus was employing a clever pedagogical device in directing his words to Philip. Instead of directly putting them all to shame, he "corrects what had to be corrected silently in their souls."[57]

Like the medieval commentators, Musculus argues that Jesus tested the disciples so that the ensuing miracle would be more evident both to the disciples and to the multitude of followers. By eliciting the responses of Philip and Andrew, Jesus in effect publicizes the fact that the disciples are not equipped to feed the crowd. Jesus therefore dispels any suspicions of trickery concerning the impending miracle. By testing the disciples Jesus also reveals, according to Musculus, a pattern of how God deals with his people. God often intensifies periods of trials and testing in order to highlight the glory of divine liberation and salvation. The servitude of the Israelites was intensified in Egypt before they were divinely rescued. Similarly, Jesus tested his disciples so that his miraculous assistance "might be imprinted on their souls" (*animis illorum infigeretur*).[58]

For Musculus the responses of Philip and Andrew have both a negative and a positive function, corresponding to the two purposes of the test. Negatively, their responses reveal the unbelief of the disciples, while positively they serve to magnify appreciation for Jesus' miracle. In their negative function, Musculus argues that no distinction should be made between the responses of Philip and Andrew; both are spoken in unbelief. In this argument Musculus opposes the medieval commentators who argue (following Chrysostom) that Andrew demonstrates more faith than Philip. For these commentators, Philip exhibits no understanding or anticipation of a miraculous remedy. Andrew, on the other hand, remembers the miracle performed by Elisha in which twenty barley loaves were multiplied to feed a hundred people (2 Kgs 4:42–44). While Andrew suspects that Jesus might perform a similar miracle and thus exhibits more faith than Philip, he errs in assuming the necessity of a ratio similar to Elisha's—namely, twenty loaves per hundred people.[59]

Musculus flatly rejects this distinction of the responses of Philip and Andrew. He argues that all of the disciples heard Philip's response, and yet none of them stepped forward to remind him of Jesus' power. Therefore, Andrew's statement expresses no more faith than does Philip's. Neither Philip, Andrew, nor any of the other disciples recognized and believed that Jesus could remedy the situation by the power of his word alone. Musculus also argues that no distinction can be made between Philip and Andrew on the basis of the fact that Andrew is identified as "one of his disciples" while Philip is not identified as such. However, Musculus is so uneasy about this possible distinction that he emends the Greek text by adding the word ἔτι. The text of verse 8, he argues, should actually read as such: λέγει αὐτῷ ἔτι εἷς ἐκ τῶν μαθητῶν αὐτοῦ. This reading would implicitly include Philip as a disciple by designating Andrew as "yet another one of his disciples." Musculus makes this textual emendation not on the basis of known variant readings but simply on his assumption that the word may have been omitted "through the sleepiness of copyists" (*per librariorum somnolentiam*). But according to Musculus one cannot exclude Philip from the company of disciples, even on the basis of the unemended text, just as one cannot exclude Peter on the basis of Mark 16:7: "Go, tell his disciples and Peter."[60]

For Musculus the responses of Philip and Andrew function positively to establish the unambiguous occurrence of a miracle. Philip declares that they do not have enough money to remedy the situation, and Andrew declares that they do not have enough food. Therefore when Jesus provides the needed victuals, no one could doubt how it happened. The unambiguous character of the miracle is strengthened by noting that Andrew speaks "through diminution" (*per diminutionem*) when describing the boy's fish: καὶ δύο ὀψάρια ("and two little fish"). According to Musculus, John the Evangelist purposely uses this expression "lest we should think that these fish were huge, of the kind that are often caught in the sea."[61]

For Musculus, the responses of the disciples are important for the knowledge and illumination of Jesus' miracle primarily because they exhibit the judgment of reason. Here, Musculus engages in an extended discourse on the role of human reason that is quite unlike anything found in the medieval commentaries. Without the judgment of reason, Musculus argues, the works of God would not be seen for what they truly are. In the case of this miracle, human reason needed to judge that five thousand people could not possibly be fed with two hundred denarii, much less with five loaves. Only when reason makes such a judgment can one be led to a true knowledge of divine power. Therefore, by testing the disciples, Jesus was eliciting the judgment of human reason in order to lead them to faith: "And for this reason the miracles were displayed, so that with human reason being led into bewilderment and wonder, he might make a place for the knowledge of divine power and faith."[62] Musculus gives an extended review of biblical figures who, faced with the works of God, judged such works to be utterly impossible. In his review, Philip and Andrew find themselves in the distinguished company of Sarah, Moses, Zacharias, and the Virgin Mary, who all make proper use of their reason in order to advance in faith. Musculus concludes, therefore, that the judgment of reason "is not extinguished in the believing, but remains unshaken, and is used for this purpose, that it might serve the admiration of the works of God."[63]

The Miracle (*Jn 6:10–13*)

On the literal level of interpretation, John's description of the miracle raises few exegetical difficulties. Having given instructions for the people to recline on the ground, Jesus offers a prayer of thanksgiving and distributes the bread and fish to the people. When everyone is sated, the disciples obey Jesus' order to gather up all of the leftover pieces, which fill twelve baskets. For the medieval commentators and for Musculus, this description of the miracle has its primary significance in what it represents allegorically or spiritually and in what it teaches morally or tropologically. In the literal exposition of the miracle, there are essentially four topics of exegetical discussion. First, why does John mention only men in his numbering of the crowd? Second, why does Jesus give thanks for the food? Third, does Jesus himself distribute the food, or does he commission the disciples to distribute it? And fourth, what is the purpose and significance of the leftovers?

The medieval commentators who deal with the first question (Theophylact, Thomas, Lyra, Denis) argue unanimously that John does not exclude women and children from the scene of the miracle. Denis even suggests that the number of women and children probably exceeded the number of men. In numbering the multitude as five thousand men, John is following the Hebrew custom of taking a census by the number of men who are at least twenty years old (Nm 1:3).[64] In addition to this argument, Thomas suggests that only the men are mentioned "because only men can be completely instructed."[65] Like the medieval commentators, Musculus argues that women and children participated in eating the food that Jesus miraculously multiplied. Their presence is undeniable since Matthew specifically mentions them (Mt 14:21). The numbering of five thousand men, Musculus explains, is simply due to Jewish custom.[66]

For Musculus and the medieval commentators, Jesus' offering of thanksgiving has its obvious tropological application. The prayer, however, troubles medieval exegetes because it seems to suggest that Jesus was in need of divine assistance. Thus, Hugh asks why Jesus prayed on this occasion when he did not pray before even greater miracles, such as when he calmed the sea and raised the dead. Summarizing the comments of Chrysostom, Hugh argues that Jesus did not need external divine assistance to perform miracles. Since he performed other miracles without praying, he obviously had the authority and power to accomplish them. Therefore, when Jesus prayed before performing a miracle, he did so in order to instruct his audience that he was not in opposition to God.[67] Thomas and Theophylact also argue that Jesus was not praying for his own sake but in order to show the people that he had come according to the will of God. Jesus performed greater miracles without praying, notes Theophylact, when there was no crowd of observers needing instruction.[68] According to Lyra, Jesus sometimes performed miracles by a simple command in order to demonstrate his own power and authority. But sometimes he prayed in order to show that he was not accomplishing his miracles by the demonic magical arts.[69]

For Musculus, Jesus' prayer is troubling, not because it suggests that Jesus was interceding for divine assistance but rather because it suggests that he did not possess all things equally with the Father. Therefore Musculus frames his question differently than the medieval commentators: How was it fitting, he asks, for Jesus to give thanks to the Father, "since all things are equally his and the Father's, and he is of the same power and honor with the Father?" The solution to this question, according to Musculus, lies not in understanding the prayer as a pedagogical medium but rather in properly distinguishing the two natures of Christ: "I respond: if you consider only the divine nature in Christ, you will not discover by what reason it was fitting for Christ to give thanks to the Father."[70] But if one considers the human nature in Christ, argues Musculus, his giving of thanks appears appropriate. By a syllogistic form of reasoning, Musculus demonstrates his point in the following manner. As a man, Jesus was subject to temptations. Since he was subject to temptations, it was appropriate for him to seek assistance from God through prayer. If it was appropriate to seek assistance through prayer, it was obviously fitting for him to return thanks for the assistance he received. Musculus offers an extended discussion of the proper understanding of the two natures of Christ and closes his argument with a long quotation from Augustine's treatment of the same topic in the *Enchiridion ad Laurentium*.[71]

The third exegetical topic in the medieval commentaries centers on the question of how Jesus distributes the food to the crowd. In the synoptic gospels, Jesus gives the food to the disciples, who then distribute it to the reclining multitude. Yet in John's account, no mention is made of the disciples' role in the distribution; Jesus appears to act independently in passing out the victuals. The medieval interpreters smooth this discrepancy simply by reading John's account in the light of the synoptic accounts. John has merely omitted a detail that is furnished by the gospels of Mark, Matthew, and Luke. According to Thomas, Jesus may be credited with distributing the food, even though he accomplishes it through others: "It says here that he distributed it because in a way he himself does what he does by means of others."[72] For Theophylact, however, no discrepancy exists between John's and the synoptics' accounts because his version of John's gospel contains a variant reading of verse 11, which harmonizes the Johannine account with the other gospels.[73] Because Musculus utilizes the same reading of verse 11 as Theophylact, he is not faced with the problem of harmonization that confronts the medieval interpreters using the Vulgate. Musculus follows the lead not only of Theophylact but also of Erasmus, who uses the variant reading in his translation of the New Testament and who justifies this reading in his *Annotationes*.[74]

The fourth topic in the literal exposition of the miracle concerns the purpose and significance of the twelve baskets of leftover food. The overwhelming abundance of leftover food invites the suspicion of extravagance on Jesus' part. Against this suspicion, Theophylact, Hugh, and Thomas state that the excess was not a gaudy, ostentatious display of power. Rather, they argue that Jesus supplied the abundant amount in order to confirm the reality of the miracle. The existence of visible and tangible leftover food would destroy any suspicion of mass delusion on the part of the crowd; the people had really been sated and had not just imagined it.[75] Second, Rupert and Denis argue that the excess food was produced for feeding the poor at a later time.[76] In a similar vein, Lyra notes that in carrying the excess food to those who had not been present, the disciples were also able to publicize effectively the miracle that had taken place.[77] Third, Jesus produced the excess food especially for the sake of the disciples, whose faith needed strengthening. Theophylact, Hugh, Thomas, and Lyra argue that twelve baskets of food were gathered not by chance but by divine arrangement. The truth of the miracle has a powerful impact on the mind of each disciple because each carries the evidence of the miracle in his own hands. It was important for the future teachers of the whole world to have the miracle impressed upon their memories. Hugh notes that Jesus himself confirms this purpose of the leftover food in Matthew 16:9 when he reminds the disciples of the baskets they carried.[78]

In his discussion of the leftover food, Musculus essentially reiterates the first and third purposes discussed by the medieval commentators. The excess food, he argues, served first to illustrate in a conspicuous manner the truth of the miracle to all who had eaten. Second, "by divine arrangement" (*divina dispositione*) each disciple carries his own basket of food so that each disciple would see with his own eyes and carry with his own hands "the most clear evidence of the displayed miracle" (*apertissimum aediti miraculi testimonium*). If the crowd had eaten all of the food, the miracle would have been easily forgotten. Therefore, in order to strengthen their faith and to place the miracle firmly in their memories, Jesus arranges for each disciple to carry a basket of the miraculous food.[79]

The Effects of the Miracle (*Jn 6:14–15*)

In John's narrative, the miracle of the feeding produces two primary effects, each of which generates significant discussion by medieval commentators. First, the people proclaim Jesus to be "truly the prophet who is to come into the world." Second, the people intend to force Jesus to be their king, an intention Jesus thwarts by withdrawing once again to the mountain. Medieval exegetes raise several questions in their interpretation of these effects of the miracle. Does the proclamation of Jesus as the prophet constitute a true confession of faith? In what sense may Jesus rightly be called a prophet? What were the people's motives in the attempt to establish Jesus' kingship? Finally, why does Jesus avoid the proclamation of his kingship by slipping away to the mountain? Does he deny that he is their rightful king? These same questions are raised by Musculus and provide the framework for his exposition of the miracle's effects.

The proclamation of Jesus as a prophet is analyzed differently in medieval exegesis. At one extreme, the Gloss argues that this confession was entirely inappropriate. The people should have confessed him to be God, but because of the weakness of their faith, they merely confer a prophetic dignity on Jesus.[80] On the other hand, Lyra argues that the confession was completely worthy of Jesus; the people were confessing him to be the true Christ. They were not putting Jesus on an equal footing with the other prophets but were recognizing the fulfillment of the prophecy in Deuteronomy 18:18: "I will raise up a prophet for them." The people understood that only this prophet had come into the world for their salvation.[81] Similarly, Hugh, Thomas, and Denis argue that the people were conferring a unique prophetic dignity on Jesus, recognizing him to be the special prophet foretold in Deuteronomy 18. According to Denis, they were not confessing Jesus to be simply a prophet but "that highest Prophet" (*summum illum Prophetam*), concerning whom Moses prophesied.[82]

Thomas, however, expresses indecision concerning the value of the people's proclamation. On the one hand, he argues that "these people seem to realize that Christ was a superior prophet"; on the other hand, he states that they did not have perfect faith because "they believed that Jesus was only a prophet, while he was also lord of the prophets." For Thomas, the application of the prophetic dignity to Christ is problematic from an epistemological standpoint. A prophet is so designated because of a special cognitive power in which "sensible species could be formed in the imagination . . . to present, future, or hidden events." Only in this type of cognition, which Thomas calls "sense knowledge," does Jesus have a kind of knowledge that may be termed prophetic. Regarding the other types of cognition—namely, "intellectual knowledge" and "divine knowledge"—Jesus shares nothing in common with the prophets.[83] Denis repeats much of Thomas's epistemological discussion and concludes that Jesus may be designated a prophet only in a limited sense: "Although truly the intellectual knowledge of Christ was perfect, and not strictly speaking prophetic, yet according to the notion of imaginative powers, he had conformity with the prophets, because sensible forms were able to be formed in the imagination of the soul of Christ, through which hidden and future things were being represented to his soul." Only in this imaginative capacity of the mind does Jesus share something in common with the other prophets. But unlike the other prophets, Jesus does not comprehend notions imperfectly but was, according to Denis, "the most excellent comprehensor" (*excellentissimus comprehensor*).[84]

Like most of the medieval commentators, Musculus commends the proclamation of the people as a proper confession of faith. They did not think Jesus was a prophet like any other but the special prophet whom Moses predicted. Because of the frequent public readings of Moses, these people were familiar with the prophecy in Deuteronomy 18. Therefore, according to Musculus "they are not at all deceived because they believe Jesus to be this prophet, concerning whom Moses made the prediction." These people err only in the fact that "they were not yet rightly understanding his majesty."[85]

Like Thomas and Denis, Musculus expresses uneasiness concerning the prophetic role of Jesus. However, his uneasiness arises not from the implied cognitive limitations of Jesus but rather because the prophetic distinction seems to add fuel to the fire of the Jewish and Islamic polemics against Christianity. The Jews, according to Musculus, argue that the prophets Elijah and Elisha performed miraculous signs similar to those of Jesus, and yet these prophets are not worshiped or given divine honor. The Turks, he argues, believe that Jesus was merely a messenger and prophet of God and therefore should not be worshiped as God. Musculus concedes that if no greater honor applied to Jesus other than the prophetic distinction, he should not be worshiped. But the designation of Jesus as prophet is only one of many honorific titles given to Jesus in the Bible. Therefore, his prophetic dignity should never be isolated from his other roles:

> In diverse respects the same Christ is a prophet and lord of prophets, a king, a priest, a shepherd, a teacher, a servant, a lord, a man, God, flesh, Word, son of God, an apostle, etc. He is not denied therefore to be the lord of prophets, if at times he is called a prophet, just as he is not denied to be the son of God when he is called a servant, minister, apostle, and priest, nor is he denied to be God when he is called man and the son of man. In these titles no one will err except those who do not understand the two natures in Christ and the matter of the dispensation which is undertaken.[86]

In order to show that Jesus is both a prophet and also greater than a prophet, Musculus interrupts his commentary with an extended comparison of Jesus and Moses. He divides his discussion into two sections with the titles "Christ Similar to Moses" (*Christus Mosi Similis*) and "Christ Higher than Moses" (*Christus Mose*

Sublimior). In addition, Musculus devotes considerable space to a polemic against Islam. All of history, he argues, is divided into two testaments or dispensations, each with a primary prophet and mediator—namely, Moses and Jesus. Since Christ was not only a prophet but the very son of God, it is absurd, according to Musculus, to propose the notion of a third testament with Muhammad as its mediator.[87]

The second effect of the miracle—the attempt of the people to make Jesus their king—receives less attention by medieval commentators than the proclamation of Jesus as prophet. Some medieval exegetes even pass over this effect in silence, finding little that needs elucidation. Of the commentators utilized in this study, only Thomas and Lyra analyze the topic in any detail. Both Thomas and Lyra affirm that the people rightly understood Jesus to be the true king prophesied in the Bible, but they did not understand the true nature of his kingdom. This misunderstanding, Thomas argues, was a manifestation of their carnality, which blinded them to the true spiritual nature of Christ's kingdom. They merely wanted a ruler who would "provide them with temporal things." According to both Thomas and Lyra, Jesus withdrew from the people in order to show that his kingdom could only be manifested at the opportune time. Lyra also adds, following Chrysostom, that Jesus withdrew in order to give his followers an example of fleeing earthly honors.[88]

In his interpretation, Musculus basically repeats the same observations that are sounded by Thomas and Lyra. The Jews, Musculus argues, wanted an earthly kingdom that would enable them to throw off the yoke of servitude imposed by the Romans. They knew from the many biblical prophecies that the Messiah would establish a kingdom, and having confessed Jesus to be the Christ, they hoped to force him to reestablish the kingdom of Israel. Their attempt, Musculus argues, is an example of the carnal nature of human beings, which neglects the spiritual salvation of the inner person and seeks an earthly salvation of the outer person. Having confessed Jesus to be the Christ, they should have pleaded to hear his teaching concerning the kingdom instead of aspiring to yet another earthly kingdom. Jesus withdrew from the people, not to deny his true kingship but rather to show that his kingdom is spiritual, not worldly. Like Lyra, Musculus also notes Chrysostom's argument that Jesus was giving an example of refusing worldly honors.[89]

The Spiritual Interpretation

In medieval exegesis of John 6:1–15, one finds an extraordinary wealth of spiritual interpretations. According to Denis, other expositors have written so much allegorically on this pericope that he finds it difficult to add something new. But since Scripture is a "bottomless pit and an inexhaustible sea" (*infinita abyssus atque inexhausibile pelagus*), he confidently asserts his ability to contribute something useful.[90] Like his medieval predecessors, Musculus also sees multiple layers of spiritual signification in the miracle story. Not only does he present moral observations, a standard component of all of his exegesis, but he also presents anagogical and allegorical interpretations. Yet in many ways Musculus's exegesis appears unique in the area of spiritual interpretation. Certainly there are similarities to medieval exegesis, but Musculus forges new paths and abandons old and well-trodden ones in his effort to discover the spiritual depths of the story.

Tropology

Musculus's preoccupation with the moral or tropological significance of Scripture dominates his interpretation of the feeding miracle. Nearly every phrase of the story suggests to Musculus an important moral truth. Even the most seemingly inconsequential detail may serve as the springboard for a tropological discussion, yet three topics receive extended treatment by Musculus in his exposition of the moral significance of the story. He discusses first what the story teaches about wealth and its dangers; second, he offers a long treatment on the subject of thankfulness; and third, he uncovers the story's implied warning against wastefulness. In all three of these areas, one finds the seeds of Musculus's observations in medieval commentaries. But none of the medieval commentators treats these subjects as extensively as Musculus.

On the subject of wealth, the medieval commentators express surprisingly little interest. Thomas notes that the story teaches the poverty of Christ, "for he did not even have two hundred denarii."[91] But beyond this comment, Thomas adds nothing on the subject of wealth. Denis exhorts his readers to see the kind of food Jesus and his disciples were accustomed to eating. The simplicity of their meal is an implied condemnation of "our delicacies, gluttony, and carnality."[92] Similarly, Hugh notes that John expresses the small quantity and the rough quality (barley) of the bread "for our instruction" (*ad instructionem nostram*). Meals, he argues, should serve utility, not the pleasures of the flesh.[93] Beyond these comments of Thomas, Denis, and Hugh, nothing is found in the medieval commentaries included in this study.

For Musculus, the mention of the two hundred denarii occasions an extended discourse on the subject of wealth. He is not certain whether or not Jesus and the disciples actually had the mentioned sum of money. They may have possessed that amount, or it may simply be a hypothetical sum mentioned by Philip. But the important point for Musculus is the moral truth implied by the mentioning of such a sum—namely, that "huge amounts of money and heaps of wealth do not satisfy the souls of mortals."[94] Wealthy people, he argues, are obsessed with acquiring things that do not offer true satiety. They already have what they need for living, and yet they think they do not have enough. "True satiety of souls" (*vera sacietas animorum*) is found among those people who are content with the things that "are necessities of nature" (*necessaria sunt naturae*). The true irony, according to Musculus, is that the wealthy are always troubled and anxious in their efforts to acquire more wealth, while those who are content with a small amount of things enjoy "tranquillity of life" (*tranquilitas vitae*). Similarly, "the stomach accustomed to a modicum of food, namely, the necessary amount, is easily sated and produces less troubles, but the stomach given to luxury demands much and is not quiet unless obtaining the usual abundance."[95]

The fish and barley bread demonstrate, according to Musculus, "how accessible, common, and frugal the way of life of the lord and disciples was." While the priests, scribes, and Pharisees "were being sumptuously delighted" (*opime delicarentur*) in Jerusalem, Jesus was content with a simple meal in the desert. However, Jesus did not demand a superstitious austerity of life, and for this reason, he includes fish in the meal, which contributes a pleasant flavor to the bread. Those people who constantly demand fasting and impose dietary laws are the very ones who normally feast gluttonously. Jesus, however, teaches the middle way between gluttonous devotion to luxurious gastronomy and superstitious devotion to excessive frugality.[96]

For Musculus, just as by the bread and fish Jesus teaches moderation and temperance of life, by his prayer of thanksgiving he shows the proper disposition he expects of his followers. Once again, in his discussion of thankfulness, Musculus goes far beyond the remarks of medieval commentators, who see the prayer simply as an instruction to begin meals with thanksgiving.[97] Certainly, Musculus sees the prayer as a model for Christians to follow when beginning a meal. Yet Musculus is more interested in discussing the giving of thanks as a general disposition in the life of the Christian.

Musculus begins his discourse on thankfulness with a definition. The giving of thanks always includes two indispensable elements: the "acknowledgment of a received benefit" (*accepti beneficii agnitio*) and the "praising of the benefactor" (*benefactoris depraedicatio*). A genuine and sincere giving of thanks may take place only when both parts are present, "so that neither an acknowledgment of a benefit without praise and blessing of God, nor a blessing of God without an acknowledgment of a benefit, constitutes the giving of thanks."[98]

Having defined thankfulness, Musculus discusses four attitudes that conflict with a genuinely thankful disposition. First, he treats the attitude of forgetfulness, an attitude that nurtures ingratitude. Many people are too absorbed in the present and never reflect upon the past; they therefore forget the benefits they have received. True gratitude requires an exercise of remembrance. The importance of memory in the giving of thanks explains why Jesus established the sacrament of the table. When the benefit of his death is continually renewed in the act of remembering, an attitude of thankfulness is produced. Second, Musculus treats the attitude of greed, which is incompatible with genuine gratitude. How can those people offer thanks to God, he asks, who are always desiring more? They are not considerate or thankful for what they already have but are constantly complaining about what they lack. Jesus only had five loaves and two fish with which to feed the multitude, and yet he does not despise the meager amount but rather praises the providence and goodness of the Father. The third attitude that hinders gratitude is envy. Those who are jealous of the benefits of others cannot be truly grateful. How is it possible that one should praise the generosity and goodness of God and also envy the greater fortune of others? True thankfulness cannot coexist with envy. Fourth, those who abuse the gifts of God in no way express thankfulness for what they have received. The person who "changes benefits into evil deeds" (*beneficia in maleficia mutat*) heaps abuse on the very name of God.[99]

Musculus ends his discourse on thankfulness with a discussion of the proper repayment of gratitude. True gratitude must always be expressed in one of two ways. First, according to the "law of repayment in kind" (*lex talionis*) one may repay gratitude by returning to the benefactor something similar to the benefit initially received. If someone is able to express gratitude in this way and yet does not, that person may be rightfully judged ungrateful. Second, one may repay gratitude by expressing thankfulness with words. The words must express both an acknowledgment of the received benefit and a praise of the benefactor. If a person is unable to express gratitude with repayment in kind, then that person must use this second method of expressing thankfulness. Because of the infinite riches of God, the second mode of repaying gratitude always governs the human response of thankfulness to God.[100]

For Musculus an attitude of thankfulness is closely related to an attitude of faithful stewardship of the gifts received from God. Jesus himself encourages this stewardship when he orders the disciples to collect all of the leftover food. Among the medieval commentators, Rupert, Hugh, and Denis briefly note that Jesus intended to teach that earthly bread should not be wasted but should be preserved and used for good.[101] Musculus argues the same point but once again stresses the general attitude or disposition that the collection of the leftovers implies. It was not necessary to save the leftover food for a future use since Jesus could certainly produce miraculous food at any time. However, he wanted to teach that where an abundance of the gifts of God is found, one must guard against the tendency to despise, squander, or waste those gifts.[102]

Anagogy

Musculus devotes an entire section of his comments to the exposition of the anagogical significance of the feeding miracle, a section that begins with the title, "concerning the anagogical meaning of this story" (*de anagogico historiae huius sensu*). This type of spiritual interpretation is necessary, he argues, because of Jesus' discourse that follows the miracle (Jn 6:26–58). Since Jesus declares himself to be the true bread of life sent down from heaven, the miracle must have been done "for the sake of a superior signification" (*significandi potioris gratia*). Through the miracle, Jesus wanted "to carry up" (*subvehere*) our minds from a consideration of earthly food to a consideration of heavenly food. Indeed, Jesus performed all of his miracles for a higher purpose—namely, to declare himself the physician and savior of souls, not just of bodies. Accordingly, Musculus argues that one must consider "how by that miraculous food, as if in a certain painting, a banquet of spiritual and heavenly food may be depicted, in which not bodies, but souls are fed with not temporary, but eternal food."[103]

For Musculus a proper appreciation and interpretation of the "painting" necessitate a correct understanding of its features. He therefore offers a menu of symbolic correspondences that form the basis of his anagogical interpretation. Christ himself is both the heavenly banquet giver and the heavenly food. But the food also represents for Musculus Christ's Word, the gospel of the Kingdom. The disciples, as the stewards of the banquet, represent the ministers of the Word, and the multitude represents all believers and disciples who partake of this heavenly food. The refreshment and satiety of the multitude represent the peace of conscience given to those who hear the Word.[104]

Although Musculus specifically terms his interpretation anagogical, in many ways his exposition is simply allegorical. The anagogical significance is limited to the correspondence between the earthly banquet and the heavenly banquet. But having pushed the symbolism heavenward, Musculus pulls it back to earth. The drama of the heavenly banquet takes place on earth whenever the gospel is preached and received by human minds. Musculus's anagogical interpretation centers therefore not so much on the future or heavenly realities suggested by the miracle but rather on the correspondence between the earthly feast and the spiritual feast—namely, the ministry of the Word. It is not surprising, therefore, that much of what Musculus purports to say anagogically conforms to what medieval commentators say allegorically.

In medieval exegesis, the bread is often interpreted as a symbol of divine teaching. Rupert argues that the bread has a twofold significance: the eucharistic bread and the teachings of God. The bread represents for Theophylact "the words of mysteries" (τοῦ μυστηρίου τοὺς λόγους) and for Denis "salutary teaching" (*salutaris doctrina*).[105] In the interpretations of the Gloss, Rupert, and Thomas, the five loaves represent more particularly the Mosaic law, found in the five books of Moses.[106]

The commentators who identify the loaves as symbols of the Mosaic law interpret the details of the miracle story in conformity with that basic identification. Accordingly, the boy symbolizes Moses, the lawgiver, or he symbolizes the Jewish people, who carry the Law but do not understand it. Jesus accepts the bread from the boy because he does not abolish the ancient Scriptures but explains and fulfills them. The bread is barley because the spiritual, life-giving kernel of the Old Testament—namely, the spiritual meaning—is tightly covered by the chaff of the literal meaning. The two fish, because they contribute a pleasant flavor to the bread, represent the Prophets and the Psalms, which moderate the harshness of the Law.

The basic identification of the loaves and fish as symbols of the Scriptures does not, however, exhaust the allegorical possibilities suggested by these symbols.

Medieval commentators delight in the symbolism of numerical quantities, and thus one finds a rich variety of interpretations regarding the five loaves and two fish. Hugh mentions the identification of the five loaves with the five books of Moses but simply refers the reader to the Gloss, where "the mystery is plain" (*mysterium planum est*).[107] Other mysteries clearly hold more interest for Hugh. Thus, he argues that the five loaves represent the five wounds of Christ. The barley signifies both the severity of Jesus' torment and the sorrow of mind that should accompany pious meditation on his passion. The fish are added to the bread to signify the consolation that is added to sorrow.[108] Yet Hugh does not stop here but goes on at great length to develop various interpretive ideas for the spiritual meaning of the loaves and fish. For Hugh, practically all of the essentials of the Christian life are contained within these symbols. His exposition uncovers the vast edifying potential of the symbols, without a narrow allegiance to the literal meaning of the text. This broadness of scope is also seen in the allegorical interpretation of Denis, who interprets the five loaves as: 1) the Godhead, which is apprehended in contemplation; 2) the body of the Savior, hidden under sacramental forms; 3) the canonical Scriptures of both testaments; 4) the grace that makes pleasing (*gratia gratum faciens*); and 5) the promise of future goods. The two fish represent the "active experience of divine sweetness" (*actualis experientia divinae dulcedinis*) and the "absorption, release, or salutary defection of the mind into God" (*absorptio, resolutio seu salutaris illa defectio mentis in Deo*).[109]

For Musculus, neither the number nor quality of the bread and fish hold any significance for his anagogical interpretation. Number allegory plays no role whatsoever in his exegesis of the story. The bread represents the Word of God because Jesus so identifies it. Yet having accepted this symbolization, Musculus wants to circumscribe it by the events related in the story of the miracle. The spiritual meaning must be tightly bound to the literal meaning of the text. Therefore, Musculus uses the main elements of the story—the diffident responses of the disciples, the reclining multitude, the distribution of the food, the satiety of the crowd, and the abundant leftovers—as guideposts for his discussion of the ministry of the Word. Furthermore, Musculus pushes all of his anagogical interpretation in a tropological direction. The story, in its spiritual depiction of the ministry of the Word, contains important moral truths pertaining to that ministry.

Thus, the responses of Philip and Andrew represent a common temptation "which frequently appears with ministers of the Word and stewards of heavenly food." Faced with so many people who are hungering and thirsting for the Word of God, preachers often despair. They err by employing their reason rather than faith in Christ. They themselves calculate how much "heavenly teaching" (*coelestis doctrinae*) is necessary for establishing true piety and thereby judge themselves unequal to the task.[110] Hugh and Rupert also interpret the disciples' response as an image of the thought processes of the preacher, but they characterize these thoughts differently than Musculus. For Hugh, Andrew's response—"What are these for so many people?"—represents the preacher's temptation to abandon the simple gospel of the crucified Christ for subtleties. Or, he argues, it may represent the preacher's proper recognition that the efficacy of the preached word depends upon the addition of grace.[111] According to Rupert, Andrew's response represents the preacher's recognition that the Old Testament must be interpreted spiritually, for "those Scriptures are not very great according to the literal sense."[112]

But for Musculus, the image represented by the response of the disciples is important because of the lesson it teaches. The preacher who doubts the effectiveness of his preaching should remember this story, for "the image of the present miracle, when faithfully considered, will beautifully heal this temptation." The story shows that when the minister faithfully dispenses the Word, God will attend to the problem of sufficiency. The primary moral lesson therefore is the lesson of obedience. Neither the disciples nor the crowd knew what would happen, and yet both obeyed Jesus' command. Similarly, Musculus argues, when the disciples were commanded to go into the whole world and preach the gospel, they obeyed even though they were ignorant of the effect of their preaching.[113]

While the disciples represent the ministers of the Word, the crowd, according to Musculus, represents the souls of those who feast on the spiritual food dispensed by the minister. Once again, Musculus develops both an anagogical image and a moral truth in his interpretation of the reclining of the multitude, an interpretation not found in the medieval commentaries. The reclining of bodies, he argues, represents the reclining of souls, which must cast aside worldly affairs in order to focus completely on the heavenly food of the gospel. Therefore, on the Lord's day it is necessary to put aside "secular business" (*negotium seculare*) because the spiritual meal of the gospel "does not fatten busied and bustling souls, but those reclining and resting."[114] For medieval commentators, the primary significance of the reclining multitude is not in the act of reclining itself but rather in the grass upon which they rest. Since grass is a symbol for flesh (Is 40:6, "All flesh is grass"), the reclining symbolizes a people who were resting in fleshly things and who were wise according to the flesh (Gloss, Rupert, Thomas, Hugh, Denis).[115] According to Rupert and Hugh, Jesus orders the people to recline on the grass because he wants them to suppress their sensual desires. For Hugh, his order is a rebuke of those who attend services of worship not to hear the Word but rather that they might see, desire, and speak with women.[116] The grass, however, reminds Musculus not of Isaiah 40:6 but of Psalm 23:2, which he translates as: "He makes me lie down in grassy places" (*in locis herbidis accumbere me facit*). Thus, for Musculus, the mystery represented by the grass has nothing to do with suppressing the flesh but rather the comfort and rest that accompany the spiritual banqueting on the Word.[117]

Seen against the medieval exegetical context, Musculus's anagogical interpretation of the distribution of the food is unique. The details of the story, he argues, represent a pattern by which the gospel is presented to the world: "Also in this matter an anagogical meaning is not lacking, that the Lord took these loaves in his hands, gave thanks, broke and distributed them to the disciples, and through the disciples to the crowd. By this image the ministry of the Word was delineated." Jesus first preached the gospel of the Kingdom himself, and in so doing, he sanctified it. Having sanctified it, he then delivered the Word to the disciples, who in turn distributed it to the world.[118] We find a similar medieval interpretation in the comments of Rupert, who argues that Jesus first takes the bread and then distributes it to the disciples in order to signify the transmission of spiritual teaching. Jesus first explained the spiritual interpretation of the Bible to the apostles, who then hand down this mystical understanding of the Scriptures to their successors.[119]

For Musculus, however, the disciples symbolize anagogically all of the future ministers of the Church. As such, the distribution of the food through the disciples signifies three important anagogical truths, each of which carries a moral lesson. First, although Jesus did not need to use bread or the disciples to satiate the crowd's hunger, he chose to use these media. Even today, Musculus argues, Jesus "is able abundantly to instruct and feed the minds of mortals without the Word and without ministers, but yet he uses both the Word and ministers."[120] Therefore, we are taught to reject the claims of the "fanatics" (*phanatici homines*) who reject the ministry of the Word and "attribute everything to an internal revelation" (*internae revelationi tribuunt omnia*). Second, Musculus emphasizes that the disciples distribute only what they receive from the hands of Jesus. They do not add anything of their own in their distribution to the crowd. The minister is thereby taught never to introduce any teaching other than that which was delivered by Christ. Third, it is significant, Musculus argues, that the disciples do not assume the disposition of lords or masters of the hungering crowd. Rather, they assume the posture of humble servants, ministering to the needs of the people. Their humility is an implicit rebuke of those ministers of the gospel who, "having repudiated the humility of ministering, seize for themselves the dignity of mastery and lordship, just as true antichrists."[121]

Musculus's anagogical interpretation of the satiety of the multitude is also without counterpart in the medieval commentaries. In fact, the phrase "now when they were filled" (Jn 6:12) occasions no spiritual interpretation at all in the medieval commentaries used in this study. But for Musculus, the phrase indicates the spiritual satiety of believers hungering for the Word. This spiritual hunger, he argues, cannot be satisfied by any substitutes for the Word: "Neither philosophy nor the law were able to remove the hunger of minds, but rather they increased it. In truth only the banquet giver, Christ himself, may restore, sate, and pacify the minds of believers with the food of his Word."[122] Nevertheless, just as the stomach when sick craves no food and thus feigns fullness, so also there is a false satiety of the soul, which Musculus describes as the "absurd unconcern of the conscience, either from impiety or from false confidence in one's own merits or the merits of others, or from a belief in God's mercy without true repentance and renovation of the mind." True satiety of the soul, on the other hand, comes "from a suitable refection" (*ex iusta refectione*)—namely, faith in the Word—and this satiety "renders consciences truly peaceful" (*conscientias vere pacatas reddit*).[123]

The leftover pieces of food signify, according to Musculus, the paradoxical and mysterious character of the partaking of the Word of God. Unlike normal food, which disappears when eaten, heavenly food increases when spiritually consumed. When the Word is faithfully imparted and received with thanksgiving, not only will believers be satisfied, but also they will have an abundance of leftovers with which to feed the spiritual hunger of others. For Musculus the leftovers also signify an important moral lesson and warning. When the Word of God abounds, he argues, there is a dangerous tendency to take that abundance for granted. Jesus orders the leftovers to be gathered up in order to warn his followers to guard against this danger. Just as the Israelites were nauseated by the manna that God mercifully and copiously supplied, so also "a loathing of heavenly food and a certain irreverence toward the plenty and abundance of the Word of Christ may sneak up on the satisfied."[124]

The leftovers also signify for Musculus the imperfect understanding of the teaching of Christ. Here, Musculus echoes the interpretations of medieval commentators (Gloss, Theophylact, Denis) who repeat Augustine's understanding of the leftover food as a symbol of the mysteries of the faith, mysteries the people do not understand.[125] Musculus, however, stresses the implied moral lesson: if something in the Word is not understood, "it should not be trampled upon contemptuously nor mangled by an eagerness for quarreling, but it should be replaced intact and unimpaired into the storehouse of the Holy Spirit, to be kept for future use."[126] If the leftover bread of the Eucharist is treated reverently and stored for future use, how much more, Musculus asks, should one maintain an attitude of reverence and respect for those parts of the Word of God which are not immediately comprehended? What is not understood should be returned "to the apostolic storehouse" (*promptuario apostolico*) until the Holy Spirit illuminates its meaning.[127]

Allegory

In the course of his commentary on the feeding miracle, Musculus offers only one explicit allegorical interpretation. The ascension of the mountain by Jesus, he argues, is a beautiful representation of the kingdom of God, for "the kingdom of God in this world is a mountain in the desert" (*regnum dei in hoc mundo mons est in deserto*). For Musculus, this allegorical interpretation is justified because Jesus himself compares the Church to a city placed on a mountain (Mt 5:14). Just as Jesus sits on the literal mountain with his disciples, so also "he sits with his people, whom he chose and transported from the base and low desert of this world to the loftiness of true faith, piety, and heavenly conversation."[128]

Various allegorical interpretations of Jesus' ascension of the mountain are expressed in the medieval commentaries, but none of these correspond exactly to the allegory given by Musculus. For Rupert, Thomas, and Denis, the crossing of the sea and the ascension of the mountain are interpreted as an allegorical drama of the events in salvation history. Jesus migrates from the Jews to the Gentiles by crossing the sea of his passion, and he climbs the mountain to signify his glorification and ascension into heaven.[129] For Thomas and Denis, however, the ascension of the mountain may also represent other things. Thomas argues that Jesus leads the disciples to the top of the mountain "to show that full satisfaction and the perfection of justice are found in spiritual realities."[130] Denis claims that Jesus ascended the mountain "so that the place might correspond to the one placed" (*ut locus corresponderet locato*). For "Christ indeed may be called a mountain on account of the excellence of his most holy life, the prominence of his miracles, the height of his contemplation, and the incomparable loftiness of his love and all his virtues." Therefore, Denis argues, "the mountain ascends the mountain" (*mons ascendit in montem*) in order to teach believers to reject "carnal things" (*carnalia*) and to seek "heavenly and divine things" (*coelestia ac divina*).[131]

Although Musculus's allegory does not correspond to any of the medieval interpretations, his moral interpretation of the allegory is similar to the one expressed by Denis. Musculus argues that Jesus, by ascending the mountain of the kingdom of God, shows the believer where to find true spiritual rest. Christians "should neither sit nor live in the vanities of this world, but on the mountain of the kingdom of God, where Christ sits."[132] Like Denis, Musculus quotes both Colossians 3:2 and Philippians 3:20 to show that believers should "seek the things that are above" (*quae sursum sunt quaerite*) since their "conversation is in heaven" (*conversatio in caelis est*). For Musculus, the primary significance of the allegory is the implicit moral exhortation to make the kingdom of God the ultimate goal in life. Certainly, the limitations of worldly existence preclude an immediate and complete dwelling in God's kingdom. But in following Jesus up the mountain, believers initiate the process of migrating from the world to their true heavenly home. That process, Musculus argues, "which commences in this life will acquire its fullness and perfection in the future life, when having been delivered from this valley of miseries and from all of the troubles of this life by the benefit and intervention of death, we will have migrated to the heavens, where we will sit and find rest with Christ forever."[133]

CONCLUSION

Based on this comparative exegetical study, we can characterize Musculus's interpretation of John 6:1–15 in the following ways. First, there are a great number of similarities between the comments of Musculus and medieval commentators, especially in the area of literal exegesis. Musculus never directly cites medieval commentators in the course of his interpretation of the pericope. Yet the large number of parallels in interpretation suggests very strongly that a positive relation existed between Musculus and the medieval exegetical tradition. In the absence of direct citations, however, it is simply impossible to prove his dependence on any of the commentators we have examined. One further caveat also dampens the possible significance of parallels in interpretation: the similarities may actually be due to the common dependence of the medieval interpreters and Musculus on the exegesis of the Fathers.

Second, the fact that Musculus makes use of medieval methods of spiritual exegesis is in itself significant. Although he criticizes and warns of the abuses and excesses associated with medieval allegorization, he demonstrates that he is unwilling to abandon this type of interpretation altogether. Indeed, in his comments he makes use of all three modes of spiritual exegesis: allegory, tropology, and anagogy. However, his utilization of two of these modes, allegory and anagogy, is bound by his criterion of "evident necessity." The importance of this criterion can be seen by comparing Musculus's comments on the feeding of the five thousand and the wedding at Cana. Both stories contain symbolism that may be pushed in an anagogical direction. Indeed, the story of the wedding feast at Cana seems to cry out even more for anagogical interpretation as an earthly depiction of the heavenly wedding feast than does the story of the feeding. Yet Musculus makes no effort to draw out the anagogical significance of the Cana narrative. For Musculus such an interpretation of the story is not evidently necessary because Jesus himself does not suggest it. However, the feeding miracle, being conjoined with a theological discourse concerning the true heavenly bread, suggests the propriety of a spiritual interpretation to Musculus. Similarly, his allegorical interpretation of the mountain is justified, he argues, because Jesus himself compares the Church to a city placed on a hill.

Third, although Musculus makes use of medieval methods of spiritual interpretation, his exegesis actually shows its greatest independence from the medieval tradition in this area. Number allegory, although a standard component of medieval spiritual exegesis, plays no role in Musculus's interpretation. Neither the six stone jars at the wedding at Cana nor the five loaves and two fish of the feeding miracle have any spiritual significance for him. The most striking characteristic of Musculus's spiritual exegesis is his devotion to the moral or tropological level of interpretation. He emphasizes this mode of interpretation more than any of the medieval commentators, plumbing the depths of the moral significance of the story. Indeed, Musculus finds rules for conduct in nearly every detail of the pericope. Often, when the story suggests a moral lesson of particular importance, he does not hesitate to interrupt his running commentary to insert extended moral discussions. Even when Musculus interprets the story allegorically or anagogically, his primary devotion to moral exegesis is evident. Allegory and anagogy simply allow him to develop a new set of symbols that are then interpreted for their moral significance. Thus, a certain pragmatic impulse inspires Musculus's work as a commentator on John: a desire to make the gospel relevant as a moral guidebook to every believer.

FOUR

Musculus and the Humanists on the Miracle at Sea

I have already noted characteristics of Musculus's training and scholarship that would lead us to suspect a strong humanist influence in his work as a commentator. His education at the Latin school of Sélestat, his training in Hebrew under Capito and in Greek under Betuleius, and his work as a translator of the classics all point to a man eager to drink at the fountains of humanist learning. Even a casual glance through the pages of his John commentary would seem to confirm this suspicion: quotations of Greek text and of classical authors, pagan and Christian, are sprinkled liberally throughout the work.[1]

In this chapter I will investigate in detail the influence of humanist biblical scholarship on Musculus's John commentary. First, I focus specifically on his use of the tools and methods of biblical humanism, as represented by the work of Desiderius Erasmus (ca. 1466–1536). Second, I examine the influence of humanist exegesis on Musculus's commentary by comparing his interpretation of John 6:16–26 to the interpretations of Erasmus and Jacobus Faber Stapulensis (Jacques Lefèvre d'Étaples, ca. 1455–1536).[2]

MUSCULUS AND THE BIBLICAL SCHOLARSHIP OF ERASMUS

The world of sixteenth-century humanist biblical scholarship is dominated by the figure of Desiderius Erasmus. In his use of critical philology to study the Bible, Erasmus became the greatest representative of the ideal of Christian humanism: the renewal of the Church based on a rediscovery of Scripture by returning to the ancient sources. His contribution to biblical studies may be classified into four main areas. First, in his *Novum Instrumentum omne*, published in 1516 by Froben's press, Erasmus offered the public the first printed edition of the Greek New Testament.[3]

This work, which Erasmus reworked for four further editions (1519, 1522, 1527, 1535), was of enormous benefit to the growing number of biblical scholars who had learned Greek. For the first time, these scholars could base their exegesis, if they so chose, on the *veritas graeca*. Second, Erasmus composed a new Latin translation of the New Testament, which he published in 1519 to accompany the second edition of his Greek New Testament. His translation scandalized many; after all, for a thousand years the Church had based its doctrine and exegesis on the wording of the Vulgate. Yet for many commentators, both Protestant and Catholic, the new translation provided fresh insight into the meaning of Scripture. Third, Erasmus combined his skills as a textual critic, translator, and interpreter in producing his *Annotationes in Novum Testamentum*.[4] First published in 1516 as an appendix to his *Novum Instrumentum*, and reworked and enlarged for each of the four succeeding editions, these "little notes" (*annotationculae*), as Erasmus called them, had enormous impact on sixteenth-century biblical scholarship. Working chapter by chapter through the New Testament, Erasmus quotes selected phrases from the Vulgate in order to discuss matters of textual criticism, such as corrupted passages in the Latin and variant readings in the Greek; matters of translation, such as the proper understanding of Greek idioms and syntax; and matters of interpretation, particularly in passages that had troubled patristic and medieval theologians. Finally, from 1517 to 1524, Erasmus produced paraphrases of every New Testament book, with the exception of Revelation.[5] The paraphrases were immensely popular among both scholars and the general public. By 1530 all of the paraphrases were available in German, by 1543 in French, and by 1549 in English. These interpretive works succeeded in propagating to a wide audience the Erasmian understanding of the essence of the gospel, an understanding Erasmus termed *philosophia Christi*.

In three of these four areas of Erasmus's biblical scholarship, we find a definite influence on Musculus's commentary on John. In the course of his commentary, Musculus explicitly mentions and uses Erasmus's Latin translation, *Annotationes*, and *Paraphrasis in Ioannem*. He also uses a Greek text when commenting on John, but whether he uses one of Erasmus's texts or another is difficult to determine with certainty.[6] It is significant, however, that Musculus demonstrates a consistent awareness of the underlying Greek as he works his way through John. My purpose here is to examine how and to what extent Musculus makes use of Erasmus's *Annotationes* and translation of John. I defer until later an examination of the influence of Erasmus's *Paraphrasis* on Musculus's commentary.

In his commentary, Musculus presents the reader with an entire text of John's gospel. His method is to quote several sentences of text (normally three to five verses), make a few general remarks about the passage, and then quote the text once again phrase by phrase, offering detailed comments after each lemma. A comparison of Musculus's text with Erasmus's translation shows clearly that Musculus does not offer a completely new translation of the gospel. He is quite content to make Erasmus's translation the basic text for his exegesis. Certainly there are disagreements, and occasionally Musculus voices his polite but firm disapproval of Erasmus's rendering of a word or phrase. But in general Musculus favors the Erasmus translation as a better reflection of the Greek than the Vulgate translation.[7]

What then are the criteria Musculus employs to correct Erasmus's translation? This question is difficult to answer since Musculus himself rarely explains his divergences from Erasmus. An analysis of the places where Musculus differs in his rendering of the text reveals no definite pattern. Occasionally Musculus prefers the Vulgate reading to Erasmus, sometimes he offers a translation different from both the Vulgate and Erasmus, and at other times he gives a differing translation even when the Vulgate and Erasmus agree.

Many of Musculus's changes of Erasmus's text are so minor as to suggest that they are not deliberate alterations at all. For example, the phrase ἐν τῷ ὀνόματί μου occurs many times in John's gospel. When it occurs, Musculus often translates the phrase *in nomine meo* while Erasmus translates it with the simple case construction *nomine meo*. Yet in other places Musculus adopts the case construction where Erasmus utilizes the prepositional phrase. Both Latin renderings are perfectly acceptable, and the difference is so minor that Latin ears would scarcely take notice.[8] The same reasoning may be applied to the phrase in John 4:23, ἐν πνεύματι καὶ ἀληθείᾳ, which Erasmus translates *spiritu ac veritate* and Musculus translates *in spiritu et veritate*. Similarly, Erasmus renders πιστεύσουσιν εἰς αὐτόν at John 11:48 as *credent ei*, whereas Musculus writes *credent in eum*. Yet at John 19:41 Musculus prefers the case construction *eo loco* for ἐν τῷ τόπῳ, a phrase Erasmus translates *in eo loco*. Because of their inconsistent nature, these minor alterations defy easy characterization on grammatical or stylistic grounds. At best one can only say that Musculus, if he actually intended to deviate from Erasmus's text, made these changes on a subjective basis; he chose the Latin construction that sounded best to his ears.

Many of Musculus's alterations, however, are stylistic decisions clearly based on analysis of Greek grammar and sentence structure. Usually Musculus draws no attention to these changes; he tacitly introduces his corrections without indicating the issue at stake. But if we analyze his changes, it is possible to discern ex post facto the probable reasons that motivated Musculus to part from Erasmus. Although his stylistic changes have a grammatical basis, they may often be reduced to a matter of personal preference. Since certain Greek constructions can be rendered by several different Latin constructions, Musculus had to decide which alternative represented the most elegant Latin without sacrificing fidelity to the Greek.

For example, Musculus occasionally departs from Erasmus's text in places where the Greek introduces an indirect statement with ὅτι. Such statements may be translated into Latin by a subordinate clause introduced by *quod* (or *quia*, as in the Vulgate) or by indirect speech utilizing a subject accusative plus infinitive construc-

tion. John 11:24 presents the Latin translator with just such a choice and is translated by the Vulgate, Erasmus, and Musculus as follows:

Vulg.:   Scio quia resurget in resurrectione in novissimo die.
DE: Scio quod resurget in resurrectione in novissimo die.
WM: Scio eum resurrecturum esse in novissimo die.

Although both the Vulgate and Erasmus render the ὅτι clause with a subordinate clause introduced by a conjunction, Musculus prefers the accusative plus
infinitive construction, utilizing the active periphrastic to convey the future sense
of the verb. Musculus's translation mirrors the structure of the Greek less precisely
than the *quod* clause of Erasmus, but it conveys the meaning of the Greek in more
elegant Latin.

A different type of stylistic disagreement occurs in Musculus's translation of the
genitive absolute of John 20:26: τῶν θυρῶν κεκλεισμένων. Both Erasmus and the
Vulgate use the parallel grammatical construction in Latin, the ablative absolute,
to translate the phrase as *januis clausis* (with/although the doors having been closed).
Musculus, however, in addition to using a different word for door (*foris*), chooses
to use a *cum* clause to express the genitive absolute: *cum fores essent clausae* (although the doors were closed). The change is subtle, for both the ablative absolute
and *cum* clauses allow for a range of possible meanings. The absolute construction
may express time, manner, means, cause, condition, concession, purpose, or description. *Cum* clauses are less versatile, expressing either time, cause, or concession. The effect of Musculus's choice is to make the concessive force ("although")
of the phrase more explicit than the absolute construction of both the Greek and
Latin.

To a certain degree, the above examples may give a misleading impression of
Musculus's work as a translator because they suggest his willingness to depart from
a strictly literal translation to convey the meaning of the Greek. Therefore, it is
important to note that Musculus frequently shows his unwillingness to sacrifice
fidelity to the Greek at the altar of elegant Latin. His departures from Erasmus's
translation are often precisely at those points where he judges Erasmus to have
strayed too far from the Greek. For example, Erasmus translates John 7:17, ἐάν τις
θέλει τὸ θέλημα αὐτοῦ ποιεῖν, as "si quis voluerit voluntati eius obtemperare"
(if anyone is willing to submit to his will). Musculus, however, departs from Erasmus at this point and gives the Vulgate rendering: "si quis voluerit voluntatem eius
facere" (if anyone is willing to do his will). Erasmus's phrase, *voluntati obtemperare*,
expresses the meaning of the Greek words perhaps more elegantly than Musculus's
voluntatem facere, but the latter expression is perfectly understandable Latin and
literally reflects the Greek words τὸ θέλημα ποιεῖν. Similarly, Musculus prefers
the Vulgate rendering of John 8:44, "et desideria patris vestri vultis facere" (and
you want to do the desires of your father), to the translation of Erasmus, "et desi-
deriis patris vestri vultis obsequi" (and you want to comply with the desires of your

father). Once again, Musculus follows the Vulgate in a literal translation of τὰς ἐπιθυμίας ποιεῖν (to do the desires) even though the effect is more wooden than Erasmus's rendering.

However, Musculus does not consistently favor a slavishly literal translation of the Greek; in fact, he usually adopts, without modification, the freer rendering of Erasmus in places where the Vulgate version is awkwardly literal. Like Erasmus, he recognizes that a literal translation has the potential to obscure the meaning of the Greek, especially in the area of Greek idiom. Yet, more frequently than Erasmus, he opts for a literal Latin translation when it does not violate or confuse the meaning of the Greek. In Musculus's view, a translation that too quickly abandons the effort to mirror Greek syntax may lose a particular nuance of meaning suggested by the Greek.

At John 6:39 Musculus levels precisely this criticism against Erasmus's translation. The Greek, the Vulgate, and the translation of Erasmus, each of which Musculus quotes, read as follows:

Gk.:   ἵνα πᾶν ὃ δέδωκέν μοι μὴ ἀπολέσω ἐξ αὐτοῦ . . .
Vulg.: Ut omne quod dedit mihi, non perdam ex eo . . .
        (So that everything which he gave me, I do not lose from it . . .)
DE: Ne quid perdam ex omnibus quae dedit mihi . . .
        (Lest I lose something from all which he gave me . . .)

According to Musculus, Erasmus violates the original meaning of the Greek in his effort to compose elegant Latin; Erasmus shows himself "more concerned with the structure of Latin discourse than with expressing the mind of the Lord's words."[9] Musculus argues that the Greek words have a "certain emphasis" (*emphasim quandam*) that is retained in the awkward, though literal, translation of the Vulgate. Christ was not simply claiming that he would lose none of the elect but also that he would lose no part—body or soul—of the elect. Musculus thus understands the statement as a subtle affirmation of the bodily resurrection: Christ claims here to be the savior "not only of souls but also of bodies, so that not even the bodies of the elect, although swallowed by death and committed to dust, indeed, having been converted into dust, should perish."[10] This understanding of the verse, Musculus notes, is adequately expressed in Erasmus's *Paraphrasis* but not in Erasmus's translation. Therefore Musculus argues that "it is better that we should read simply as the words are in the Vulgate edition."[11] Although it is difficult to see how Erasmus's translation fails in the way suggested by Musculus, the motivation behind the criticism is clear. Musculus wants a Latin translation that retains the precise force of meaning conveyed by the Greek.

Not all of Musculus's changes of Erasmus's text hinge purely on the issue of style or of a literal versus lucid translation, for occasionally he corrects Erasmus on finer points of grammar. For example, at John 8:14 both Erasmus and the Vulgate translate: "quia scio unde veni et quo vado, vos autem nescitis unde venio et quo vado" (because I know whence I have come and where I am going, but you do not know whence I have come and where I am going). In his translation, Musculus simply shifts all of the verbs into the subjunctive mood: "quia scio unde venerim, et quo vadam, vos autem nescitis unde venerim, et quo vadam." The Vulgate and Erasmus, in fact, translate the Greek literally by keeping the verbs in the indicative mood. But the result is a violation of one of the finer points of Latin grammar, which, unlike Greek, requires the subjunctive in an indirect question. Erasmus himself had made it a point to criticize the Vulgate on this very issue. As he points out, it is better in such places to depart from a literal translation in order to compose good Latin.[12]

Conditional sentences are another area in which Musculus corrects points of grammar in Erasmus's translation. At John 15:19, for example, the Greek reads: εἰ ἐκ τοῦ κόσμου ἦτε, ὁ κόσμος ἂν τὸ ἴδιον ἐφίλει. Here, the verbs in the protasis and apodosis are in the imperfect indicative, indicating a present contrary-to-fact condition. To transfer this condition into Latin necessitates a switch of mood to the subjunctive; the imperfect tense, however, should be retained to indicate present time. But Erasmus translates the sentence as a mixed condition, putting the protasis in the pluperfect subjunctive and the apodosis in the imperfect subjunctive: "Si de mundo fuissetis, mundus quod suum est, diligeret" (If you had been of the world, the world would love that which is its own). Musculus departs from Erasmus's translation at this point and gives the Vulgate version, which correctly places both clauses in the imperfect subjunctive: "Si de mundo essetis, mundus . . . diligeret" (If you were of this world, the world would love). Again, at John 11:32 both Erasmus and the Vulgate translate a past contrary-to-fact condition, κύριε, εἰ ἦς ὧδε, ὁ ἀδελφός μου οὐκ ἂν ἀπέθανεν, as a mixed condition, using the pluperfect subjunctive in the first clause and the imperfect subjunctive in the second: "Domine, si fuisses hic, non esset mortuus frater meus" (Lord, if you had been here, my brother would not be dead). Musculus spots the error, demonstrating his constant attention to the underlying Greek, and gives a reading that uses the pluperfect subjunctive in both clauses: "Domine, si fuisses hic, non fuisset mortuus frater meus" (Lord, if you had been here, my brother would not have died).

At John 10:10 Musculus offers a grammatical discussion that is interesting because it is one of the few places where he lowers the veil of anonymity and expressly informs the reader of the reasons for his translation. The Greek sentence and the translations of the Vulgate, Erasmus, and Musculus are as follows:

Gk.:	ἐγὼ ἦλθον, ἵνα ζωὴν ἔχωσιν, καὶ περισσὸν ἔχωσιν.
Vulg. & DE:	Ego veni ut vitam habeant, & abundantius habeant.
WM:	Ego veni ut vitam habeant, & abundantiam habeant.

In his comments Musculus notes that "both the old and the recent translator [i.e., the Vulgate and Erasmus] render [the phrase] 'and that they might have more abundantly'" (*& vetus & recens interpres reddidit, & abundantius habeant*). He then proceeds to show that Augustine, Cyril, Chrysostom, Theophylact, and "recent authorities" (*recentiores*) also base their exegesis on an understanding of the phrase as an adverbial construction. Yet in spite of this formidable exegetical consensus, Musculus offers a differing translation based on his analysis of the Greek:

> I prejudge no one, but I simply say how it appears to me. Since the Lord's words do not have περισσότερον, that is, more abundantly, but simply περισσόν, a word that signifies abundance, wealth, and affluence, I think the Lord was speaking about wealth of a general kind and the abundance of heavenly grace and blessing, which believers in him have together with one life, so that not only does he promise life to believers in him, but also that true happiness and superabundance of every good that accompanies true life in the kingdom of God; just as if he should say in German: ich aber bin komen daß sie leben und alles ubrig gnug habend.[13]

Musculus defends his translation not only grammatically but also exegetically. The expositors who utilize the Vulgate rendering are "twisted" (*torquentur*) in their attempts to make subtle exegetical distinctions between "having life" and "having life more abundantly." Yet a proper understanding of the Greek, according to Musculus, will make such attempts unnecessary. If the word περισσόν is understood nominally rather than adverbially, it becomes clear, he argues, that Jesus was not making a subtle scholastic distinction but rather was speaking "simply and commonly" (*simpliciter ac populariter*).[14]

Several of Musculus's divergences from Erasmus's text involve the simple choice of a different Latin word to express the meaning of a Greek word. These changes are often of minor importance, indicating nothing more than the personal preference of the translator for one synonym over another. Thus, at John 5:14 the Vulgate, Erasmus, and Musculus each offer differing translations of the Greek expression μηκέτι ἁμάρτανε:

Vulg.: Iam noli peccare.
        (Do not sin anymore.)
DE: Ne posthac pecces.
        (Do not sin hereafter.)
WM: Ne pecces amplius.
        (Do not sin any further.)

Here, Musculus follows Erasmus in changing the simple imperative of the Vulgate into a jussive subjunctive, but he utilizes a different adverb and word order than Erasmus. The change has little, if any, effect on the meaning of the phrase itself. Similarly, at John 6:27 we find three different translations for the word ἐσφράγισεν:

Vulg.: Hunc enim Pater signavit deus.
DE: Hunc enim Pater consignavit deus.
WM: Hunc enim Pater obsignavit deus.

Again, Musculus's choice of the verb *obsignare* does not alter the meaning of the phrase in any significant way. While this verb has a narrower range of meanings than the Vulgate's *signare* and Erasmus's *consignare*, all three verbs express the basic meaning "to seal." Musculus may have had something in mind that directed his choice of verb, but since he makes no comment on his choice, we can only speculate.

At John 10:16, however, Musculus introduces a similar subtle change in translation, which he explains to the reader. In Erasmus and the Vulgate, the verse reads: "Et alias oves habeo, quae non sunt ex hoc ovili: illas quoque oportet me adducere" (And I have other sheep that are not of this fold; I must also draw them together). Musculus's translation makes only one alteration by substituting the verb *ducere* for the *adducere* of Erasmus and the Vulgate. Once again, he defends his choice on both grammatical and exegetical grounds. The Greek verb, he points out, is not εἰσαγαγεῖν or προσαγαγεῖν but rather ἀγαγεῖν, which he asserts should be translated by the Latin verb *ducere* (to lead), not *adducere* (to draw together). He also argues that the meaning of the verse is better conveyed by *ducere* since the verb is more general and comprises in itself all kinds of leading that Christ, the good pastor, employs. Christ not only draws his sheep together (*adducere*) but also leads them out to pasture (*educere*) and back to the sheepfold (*reducere*).[15] Here Musculus shows himself an observant student of language and indicates that his changes of Erasmus's text, even seemingly minor ones, are rooted in a careful consideration of the grammar and meaning of the underlying Greek.

Because the meaning of the Greek is an important criterion for Musculus's translation, he often shows himself unwilling to follow Erasmus's translation in places where he thinks Erasmus has made the meaning of the Greek clearer than it really is. Thus, at John 3:17–19, Erasmus translates: "Non enim misit deus filium in mundum, ut *condemnet* mundum, sed ut servetur mundus per eum. Qui credit in eum, non *condemnatur*. Qui vero non credit iam *condemnatus est*, quia non credidit in nomen unigeniti filii dei. Haec est autem *condemnatio*" (my emphasis). Musculus precisely follows this translation, except where Erasmus renders the Greek κρίνειν/κρίσις as *condemnere/condemnatio*. In these places Musculus prefers the Vulgate's choice of *judicere/judicium*, a translation based on the broadest sense of the Greek words. Erasmus chooses the more particular word "condemn" because he believes the context suggests the propriety of the word. Believers may be judged, but they will be acquitted—that is, they will not be condemned. Erasmus likely has John 9:39 in mind, where Jesus says that he came into the world for the very purpose of judgment. In his own comments, Musculus shows that he understands the verses just as Erasmus does: judgment really means condemnation.[16] However, for Musculus, the place to explain the specific meaning of the Greek is not at the level of translation but at the level of exegesis.

A similar force operates in Musculus's translation of the phrase ἐκ τούτου (Jn 6:66), which the Vulgate translates *ex hoc* (because of/from this) and which

Erasmus translates *ex eo tempore* (from that time). In his *Annotationes* Erasmus defends his translation as the proper reading of a Greek temporal idiom. Musculus, however, translates the phrase *ex eo*, demonstrating his unwillingness to clarify the ambiguity of the phrase by introducing the word *tempore*, a word that does not occur in the Greek. In his comments Musculus reveals that he agrees with Erasmus's understanding of the phrase; the words, he argues, have a "temporal connotation" (*temporis connotatione*).[17] Yet for Musculus it is the work of the commentator, not of the translator, to elucidate the meaning of the phrase.

In the matter of word selection, the most striking difference between Musculus and Erasmus concerns the translation of λόγος in the first chapter of John's gospel. Much of the theological uproar that greeted Erasmus's translation of the New Testament was precipitated by his abandonment of the Vulgate's *verbum* (word), in favor of *sermo* (speech/discourse) at John 1:1 and 1:14.[18] The controversy was so fierce that Erasmus significantly expanded his defense of this translation in each of the succeeding editions of his *Annotationes*. Even the Protestant theologians disagreed in their estimation of the new reading. Zwingli and Calvin strongly supported Erasmus, while Bucer, who used Erasmus's translation for his own John commentary, nevertheless flatly rejected *sermo* in favor of the traditional wording. Musculus, perhaps influenced by the judgment of Bucer, his former teacher, also translates λόγος as *verbum*. Although the reasons for Musculus's choice are not fully explained in his commentary, it is clear that his choice is not based on a firm rejection of Erasmus's translation. Musculus mentions in a parenthetical remark that Erasmus renders λόγος as *sermo*, and he proceeds to argue that the word may in fact be rendered by several Latin terms, such as *ratio* and *sapientia*, as well as by *verbum* and *sermo*.

The only statement Musculus makes against Erasmus's use of *sermo* is based not on the theological or linguistic inadequacy of the term but rather on the resulting ambiguity of the demonstrative pronoun *hic* at John 1:2. In order to make his reasoning clear, it is necessary to present the versions of Erasmus and the Vulgate for John 1:1–2:

> Vulg.: In principio erat verbum, et verbum erat apud deum, et deus erat verbum. *Hoc* erat in principio apud deum.
>
> DE: In principio erat sermo, et sermo erat apud deum, et deus erat ille sermo. *Hic* erat in principio apud deum. [My emphasis]

Since *sermo* and *deus* are both masculine, Musculus argues that the masculine demonstrative *hic* in Erasmus's version has an unclear antecedent. This ambiguity may be avoided, he argues, if the Vulgate reading is retained since the neuter pronoun *hoc* can only refer to the neuter *verbum*. Musculus writes:

> The version of Erasmus, which has "hic erat in principio apud deum," is ambiguous since the demonstrative "hic" is able to be expounded both of God and his word, and may be understood both that God was in the beginning with God, and that speech was

in the beginning with God. But I pointed out above that the Evangelist with singular care does not say "and God was with God," but "and the word was with God." Accordingly, I prefer to read according to the old version: "In principio erat verbum . . ."[19]

Although Musculus once again shows himself attentive to the fine points of Latin grammar in his decisions as a translator, his argument here is unconvincing. Erasmus's translation is, in fact, no more ambiguous than the original Greek where the masculine demonstrative οὗτος also may refer to either θεός or λόγος, both of which are masculine in gender.

In his alterations of Erasmus's translation, Musculus is attentive not only to the Greek and the Vulgate but also to the linguistic aids in Erasmus's *Annotationes*. In his glosses of Greek words and phrases in the *Annotationes*, Erasmus usually offers several possible Latin equivalents. Musculus frequently chooses one of these glosses instead of the term that appears in Erasmus's translation. For example, at John 10:24, Musculus appears to offer a translation independent of Erasmus and the Vulgate:

> Vulg.:   Si tu es Christus, dic nobis palam.
> DE: Si tu es Christus, dic nobis ingenue.
> WM: Si tu es Christus, dic nobis libere.

Yet the term chosen by Musculus is suggested by Erasmus in the *Annotationes* in his discussion of the word παρρησία, a term he glosses "libere sive ingenue." A similar example occurs at John 4:6:

> Vulg.:   Iesus . . . sedebat sic supra fontem.
> DE: Iesus . . . sedebat sic super fontem.
> WM: Iesus . . . sedebat sic ad fontem.

In the *Annotationes*, Erasmus argues for the superiority of *super* to *supra* but suggests additionally that *ad fontem* is "better than supra fontem" (*melius quam supra fontem*). Although Musculus does not identify the *Annotationes* as the source for these changes, the number of examples precisely like the two above strongly suggests that Musculus corrects the Erasmian translation by Erasmus himself.[20]

In the course of his commentary, Musculus makes frequent use of the *Annotationes*, sometimes acknowledging his dependence and sometimes not. Occasionally, he does not bother to repeat Erasmus's arguments but simply directs the reader to the *Annotationes* as a source of useful information on a particular word or phrase.[21] In places where he actually summarizes information gleaned from the *Annotationes*, his borrowings may be classified into four main areas. First, he uses the *Annotationes* as a lexicographical source to explain the precise meaning of Greek words. Second, he draws upon Erasmus's linguistic expertise in the explanation of Greek syntax and grammar. Third, he finds the *Annotationes* a valuable aid in the explanation of textual problems. And finally, Musculus occasionally uses the *Annotationes* as a source for patristic exegesis, especially in places where Erasmus neatly summarizes the contrasting views of the Fathers on certain problematic passages.

The very fact that Musculus includes lexicographical discussions of the Greek in his commentary shows the influence of humanist biblical studies on his method of interpreting John. Although some of his technical linguistic arguments are not based directly on the work of Erasmus, his method of glossing Greek words and expressions with several Latin counterparts owes its inspiration to humanist ideals of biblical scholarship.[22] Usually, however, when Musculus cites the Greek, he cites and discusses precisely those words or expressions that Erasmus highlights in the *Annotationes*. At John 8:7, for example, Musculus gives Erasmus's definition of the word ἀναμάρτητος, a definition he finds useful for exegetical purposes.[23] But more frequently, Musculus summarizes lexicographical information from the *Annotationes* without acknowledging his borrowings. Thus, at John 14:16 he repeats Erasmus's argument that παράκλητος means *advocatus* as well as *consolator*.[24] Similarly, at John 3:3 and 3:7, Musculus shows his dependence on Erasmus's explanation of the meaning of the word ἄνωθεν. Erasmus argues that the word may be understood as a temporal adverb meaning *ab integro* (anew) or *iterum* (again) or as a spatial adverb meaning *superne sive de supernis* (from above). Musculus states that the word may mean "vel iterum, vel ab integro, vel e supernis" and proceeds to explain the exegetical implications of each possibility.

In addition to simple lexicography, Musculus uses the *Annotationes* to identify phrases that pose grammatical and syntactical problems. For example, at John 1:14 Erasmus alerts his readers to a difficulty in the sentence: "et vidimus gloriam eius, gloriam quasi unigeniti a patre, plenum gratiae et veritatis." The problem, he notes, is associated with the word *plenum*, which has no obvious antecedent. Since the Greek word πλήρης is indeclinable, the Latin translator must make a grammatical and interpretive decision. Erasmus concedes that most interpreters have understood the word to apply to Christ; *plenum* in this case would modify *verbum*. Yet Erasmus is not satisfied with this solution because *plenum* is separated from *verbum* by so many words that it "coheres rather awkwardly" (*duriuscule cohaeret*). He argues that the word coheres better with what immediately follows—namely, John the Baptist. Therefore, Erasmus proposes the reading: "Plenus gratia et veritate Ioannes testificatur de illo" (Full of grace and truth, John bore witness concerning him). Musculus agrees with Erasmus's assessment of the problem but is reluctant to endorse his solution:

> It is certainly rather awkward that he does not say "plenam" so that it might refer to "gloriam," or "pleni" so that it might refer to "unigeniti," but "plenum." As if all these things—"and we have seen his glory, glory as of the only-begotten of the Father"— are inserted as a parenthesis, so that Erasmus, by no means without cause, suspects these words to relate to those things which follow concerning John. But let us follow the received reading so that we may understand the Evangelist here to speak not of John, but of Christ.[25]

At John 8:25, however, Musculus enthusiastically endorses a grammatical argument of Erasmus. The word ἀρχήν, Erasmus notes, should not be understood nominally as in the Vulgate translation: "Principium qui et loquor vobis" (the beginning, which I also speak to you). Rather, the word should be understood adverbially as *primo* or *principio* (at/in the beginning). Furthermore, Erasmus argues that the adverb need not be understood temporally but rather in the sense of *primo loco* (in the first place). This sense of the word is expressed in Erasmus's translation of 1519: "In primis quod et loquor vobis" (primarily what I also say to you). Musculus translates the sentence in the same way and defends the translation in terms suggested by Erasmus's *Annotationes*: "That τὴν ἀρχήν, which Erasmus renders 'in primis,' signifies nothing else but 'chiefly,' or 'above all,' or 'in sum.' . . . And therefore I judge that the Evangelist wanted to express this meaning of the Lord's words by this formula . . . that is, 'I am this above all and in sum what I now so often say myself to be.' If anyone should desire other things, let him read Erasmus."[26] Like Erasmus, Musculus recognizes that ἀρχή is a theologically charged word in John's gospel and that many interpreters have understood John 8:25 as a statement concerning the preexistent logos. But in this case, Musculus argues that "it is not necessary to philosophize in a lofty manner" (*necesse non sit sublimius philosophari*) since Jesus was speaking "in a very straightforward manner" (*simplicissime*). Musculus defends this assertion with a linguistic argument based not on the *Annotationes* but on his knowledge of Hebrew: "Without doubt the Lord was speaking not in Greek, but either in Hebrew or Syriac, so that it is likely that he said either ברשונה or ברשיח, which not only signifies 'in the beginning' so that it must be related to the order and succession of things, but also signifies 'in sum' and 'head.'"[27]

This speculation concerning the Hebrew background of New Testament Greek is a recurring theme throughout Musculus's John commentary. He suggests repeatedly that John's Greek presupposes or veils an underlying Hebraism.[28] Strange expressions and grammatical constructions often can be explained, Musculus argues, by examining the particularities of Hebrew grammar and idiom that lie behind the Greek. The *Annotationes* never provides the direct inspiration for these arguments, for Erasmus examines Hebrew only when discussing the etymology of loan-words or when comparing John's Old Testament quotations with the original.[29] Yet Musculus's study of latent Hebraisms certainly reflects the spirit of the *Annotationes* in an area where he held a technical advantage over Erasmus, who never mastered Hebrew.

For Musculus, the *Annotationes* was a rich source of information regarding textual problems, and he occasionally incorporates Erasmus's textual remarks in his commentary. At John 8:3, for example, Musculus repeats Erasmus's explanation that the story of the woman taken in adultery is not included in all manuscripts. Like Erasmus, Musculus refers to Book 3 of Eusebius's *Historia ecclesiastica* to explain that the story was taken from the apocryphal Hebrews gospel. Although

Musculus concedes that the story may not be original, he expresses little concern over the matter: "We are not very worried here" (*Nos hic non admodum anxii sumus*).

At John 19:13 Erasmus notes that the location of Pilate's court is wrongly termed *lithostratus* by the Vulgate. The correct reading, he argues, is given in other Latin manuscripts as *lithostrotos*. Musculus repeats this argument but adds his own explanation for why the error occurred. The Vulgate translator, he argues, simply "joined a Latin pronunciation to the Greek" (*latinam vocem graecae coniunxit*). Musculus also repeats Erasmus's etymology of λιθόστρωτος as "a place paved with stones" (*locus lapidibus stratus*). A similar example occurs at John 1:28, where Erasmus proposes on the basis of patristic evidence the reading *Bethabara* instead of the Vulgate's *Bethania*.[30] Musculus adopts the change for his own translation and confidently asserts that the new reading has won the day: "The old translation incorrectly has 'Bethania.' Although it is beginning to be corrected now, even by those who reject Erasmus."[31] Musculus admits that *Bethabara* occurs nowhere else in the Bible, but he claims to have seen it in certain maps of the Holy Land. The city is located, he argues, in the region where Joshua led the Israelites across the Jordan, a fact that explains the meaning of *Bethabara* as "house of passage" (*domus transitus*). Musculus argues, in opposition to Erasmus, that Jerome in fact supports the reading *Bethabara* in the *Loca Hebraica*. Erasmus had criticized Jerome's term, *Bethaibam*, but Musculus claims to have seen a copy of Jerome's work that has the reading *Bethbaara*. This word, Musculus argues, is likely due to the error of a printer "who by metathesis incorrectly rendered *Bethbaara* for *Bethabara*."[32] It is also possible, he suggests, that "some sciolist" (*sciolus quispiam*) who did not understand the significance of the meaning of *Bethabara* intentionally altered Jerome's word in order to create a place name corresponding to John's baptismal activity; therefore the ignorant redactor changed *Bethabara* to *Bethbaara*, which means "house of purification" (*domus purificationis*).

In the above examples, Musculus shows not only his dependence on Erasmus's *Annotationes* but also his familiarity with principles of textual criticism. Musculus uses the data in the *Annotationes* as the basis for his own textual observations. A further example of this is seen at John 12:38, where Erasmus notes that the word *domine* in John's quotation of Isaiah 53:1—"Domine quis credidit auditui nostro"— does not occur in the Hebrew. Erasmus argues that the addition of the word merely indicates that John cites Isaiah from the Septuagint rather than from the Hebrew Bible. Yet Erasmus notes that the quotation of Isaiah 6:10 at John 12:40 does not reflect the wording of either the Septuagint or the Hebrew text. Musculus repeats these observations concerning the two Isaiah quotations and contributes his own discussion based on analysis of the Hebrew. The peculiar quotation of Isaiah 6:10 may be partially explained, Musculus argues, if John's Hebrew text was unpointed. Regarding the quotation from Isaiah 53:1, Musculus proposes in fact a new reading of the text. Since Isaiah was speaking in a prophetic voice, Musculus argues, the verbs may be translated with the future tense: "The speech of the prophet was constructed here in the past tense, according to the custom of the Hebrew language, yet it is able to be read in the future as 'who will believe the report,' that is, our speech, 'and to whom will the arm of the Lord be revealed?' For the prophet was speaking in that chapter about the passion and death of Christ.[33]

In addition to this interpretive argument, Musculus adds a textual-grammatical analysis to change the text even further: "If you get rid of the points in the Hebrew, you will be able to read both 'who will believe his report,' namely Christ's, and 'who will believe our report.' For the article נ not only signifies us and ours, but also him and his; and therefore the phrase לשמועתנו is able to be read as 'our report' and, if there is a dagesh in the letter nun, 'his report.'"[34]

The effect of Musculus's analysis is a new reading that makes the christological force of the verse less ambiguous: "Who will believe his report, and to whom will the arm of the Lord be revealed?" He does not argue that this reading of Isaiah 53:1 is John's text, for John clearly follows the Septuagint reading. Rather, by using textual analysis, Musculus argues for a reading that *should* have been John's text, for "the reading certainly would have squared very beautifully with the purpose of the Evangelist."[35] Yet having made this rather bold proposal, Musculus sounds a note of caution since, as he admits, no other interpreter, including the Evangelist himself, has ever read the text as "his report." Although the new reading is edifying, Musculus refuses to give it his full endorsement, "chiefly on account of the authority of the gospel" (*maxime propter autoritatem Evangelii*).[36] In his analysis of the the text at John 12:40, Musculus goes far beyond the notes made by Erasmus, perhaps even too far, as he himself suggests. Yet Musculus demonstrates not only his willingness to appropriate basic data from the *Annotationes* but also his ability to use methods of textual analysis to evaluate and build upon that data.

Much of the textual, lexicographical, and grammatical data in the *Annotationes* is supplemented by Erasmus with testimonies from patristic literature. Additionally, Erasmus uses the Fathers as exegetical guides in particularly knotty passages. Musculus also consults the patristic writings throughout his John commentary, usually for exegetical insights, but occasionally he gleans his information secondhand; he borrows from or refers to summaries of patristic opinion located in the *Annotationes*. Musculus acknowledges his dependence only in places where he does not actually repeat the patristic data given by Erasmus; he simply refers the reader to the *Annotationes* as a source of useful information. Thus, at John 7:1 Musculus gives a textual variant from Chrysostom without further comment and simply directs the reader to the *Annotationes*, where the variant reading is treated at length.[37] Similarly, at John 14:1, Erasmus notes that the sentence πιστεύετε εἰς τὸν θεόν, καὶ εἰς ἐμὲ πιστεύετε has four possible readings, depending on whether the verb in each phrase is understood to be in the indicative or imperative mood. Erasmus assigns the various readings to different Fathers and discusses the exegetical implications of each interpretation. Musculus also notes that the ambiguity of the Greek has raised interpretive problems that are treated by the Fathers, but he does not present the patristic arguments. Rather, he abbreviates his discussion with a reference to the *Annotationes*: the words "are able to be read in four ways as has been noted by Erasmus."[38]

When Musculus presents the actual substance of patristic opinion gleaned from the *Annotationes*, he usually does so without acknowledgment. Thus, at John 13:5–6, Musculus relates a disagreement between Chrysostom and Augustine concerning the foot-washing scene. Chrysostom believes that Jesus first began to wash the feet of Judas and then proceeded to Peter and the other disciples. Augustine, however, believes the text suggests that Jesus began the ceremony with Peter. Musculus almost certainly takes this information from the *Annotationes*, where Erasmus summarizes the disagreement between the two Fathers.[39] In their assessment of the disagreement, however, Erasmus and Musculus go their separate ways. Erasmus sides with Chrysostom: "The suspicion of Chrysostom is more pleasing to me [than Augustine's opinion]" (*Mihi tamen magis arridet Chrysostomi suspitio*). But Musculus sides with Augustine against Chrysostom: "Augustine refutes this opinion, and neither does it [Chrysostom's opinion] seem likely to me" (*Verum refutat hanc opinionem Augustinus, nec mihi videtur probabilis*). Once again, Musculus demonstrates his reliance on the basic data in the *Annotationes*. But the fact that he presents this data, be it patristic opinion, textual problems, or grammatical difficulties, does not mean that Musculus uses or interprets it in the same way as Erasmus.

The foregoing catalog of borrowings firmly establishes Erasmus's *Annotationes* and translation of John as important sources for Musculus's commentary. Yet in these borrowings Musculus consistently shows himself to be more than a mere epigone of Erasmus. He adopts Erasmus's translation as his basic text, but not without important modifications and corrections. He reproduces linguistic and textual data from Erasmus's *Annotationes* but often adds his own assessment of that data. Yet the fact that Musculus includes problems of text, translation, and grammar in the course of his commentary shows not only his indebtedness to Erasmus but also his recognition of the new set of priorities for commentary-writing that biblical humanism engendered.

THE MIRACLE AT SEA (JN 6:16–26)

We have determined that Musculus uses the critical philological and textual tools of humanism in the composition of his John commentary. We turn now to an examination of his exegesis of John 6:16–26 in the context of humanist interpretations. There are two humanist commentaries on John that may serve as candidates for this comparative study: the *Paraphrasis in Evangelium secundum Ioannem* of Erasmus, first published in 1523, and the *Commentarii initiatorii in quatuor Evangelia* of Faber Stapulensis, which first appeared in 1522.

Erasmus's *Paraphrasis* does not share all of the characteristics of a traditional biblical commentary. As a paraphrast, Erasmus does not attempt to solve all of the exegetical problems in the text. Synoptic difficulties are rarely discussed, theological discussions are kept to a minimum, and the opinions of previous commentators are never explicitly summarized. In short, Erasmus produces a fairly continuous narrative that allows for few of the traditional interruptions in the exposition of the text.[40] Yet these differences alone do not distinguish the paraphrase and the commentary as entirely distinct literary genres. Erasmus himself, in the preface to his *Paraphrasis in Ioannem*, argues that "a paraphrase too is a kind of commentary."[41] Although a paraphrase has an expository function that is narrower in scope than that of a commentary, it represents an important mode of explanation found in many biblical commentaries. Musculus makes consistent use of paraphrase throughout his John commentary, usually with the formulaic *quasi dicere* (as if to say).[42] He also frequently uses false paraphrase in order to make the positive meaning of a statement more explicit: "Non dicit . . . sed dicit . . ." (He does not say . . . but says . . .). Furthermore, Erasmus's *Paraphrasis* often blurs the distinction between paraphrase and commentary by its occasional inclusion of allegories and moral observations. Therefore, the *Paraphrasis* has an explanatory value that has allowed it to enter the stream of Johannine exposition consulted by commentators on John.

Musculus indicates his familiarity with Erasmus's *Paraphrasis in Ioannem* by two explicit references, one expressing his agreement and the other his disagreement.[43] Whether he utilized Faber's *Commentarii* is not clear. Although he never explicitly mentions the work, there is at least one piece of evidence that suggests his acquaintance with it. At John 7:28 Musculus mentions the interpretation of *recentiores* who interpret the words of Jesus—"Me nostis et unde sim nostis" (You know me and you know where I come from)—as an ironical statement (*verba per ironiam dicta*). According to these interpreters, the statement actually means the opposite of what it seems to affirm. This interpretation of 7:28 is first proposed by Faber in his *Commentarii*, and the explanations of Musculus and Faber do indeed have a strong verbal similarity:

FS: Ac si diceret: Dicitis quod me scitis, & unde sim: at neque me scitis, neque unde sim scitis.
(As if he said: You say that you know me and where I am from, but you neither know me nor do you know where I am from.)
WM: Quasi dicat, Nec me nostis, nec unde sim scitis.
(As if he says: You neither know me nor do you know where I am from.)[44]

Yet the fact that Musculus, unlike Faber, calls this interpretation "ironia" suggests his reliance on another source—namely, either Melanchthon or Bucer. In his comments on the verse, Melanchthon writes: "I do not think it is irony, but rather a simple statement."[45] Bucer, on the other hand, embraces the ironical interpretation: "He answered them by irony, whereby he was indicating that they were deceived and that they did not know what they were bragging about."[46] Therefore, when Musculus indicates that *recentiores* interpret the verse as ironical, he may mean Faber or Bucer or both. While this example does not firmly establish Musculus's dependence on Faber, it does suggest a ground for suspecting his acquaintance with Faber's John commentary.

The Literal Interpretation

If we were to confine ourselves strictly to the areas of common interest in the interpretations of Musculus, Erasmus, and Faber on the sea miracle (Jn 6:16–26), our comparative study would be limited almost entirely to literal exegesis. Even at this level of interpretation, thematic points of contact are surprisingly few in number. Yet interesting similarities and differences can be demonstrated in three general areas of the literal exposition of the story.

First, problems of chronology and geography are treated by our three commentators. If read superficially, the story seems to present no difficulties in this area. The disciples, we are told, go down to the lake in the evening with the intention of crossing to Capernaum. Jesus, who has withdrawn from the multitude eager to make him king, is left alone in his mountain retreat. While the casual reader might find these details clear enough, the commentator eager for precision will sniff out discrepancies and expose ambiguities in the details of the story's setting. A critical and contextual reading raises questions in need of interpretive solution.

Second, the purpose of Jesus' miracle is a common area of exegetical investigation. Walking on the water, Jesus approaches the frightened disciples, who are struggling against a rough sea driven by a fierce wind. He calms the disciples' fear, and the boat suddenly reaches its intended port. Our commentators want to know why Jesus performed the miracle as he did. What point was he making? And who are the real beneficiaries of the miracle?

Third, the three commentators discuss the role played by the multitude in John's account of the miracle. Unable to find Jesus in the place where they had been miraculously fed and puzzled by his absence since the disciples had left in the only available boat, the multitude travel to Capernaum in hope of finding Jesus there. When they find Jesus, they question him concerning the time of his arrival, a question that prompts a sharp rebuke from Jesus. Certainly, this rebuke indicates that something was wrong with the motives of the people. Therefore, Musculus, Erasmus, and Faber each explore the nature and cause of their faulty disposition. Was their attitude entirely reprehensible? If so, in what way? If not, why does Jesus reprimand them so severely?

Chronological and Geographical Problems

The issue of chronology centers on the time of the disciples' departure. They go down to the sea, according to the Vulgate, when "it was late" (*sero factum est*).

According to Erasmus, this temporal expression simply means the evening. The disciples, he argues, were looking for Jesus on the mountain, but as night began to fall, they gave up their search and prepared for the trip to Capernaum, being unwilling to spend the night in the desert. By the time they were ready to begin their journey, "it was already dark" (*iam erant tenebrae*).[47]

Faber, however, argues that when the disciples boarded their boat, it was not yet evening, but "the day was turning toward evening" (*dies vergebat in vesperam*). The Greek phrase ὡς δὲ ὀψία ἐγένετο, he concedes, may be translated as in the Vulgate: "Ut autem sero factum est" (now as it was late). But a better translation would be: "ut autem sero fiebat" (now as it was becoming late). Although Faber concedes that the Latin perfect tense corresponds to the Greek aorist, he argues for using the imperfect tense strictly on the basis of exegetical necessity; the disciples could not have departed in the evening since, according to Matthew and Mark's account, Jesus dispatched them before nightfall. John himself implies that the multitude watched the disciples depart (Jn 6:22), indicating good visibility. Therefore, the use of the imperfect tense is entirely appropriate: "For an indefinite should sometimes be understood even when the imperfect is omitted, especially when the matter requires it, which seems to be the case here."[48]

Like Erasmus, Musculus argues that the disciples departed on their journey in the evening. He repeats Erasmus's translation of John 6:16, a translation that makes this point unambiguously: "at ubi iam vespera esset" (but when it was already evening).[49] Yet the matter does not end here because Musculus, like Faber, recognizes that an evening departure seems to conflict with the synoptic account of the story. However, Musculus and Faber see this tension differently. Faber believes that evening indicates nightfall; since Matthew and Mark relate that Jesus dispatched the disciples before he had even dismissed the multitude, and since John states that the multitude watched the disciples depart, the time of their departure must have been earlier than evening. Musculus, on the other hand, argues that the disciples seem to have departed at a time later than evening since Matthew relates that the evening was drawing near before Jesus had even fed the five thousand (Mt 14:15). Musculus identifies the problem as follows: "If it was already evening, before he was consulted about feeding those crowds, how is it that our [Evangelist] says here that the disciples left to board the boat when evening came? For certainly it must be believed that several hours were spent in feeding the crowds."[50] The resolution of this problem depends, Musculus argues, on a correct understanding of the term "evening" (*vespera*), which "is not the space of just one hour but commonly includes all the time that is from three in the afternoon to night, up until dark."[51] Therefore, the multitude was fed in the early part of the evening—namely, late afternoon—and the disciples departed in the late part of the evening as nightfall approached.

The geographical information in the story elicits little discussion in Erasmus's paraphrase. The disciples, he argues, having been unable to find Jesus on the mountain, simply decided to go to Capernaum because they knew Jesus had a residence (*domicilium*) there.[52] For Faber and Musculus, however, the designation of Capernaum as the intended destination of the disciples is problematic. Once again, they define the problem differently.

For Faber the difficulty arises from the Vulgate translation of verse 17: "Venerunt trans mare in Capernaum" (They came across the sea to Capernaum). This translation, he argues, may be misconstrued to suggest that the disciples completed the action of crossing and arrived in Capernaum before their encounter with Jesus. This interpretation must be rejected, for "it is unlikely that they were in Capernaum and then returned to the sea, rowing again whence they came. For if they had been across the sea, they would have waited there for the Lord."[53] Therefore, Faber offers a translation that makes the durative force of the verb less ambiguous: "Ibant trans mare in Capharnaum" (They were going across the sea to Capernaum).

For Musculus, the problem lies in the apparent discrepancies between the geographical information given by John, Matthew, and Mark. John relates that the disciples were headed toward Capernaum, but Mark says that Jesus ordered them to go to Bethsaida. Furthermore, both Mark and Matthew state that the disciples landed in Gennesaret. The exegetical challenge for Musculus is to harmonize this information: "If you consider [the matter] carefully, there will be no discrepancy here."[54] The fact that the disciples landed in Gennesaret in no way conflicts with John's account since Gennesaret is the name of the geographical district in which Capernaum lies.[55] But the fact that Jesus orders the disciples to Bethsaida, not Capernaum, in Mark's gospel is not so easily explained. Musculus suggests that the accounts may be harmonized if Bethsaida is understood not as the final destination but rather as a transit point on the way to Capernaum. In ordering the disciples to Bethsaida, Jesus was simply giving navigational directions. He wanted the disciples to travel toward Bethsaida and then to turn off from Bethsaida toward the far shore where Capernaum was located. Why would Jesus make such a strange command? Musculus confesses his ignorance: "Perhaps [the sea] was crossed more advantageously that way, or perhaps because he intended something else in this command, unknown to us."[56]

The Purpose of the Miracle

Regarding the purpose of Jesus' miracle, we find a greater degree of unanimity between our three commentators. Each argues that Jesus performed the miracle in order to demonstrate his lordship over nature. According to Faber, by walking on the sea, by stilling the storm (as is clear from the synoptic accounts), and by transferring the boat suddenly to land, Jesus shows himself to be "lord of the earth, sea, waves, and wind" (*terrae, & maris, & fluctuum, & ventorum dominum*).[57] Similarly, Erasmus states that Jesus was "walking on the waves of the lake, just as if treading upon solid ground in order to declare himself lord not only of the earth, but of all elements."[58] Musculus makes the same point: "That the Lord walked over that stormy sea produces a declaration of his divine strength and power, which inanimate things not only recognize but are even compelled to revere, that they obey him even against their own nature."[59]

Unlike Faber and Erasmus, however, Musculus emphasizes the divine economy of the miracle that demonstrates in the best conceivable fashion the lordship of Christ over nature. Jesus could have proceeded to the disciples in another manner; but any other method would have diminished the force of the point he was making. He could have flown through the air, untouched by the turbulent sea. He could have parted the waters and walked on the dry bottom, untroubled by the adverse wind. But Jesus preferred to walk on the surface of the tempestuous sea directly into the rushing wind in order to demonstrate his lordship in a concrete fashion. "What else do the winds and sea proclaim by this example but that this Christ is the Son of God and their very creator?"[60]

Furthermore, Musculus argues that the ultimate purpose of the miracle is not simply to demonstrate Jesus' lordship over nature. Rather, by showing his authority over inanimate things, Jesus intends to reveal *a fortiori* his authority and lordship over human beings.

> A human being also has authority among human beings, but no mortal, however powerful, will command the sea and wind except the one here, king and lord of all things. Therefore, how much easier is it for Christ to command mortals, whom the winds and sea very often overturn and destroy, since he imposes a bridle with such ease on those wild elements, the subduers of mortals, and uses them according to his will, even against their nature?[61]

Accordingly, Musculus argues that those who resist the rule of Christ act not only impiously but also unnaturally, resisting the very course of nature.

For all three commentators, the miracle expresses a timeless truth in teaching the lordship of Christ. This purpose of the miracle should be noted by any reader of the story. Yet Erasmus and Musculus stress that on the literal level this didactic purpose was aimed primarily at the disciples. Both emphasize the psychological disposition of the disciples, whose flagging faith was the immediate cause of Jesus' miracle.

According to Erasmus, the disciples "are tortured" (*cruciarentur*) by their longing for Jesus. Terrified, they find themselves in the midst of a turbulent sea and, what is worse, at night, a fact that only increases their horror. When the disciples finally see Jesus, they are frightened out of their wits because they think him to be a "nocturnal specter" (*nocturnem spectrum*). Yet the primary cause of their fear is a "weak and vacillating trust" (*imbecillis ac vacillans fiducia*) that is exposed by the storm. Therefore, Jesus not only calms the storm but also miraculously transfers the boat to land in order to show the disciples that everything had taken place by divine power. The perilous circumstances and the miracle itself were divinely arranged in order to address the matter of the disciples' faith. "By these proofs, this miracle was carefully imprinted on the souls of the disciples, whose faith had to be formed and confirmed in every way."[62]

Musculus, even more than Erasmus, emphasizes the fear that consumes the disciples. Drawing upon the synoptic accounts and his own imagination, he enumerates the circumstances that bring about a situation fraught with danger and terror. First, the disciples are confronted by a fierce headwind that not only impedes their progress but threatens to overturn the boat. Second, violent and huge waves generated by the wind threaten at any moment to bury the boat. Third, the disciples find themselves in the middle of the sea, not along the coast. Fourth, the darkness of the night, cutting off every view of the shore, doubles the horror. And finally, the disciples encounter this situation alone, for Jesus is not yet present with them. Because of their fragile disposition, they scream out in terror when Jesus finally appears, thinking him to be a specter.[63]

Like Erasmus, Musculus argues that the disciples encounter this frightful situation not by chance but rather by providential arrangement. Jesus sends them on the journey in order to prepare them for a miracle that is necessitated by the weakness of their faith. The disciples had already seen many miracles, but they did not have their intended effect. Indeed, having just witnessed the miraculous feeding of five thousand people, the disciples were still cold to Jesus' power, as noted in Mark 6:52: "For they did not understand concerning the bread. Indeed, their heart was blinded." This obduracy, which does not go unnoticed by Jesus, is the primary reason for the miracle at sea: "Therefore what else was there for the Lord to do but by a special and effective miracle to banish this blindness of their hearts and to impart an understanding of his power?"[64] Certainly, the disciples do not entirely lack faith, but their faith is not based on a proper estimation of who Jesus really is. The miracles they had witnessed should have long since convinced them of Jesus' divinity, but they continue to think of him in a worldly manner:

> They believed him to be the Messiah promised in the prophets, and the son of David, and they were hoping for him shortly to occupy the kingship of Israel. They followed him in this faith; they were not even dreaming that he was the son of God. . . . Therefore Christ performed that miracle, not only performed it, but also effected that the disciples might grow in faith toward him and recognize him truly to be the son of God and the lord of the winds and the sea and the entire universe.[65]

To sum up, we find a basic similarity between the interpretations of Musculus, Erasmus, and Faber regarding the primary purpose of the sea miracle: the revelation of Christ's lordship over nature. However, Musculus uniquely stresses that the miracle demonstrates Christ's lordship over humankind. While Musculus and Erasmus both emphasize the role of the disciples as the intended audience of the miracle, Faber makes no mention of this seemingly obvious point. Musculus and Erasmus both implicate the disciples' lack of faith as the immediate cause of the miracle, but Musculus alone explains the nature of this deficiency: the disciples simply do not understand who Jesus is.

The Role of the Multitude

Concerning the role of the multitude in the sea miracle, we find once again a general similarity in the interpretations of Musculus, Erasmus, and Faber. Each argues that the multitude searching for Jesus comes by degrees to a realization of the miracle, and each accuses the multitude of an improper attitude in following Jesus. This level of interpretive agreement, however, remains at such a basic level that it is hardly notable; almost any commentator on the story would make these same general arguments, which scarcely go beyond a recitation of the obvious. At a more particular level, we find that the interpretations of the three commentators, although by no means entirely contradictory, emphasize certain distinctive themes in characterizing the disposition of the multitude.

All three commentators characterize the initial state of the multitude as one of bewilderment. The people expect to find Jesus in the vicinity of where they had been fed the previous day. They are amazed at his absence because they know that the disciples had taken the only available boat. According to Erasmus and Faber, the multitude initially has no inkling of a miracle; the people begin to suspect a miracle only after they find Jesus in Capernaum. Faber writes that when they see Jesus they finally realize that a miracle must have taken place because an overland route would have taken too long and a sea route would have been impossible without a boat. Filled with admiration, they ask Jesus when he arrived.[66] According to Erasmus, even after the people find Jesus in Capernaum, they still find it hard to believe that a miracle has occurred. The joyful exuberance and loyalty expressed by the people upon witnessing the miraculous feeding have been replaced by a perverse cynicism: "But now that heat of the previous day has become cool."[67] For Erasmus, it is skepticism, not admiration, that characterizes their questioning of Jesus. Musculus alone argues that the people suspect a miracle from the very beginning. Even before setting out across the lake in search of Jesus, they sense that Jesus must have transported himself by miraculous power. Therefore, they question him in order to confirm their suspicion: "And having found [Jesus] when they had arrived there, they questioned him, by which questioning they certainly signified their suspicion of a miracle that they conceived from their first conjectures."[68]

Although Erasmus, Faber, and Musculus differ regarding the precise moment of the multitude's cognizance of the miracle, they agree that the multitude is governed by an improper attitude in following Jesus. This faulty disposition is made obvious by the response of Jesus, who not only refuses to answer the people's question but also chastises them with the stinging remark: "You seek me not because you saw signs, but because you ate of the bread and were filled" (Jn 6:26, Vulg.). Each of our commentators, however, characterizes both the response of Jesus and the attitude of the multitude in different terms.

For Musculus, the fact that Jesus refuses to answer the question indicates that the multitude is partially motivated by an empty curiosity concerning the spectacular. They respond to the miracle as an audience to a magician's sleight of hand;

they want to know how the trick was done. Jesus could have satisfied their curiosity and brought glory to himself if he had explained the miracle or directed them to the disciples for eyewitness testimony concerning what had happened. Yet to do so would have been to neglect the spiritual sickness that afflicted the multitude: "In responding, he preferred, as was befitting him, to do what was more necessary for the salvation of those people than to serve his own glory and their curiosity."[69]

Erasmus also states that Jesus was unwilling to serve his own glory by giving a public explanation of the miracle. But this unwillingness, he argues, is motivated solely by humility. Jesus in fact wants the people to learn about the miracle, but he does not want "to make a boastful display of his power" (*ostentare virtutem suam*). Therefore, he directs them to the disciples, who give eyewitness testimony concerning everything that happened.[70] Similarly, Faber argues that the people should not have asked Jesus something that they could have learned "from others" (*ab aliis*).[71]

Musculus, Erasmus, and Faber each argue that the multitude, because of its defective disposition, deserved the severe rebuke from Jesus, but each commentator characterizes this disposition differently. For Faber, the people are rebuked because they are motivated by an attitude of selfishness. They seek Jesus not because of who he is but because of what he can do for them. Having been sumptuously fed in the desert, they seek him in order to procure further worldly benefits. The multitude seeks Jesus, motivated solely by consideration of self: "And in this manner they were considering themselves alone, and for the sake of themselves alone they were doing everything."[72] Although they had witnessed the miracle of the feeding, they had failed to see its signifying intent. As a sign, the miracle should have convinced them of Jesus' divine status and prompted them to follow "because he was God" (*quia deus esset*).

According to Erasmus, the people are rebuked not for their selfishness but for their stupidity. Enchanted by the food that Jesus had provided, they crassly assume that bodily nourishment was the purpose of the miracle. The people completely miss the miracle's pedagogical purpose: to lift their minds to a consideration of Jesus' teaching, the true spiritual food that pertains to eternal salvation. Erasmus writes: "By a severe scolding, he corrects the disposition of the multitude, not only fickle but also stupid and certainly not worthy of gospel teaching. Because although they had seen great miracles revealing divine power, nevertheless the satiety of the one banquet stirred them more than the longing for eternal salvation."[73] According to Erasmus, Jesus' miracles are never an end in themselves but always present a sensible and bodily reflection of an insensible and spiritual reality. In essence, the miracles are a condescension to human ignorance. Any teacher, Erasmus argues, would prefer to have students able to move directly into the most advanced areas of a particular discipline. Yet in reality every teacher must "shape and form the rough intelligence with certain first principles until he has led it to an accurate knowledge of the discipline, so that no longer will there be any need of those rudiments."[74] Jesus therefore rebukes the multitude, much as a teacher might rebuke a student unable or unwilling to make progress beyond the introductory lessons.

Musculus's interpretation certainly does not conflict with those of Faber and Erasmus, for he acknowledges the selfish concerns of the people and explicitly censures their "stupidity" (*stupiditas*). Yet for Musculus, selfishness and stupidity are the secondary effects of a primary spiritual sickness, which he terms the "sickness of the carnal soul" (*morbum carnalis animi*). The people appear to follow out of religious devotion to Jesus, but in fact they are controlled and motivated by carnality: "They were carnal, controlled not by an eagerness for piety, but by an eagerness for the stomach."[75] Furthermore, the people are not even aware of their own spiritual sickness; they honestly believe themselves pious seekers of Jesus. Therefore, in responding, Jesus "reveals the latent sickness of the soul in those carnal people and brings it out into the open." Jesus rebukes the multitude, not as a teacher irritated by the slow progress of a dull student but as a physician confronted with a sick patient feigning wellness and "presuming very much concerning a health he does not have."[76]

The Spiritual Interpretation

As noted above, the topics of common concern in the interpretations of Musculus, Faber, and Erasmus are limited almost entirely to the level of literal exegesis. While Musculus expends a great deal of creative energy in explicating a wide range of allegorical and moral meanings of the sea miracle, Faber and Erasmus all but ignore the spiritual significance of the story. Therefore this study is not limited to thematic points of contact in the interpretations of Musculus and the two humanists. To limit the study in this way would grossly misrepresent the situation, for in comparing the spiritual interpretations of these commentators, the impressive feature is not the occasional similarity of argument but the striking contrast in the quantity and scope of spiritual meanings. Furthermore, it is simply impossible to appreciate Musculus's interpretation of the story without recounting the rich mosaic of allegorical images and moral truths that he finds below the surface of the literal meaning. Spiritual exegesis dominates his reading of the story, easily accounting for two-thirds of all his comments. Therefore, I present here a summary of some of the major themes in Musculus's spiritual interpretation, including those themes that correspond to ideas found in the commentaries of Faber and Erasmus.

The storm, according to Musculus, has great instructive value as an image (*imago*) of the moral maxim, "Hardship yields understanding" (*Vexatio dat intellectum*). God frequently allows his people, represented by the disciples, to encounter satanic opposition, represented by the storm, in order to promote their faith and understanding. For Musculus, each element of the storm—the darkness, the rough sea, the wind, and the waves—represents a different facet of the satanic tyranny that rages against the elect.

The darkness of the sea voyage represents the darkness of the soul that descends upon those destitute of Christ. When Jesus finally appears to the disciples, it is still physically dark, but the darkness of their souls is lifted: "As indeed the presence of the sun brings in day, and its absence night, so also the presence of Christ, who is the true light, brings illumination of hearts, but his absence brings a darkening of hearts."[77] Erasmus, in one of his rare moments of allegorical speculation, offers a similar argument. The fact that the disciples see Jesus approaching signifies the spiritual illumination of those to whom Jesus is present: "But the love of the gospel also has eyes in the dark, and there is no night where Jesus is present, nor is there a deadly storm where he, who calms all things, is nearby."[78] Here we have Erasmus's sole allegorical observation regarding the sea voyage. Faber is even more reticent, interpreting all the details of the storm, the voyage, and the miracle in a strictly literal fashion. But for Musculus, the allegorical significance of the darkness is only the beginning of an extended spiritual exposition.

Musculus argues that the stormy sea produces in general an image of the satanic opposition facing those who preach the gospel. The sea, initially calm and tranquil, becomes turbulent as soon as the disciples set sail at the command of Christ. Ministers of the Word should therefore expect immediate and ferocious opposition as soon as they begin to preach, at Christ's command, the gospel of God's kingdom. The wind and the waves represent more particularly, according to Musculus, the nature of Satan's opposition to all Christians, especially to those entrusted with the ministry of the Word.

The wind opposes the course of the disciples' voyage, just as the kingdom of Satan perpetually opposes the course of the kingdom of God. Since wind is invisible, it presents a fitting image of Satan's power. Wind also may be compared to the Holy Spirit, but that wind is of a different sort: it blows calmly and refreshes the earth, unlike the satanic wind, which blows violently and threatens destruction. The hostile wind opposes the disciples in the dark because Satan's rule "is in the darkness of ignorance and all kinds of errors and lies." For this reason, Paul refers to the evil spirits as the "rulers of darkness" (Eph 6:12) and to Satan's kingdom as the "power of darkness" (Col 1:13). The fact that the wind not only opposes the course set by the disciples but also whips the sea into an agitated state "teaches beautifully whence the rousing and agitation of this age is, which arises at the preaching of the truth." The disciples in their one little boat certainly do not cause this agitation, for they would have preferred to sail peacefully on a calm sea. Similarly, those who preach the gospel "do not rouse the world to dissension, which they prefer to exist in peace . . . but Satan, the prince of this world, is in an uproar in his kingdom, being unable to endure the teaching of truth."[79]

Musculus also interprets the stormy sea as an image of worldly princes and magistrates who oppose the proclamation of the gospel. The sea was not agitated "just in any way" (*utcunque*), but "great mountains of waves" (*magni fluctuum montes*) were towering over the disciples. The huge waves represent both the cruelty and arrogance of rulers who, swollen by a haughty spirit, rage from on high against the humble teachings of Christ. These rulers appear to act of their own power and authority, but in fact they are captives to Satan's tyranny. Their captivity is represented by the stormy sea since the waves "did not rise up of their own accord" (*non suapte sponte exurgebant*) but were driven and controlled by the fierce wind. "Clearly," writes Musculus, "in this manner the tyrants of this world, raging against the teaching of Christ, are to be compared. They are captives of Satan, subject to his blowings and impulses. They are not roused to raging of their own accord, nor are they brought down to mildness of their own accord. . . . They do not their own, but Satan's business."[80] The captivity of these tyrants is such that they rage not only against the teachings and teachers of Christ but also against each other, just as the waves driven by the wind crash violently together. Such rulers are more to be pitied than to be detested or feared for they harm themselves more than they harm anyone else. Yet one should recognize that the cruel and haughty spirit that controls the tyrants of the world also threatens to tyrannize pious souls. Consequently, Musculus argues that the image of the waves carries an implicit moral admonition:

> Therefore, as often as we see, whether in ourselves or others, a swollen and raging motion of the soul, just like the high and raging waves of the roused sea, let us recognize this adversarial wind, by its impulse agitating, rousing, raising, and carrying off calmness and humility of souls to ferocity, and let us beseech the Lord, who is able to restrain the motion of both the sea and hearts, that in restraining this adversarial wind, and with the storm having been calmed, he might restore tranquillity and submission of souls.[81]

Musculus consistently develops moral lessons from the images represented by the sea miracle, attempting to demonstrate not only what the latent images represent but also what they teach. This moralizing tendency is seen especially in another theme in Musculus's spiritual interpretation: the disciples as an image of followers of Christ. The behavior and attitudes of the disciples function both positively and negatively as moral exhortations and admonitions to Christians of all ages.

First of all, the disciples give an example of true obedience. As is clear from the accounts of Matthew and Luke, the disciples did not set out on the voyage on their own initiative but rather at Jesus' command. Although they were completely ignorant of what would happen, they demanded no explanation for the command nor did they hesitate; they simply obeyed. Musculus argues that their behavior demonstrates the type of obedience required of all followers of Christ. Even if a command seems puzzling or unrealistic, simple obedience is required, for "obedience alone preserves pious and faithful souls . . . even when they are quite unaware of God's plans."[82] Human reason has no right to issue demands of God, but all too often it seeks to quench its own curiosity, resisting obedience until satisfied with the reasonableness of divine counsel. But believers should simply and immediately obey, just as the disciples did, in the confidence that God's providential care directs everything both for their own good and for his own glory.

The disciples also exemplify the type of irrational fear that continually plagues Christians. They thought they were seeing a specter when Jesus first appeared, and consequently, they were consumed by a groundless fear. Even if they had seen a specter, there would have been nothing to fear since "a specter is certainly nothing but an illusion and a false apparition, and for this reason, it is called φάντασμα in Greek."[83] Their fear presents an image of a common human malady that arises from the deception of the human heart. According to Musculus, this deception manifests itself in a complete disorientation of our fears. We fear things that are not truly evil but are merely the "empty specters of evil things" (*inania malorum spectra*). Yet in fleeing the things that threaten no real harm, we eagerly run after and embrace things that appear as "phantasms of good things" (*bonorum phantasmata*), things that are truly evil and harmful. More saliently, Musculus writes: "Sickness of the body, lack of worldly possessions, scorn in the world, and even death itself are not truly evil but are the phantasms of evil things. Those who are frightened by these, are frightened by empty specters. On the other hand, health of the body, wealth, fame, a long life, etc., are not truly good but are the specters of good things. Whoever is delighted by these, is delighted by specters."[84] Therefore, for Musculus, the image of the terrified disciples serves to warn us of the seduction of human reason, which causes, even in followers of Christ, a disorientation of proper spiritual values.

In his spiritual interpretation, Musculus develops another major theme concerning the saving power of Jesus, who rescues all of his followers from the onslaughts of Satan, just as he rescued the disciples from the storm. The image presented is one of great consolation because the story shows that no matter what Satan attempts to do against Christians, Jesus will not be hindered from bringing deliverance. But the story presents much more than a general image of salvation, for each detail of Jesus' behavior symbolizes in particular how Jesus saves those who endure distress of the soul. Jesus sees the disciples from the shore; he delays the moment of liberation; he speaks a word of comfort. Each of these elements in Jesus' rescue mission has symbolic importance in Musculus's interpretation.

When Jesus stood on the shore and watched the troubled circumstances of the disciples (as is related by Mark's gospel), he was sustaining them "by the power of this looking" (*virtute aspectus huius*). Although the disciples had no idea that they were being observed, they were in fact being protected from sinking by the "eyes of his majesty" (*oculos maiestatis suae*). In the same way, Christians in the midst of trials are protected from danger by the sustaining power of Christ. When believers recognize the fact that Jesus, although absent in body, sees their distress in times of trial, they will be comforted by this fact and will attempt all the more to resist temptation.[85]

The fact that Jesus delays his rescue mission indicates, according to Musculus, that God uses trials and tribulations in order to benefit the faithful. Jesus could have come immediately to the disciples' aid, but he allowed them to struggle at the oars for several hours. He wanted them to come to a recognition of the utter hope-lessness of their situation because only then would they experience and understand the power of salvation. Similarly, God allows the elect to endure testings for a time, until by his providential wisdom he brings deliverance. If God were to rescue be-lievers as soon as troubles first appeared, then he would manifest a love that is blind (*caecus amor*). But God reveals a love (*dilectio*) that "is conjoined with wisdom and prudence" (*sapientem ac prudentiam habet adjunctam*). Therefore, God always perfectly times the testings and deliverance of the elect so that they will grow in knowledge and faith.[86]

Finally, Musculus analyzes the act of deliverance itself. Jesus did not simply watch the struggling disciples, nor did he delay forever, but eventually he came to their aid. This fact presents a further image of consolation: "Not only does Christ know and see our trials, and . . . conserve us lest we perish, but at an opportune time he also runs and liberates with the highest consolation and grace those experiencing troubles."[87] For Musculus, the significant aspect of this act of deliverance lies in the act of speech. Jesus did not simply appear to the disciples, but he calmed their fear with the words: "It is I, do not fear" (*Ego sum, nolite timere*). As long as he was silent, the disciples considered him a specter, an object of terror, but as soon as he spoke, they recognized him to be their beloved teacher. For Musculus, this part of the story signifies that Christ never presents himself to those laboring in the sea of this world without his Word. Indeed, Christ did not appear in the world with bald demonstrations of miraculous power, but he added the dispensation of his Word in order to make himself known to mortal minds. The Church continues to present Christ with the Word because the need for speech is written into the very fabric of human psychology. Imagine, Musculus suggests, meeting a stranger in the middle of the night during a solitary walk. If the stranger does not speak, neither giving nor acknowledging a greeting, the encounter will produce fear. Or imagine a king who never speaks to his subjects; will he not become an object of fear, a "terrible specter" (*formidabile spectrum*)? If the need for speech is so established in worldly affairs, it is much more necessary in spiritual matters. Thus, when the sacraments are presented without the Word, they become the objects of a superstitious fear; "they strike fear and horror in the ignorant, although they were instituted not for the purpose of frightening but for consoling and confirming." The true Christ is found wherever his Word is proclaimed.[88]

Erasmus also sees a spiritual meaning in the act of deliverance, but unlike Musculus, he does not argue that Jesus' speech is a symbol of the proclaimed Word. By speaking to the disciples, Jesus simply showed them he was present and assuaged their fear. Jesus' presence with the disciples signifies "that no fierce tempest of the world should be feared by those to whom the Lord Jesus is present." While for Musculus Jesus' words indicate where Jesus is to be found—namely, in the pro-claimed Word—for Erasmus Jesus' words simply indicate that he is always present to those "who, by a simple and firm trust, depend on him."[89]

The final theme of major importance in Musculus's spiritual interpretation concerns the allegorical significance of the disciples' boat. He argues that the boat that transported Christ and the disciples presents a clear "type of the Church" (*typus ecclesiae*). Musculus makes no claims to originality here, for he concedes that this interpretation has been maintained "for a long time now" (*iam olim*).[90] But the longevity of the interpretation makes it no less compelling to Musculus, for the boat has features that perfectly image the characteristics of the one true Church.

> There is then one boat of Christ; his true Church is also one. Which one? Clearly the one in which Christ is transported with his people, in which there are those who comply with the Word of Christ and set sail at his command, in which Christ is acknowledged as the true son of God and worshiped. The one that lacks Christ, the Word, and the apostles, in which Christ is neither rightly known nor suitably worshiped, ought not to be known by the name of the Church of Christ but ought to be classed among mercenaries.[91]

Musculus characterizes the boats that transported the multitude as mercenary because he believes they were piloted by sailors eager to make a quick profit in transporting the people to Capernaum. Therefore, these boats present an image of the multitudinous pseudo-churches that pretend to seek Christ but actually seek worldly gain. The pseudo-churches are allied more with Satan than with Christ, a fact that is demonstrated by the peaceful voyage of the boats to Capernaum. There is no mention of a headwind, of waves, or of a storm of any kind; Satan offers no opposition, causes no trouble. Therefore, Musculus concludes that the multitude represents "an image of carnal Christians, for whom the prince of this world makes no trouble."[92] Christians of this kind seem to follow Christ in true devotion, but in truth they are motivated by an eagerness for carnal pleasures and worldly things; they seize upon the gospel of Christian liberty as an occasion for the liberty of the flesh.

For Musculus, the pitiable disposition of these pseudo-Christians stands as a warning to all true followers of Christ: the "sickness of the carnal soul" is an infectious disease, threatening to kill sincere piety and genuine faith with its deadly poison. There are people, Musculus believes, who think themselves "truly evangelical" (*vere evangelicum*), who deserve, like the multitude, to be rebuked by Christ for an allegiance to Christianity informed by a carnal disposition. The image of the multitude thus serves as a reminder of the need for habitual introspection: "Therefore let each one test oneself, by what disposition or to what end he hears the Word and gospel of Christ."[93]

Like Musculus, Faber also develops a moral lesson from the faulty disposition of the multitude. Motivated solely by selfish desires, they demonstrate an attitude entirely inappropriate to true seekers of God. We are taught, Faber argues, that God must be sought "on account of God himself and on account of nothing else" (*propter deum ipsum & propter nihil aliud*).[94] This moral observation is the only point where Faber and Musculus offer a similar spiritual interpretation. Even more striking, however, is the fact that this observation is the only place in Faber's entire exposition of the sea miracle where he goes beyond a strictly literal interpretation.

CONCLUSION

We have seen that Musculus's John commentary owes a significant debt to the humanist biblical scholarship of Erasmus. Musculus uses Erasmus's Latin translation as the basis for his exegesis, and he consults Erasmus's *Annotationes* for linguistic, textual, and interpretive information. This study has also shown that Musculus's dependence on the great Dutch humanist is much more extensive than his occasional citations of Erasmus would suggest. When Musculus treats matters such as the meaning of the Greek, problems of translation, or textual difficulties, his discussion is almost always occasioned by the work of Erasmus.

Yet Musculus's dependence on Erasmus is not marked by a ready agreement with all of Erasmus's conclusions. He appropriates Erasmus's scholarship as a critical analyst, not as a deferential copyist. Therefore, the data in the *Annotationes* function positively to alert Musculus to problematic areas in the interpretation of John's gospel. But Musculus frequently exercises his own independent skills in linguistic and textual analysis to evaluate the data differently than Erasmus. Indeed, Musculus could do so because he himself had mastered the technical and philological tools of biblical humanism. Most important, Musculus embodied the humanist ideal for the biblical scholar as a *trium linguarum gnarus*; he had mastered the three sacred languages of Hebrew, Greek, and Latin. Therefore, while Musculus uses Erasmus's Latin translation as the basis for his exegesis, he constantly evaluates and sometimes corrects it by comparing it to the Vulgate and to the Greek. Musculus corrects Erasmus not as a traditionalist responding to dangerous innovation but as a scholar appropriating the basic tools and methods of humanism itself.

When we turn to Musculus's exegesis of the sea miracle, we find that his commentary has little in common with the humanist commentaries of Erasmus and Faber. Given Musculus's significant reliance on Erasmus's biblical scholarship, this is certainly a striking fact. On the literal level of interpretation, there are a few basic areas of agreement, but these areas are so general and commonplace that they do not suggest an important link between Musculus and the humanist commentary. On the spiritual level of interpretation, we find a vast disjuncture in the interpretations of Musculus, Erasmus, and Faber. The abundance of moral observations and allegorical images in Musculus's interpretation contrasts vividly with the interpretations of the two humanists, who express little interest in this mode of exegesis.

An important difference of purpose lies at the heart of this contrast in interpretations. While Musculus agrees with the humanist emphasis on the need for linguistic and textual analysis in order to establish the literal interpretation of the biblical text, he does not believe that this type of analysis constitutes the sum of what it means to interpret the Bible. In writing his John commentary, Musculus is not interested in producing an academic reference book devoid of theological concerns and practical issues. Certainly, it is important to get the story straight, and for this reason, Musculus employs sound scholarly methods to explicate the literal historical sense. But Musculus is primarily interested in producing a work that will edify faith and promote piety in his readers. Furthermore, he recognizes that his commentary will be read by ministers eager for insights as they prepare their sermons. Textual problems, etymologies, and grammatical analysis may be interesting reading material to a group of biblical scholars, but they make for rather poor sermon material. By offering a rich variety of allegorical and moral observations on the sea miracle, Musculus's interpretation suggests various directions the minister might take at the pulpit.

Read in the context of humanist biblical scholarship, Musculus's interpretation of the sea miracle manifests features that are both old and new. His spiritual interpretation is based on methods of exegesis developed in centuries past. Placed in a medieval or patristic context, his allegorical images and moral observations would appear much less novel than they do in a humanist context. But Musculus's commentary brings together the tried and true spiritual methods of interpretation with the new tools and methods developed by the biblical humanists.

FIVE

Musculus and Sixteenth-Century Catholic Commentators on the Healing at the Pool of Bethesda

In this chapter we examine Musculus's exegesis in the context of commentaries written by Roman Catholic contemporaries of Musculus. We focus here on interpreters of John who—unlike the Catholic commentators treated in the previous chapter—shared no sympathy for the Protestant cause or for humanist methods of exegesis. The number of such commentators is surprisingly small. When Musculus published his John commentary in 1545, he had been preceded in this work by eight different Protestant commentators. Yet prior to 1545, only three nonhumanist Catholic commentators authored works on John: John Major, Antonius Broickwy von Königstein, and Francis Titelmans.

In addition to these three relatively obscure figures, there is the John commentary first published in 1530 by Tommaso de Vio (Cajetan, 1469–1534), master general of the Dominican order, and arguably the most famous Catholic theologian of the early sixteenth century.[1] Cajetan's commentary is not treated in this comparative study because we are focusing here on Catholic interpretations of John that reflect a different perspective than the Catholic humanist commentaries of the previous chapter. Although Cajetan is not usually classified as a humanist, his biblical studies in fact are based upon humanist methods of interpretation.[2]

The humanist character of Cajetan's biblical commentaries did not go unnoticed by his contemporaries. He was accused by the Sorbonne faculty of teaching Erasmian and Lutheran ideas, and he was attacked by a fellow Dominican, Ambrosius Catharinus (1484–1553), who published a stinging rebuttal of Cajetan's exegesis.[3] Although Cajetan defended himself against the charge of Protestant sympathies, there is no escaping the decidedly humanist character of his commentaries.[4] He believed that the Protestant heresies could be effectively battled only when Catholic theology rooted itself firmly in the historical-grammatical meaning of Scripture.

Cajetan's John commentary is so literal in its interpretation that it would be of little value even if we were to include it in this study. His comments rarely go beyond a terse rephrasing of the Evangelist's words. He does not raise theological questions, and he rarely offers learned speculation even concerning the literal level of meaning; spiritual interpretations are nonexistent. The commentaries of Major, Broickwy, and Titelmans are quite another matter. These men shared not only a hostility toward the Reformation but also a deep-rooted suspicion of the humanist program of biblical scholarship. They believed that the humanists were dangerous, although perhaps unwitting, allies of the Reformation.

SIXTEENTH-CENTURY CATHOLIC COMMENTATORS ON JOHN

The commentaries of Major, Broickwy, and Titelmans have received very little study by modern investigators. Indeed, little is known about the authors themselves, who remain shadowy figures at best to most historians of the sixteenth century. Therefore, before beginning a comparative exegetical study, I present here a brief introduction of these figures, situating them historically and offering some general observations about the character of their works on John.

In 1529 the first nonhumanist Catholic John commentary appeared in print, authored by John Major (1467–1550) as part of his exposition of the four gospels. Judging by its printing history, the work was not a huge success.[5] Major took up his biblical studies relatively late in life after he had firmly established his reputation as a philosopher, theologian, and historian.[6] A prolific writer on an impressive range of subjects, he is best remembered for his *Historia Majoris Britanniae*, his expositions of Aristotle's *Logic* and *Ethics*, and his commentary on Lombard's *Sentences*.[7] As a logician, Major made outstanding scholarly contributions, attracting many gifted students from across Europe.[8]

Major was educated at Cambridge and at Paris, where he took his arts course at the Collège de Sainte-Barbe. He studied theology and logic at the Collège de Montaigu and graduated doctor of theology in 1505. He taught at Paris for nearly thirteen years (at Montaigu, Navarre, and the Sorbonne), after which time he moved to his native Scotland to teach at the University of Glasgow (1518–1523), and at St. Andrews University (1523–1526). He reassumed his teaching post at Montaigu in 1526, remaining four years before returning once again to Scotland, where he spent the last twenty years of his life in relative obscurity.[9]

Despite the growing influence of humanism during Major's second tenure in Paris, he remained to the end a loyal adherent to the old methods of theology. As a thoroughly scholastic theologian, his writings especially show the influence of Duns Scotus and William Ockham.[10] Major cannot, however, be dismissed as a reactionary or as a man with his head in the sand. He opposed the Protestant Reformation in no uncertain terms, but he recognized the need for reform and vigorously advocated the conciliar theory.[11] He defended the teaching of the Roman Church against the Protestant assaults, but he himself challenged the Church's teaching on sexuality.[12] Yet many of his contemporaries derided Major as a man hopelessly behind the times. His detractors accused him of being an obscurant, a living relic of a discredited mode of learning.[13]

After Major's work on John, we have the commentary of Antonius Broickwy von Königstein (ca. 1475–1541), which was published in 1539 as part of his exposition of the four gospels.[14] Unlike Major's commentary, Broickwy's seems to have generated considerable interest; from 1539 to 1555, it was printed at least sixteen times. Yet the man behind the commentary remains an extremely obscure figure, easily the least known of the three Catholic commentators. Even concerning the basic matter of his origins, one finds disagreement in the secondary literature: he has been described variously as a Belgian, a Hollander, and a German.[15]

Although little is known about Broickwy's early years, Benjamin De Troeyer demonstrates that his signature clearly makes him a German, a native of the Hessen town of Königstein-am-Taunus, situated on the outskirts of Frankfurt-am-Main.[16] Concerning Broickwy's later years, more information is available. He was a member of the Cologne Province of the Friars Minor and spent his adult life in and around Cologne. Before 1529 he preached frequently in the Cologne cathedral and was known for his sermons against Lutheranism. After 1529 he devoted himself to his writings and served as Guardian of Franciscan houses in Brühl (1529–1530), Koblenz (1531–1537), and Nijmegen (1539–1540).

Broickwy's primary vocation was to the pulpit, and his writings reflect this fact. His books were intended primarily for fellow preachers in need of organizational aids and material in the preparation of their sermons. His first and most popular writing, an alphabetically organized concordance to the whole Bible, explicitly reflects this objective.[17] But Broickwy's biblical commentaries are no exception to this purpose.[18] To his John commentary, for example, he appended an index in which the reader can locate sermon material organized according to the Church calendar. His writings contain muted polemics against Protestant theology, yet these arguments were not intended for the debate of the classroom but for the preacher seeking to defend Catholic doctrine to the common flock of the local parish.

Finally, we have the John commentary of the Dutch Franciscan Francis Titelmans (1502–1537), published posthumously in 1543 by his brother Pieter Titelmans.[19] Although he died at a young age, Titelmans managed to author an extraordinary number of works in philosophy, theology, and exegesis.[20] Much of his exegetical work is defined by an overarching concern to combat the biblical humanism of Erasmus. Titelmans had been well prepared to debate Erasmus during his student years at Louvain, where he came under the influence of Jacobus Latomus (ca. 1475–1544), who was known for his polemical writings against Protestant theology and humanist biblical studies. Titelmans was a distinguished student at Louvain, taking his bachelor of arts degree in 1521 as the first of 162 candidates. Soon thereafter, he began studying theology while teaching philosophy in the arts faculty. In 1523 he entered the Observants' house of the Franciscans in Louvain, and by 1525 he was instructing his brother friars in philosophy and the Bible. Titelmans remained in Louvain until 1535, when, attracted by the stricter rule of the newly founded Capuchin order, he obtained a transfer and departed for Italy, teaching theology at Milan and serving in a hospital for the incurably ill in Rome. His body weakened by the rigors of ascetic ordeals, Titelmans died after a brief illness in 1537.

In his lectures on the Bible at Louvain, Titelmans made it a point of emphasis to demonstrate the errors of the humanists, whose biblical studies, he believed, served to arm the Protestant heretics with further ammunition in their attacks on Catholic theology. During this period, Titelmans published his *Collationes quinque super epistolam ad Romanos*, in which he presented himself in a dialogue with Lorenzo Valla, Faber Stapulensis, and Erasmus.[21] In the work Titelmans presents various arguments of the humanists, excerpted from their writings, for emending the text of Romans. Titelmans responds in each case with arguments for the superiority of the traditional reading; the Vulgate, he believed, was a divinely inspired translation that should remain the basis for exegesis and doctrine.

Titelmans expresses his hostility to humanist biblical scholarship more openly than either Major or Broickwy, but all three men share a cautious attitude toward the humanist philological and textual approach to biblical scholarship. For these scholars, to begin to question the trustworthiness of the Vulgate is to open the door to a flood of uncertainties that can only threaten traditional teaching and piety. Although Major, Broickwy, and Titelmans share this attitude, it would be a mistake to conclude that their commentaries share much in common. Indeed, both in style and in polemical content, the John commentaries of these three men are quite distinct.

Major's work on John is certainly the most polemical of the three Catholic commentaries. His polemical purpose is clearly expressed in the title of the book: *Disquisitiones et disputationes contra haereticos plurimae.* In the preface to the entire work on the four gospels, dedicated to James Beaton, archbishop of St. Andrews, Major explains the purposes of his commentaries. First, he intends to demonstrate the harmony of all four gospels, as well as the inner consistency of each individual gospel. Second, Major claims that he will uphold the "ancient translation" (*antiquam tralationem*) and Catholic traditions as handed down by the established doctors of the Church. Third, Major names the opponents he intends to refute in the course of his commentaries. He will expose the errors of Theophylact's gospel interpretations, and he will uproot "the pestiferous tares of the Witcliffites, the Hussites, and their followers, the Lutherans."[22] Major has other opponents whom he refuses to name because "Christians are instructed not to say racha to a brother" (*Christiani esse instituti, ne racha quidem fratri dicere*). These unnamed opponents are not heretics but men who have erred through "human accident" (*humano casu*). In this last category of opponents, Major certainly has Erasmus in mind (as well as others), for in the course of his John commentary, he opposes views expressed in Erasmus's *Annotationes.*[23]

Major's commentary, however, is not dominated at every turn by polemical concerns. In fact, he reserves most of his polemic remarks for an extended discussion of transubstantiation at John 6:48–58, a defense of the adoration of the saints at John 16:23, and a defense of auricular confession at John 20:23.[24] For the most part, Major concentrates on a positive presentation of the meaning of John's gospel, using scholastic modes of exposition. The method of question and response dominates his method of interpretation. He places objections or questions in the mouth of the reader (e.g., *quaeris, percontaris, fluctuas*) and responds with syllogisms or series of propositions. Frequently, he lists a whole series of difficulties to which he responds in systematic scholastic fashion (*ad primum, ad secundum,* etc.). The scholastic character of his commentary is also revealed by the types of questions he raises, questions that would occur only to a schoolman.[25] Furthermore, Major demonstrates his indebtedness to scholasticism by the authorities he cites: Aristotle is quoted as frequently as Augustine.[26]

Unlike Major, Broickwy does not make refutation of Protestant teachings an explicit purpose of his commentary on John. Certainly, there are places where one senses an implicit polemical intent, as, for example, in his discussion of the doctrines of free will, transubstantiation, purgatory, and soul sleep.[27] But for the most part, Broickwy's commentary is surprisingly noncombative for a man who largely made his living attacking Protestant errors from the pulpit. In no place does Broickwy directly mention his Protestant opponents, nor does he ever refer to the "heretics" or "false teachers."[28] Similarly, Broickwy nowhere explicitly attacks Erasmus or humanist biblical scholarship; in fact, he occasionally borrows information from Erasmus's *Annotationes.*[29] Broickwy, as De Troeyer has noted, avoided polemical outbursts and limited himself to a proclamation of Catholic doctrinal positions.[30]

Broickwy's commentary on John is in large part a mélange of scriptural and patristic quotations. Indeed, if one were to excise these quotations, Broickwy's commentary would be a very small book. As a commentary written by a preacher for preachers, it is intended to show the interconnections between the words of John's gospel and the rest of the Bible. A word or theme expressed by John often triggers a whole stream of scriptural quotations that serve to explain John's meaning. Frequently, Broickwy's quotations are the only commentary he presents on passages from John. For passages presenting interpretive difficulties, Broickwy prefers to expose the exegetical tradition, quoting the interpretations of Augustine, Chrysostom, and Cyril.[31] Thus Broickwy's commentary is a very traditional sort of work, but it is traditional in a different sense than Major's scholastic commentary. It does not reflect the speculative tradition of the academy but the practical spiritual reading of the monastery. Broickwy's commentary resembles, in fact, the traditional monastic literary genre of the *florilegium*, in which choice biblical texts and *dicta Patrum* are assimilated into a single work.[32] The text of John's gospel remains the skeleton on which Broickwy hangs these *florilegia*, which provide the preacher a wide selection of texts useful for meditation and sermonic exposition.

Titelmans's work on John is an entirely different sort of commentary, and it is not accidental that he adopts the favorite modes of humanist exposition: paraphrase and annotation. For each chapter of the gospel, he first provides a straightforward paraphrastic commentary, followed by annotations on selected words and phrases of the chapter. Although his paraphrase is remarkably free of polemical content, his notes are frequently directed against the biblical studies of Erasmus. Citing patristic authorities and his own gospel manuscripts, Titelmans attempts to prove that many of Erasmus's textual emendations are simply unnecessary. The Vulgate translation occasionally errs, he concedes, but only because of the carelessness of scribes; the original translation produced by divine inspiration was free of error. Furthermore, Titelmans argues against Erasmus that the errors that have accrued over the centuries are few and of no interpretive consequence. Thus, in Titelmans's work on John's gospel, we find an overriding polemical purpose that defines his imitation of Erasmus's studies of the gospel: he uses paraphrase and annotation in order to provide a Catholic antidote to the poisonous conclusions of humanist biblical scholarship.

THE HEALING AT THE POOL OF BETHESDA (JN 5:1–16)

The proper interpretation of John's gospel played an important part in the doctrinal disputes that divided Catholics and Protestants in the sixteenth century. The correct understanding of the eucharist (Jn 6:48–58), the authority of tradition (Jn 16:12–15), and the Petrine foundation (Jn 21:15–17) were all matters that were debated on the basis of Johannine proof texts. Yet it is not altogether clear how Protestant and Catholic interpreters might differ on passages in John that appear less pertinent to the disputed doctrinal issues that divided them.

The story of the healing at Bethesda is a good example of a text concerning which it is difficult to predict how such interpreters might differ (or in fact agree). There are no obvious doctrinal issues at stake in the story. Jesus approaches a man, sick for thirty-eight years, who is reclining at a pool in Jerusalem renowned for its occasional healing powers. Jesus asks the man whether he desires health and, after patiently hearing the man bemoan his circumstances, orders him to rise, take up his pallet, and walk. The man obeys Jesus and by so doing precipitates a controversy with the Jews, who take offense at the man's violation of the law against carrying burdens on the Sabbath. They demand to know who gave such a command, but the healed man is utterly ignorant of Jesus' identity. Jesus later finds him in the temple, confirms his health, and warns him against future sin. The healed man immediately departs in search of the offended party in order to report that Jesus is the one who had accomplished his miraculous healing.

Would a Catholic reading of this story differ significantly from that of a Reformer such as Musculus? If so, how? Do the doctrinal differences of the sixteenth century form a hermeneutical divide that dictates the approach a commentator will take with a story such as the Bethesda healing narrative? Or are differences in interpretation simply due to the individual exegetical preferences of each commentator? These questions constitute the backdrop of this comparative study of the interpretations of Musculus, Major, Broickwy, and Titelmans. We can safely place the question of direct influence to one side, for there is no firm evidence that Musculus was familiar with the commentaries of these men.

The Pool (Jn 5:1–4)

In his description of the pool, the Evangelist gives two names associated with the place, the Greek term *probatica* and the Hebrew term *Bethesda*. Each of our commentators discusses the meaning and significance of these terms in relation to the function of the pool. Major, Broickwy, and Titelmans agree that the Greek term generally means "of livestock" (*a pecudibus*), more specifically, "of sheep" (*a ovilis*) or "of cattle" (*a pecualis*). The pool was given this name, according to Major, because it was not a "fish pond" (*vivarium piscium*) but "a kind of reservoir in which sheep and cattle were washed. . . . Disemboweled sheep suitable for sacrifice were cleansed there."[33] Broickwy and Titelmans echo this explanation of the pool's association with the sacrificial rites of the temple, an explanation that has its ultimate source in Jerome's *De locis hebraicis*. This function of the pool also corresponds to the Hebrew name of the pool, Bethesda, which Broickwy and Titelmans explain to mean "house of sheep" (*domum pecudum*).[34]

To this discussion of the pool's names and function Musculus adds a voice of skepticism. He concedes that the Greek term signifies sheep but argues that this definition alone does not explain the purpose of the pool. Sheep may have been washed there, but it is also possible, he suggests, that in the vicinity of the pool there was a holding pen or a market place in which animals were sold. Musculus mentions Jerome's argument concerning the liturgical function of the pool but casts serious doubt on this explanation. How could the pool have served as a bathing place if it was polluted by the blood and entrails of sacrificial victims? The question, he asserts, must remain unanswered, for "in a matter so uncertain, it is not agreeable to divine" (*in re ita incerta, divinare non lubet*). Similarly, Musculus argues that the meaning of the Hebrew name is unclear. He claims that he has consulted both ancient and recent authors on the question but has found no convincing explanation concerning the term. Furthermore, it is imprudent to offer a definition of the word when even the spelling of the word is uncertain, for it has been written variously as Betzaida, Bethseda, Bethesda, and Betheder. Therefore, Musculus argues that meaning of the word must remain unknown until it is established how the word was actually written in Hebrew. In sum, Musculus believes that the traditional explanation of the pool's function asserts too much on the basis of too little information. John's description of the pool does not permit any definite conclusions, except of the most general sort. "It is simpler," Musculus concludes, "that we understand that the place was in Jerusalem, designated for keeping, selling, or washing sheep, which on account of its use they called προβατικόν."[35]

For all of our commentators, the healing power of the pool is significant because of what it symbolizes spiritually or typologically. Only Major and Musculus offer any noteworthy discussion of the historical significance of the pool's healing power. Major states that the only available information concerning this pool comes from John's gospel; there is no mention of it in the Old Testament. Therefore John appropriately describes the healing pool "because it is worthy of memory" (*quia est memoria dignum*). The five porticos were constructed around the pool, he suggests, to protect the sick from the elements and to provide ample space so that the sick would not be in the way of those purifying sacrificial animals. Although John mentions the presence only of the blind, lame, and withered, Major argues that these three groups represent all who were diseased. The triple number is appropriate because "they were being healed by the indivisible Trinity" (*ab individua trinitate sanabantur*). The pool had no curative power in itself, nor did the angel who disturbed the waters; the person who plunged first into the pool of seething water was healed by God, who in his wisdom established this particular healing mechanism. Here Major raises the sort of question that would occur only to a schoolman: What would happen if two or more people threw themselves into the water at precisely the same moment? Which person would receive the gift of health? Major responds that a proper procedure had probably been established by the rulers of the synagogue to avoid this possibility. Since it was well known that only one person could be healed after each angelic disturbance, the rulers had established an order among those waiting so that only one person would enter the pool at the appropriate moment.[36]

Like Major, Musculus argues that the porticos were constructed for the benefit of the sick lying around the pool. From these porches, the sick could descend by steps into the pool. Those reclining at the pool were not limited to the three groups explicitly mentioned by the Evangelist but included those who were afflicted by all sorts of illnesses. Musculus also argues that the water had no natural curative powers, as found in pools fed by thermal springs, but was ordained by God's will alone to confer its curative effect. Certainly the health that is provided by thermal baths is also a gift of God, but the miracles associated with this pool have no natural cause. Indeed, God could have conferred health without the external means of an angelic disturbance of water, but by his sovereign will, he established this particular method "so that there would be a greater sense of the miracle." The angel did not confer

health, nor did it descend of its own volition, but it was sent by God as a ministering spirit. Here, Musculus seizes the opportunity to condemn "that inexcusable
idolatry of heavenly saints" (*inexcusabilem illam coelendorum sanctorum idolatriam*).
In numerous places in the Bible, God is seen to have used angels to minister to
mortals; but in no place is he seen to have used the ministry of dead saints. In the
time of the New Testament, God did not hand over the function of angelic ministry to dead saints; "that error," Musculus asserts, "is rightly rejected" (*merito error
ille rejiciatur*).[37]

The fact that only one person could be healed after each angelic disturbance
is no indication of the weakness or imperfection of the miracle but suggests to
Musculus the ultimate purpose of the healing pool. God did not establish this
miraculous pool so much for the healing of sick bodies as for the demonstration of
his continuing providence for his people; his primary purpose was "more to cure
souls than bodies" (*magis animos quam corpora curaret*). Furthermore, by limiting
the gift of health to the first person to reach the pool, God intended to show that
his gifts are bestowed on those who eagerly and quickly embrace them; heavenly
gifts rarely come to the "hesitating, tardy, and slow" (*haesitantibus, tardantibus, ac
pigris*).[38]

As for the symbolic meaning of the pool, it is hardly surprising that many commentators have traditionally argued for a baptismal analogy.[39] For Titelmans and
Broickwy, this understanding of the healing pool is the primary area of exegetical
concern. Titelmans argues that God purposefully established the miraculous pool
in order to demonstrate to the Jews a "type" (*typum*) of Christian baptism, a sacrament soon to be established in the time of grace. The pool thus served as a divine
pedagogical device; by experiencing the healing powers of the bath, they were
"gradually" (*paulatim*) being prepared for receiving the spiritual healing of that
most sacred bath:

> For having been taught by ancient experience that the water of the pool mixed with
> the blood of ceremonial victims, by the working of an angel, cures of every infirmity
> those who dip in it, they were being disposed to believe that in the baptismal bath,
> by water mixed with the blood of that true sacrificial victim sacrificed for the salva-
> tion of the whole world, by the working of the Holy Spirit, a full remission of all sins
> is entirely conferred and perfect health is given to their souls.[40]

Offering this same motif, Broickwy uses the baptismal symbolism as the
hermeneutical key for unlocking the meaning of all of the features associated with
the healing pool. Thus, the angelic disturbance of the water is interpreted as the
joining of Word and element to form a sacrament. Just as the water of the pool
had no healing power in itself but only gained such power when it was moved by
an angel, "so also plain water is not effectual in us, but when it receives the grace of
the Spirit it washes away all sins."[41] Similarly, Broickwy argues that salt, water,
plants, and grains have no inherent power to drive away demons but become

effectual instruments in exorcisms by the presence of "the power of the divine name" (*virtus divini nominis*). The five porticos represent the five wounds of Christ, by whose passion the sickness of the soul is healed. Those who suffer with diseases of the soul are represented by the sick reclining around the pool. Broickwy argues that five different kinds of sinners are represented by John's description of the sick. The languid represent those who sin through laziness and idleness, and the blind are those who sin through ignorance. The lame are those who "do not have a firm step" (*non habent firmum gressum*) in doing good works, and the withered are those who lack the fullness of charity in their works. Finally, the man who was sick for thirty-eight years represents the kind of inveterate sinner who sins by long habit.[42]

Major also endorses the baptismal symbolism, but his interpretation follows a different course than those of Titelmans and Broickwy. He does not stress the correspondences between the healing pool and baptism as much as the dissimilarities. The pool points to baptism but only by way of contrast. The pool, after all, could heal only one person after each aquatic disturbance; those who were healed in this pool therefore represent the Jewish nation, which was in bondage to the Mosaic Law. By way of contrast, "the baptism of Christ rejects no one" (*neminem Christi baptismus rejicit*). Furthermore, baptism is not limited in its power to certain appointed times, but "by night and day its remedy is at hand." The pool of Bethesda and baptism, however, share one important characteristic in Major's interpretation: neither heals by its own nature but only when divine power is conferred upon the water.[43]

Musculus introduces the baptismal motif in his interpretation of the pool only to stress one theme expressed by each of the Catholic commentators: neither the water of the pool of Bethesda nor the water of baptism has any intrinsic magical potency. "Who is so insane," Musculus asks, "to think that the element of water, in which the body is dipped, is able by its own power to cleanse and renew the soul, which it is unable to touch?"[44] The gift of regeneration is dispensed, like the healings at the pool of Bethesda, "with the external covering of water" (*cum externo involucro aquae*), but the water has no "singular and unusual efficacy from nature" (*ex natura singularem & insolitam efficaciam*). The gift of regeneration must never be ascribed to any earthly element but to God alone, who, using the external means of water and the Church, confers this gift "by the Holy Spirit in the hearts of the elect" (*per spiritum sanctum in cordibus electorum*).[45]

The Healing of the Man Sick Thirty-Eight Years (Jn 5:5–9a)

As a prelude to the miraculous healing, a brief dialogue takes place between Jesus and the man that raises several interpretive questions. First, why does Jesus ask the man whether he desires health? The question could almost be considered absurd, as Musculus states: "For what sick man does not desire to be made well, especially one afflicted by sickness for such a long time?"[46] Assuming Jesus' omniscience, every interpreter seeks to understand this question not as a factual inquiry but as a question with some other purpose, a purpose unstated by the Evangelist but discernible through interpretive speculation. The response of the sick man to Jesus' query also raises important questions. He does not respond directly to the question but relates the pitiable circumstances that have hindered him from approaching the waters of the pool at the opportune moment. Is this response commendable or otherwise? Is the man to be reproached as a complainer, or is there a way to read his response in a more favorable light? In short, what does the response indicate about the character of this sick man?

First of all, each of our commentators notes that Jesus was moved by compassion for the sick man and singled him out upon his own initiative. Quoting Cyril, Broickwy notes the "great mystery of mercy" (*magnum misericordiae sacramentum*) in the fact that Jesus does not always wait for the prayers of the suffering before coming to their aid. Jesus chose this man because, of all of the sick people lying around the pool, he was "especially hopeless" (*maxime deplorandum*). Titelmans argues that Jesus also chose this man in order to make the miracle more impressive; "for that future miracle was so much more glorious, the more lamentable and inveterate the sickness was."[47]

Musculus echoes these sentiments but argues that a more important purpose lies behind Jesus' selection of the sick man. The healing of bodies was not the primary reason Jesus visited the pool, for he certainly could have healed all of the people of their afflictions. But Jesus came into the world to heal souls, and for this purpose, he chose one who was more unfortunate than the others. By healing this man, he provided the occasion for the others to receive him "at the fountain of all salvation" (*ad fontem omnis salutis*).[48] Furthermore, Musculus argues that it is not proper to question why this man was elected while the others were not. Rather, one should simply admire divine providence with reverence and fear of God. The gift of health, according to Musculus, is always "administered by the free dispensation of divine providence whether it occurs by a miracle or through the medicinal art."[49]

Concerning Jesus' question to the sick man, we find similar explanations in the interpretations of Major and Broickwy; Titelmans does not address the matter. According to Major, Jesus asked the question "in a friendly manner" (*benigne*), knowing full well that there was nothing on earth the man desired more than a restoration of health. But by asking the question, Jesus intended "to excite his passion" (*ut fervorem eius excitaret*) to move him to a proper disposition for receiving the miraculous healing. Broickwy similarly argues that Jesus knew the man's deep desire for wellness but asked him the question in order to inflame this desire even more. Jesus wanted the man to request assistance so that he would be prepared for receiving grace.[50] Musculus, however, explains the purpose of the question differently. Jesus was not trying to elicit any particular response from the man but was simply expressing kindness by a polite form of address. By asking this rhetorical question, Jesus wanted to show his compassion and his willingness to help. This manner of speaking, Musculus argues, is a common form of everyday parlance. If we see a hungry man whom we desire to help, we might appropriately ask him if he would like some food. "Speech of this kind smacks of a feeling of compassion, born of an eager and singular consideration of someone's present misery."[51]

In his response, the sick man does not directly answer Jesus' question but relates the particular misfortunes that have prevented him from attaining the benefit of the pool's powers. Yet for each of our commentators, this response is entirely commendable, revealing a man who exhibits remarkable patience. According to Broickwy, the man could have understandably thought that he was being ridiculed by Jesus. He might have denounced Jesus as one making fun of his circumstances, or he might have cursed the day of his birth, but instead he answers "gently and calmly" (*mansuete & placide*) even though he did not know who Jesus was.[52] Titelmans also argues that the man should be praised for simply explaining his need "with patience and modesty" (*cum patientia & vercundia*). Most people in his condition would respond by cursing themselves or others, but this man understands Jesus' question for what it really was: an offer of assistance. Since Jesus spoke to him "in such a friendly manner" (*tam amice*), and since he saw that Jesus was a strong young man, he concluded that here, at last, was someone who could and would help him to the pool. Therefore the sick man appropriately makes a tacit request for help by reciting his misfortunes.[53] Major argues that the sick man exhibits "amazing patience" (*inaudita patientia*) because an impatient person desperately longing for health would have considered Jesus' question "inopportune" (*intempestivam*). Those who are impatient merely increase their own pain and suffering. They are "so broken by adversities" (*ita adversis franguntur*) that they become enraged, giving themselves over to impieties and blasphemies. On the other hand, those who bear their sufferings with patience diminish their own grief, for "sickness is soothed by equanimity" (*aequanimitate languor dilinitur*). The sick man of this story, representing the ideal patient sufferer, responds to Jesus "very calmly" (*placidissime*) by indicating his desire to be helped into the pool. By responding in this way, he made himself worthy of divine assistance, for "Jesus was not wont to deny his aid to such so very mild."[54]

In his discussion of the sick man's response, Major introduces two other themes that distinguish his interpretation from Broickwy's and Titelmans's. First, he notes that the response indicates the mercilessness of the man's neighbors. The man lay next to the pool for many years, yet no one ever offered him any assistance. Just as the man is to be praised for his patience, so his neighbors are to be condemned for their callousness. Second, Major states that the extraordinary patience of the sick man raises an important theological question—namely, "whether the scourges placed upon us, as nephritis, colitis, and others of that kind, are able to atone for our failings."[55] This question, Major argues, may be answered by a logical progression through a series of five propositions: 1) an impatient act is sin; 2) a patient act is morally good; 3) a patient act is meritorious; 4) patience is a great merit; 5) therefore, hardships that are patiently sustained "are able to atone" (*sunt satisfactoriae*) and are expiative (*expiativae*) for our failings. Thus, for Major the sick man demonstrates the proper and meritorious response to divinely inflicted punishment, a response that is "reorientive of guilt" (*culpae reordinativa*).[56]

Not surprisingly, Musculus offers no argument for the meritorious disposition of the suffering sick man, yet like all of the Catholic commentators, he praises the man's patience. Since the man did not know who Jesus was, he must not be condemned for his response. When Jesus addressed him in such a friendly manner, the man simply expressed his need, hoping that Jesus might help him to the pool. This sick man, Musculus argues, demonstrates a remarkable "perseverance of hope" (*pertinacia spei*). Although ill for so many years and lacking the means to acquire the benefit of the pool, he nevertheless persevered in that place, hoping against hope that he might somehow be healed. The man does not grumble about divine injustice, nor does he blame anyone for his misfortunes. He represents, therefore, a model of the proper attitude in those who suffer various ills. Yet, like Major, Musculus also sees in the sick man's response an indictment of his neighbors, who refused for so many years to offer any assistance. It is truly ironic, Musculus argues, that mercilessness and inhumanity abounded in a city where the sacrificial worship of God was centered.[57]

Turning to the literal explanation of the miracle itself, we find identical interpretations in the commentaries of Musculus and the three Catholic commentators. Jesus healed the man by three simple commands, which were intended as a public confirmation of the miracle's occurrence. Jesus could, Musculus suggests, have simply said "be healed," but instead "he prescribes for him certain and visible proofs of a true and indubitable health, which would be a public demonstration of divine power."[58] By these proofs, any suspicion of a fake or imaginary healing would have been removed. Major, Broickwy, and Titelmans each give the same explanation for the method Jesus used to heal the sick man.[59]

However, while our commentators are unanimous concerning the literal significance of the miracle, they offer widely disparate interpretations concerning the miracle's symbolism. Musculus offers an extensive exposition of the spiritual meaning of the miracle quite unlike anything found in the Catholic commentators. In fact, Major and Titelmans give a strictly literal explanation of the miracle, saying nothing about what the miracle represents symbolically. Broickwy does not explicitly explain the spiritual meaning of the miracle, but his understanding of the symbolism is discernible by examining the Scripture he quotes in explaining the meaning of Jesus' commands. After the command "rise," Broickwy quotes Ephesians 5:14: "Rise, you who sleep, and arise from the dead and Christ will shine on you." After the command "take your bed," Broickwy quotes Romans 6:19: "Just as you presented your members to serve impurity and iniquity upon iniquity, so now present your members to serve righteousness to sanctification." And after "walk," he quotes Psalm 34:14: "Turn from evil and do good." These scriptural quotations imply that Broickwy understands the miracle to symbolize the conversion of the sinner, who rises from the deadness of sin (symbolized by the illness) carrying a body (symbolized by the bed) for good works (symbolized by walking).[60]

While this symbolism is implicit and undeveloped in Broickwy's interpretation, in Musculus's comments it emerges quite explicitly as the primary area of exegetical concern. The miracle, he argues, presents an image of the power of Christ's Word "in healing the interior human being" (*in sanando interiore homine*), which when sick can do nothing but sin but when cured can excel in true piety. Christ's Word has a curative effect in the fact that it not only commands but also gives the will and ability to comply with the command: "When it is said to our minds through the spirit of Christ, 'love God,' we will love God; 'love neighbor,' we will love neighbor; 'fear the Lord,' we will fear the Lord."[61] But when these things are taught "by a human voice" (*humana voce*), they are like a tale narrated to a deaf man. Therefore, those who argue that the natural human being has the power to fulfill the commands of God and that God never prescribes impossible commands sin against the power and grace of Christ. The natural human being is a slave of sin and cannot even recognize the things of God, let alone excel in performing the works of God. But at the same time, Musculus argues that one must reject the argument of those who claim that Christians are unable to resist sins, to love God, and to advance in piety:

> If we have been cured from the sickness of the interior human being through the power and spirit of Christ, it is not proper for us to say that we are taught things impossible for us through the Word of Christ. And this sick man did not say, "You command me to do what I am unable to fulfill," but immediately by the power of Christ's Word the old man got up, took his pallet, and walked, that is, he obeyed the Word of Christ and displayed things that as they are characteristics only of healthy people, are thus impossible for paralytics.[62]

Christians who claim their inability to obey God simply show themselves not yet healed by the power of Christ; they are still bound by the chains of sin. For "as long as we are held in this corruption and servitude of sin, those things are impossible for us that are divinely prescribed."[63] But when Christ heals the sinner, he destroys the bondage of habitual sin, providing liberty for true obedience.

For Musculus, the three commands issued by Jesus each represent different stages in the process of conversion. "They beautifully present," he states, "an image of the new human being" (*Novi hominis imaginem pulchre praeferunt*). The command to rise corresponds to the act of repentance because those who are controlled by sin are spiritually flat on their backs. Repentance is required in order to break the bonds that fasten sinners to their beds, but this is not humanly possible: true repentance is given only by the power of Christ's Word. The second command, "take your pallet," is also "not without a mystery" (*mysterio caret*), for the pallet of the soul, according to Musculus, is the body. When the sick man is healed, he does not simply discard his pallet but carries it about freely by the power of health given by Christ. In the same way, sinners who rise through repentance are not able immediately to relinquish the body of sin to which they were formerly held captive. They are no longer governed by the sinful dictates of the body but are able by the power of Christ to control and guide it until the time comes for laying it aside. Christians are called to pursue righteousness and to walk in newness of life. The final command, therefore, symbolizes this active process of the Christian life: "It is not enough to rise from sins through repentance and to carry around a body no longer slavishly subject to the power of sin, but it is also required that we walk, namely, that we undertake the journey to the heavenly homeland through zeal for true piety and by a firm faith and love."[64]

Since the healing of the man represents an image of individual conversion, it is fitting, Musculus argues, that this healing took place on the Sabbath. In the hearts of the elect, a true Sabbath is established, which is foreshadowed by the Jewish Sabbath day. The Jews were to rest from labor on this day in order to consecrate their minds to God. Similarly, Christians are consecrated and sanctified by the work of Christ, which is the work of the true Sabbath, and they in turn become "a sabbath delightful to the Lord" (*domino sabbatum delicatum*). The healing of the man on the Sabbath therefore represents the spiritual sabbath that the converted experience: they are freed from servile works and through faith are rendered "peaceful and at rest in their consciences" (*in conscientiis pacati & quieti*).[65]

For Musculus, the healing of the man at Bethesda is useful not only as an image of individual conversion and sanctification but also as an image of salvation history. The sick man therefore not only symbolizes the individual sinner but also "produces an image of humankind, held back in servitude to sin, and the work of Christ . . . expresses an image of human redemption."[66] Musculus elaborates this interpretation with a list of correspondences between the healing of the man and the process of redemption set in motion by the Adamic fall of the human race. The sick man, formerly healthy, was able and free to walk, but by abusing that liberty for sinful purposes he was cut off from God and made a paralytic. With his former liberty now lost, the man was able neither to rise nor even to do the things that would allow him to recover health. In the same way, Musculus argues, the human race was initially free to do good. Its liberty, intended for obedience to God, was abused for sinning. Because of this abuse, the human race became a captive to sin and lost its liberty to do good. Just as the paralytic lay captive for thirty-eight years, cured by neither angelic nor human assistance but only by the arrival and power of Christ, so also the human race was imprisoned by sin for many years, unable to be set free until the advent of Christ on the day of Sabbath—namely, the time of the New Testament. When the sick man was healed, he regained his former liberty, the liberty that he lost through sin. Similarly, the human race recovered its liberty to rise from sin and walk in obedience to God.[67]

The Sabbath Controversy (Jn 5:9b–13)

In the aftermath of the miracle, the Jews, disturbed by an apparent violation of the Sabbath, interview the healed man in order to ascertain the cause of the sacrilege. Each of our commentators discusses the nature of the charge made against the man and indirectly against Jesus. What motivates them to make the legal challenge? And is there any truth in their accusation? Additionally, the commentators discuss the nature of the healed man's response and the reasons for Jesus' disappearance from the scene of controversy. Musculus and the Catholic interpreters offer similar lines of interpretation in treating these matters. Only in the scope of interpretation may we distinguish Musculus from his Catholic peers. Quite simply, Musculus has much more to say on these topics. His interpretation is not only more elaborate, however, but frequently more practical; Musculus draws moral applications from this part of the story that are absent in the Catholic commentaries.

Broickwy and Titelmans each accuse the Jews of a superstitious religiosity that blinds them to matters of true spiritual importance. Titelmans states that the Jews were "scrupulous in lesser things" (*in rebus minimis scrupulosi*) but were negligent of the greater and principal matters pertaining to the law. They were, argues Broickwy, carefully observing the temporary "carnal matters" (*carnalia*) of the law but were neglecting the eternal matters of the law. They considered a violation of the Sabbath rest an odious crime, but the defrauding of a neighbor on the Sabbath they judged of no importance. Therefore, they did not ask the man who had made him well but asked who had told him to carry his pallet. Major, without elaboration, simply accuses the Jews of stubbornness. But for all three Catholic commentators, the defective religious disposition of the Jews reveals the nature of their accusation: it is a "false charge" (*calumnia*). Only Major, however, attempts to explain how Jesus may be defended from their charge. The healing of the man "redounded to divine glory" (*in divinam gloriam redundabat*) and therefore in no way violated the Sabbath laws. Even if Jesus had violated a legal custom, he would be free of blame, for "the Lord was not obliged to observe legal matters" (*dominus legalia observare non erat obnoxius*).[68]

Musculus's comments agree at a basic level with the Catholic interpretations, but they include a much more detailed discussion of what he terms "the superstitious religion of the Sabbath" (*superstitiosam sabbati religionem*), a discussion that leads to a more extensive legal defense of Jesus' behavior. First of all, Musculus argues that since the Sabbath laws were based on divine mandate, one must recognize the sacredness of this holy day. The Sabbath observance in itself must never be condemned. Therefore, the fact that the Jews reminded the healed man of the Sabbath, Musculus argues, "is without fault" (*repraehensione caret*). But while these guardians of the Sabbath want to appear as zealous observers of its laws, they show themselves ignorant of the true intent of the Sabbath religion, for it was not the intention of the law to make an act done for the glory of God illicit. Therefore, the

Jews were wrong to accuse the man carrying his pallet of violating the Sabbath, for Jesus ordered this act in order to prove the miracle and ultimately to bring glory to God.

The true purpose of the Sabbath, Musculus argues, is discovered in the proper relationship of the two principal elements in the Sabbath religion: "rest" (*otium*) and "sacredness" (*sanctimonia*). God did not establish the sacredness of the Sabbath for the sake of rest but prescribed rest for the sake of sacredness. Yet the Jews have in effect turned the true intention of the Sabbath on its head. Having neglected the true purpose of the Sabbath, they considered bodily rest the ultimate goal of Sabbath observance; but this understanding was "against the intention of God" (*contra mentem Dei*), for bodily rest was simply a means to a greater end. Cessation "from the business of life" (*ab negociis βιοτικοί*) was "not in itself pleasing to God" (*per se non erat Deo gratum*), nor did it constitute in itself the sacredness of the Sabbath. Rather, the true sacredness of the Sabbath consisted in the sacredness of souls—namely, when minds were established in faith, piety, and love.

Jesus' healing of the man at Bethesda, far from being a violation of the Sabbath, was in fact "truly a work of the Sabbath" (*vere sabbati opus*). Although the Jews want to appear as zealous defenders of God, they themselves are the real violators of the Sabbath. If they were willing to consider the context of the man's pallet-carrying, they would, or at least should, have glorified God and praised divine power. But they refuse to consider any mitigating circumstances. They do not ask the man, "Who made you well?," but only, "Who ordered you to take your pallet and walk?" Seeking only evidence that would be useful for a malicious accusation against Jesus, they ignore any information that would weaken their case.[69] Furthermore, the Jews were not only "irreligious against God" (*irreligiosi contra Deum*) but also "inhumane toward the healed paralytic" (*inhumani erga sanatum paralyticum*). At the very least, Musculus argues, they should have congratulated the man on his restored health. Instead, by accusing him of violating the Sabbath, they merely seek to burden his conscience.[70]

The response of the sick man to his accusers is interpreted as entirely commendable by each of our commentators. The healed man explains that he is simply following the command of his healer. When pressed to identify the man who had commanded him to carry his pallet, he cannot respond; he is not only ignorant of Jesus' identity but cannot even point him out, for Jesus has retreated from the scene. According to Broickwy and Major, the man is to be admired for his open declaration of the benefit he had received. The man, argues Broickwy, signified by his response the conviction that a man who could heal by his word must have greater authority than the Sabbath laws. Titelmans praises the man because he wants to obey Jesus more than he wants to please the Jews. The man believed that his healer, as a holy and divine man, would not have ordered him to carry his pallet if he had judged it illegal and contrary to God's glory. After receiving such a wonderful benefit from Jesus, it would have been a monstrous crime to refuse obedience.[71]

In a similar fashion, Musculus argues that the man offered the best possible response. The healed man does not enter into a theoretical disputation concerning Sabbath observance or offer a lengthy defense of the legality of his action but simply refers his accusers to the authority of Jesus. He freely declares the restoration of his health and claims his indebtedness to his healer. This response is all the more admirable given the fact that the man does not even know who Jesus is. Although ignorant of Jesus' identity, he knows that he has been healed by someone with an authoritative word, and on this basis alone, he is willing to obey and defend Jesus against his detractors.

For Musculus, however, the response of the healed man is to be not only praised but also emulated. In typical fashion, Musculus shows the practical and moral application of the man's response; and in this emphasis, Musculus's comments may be distinguished from the Catholic interpretations. First, Christians should imitate the healed man in declaring themselves beneficiaries of Christ. Those who have received the benefit of salvation can have no less certain a sense of their spiritual restoration than the healed man's sense of his bodily restoration. Second, not only should Christians recognize and acknowledge the gift of salvation, but like the healed man, they should immediately and constantly obey the Word of Christ. Some will certainly oppose and take offense at this obedience. But to these opponents of Christian obedience, the faithful should respond just as the healed man: "He who healed me, indeed, he who redeemed me by his blood, he ordered me to do what I do."[72]

Finally, each of our commentators attempts to explain Jesus' disappearance from the scene of controversy. By withdrawing himself from the crowd, Jesus leaves the man to his own devices in answering his accusers. Why did Jesus do this? Musculus and the three Catholic commentators each offer two similar explanations. First, they repeat Chrysostom's argument that Jesus left the scene because he did not want to cause any further irritation of the malice and envy of the Jews. The sight of Jesus, Major states, would have simply added fuel to the fire of their jealousy. Second, each commentator argues that Jesus left the scene because he wanted to avoid the appearance of seeking after glory and fame. According to Musculus, he was not seeking "common applause" (*vulgarem applausum*) for himself but wanted the miracle to stand by itself as a testimony to divine power. Each commentator claims that by avoiding the crowd, Jesus gives an example to all Christians of fleeing glory.[73]

Jesus and the Healed Man in the Temple (Jn 5:14–15)

According to the gospel text, Jesus finds the healed man in the temple, where he confirms his healing—"You have been made well"—and warns him against future sin: "Sin no more lest something worse befall you."[74] Although the text does not indicate what the man was doing in the temple, each of our commentators argues that he went there to offer thanks to God. Broickwy reveals the source of this interpretation by his quotation of Chrysostom, who commends the man for his action. He did not go to the market or give himself over to the pleasures of his newly healthy body but went straight to the temple to express thanksgiving to God. Musculus argues that since the man did not know the person who had healed him, he rightly referred the benefit to God and went to the temple to make a votive offering.[75]

From a commentator's standpoint, however, the most interesting point in this part of the story lies in Jesus' warning against further sin. The warning, after all, implies that the initial cause of the man's sickness was sinful behavior. Major, Broickwy, and Musculus each analyze this implication in the context of extended theological discussions concerning the the relationship of sin and affliction. Titelmans, by contrast, has little to say on this point, but he does argue that Jesus' statement indicates that the man had been healed, not only of his bodily illness but also of the "evils of the soul" (*malis animi*) that had caused the illness.[76]

The essential argument in the discussions of Major, Broickwy, and Musculus is the same: Jesus' warning indicates that the man contracted his sickness as a divinely inflicted punishment, but not all sins are punished in this way, nor are all sicknesses due to sin.[77] This is obvious, according to Broickwy, because one sees so many wicked people who live in sinful delights but who nevertheless enjoy a healthy and prosperous life. Their health and prosperity should be no cause of envy because the Lord truly shows his favor on those whom he chastens and disciplines. Broickwy argues that when God inflicts suffering upon his people, he does so not for reasons of vengeance but for the purpose of admonition; sickness therefore can have a corrective function. Many sicknesses, however, have nothing to do with sin but have other causes. Some simply have a natural cause; that is to say, they arise "from a natural defect" (*ex naturali defectu*). Others, like those of Job and Tobit, are inflicted "for the sake of a testing" (*ob probationem*), and still others are inflicted simply for the sake of God's glory, as was the case with the man born blind (Jn 9).[78]

Major also argues that the story of the man born blind proves that not every sickness arises from the guilt of sin. Conversely, absence of sickness does not prove absence of guilt, for even the most monstrous criminals sometimes enjoy bodily health. But why, Major asks, does God allow Muslims and other infidels to enjoy a long life when he so shortens the lives of other evildoers? The answer, according to Major, lies in a proper understanding of the medicinal character of divinely inflicted afflictions. Like Broickwy, Major argues that the sicknesses caused by sin are inflicted not out of divine vengeance but out of divine admonition. A schoolmaster, Major suggests, will often focus his discipline and correction on those students whom he especially loves, while students who are unteachable are simply expelled from the school. They are permitted "to go about in their wickedness" (*in sua malitia grassari*). But there is also a second reason why the infidels often enjoy better health and prosperity than citizens of Christendom: "Those not accepting the orthodox faith sometimes conduct their lives moderately; they defraud a neighbor less than many of our countries."[79] Therefore it is moral superiority, not divine indifference, that may account for the health and prosperity of some infidels. Nevertheless, the good fortune of unbelievers should never be envied, for a severe torture awaits them in the afterlife; "with good health, they run over a cliff" (*valetudine in praecipitium currunt*).

According to Major, there are two respects in which sickness may result from sin. First, some sins are the "immediate causes" (*causae propinquae*) of illness. That is to say, sickness often results as the natural consequence of sinful indulgence in bodily pleasures. "Intemperateness" (*intemperies*), "sumptuous victuals" (*lauta obsonia*), and drunkenness all produce sicknesses that are the natural result of such overindulgence. Gastronomic pleasure is especially dangerous, for "it begets a deadly gluttony" (*exitialem ingluviem procreat*), which ultimately shortens the human lifespan.[80] Sexual pleasures have the same deadly effect. How else can one explain the fact that "sterile mules" (*mulae steriles*) live so much longer than horses? In the second respect, sicknesses may result not as the natural consequence of sinful behavior but as divinely inflicted punishments. Such sicknesses are not injurious if they are accepted with the proper disposition. In fact, when patiently and joyfully received, these sicknesses are divinely dispensed medicines that are capable of reorienting the guilt of sin. Therefore, those who complain and remain unrepentant in the midst of their afflictions merely add to their own guilt because they "do not receive the medicine with joy" (*medicinam haud gratanter acceptant*).[81]

In his discussion of the relationship between sin and sickness, Musculus repeats many of the same themes expressed by Broickwy and Major. He argues that sicknesses caused by sin are inflicted by God in order to admonish, and hence benefit, those whom he especially loves. Thus, while not every sickness may be considered a direct consequence of sinful behavior, it frequently happens "especially among the children of God" (*praesertim inter filios dei*) that God corrects sins with sickness in order to spare his people from future condemnation. Like Major, Musculus distinguishes between sicknesses that are a biological consequence of sinful behavior and those that are inflicted solely by the will of God. The causal relationship between sin and illness is written into the very fabric of nature, at least in regard to the sins of bodily pleasures. A sin of this kind "does wrong not only against the will and precepts of God but also against the very constitution of our nature." As examples of such medically hazardous sins, Musculus mentions luxurious living, drunkenness, and, interestingly, wrath and envy.[82]

In one respect, Musculus contributes a unique addition to the discussion of the relationship between sin and sickness. He argues that some degree of proportionality must exist between the wickedness of the offense and the severity of divinely inflicted punishment. In warning the man against future sin, Jesus did not specify the sin that had caused the man's debilitating disease. This suggests that the man's sin was not "anything ordinary" (*vulgare aliquod*) but was such a heinous and extraordinary sin that there was no need to mention it; the man knew very well the sin that had caused his sickness. The fact that the man had been afflicted for thirty-eight years also suggests his guilt of some atrocious sin, "for it is not credible that on account of some trivial offense such a grave and long sickness would have been inflicted by God on him."[83]

When Jesus warns the healed man against future sin, he states that "something worse" (*deterius aliquid*) may happen if the man fails to heed the warning. Each of the commentators attempts to explain this statement as a warning of the future punishments of hell. Broickwy argues that the afflictions of the present life are *admonitiones* that are rooted in the mercy of God. Those who refuse these divine disciplines are condemned as irrational brutes and despisers of God's mercy. They are led to the afflictions of the future life that are rooted in the justice of God. The tortures of hell are "punishments" (*supplicii*), not admonitions; there is no longer any opportunity for repentance. Major argues similarly that those who refuse the discipline of this life have a greater torment waiting for them in hell. In his mercy, God uses sickness and other afflictions as disciplines to correct sinful behavior and to prevent his people from the horrible tortures of the future life. Titelmans states that if those who are liberated from affliction fall back once again into sin, they will be condemned "on account of their ingratitude" (*propter ingratitudinem*). They face the prospect of eternal suffering in the "future retribution." But Titelmans also suggests that the warning of "something worse" may also indicate a threat of a future illness in the present life much graver than the man's original disease.[84]

Like Titelmans, Musculus argues that Jesus' warning is a threat either of more severe afflictions in the present life or of the punishments of hell. It is hard to imagine, Musculus concedes, a more severe illness than the one that had afflicted the man by the pool for so many years; even death itself would hardly seem worse than the man's sickness. But no matter how severe and bitter the pain of present sufferings may be, "it is not impossible for God to add to our afflictions." Even if the severity of suffering cannot be surpassed in this life, the punishments of hell are always "something worse." We are taught, Musculus argues, never to despise the disciplines of the present life lest we are handed over to the future judgment of God, which is not a corrective and medicinal discipline but a discipline of condemnation and perpetual perdition. Therefore, Jesus' words to the sick man constitute an important warning to all Christians, for "we are never more disposed for sinning than when we are healthy and without affliction."[85]

CONCLUSION

The theological presuppositions that divided Musculus from his Catholic peers defined nothing less than the central meaning of the Christian gospel. The debate over these issues severed the unity of Christendom into various theological camps, precipitated armed conflict, and contributed to the emergence of the modern nation-states. Given the power and virulence of the debate, it is striking how much the interpretations of Musculus and his Catholic peers share in common. The exegetical tradition clearly exerts a centripetal force that to a certain degree mitigates the forces driving Catholics and Protestants apart. On any given passage, this tradition defines the appropriate topics for discussion, identifies the central problematic issues, and suggests possible exegetical solutions.

One of the purposes of this comparative exegetical study has been to identify characteristics that would distinguish Musculus's interpretation from the interpretations of his Catholic contemporaries. Yet repeatedly we have found that Musculus offers many of the same themes, arguments, and questions that are expressed by the Catholic commentators. For example, all four commentators explain the motives of Jesus in similar fashion. Why Jesus singled out the man for healing, why he issued three separate commands, and why he left the scene of controversy are questions that find the same basic answers. Our commentators also offer very similar characterizations of the sick man and of the offended Jewish party. They praise the patience of the sick man and commend him for his responses both to Jesus and to the Jewish inquisitors. The Jews are condemned for a superstitious allegiance to Sabbath regulations because their allegiance is based on a faulty understanding of the true nature of the Sabbath. Additionally, with the exception of Titelmans, each commentator interprets Jesus' warning to the healed man through a similar theological discussion on the relationship between sin and sickness. Most striking, however, is the fact that Musculus joins the Catholic commentators in repeating the traditional baptismal symbolism associated with the pool at Bethesda.

The characteristics that distinguish Musculus's comments on this story from the Catholic interpretations are those that we have repeatedly seen to distinguish his exegesis from that of other commentators. His tendency to interrupt the flow of his comments with extended theological discussions is seen once again in his interpretation of the Sabbath controversy. He presents a thorough treatment of the true nature of Sabbath observance in a manner unparalleled by the Catholic commentators. His passion for moral exposition also comes to the fore. Like the Catholics, Musculus praises the disposition of the sick man as worthy of emulation, but he develops this and other moral admonitions much more extensively than the Catholic interpreters. The command to carry the pallet becomes a moral exhortation for Christians to properly govern their bodies; the command to walk becomes an exhortation to pursue piety and obedience. Similarly, the man's public confession of his healing reminds Christians of their duty to proclaim their spiritual healing by Christ. We also find that at least in one area, Musculus's interpretation distinguishes itself from the Catholic interpretations because of the influence of humanist modes of exposition. Major, Broickwy, and Titelmans each give the standard etymologies for the Greek and Hebrew names of the pool, etymologies rooted in the work of Jerome and appearing throughout the exegetical tradition on the story. Musculus, however, here parts company with the exegetical tradition, offering his own analysis of the Greek and Hebrew.

The most significant difference in the interpretations of Musculus and the Catholics, however, lies in the area of spiritual exegesis. But it is not the case, as one might have expected, that Musculus shows himself a more restrained allegorist than his Catholic counterparts. The allegorical interpretation of the miracle as an image of human salvation is in fact the major theme of Musculus's comments on the story. The miracle images the healing of the inner human being, and the three commands represent three distinct stages in the process of conversion. On a grander scale, the miracle also represents for Musculus an image of salvation history. The sick man thus images fallen humanity, while the miracle symbolically portrays the process of human redemption. In contrast, Broickwy merely hints at the allegory of individual conversion, while Major and Titelmans have nothing at all to say on the matter. Even more striking is the fact that Musculus makes use of allegorical exposition to express the one theme that would distinguish his interpretation as Protestant. The impotence of the human will before it is transformed by the grace of Christ is represented, Musculus argues, by the image of the sick man lying by the pool who can do absolutely nothing to contribute to his own healing. This Augustinian theme contrasts vividly with the interpretation of Major, who argues for the meritorious disposition of the sick man in reorienting the guilt of his sin. For Musculus, salvation is completely one-sided; human beings are redeemed just as this man was healed, not by any meritorious act or disposition but by the free and gracious election of God. Musculus expresses this idea, so central to the Protestant Reformers, as a new wine poured into the old wineskin of the spiritual method of exegesis.

SIX

Musculus and the Lutheran Commentators on the Healing of the Man Born Blind

In his commentary on John, Musculus openly acknowledges his reliance on patristic exegesis, citing the commentaries of Augustine, Chrysostom, and Cyril throughout. We have also seen that Musculus makes systematic use of Erasmus's translation and *Annotationes* in the composition of his commentary. There can be little doubt that Musculus consults some of the sixteenth-century commentaries on John authored by Protestant theologians as well, but it is surprisingly difficult to determine these sources with precision. This difficulty stems from the fact that he never cites by name the opinions of his contemporaries (with the exception of Erasmus), preferring to refer to the opinions of "recentiores" or "quidam."[1] Having examined these anonymous references to "recent authors," however, I have found no evidence that Musculus makes programmatic use (either as source or adversary) of any contemporary Protestant exegete.

Insofar as Musculus reacts to the ideas of his contemporaries, his remarks are directed mainly against Anabaptist teaching and the doctrines of Roman Catholic theology. There are muted critiques of Lutheran christology and sacramental doctrine in places where one would expect them (such as at Jn 6:53–59 and Jn 20:26), but these critiques are not directed against any particular exegetical opponent. Unlike the John commentary of his mentor Bucer, who systematically refutes many of the exegetical positions of Brenz in order to disprove the teachings of the "new Marcionites," Musculus's commentary steers clear of such polemic. Indeed, in his prefatory letter to the reader, Musculus expressly declares his intention to avoid contentious remarks in his commentary. The writings that best serve the truth and Christian piety are those "in which each person, according to the grace that he receives from the Lord, calmly relates his sense of the truth to others without any stomach for slanderous and brash insulting."[2]

One cannot, however, rule out the possibility that Musculus makes positive use of the commentaries of contemporary Protestant theologians. Indeed, if similarity of ideas could serve as an adequate criterion for determining a source, then the possibilities for contemporary influences would be numerous. Focusing here on the "Lutheran" commentators on John, we find that there are three commentaries that antedate Musculus's: those of Philip Melanchthon (1497–1560), Johannes Brenz (1494–1570), and Erasmus Sarcerius (1501–1559).[3] Melanchthon holds the distinction of having authored the first Protestant John commentary (1523), a work that was extremely popular, judging by its printing history.[4] Brenz, the reformer of Schwäbisch Hall and adviser to Duke Ulrich of Württemburg, authored the second Protestant commentary on John in 1527, a work that was published at least twelve times between 1527 and 1554. The less popular commentary of Erasmus Sarcerius, who served Landgrave Wilhelm von Nassau as superintendent of the Lutheran churches, was published in 1540, just five years before the publication of Musculus's own commentary.

Although there is no indication that Musculus makes systematic use of any of these Lutheran commentaries, one piece of evidence suggests his familiarity with either Melanchthon's or Brenz's commentary. Commenting on John 1:16 ("And from his fulness we have all received grace upon grace"), Musculus summarizes the various attempts by expositors to distinguish the two graces indicated by the phrase "gratiam pro gratia." After presenting the views of Augustine, Chrysostom, and Cyril, Musculus notes that "certain recent writers understand the first grace as that which is of the Father toward the Son, and the latter as the grace of the Son toward us by which we have been made pleasing and acceptable to the Father."[5] This understanding of the phrase is presented by both Melanchthon and Brenz, who argue that the grace that believers receive from Christ is anticipated by the prior grace that Christ receives from the Father.[6] Furthermore, of all of the other sixteenth-century commentators I have examined, none offer this distinctive interpretation of the phrase. Therefore, there is reason to believe that Musculus may have consulted either or both of these Lutheran commentaries on John.

Having addressed the question of direct influence, we turn now to the main focus of this chapter: a comparison of the exegesis of Musculus and the three Lutheran commentators on the story of the healing of the man born blind (Jn 9). Before beginning this analysis, one should note the sharp distinction between the commentary of Musculus and his Lutheran counterparts as indicated by the respective length of their treatments of this story. This distinction is most clearly seen when one compares the length of Melanchthon's exposition, which fills a mere two columns of the *Corpus Reformatorum* edition, to Musculus's comments on the story, which run to forty-eight folio-sized pages. In the case of Melanchthon's commentary, this contrast is largely due to the fact that Melanchthon's method of exegesis does not entail a verse-by-verse exposition but rather a focus on selected verselets that point (in his view) to the central theological themes, or *loci*, of a given text.

But Musculus's interpretation of the story also vastly exceeds the running commentaries of Brenz and Sarcerius, whose comments fill sixteen and thirty-one octavo-sized pages, respectively.

The remarkable profuseness of Musculus's comments precludes an exhaustive treatment of his interpretation of the healing of the blind man, a story that occupies the entire ninth chapter of John's gospel. Therefore, this comparative study focuses solely on the first seven verses of chapter 9. First, we will examine how Musculus and the Lutheran commentators interpret the discussion between Jesus and the disciples concerning the causes of the blind man's affliction. Second, we will consider their interpretations of the healing miracle itself and what it represents.

THE RELATIONSHIP BETWEEN SIN AND SUFFERING

The conversation between Jesus and his disciples at the beginning of John 9 produces two basic interpretive questions. First, how should the disciples' question be characterized? Seeing a man blind from birth, the disciples ask Jesus: "Who sinned, this man or his parents, that he was born blind?" Each of our commentators discusses the assumptions that informed the disciples' question, and in turn each offers some evaluation of the question's validity. Second, how should one interpret the response of Jesus? What does Jesus mean when he says: "Neither this man sinned nor his parents, but that the works of God might be displayed in him"? From an exegetical standpoint, however, the following statement of Jesus is even more problematic: "We must work the works of him who sent me, as long as it is day. Night is coming when no one can work. While I am in the world, I am the light of the world." Each of our commentators struggles to explain Jesus' use of the metaphors of night and day, seeking in various ways to weaken the suggestion that the work of the gospel would cease after the death or ascension of Jesus.

In their interpretation of the disciples' question, the Lutheran expositors each conclude that the disciples were prompted by a common judgment of reason concerning the relationship between sin and suffering. When reason sees affliction or hardships of any kind, it naturally concludes that sin is the cause. Sarcerius states that such reasoning is not a relic of an outmoded way of thinking, for there is still a natural impulse in all of us to make an immediate connection between suffering and sin. Indeed, he states, reason can find no other explanation for human miseries than to conclude such miseries to be penalties for sin.[7]

Melanchthon and Brenz, however, argue that it is not reason alone that makes such a judgment, but reason informed by the law. Since the law, Melanchthon states, promises good things to the righteous and harsh things to the wicked, "reason infers thus: this man is afflicted, therefore he is a sinner and rejected by God; this man is well-off, therefore he is pious and dear to God." The problem of theodicy arises, according to Melanchthon, when the state of human affairs fails to corroborate this inference of reason informed by the law. The prosperity of the wicked and the hardships of the righteous lead reason to condemn the judgment of God and to deny the governance of divine providence.[8] The law, Brenz notes, provides abundant evidence that "curses, infirmities, plagues, calamities, and death itself entered into the world on account of sin," and he refers the reader to Leviticus 26 (verses 14–39) and Deuteronomy 28 (verses 15–68) to demonstrate this threatening aspect of the law. Therefore, whenever human reason is instructed in the law apart from the knowledge of Christ, it always concludes that human sufferings are punishments for sin. Thus the disciples, indoctrinated in the law apart from a knowledge of the cross of Christ, thought it entirely necessary that the man's blindness had resulted from sin. The disciples reveal themselves—as Melanchthon and Sarcerius also argue—to stand in the same error as the friends of Job.[9]

Yet according to Sarcerius, the disciples were only partly wrong in their assumption that sin is the cause of affliction. They failed to realize that the *righteous* are not always afflicted on account of sins; but their assumption was in fact true in regard to the *unrighteous*: "Among the impious it is always true that they are afflicted because of their sins. Among the pious it is not always true." Therefore, by implication—though he never states this explicitly—Sarcerius makes the blind man a type or figure of the righteous sufferer, whose afflictions may have other causes than sin. But for Sarcerius the causal relationship between suffering and sin remains axiomatic for the unrighteous sufferer. In positing this distinction, Sarcerius's exegesis stands out from the other Lutheran commentaries.[10]

Brenz's interpretation stands out in another way. Unlike Melanchthon or Sarcerius, Brenz fully explicates the disciples' understandable perplexity. On the one hand, they realized that God had promised to vindicate himself on the children of sinners to the third and fourth generation (Dt 5:9; Ex 20:5). Therefore, they could not safely dismiss the possibility that the blind man had been punished for the sins of his forebears. On the other hand, the words of the prophet were ringing in their ears: "The son will not bear the iniquity of the father" (Ez 18:20). But if the blind man was himself to be blamed for an affliction from birth, how could he have sinned before he was born? Even though the disciples believed it unfair that God would take vengeance on the children of sinners, they could at least understand this possibility. That each individual should bear the responsibility of his or her own sin seemed fair but, in the case of one born with a congenital defect, totally incomprehensible. How could the fetus act wickedly "who was not yet able to do anything" (*qui nondum quicquam agere potuit*)?[11]

In his characterization of the disciples' question, Musculus's comments go well beyond those of the Lutheran commentators. Like Brenz, he attempts to explicate fully the context for the disciples' question—namely, what were the real questions and assumptions behind the question? But Musculus develops an extensive and nuanced interpretation of this context, raising issues not treated by Brenz, Melanchthon, or Sarcerius. In fact, Musculus presents two possible ways of understanding the disciples' question, and in presenting these two possibilities, Musculus's interpretation focuses squarely on the question of the disciples' disposition and motives for posing the question.

The first possibility is that the disciples asked the question "simply" (*simpliciter*). They honestly believed that human sufferings are inflicted by God because of sin, and they sincerely wanted to know to whom the sin should be ascribed. But if in fact they asked "simply," then their question has an element of absurdity, for how could the blind man have caused his own blindness through sin when he was born with that defect? The disciples could have asked the question sincerely only if they were informed "by the common opinion" (*vulgata opinione*) that the soul of the blind man had sinned in some antenatal existence. Otherwise, the absurdity of the question would belie the fact that it had been sincerely asked.

The second possibility, according to Musculus, is that the disciples asked the question "in an argumentative fashion" (*per modum argutandi*). Since they had heard Jesus say to the healed paralytic, "Sin no more lest something worse befall you" (Jn 5:14), they assumed that Jesus was indicating such serious illnesses to be punishments for sin. Unhappy with this correlation, and seeing the blind man, the disciples seize the opportunity to initiate a quarrel with Jesus. The question, then, is not posed simply and sincerely but only as a pretext for expressing their displeasure with Jesus' earlier statement. In Musculus's words, it is as if they were saying: "If troubles of this kind are divine vengeances inflicted on account of sins, what will we say about this blind man who was born blind before he sinned? For to whose sin will we attribute this blindness? To the blind man? But that seems absurd. For how could he have sinned, who was not yet born? But by what fairness would an infant have been punished for the sins of parents since it is written that the son does not bear the sins of his parents?"[12] Unlike the Lutheran commentators, who characterize the disciples' question as a theoretical query based on the judgment of reason or of reason informed by the law, Musculus here portrays the question as argumentative, tinged with indignation, and occasioned by Jesus' own words to the healed paralytic.

Musculus does not, however, finally declare which of his two possible interpretations of the disciples' question is preferable. Since the intention of the disciples is not clearly expressed by the Evangelist, Musculus concedes the final interpretation to the judgment of the reader "to embrace the opinion that seems more probable" (*amplectendi sententiam, quae vero videatur propior*). In either case, Musculus argues that the disciples reveal a defective disposition that should be avoided by believers in Christ. As is so often the case, Musculus here draws a moral lesson from the story whereas other commentators express none.

If the disciples asked "simply," sincerely wanting to know whose sin had caused the man's blindness, then they must be reproached for their curiosity. Paraphrasing Augustine, Musculus states that curious people are always eager to know about the sins of others but are negligent and lazy concerning their own.[13] Since they believed that Jesus knew the sins of all people, they would have done better to ask Jesus concerning their own sins. And if in fact they were truly concerned about the blind man, they would have simply interceded on his behalf, asking Jesus to remove his infirmity. Thus, their prurient interest in the sins of others not only was misplaced but also revealed their lack of charity toward the man. But if the disciples asked "in an argumentative fashion," then they must be reproached for their temerity, for in effect they were calling into question God's justice. They rashly accuse God either of unfairly punishing the innocent (i.e., an infant) or of unfairly imposing the guilt of the parents' sin upon an innocent child. We see here, according to Musculus, a splendid example of how "the temerity of human reason argues against God" (*humanae rationis temeritas contra Deum arguatur*). To this reckless arrogance of reason, Musculus argues, the words of Paul are a fitting response: "Who are you, man, who responds to God?"[14]

In interpreting the response of Jesus, each of the Lutheran commentators argues that the blind man and his parents are not made sinless by the words, "Neither this man sinned nor his parents." Jesus' words must be carefully restricted to the immediate context of the disciples' question: "Who sinned, this man or his parents *that he should be born blind*?" Jesus declares simply that they had not sinned so as to cause the blindness. But certainly they, along with all human beings, were sinners, as the rest of Scripture makes abundantly clear.[15] This exegetical commonplace, affirmed by nearly every commentator on the passage, is also echoed by Musculus, who argues that Jesus was really saying, "Neither this man nor his parents sinned *that he should be born blind*." Even if he did not say this "word for word" (*ad verbum*), there can be no doubt that this is what he meant.[16]

When Jesus states that the purpose of the blindness was "that the works of God might be manifested in him," he affirms that the affliction was not based in retribution or punishment but rather in the purpose of bringing glory to God. This is the basic point made by all of our commentators. Melanchthon states that by these words Jesus teaches believers to endure afflictions patiently in order to arrive at the fruit of such testings—namely, the recognition of God's will. When God's will is recognized in the midst of such trials, his name is glorified.[17] Sarcerius and Brenz, on the other hand, do not stress the knowledge of God's will as much as the act of liberation itself in bringing glory to God. According to Sarcerius, God is glorified when the suffering are powerfully and unexpectedly liberated. The "works of God" then are "signs and marks of God's power" (*signa sunt & notae potentiae dei*), which when recognized bring glory to God.[18] Brenz argues that just as the great and famous men of the past acquired renowned names for their heroic and often brutal deeds, so also God acquires a glorious name and fame through his acts of liberation. Scipio is known as "the African" (*Aphricanus*) because of his conquest of the Carthaginians. Manlius, who wore the neck-chain of a Gaul he killed in combat, is known as "Torquatus" ("adorned with a neck-chain"). God also is known by titles that commemorate his glorious acts, although these titles are far more honorable and praiseworthy than those of the cruel tyrants of history: "For when he brings his people down into the utmost misery and afterward rescues them, he acquires this title, 'God the Liberator and Helper in Times of Need' (*ein Nothelfer*), which is a most magnificent title, inviting all men to call upon God."[19] Brenz stresses that such human calamities do not happen by chance but by the will of God in order to bring glory to himself. God afflicted Joseph so that he might acquire glory in liberating him from prison. God afflicted the Israelites so that in freeing them from the tyranny of Pharaoh he might acquire praise among all the nations. In a similar fashion, God afflicted the blind man with blindness in order to bring glory to himself by a powerful act of liberation. Therefore, Brenz argues, anyone who impatiently "rejects a cross from himself" (*crucem a se reijcit*) in effect rejects the very glory of God.[20]

Like Brenz, Musculus emphasizes the fact that the man's blindness occurred not by chance but by the will of God; indeed, it was "determined from eternity" (*ab aeterno destinatus*) that the man would be born blind in order to give Christ the opportunity to manifest the works of God. But in distinction to the Lutheran expositors, Musculus also explains why such extraordinary works are necessary to arouse praise and glory to God. For in truth, it is a work of God that human beings are born with sight; this gift of vision alone should be enough to lead human beings to sing God's praises. But because of its ordinariness, the gift is not perceived to be a work manifesting God's glory. The same can be said of the gifts of health and life itself. Therefore, God afflicts individuals with infirmities and restores them by extraordinary works in order to break through the spiritual blindness that prevents human beings from seeing the works of God all around them: "And in this way we serve the glory of God by our infirmities, while as long as we are well, we obscure it."[21]

That human sufferings often occur simply as a vehicle for manifesting God's glory is, according to Musculus, a great consolation for believers. This point is not new, for Melanchthon, Brenz, and Sarcerius all make the same argument: the story teaches us to remain steadfast in faith in the midst of afflictions, knowing that patient endurance leads ultimately to God's glory.[22] Yet Musculus once again goes well beyond the Lutheran commentators, expanding this basic observation into an extended discussion of the various causes of affliction. The consolation offered by the story, in Musculus's reading, extends only to those whose suffering has no other cause save the glory of God. Those who are afflicted for other reasons should not hastily flee to this story for comfort, because personal responsibility for suffering is not universally ruled out by Jesus' response to the disciples.

Musculus enumerates three basic causes for human afflictions. The first and most general cause is sin. In many places the Scriptures declare that God punishes individuals for their transgressions.[23] Such punishment is not simply rooted in retributive justice but aims at correction and reform of life as 1 Corinthians 11:32 and Hebrews 12:6 make clear. Yet the Scriptures also declare that individuals are occasionally punished for the sins of others. Here, Musculus quotes Exodus 20:5, where God threatens to visit the sins of parents on their children to the third and fourth generation. But Musculus immediately blunts the edge of this dictum by explaining that the statement applies only to those who imitate the wickedness of their forefathers. The second cause of afflictions is "that we might be exercised, tested, and made careful not to sin" (*ut exerceamur, probemur, & ne peccemus cauti reddamur*). When patiently received, such afflictions are beneficial to piety: "Faith grows in tribulations, prayer becomes more fervent, the soul is humbled and lives soberly, and in sum the old man is killed and the new man grows."[24] The third cause is that which Jesus declares in the present story—namely, "that the glory of the power and goodness of God might be declared in us" (*ut declaretur in nobis gloria potentiae ac bonitatis Dei*). Musculus finds examples of this purpose in the afflictions of Job and Lazarus, whose sufferings served to reveal God's glory.

This extended discussion of the causes of affliction represents a significant feature of Musculus's method of commenting, a feature that consistently distinguishes his exegesis from the Lutheran interpretations. Throughout his comments on John 9, Musculus presents lengthy discussions of topics suggested by certain key words and phrases in the text. Thus, in his treatment of John 9:22 ("If any one should confess him to be Christ, he was to be put out of the synagogue"), Musculus introduces a broad treatment of the subject of excommunication discussing what constitutes a true versus a false excommunication, and what constitutes a laudable versus a blamable fear of excommunication.[25] At John 9:24 ("Give glory to God; we know that this man is a sinner"), Musculus first presents an extraordinarily lengthy discussion of "what it is to give glory to God" (*quid sit Deo gloriam dare*) and then engages in an extended epistemological discussion of the nature of human cognition.[26] At John 9:31("but if anyone . . . obeys his will"), he gives a lengthy discourse on the will of God and how it is known.[27] These examples (and others could be included) point to an important difference between the interpretations of Musculus and those of his Lutheran counterparts. Only on the subject of excommunication do we find a brief discussion by Brenz, but even this is dwarfed by the treatment by Musculus.[28] In none of the other cases do Melanchthon, Brenz, or Sarcerius offer any discussion similar to that of Musculus. This difference is significant, for it points to a different understanding of what properly constitutes biblical commentary itself. Musculus says nothing in his discussion of various topics that is particularly exceptional or innovative; the Lutherans would likely agree with almost everything he writes. But the Lutheran commentators would likely assess such topical discussions as unnecessary and extraneous intrusions that have the potential to distract from the plain and sensible meaning of the story at hand.[29]

The second part of Jesus' response to the disciples' question reintroduces the Johannine themes of light and darkness. Jesus states that "we must work . . . while it is day" and further explains the metaphor of "day" by identifying himself as "the light of the world." This much of Jesus' statement is clear and would pose no interpretive difficulties were it not for the limitations that Jesus seemingly places on the duration of the day and the effectiveness of the light. Jesus is the light of the world but only as long as he is in the world. And the night is coming, when no one may work. In the history of exegesis, one finds various explanations of the metaphors of night and day that attempt to show that Jesus' role as light of the world was not limited—as the text seems to suggest—to the time of his earthly ministry.

Among the Lutheran expositors, we find two basic explanations. Melanchthon claims his agreement with the "general view" (*generali sententia*) that "day" means the gospel, "night," ignorance of the gospel. When Jesus states that no one may work at night, he indicates that when the Word of God is not present, it is impossible to work the works of God. "Therefore whatever reason unillumined by the Word of God is able to do is condemned."[30] The second explanation is found in the comments of Brenz and Sarcerius, who concede that "day" does in fact mean the time of Jesus' ministry on earth but assert that Jesus does not thereby limit his role as light or restrict the work of his followers to the time of his earthly ministry. Since Christ is eternal, Sarcerius argues, so also "his workings are eternal" (*operationes eius aeternae sunt*); that is, he continues to be the light of the world even after his ascension. Those who think otherwise succumb to a falsehood of reason, for Jesus does not limit his working absolutely but only his working of miracles in the flesh. Therefore, according to Sarcerius, "night" may refer to the cessation of Jesus' miracle-working, to the future "privation and obfuscation of the gospel under antichrist" (*privationem Evangelii & obfuscationem sub Antichristo*), or, in a general sense, to the unbelieving rejection of the gospel. Here Sarcerius expresses a view close to that of Melanchthon: "Christ is a light to the world as long as it holds him by faith, but where faith in Christ ceases, there Christ is no longer the light of the world."[31] Brenz comes to a different understanding of the term "night." Just as "day" refers to the time of Jesus' earthly ministry, so also "night" refers simply to the cessation of that ministry. However, Brenz argues that Jesus calls this time "night," not because he would cease to be the light of the world or because the disciples would truly be unable to work but because it would *seem to the disciples* that the work of the gospel had ceased and that Jesus was no longer the light of the world. In essence then, Jesus simply warns the disciples of the stumbling-block they would experience in his humiliation and death, saying in effect: "I am the true light of the world, although by no means will it appear so on the cross when my ministry ceases and the power of darkness prevails." Yet Brenz notes that there is also "another opinion" (*alia sententia*) concerning the meaning of "night" and "day," and here he gives the interpretation of Melanchthon. "Day" simply means the presence of Christ by the Word received in faith, and "night" is the spiritual darkness that envelops those who reject the Word.[32]

In his interpretation, Musculus explains the metaphors of day and night similarly to Brenz and Sarcerius. "Day" refers to the time of Jesus' bodily presence in the world, while "night" refers to the time of his passion and death. Musculus notes that some interpreters explain night as a prophetic reference to the divine abandonment and dispersion of the Jewish people, but he thinks this view strains the plain sense of the metaphors.[33] But if the metaphors are to be taken in their "simple sense," it does not necessarily follow, Musculus argues, that after his death Jesus would no longer be the light of the world. Christ promised his perpetual presence to the end of the age, and he continues to operate in the world by the power of his spirit (Mt 28:20). Musculus explains—and here his interpretation distinguishes itself from the Lutherans—that in interpreting the terms "night" and "day," one must pay careful attention to the kind of language being used. These terms are "similitudes" (*similitudines*), and as such "they should be understood in their simple sense, not drawn out beyond their purpose."[34] The terms "night" and "day" should not be used to fuel the fire of debate concerning whether or not Jesus continues to be the light of the world after his death, for this question "was not in the mind of Christ" (*in mente Christi non fuit*). If the similitudes are understood in their straightforward sense, it is clear that Jesus did not use the term "night" to express "times of perpetual blindness and darkness" (*perpetuae excaecationis tempora ac tenebrae*) but simply to indicate that his death was fast approaching and that the disciples should therefore busy themselves with the work of the gospel while he is bodily present.[35]

THE MIRACLE: SPIT, CLAY, WATER, AND OBEDIENCE

We come now to the account of the illumination of the blind man, focusing our attention on what the commentators say about the particular method Jesus used to accomplish the miracle. Unlike the healing of the ruler's son and the healing of the man at the pool of Bethesda, Jesus does not heal here by his Word alone but employs particular means to restore the man's vision. The standard question is why Jesus used these means when he could, it is assumed, have simply commanded the restoration of sight. While each of our commentators attempts to answer this question at the literal level of interpretation, the very strangeness of the means employed suggests a deeper symbolic level of meaning. Jesus spits on the ground, making a mud ointment that he applies to the blind man's eyes. He then instructs the man to wash in the pool of Siloam, where he finally receives his sight. The details of this account—the spit, clay, and waters of Siloam—are rich in symbolic potential, and the Evangelist himself seems to point to a latent level of meaning when he interprets Siloam as "sent." Not surprisingly then, the exegetical tradition abounds with attempts to ferret out the latent symbolism in the story of this miracle. For the purposes of this study, the question is how and to what degree Musculus and the Lutheran expositors exploit the symbolic potential of this passage. Here, however, we must lay aside the interpretation of Melanchthon, for he writes nothing at all about the miracle of the blind man's illumination.

At the literal level of interpretation, there is one basic argument common to Brenz, Sarcerius, and Musculusa: all three exegetes insist that the means Jesus employed were not essential for the performance of the miracle. The employed means, Brenz and Sarcerius argue, should not distract from the fact that the healing occurred by the power of the Word. Brenz states that Jesus sometimes healed by his Word alone, and at other times he added "instruments" (*instrumenta*), not by any necessity but "according to his mere pleasure" (*pro mera sua libidine*). Musculus argues that it would be ridiculous to think that the clay or water contributed anything to the actual healing, since clay smeared on the eyes hinders rather than promotes vision, and water in itself cleanses only the external filth of the body.

If the means were not essential for the miracle, why then did Jesus employ them? Here, we find a diversity of opinions among our commentators. According to Sarcerius, Jesus made use of spit, clay, and water in order to commend the ordinary means that God has established for accomplishing healing. Specifically, Sarcerius has in mind the study of medicine, "which God created from heaven and which 'the wise man will not despise'"(Ecclus 38:4).[36] But by employing certain means, Jesus also advocates the necessary use of the sacraments. By sending the blind man to the pool of Siloam, Jesus directs him to a "type" (*typum*) of Christian baptism. The story demonstrates, according to Sarcerius, that the sacraments confer grace not in themselves or "by the work performed" (*ex opere operato*) but only by the presence of the Word seized in faith. Without Jesus' command, the blind man would have never recovered his sight, no matter how many times he washed in the pool of Siloam. It was only by the response of faith and obedience that the water became an effective means for conferring grace. God certainly may save anyone apart from sacramental means, and in fact he does so in emergency situations. But the empty fable (*vana fabula*) of the heretics, who assert that the sacraments are not necessary in the Church, cannot stand against the example of Jesus, who employed specific means in healing the blind man.[37]

Brenz states that Jesus utilized spit, clay, and water in order to show that "the just means offered to us by the Lord must be used." Although he does not give examples of these "just means," as Sarcerius does in pointing to medicine and the sacraments, the essential point is the same. But Brenz proceeds to give another explanation that centers on the effectiveness of "intermediary instruments" (*media instrumenta*) in making known the works of God. The means appointed by God are often those that run counter to human expectations and thus serve as forceful demonstrations of God's power. "For God is not willing to distribute his goods to us by the means which we choose, but [by those] which he himself chooses."[38] Here Brenz notes the example of the healing of Naaman, the leprous captain of the Syrian army (2 Kgs 5:1–14). Naaman's expectation and hope that Elisha would greet him and lay his hands on him were disappointed when he was instructed by a messenger to dip himself seven times in the filthy waters of the Jordan. But it was precisely because these means ran counter to the expectations of reason that the work of God was "more celebrated" (*celebrius*). If Elisha had greeted Naaman and touched the leprosy, then the healing would have been ascribed partly to the prophet and not to God alone. In a similar fashion, Jesus healed the blind man employing means that neither the man himself nor the spectators would have expected. Yet these means were perfectly suited to the objectives of the miracle—namely, to make the power of God known and to lead the blind man to faith: "Christ heals a blind man with a poultice made from clay and spit so that by the strangeness of this poultice the miracle and the power of his word would become more celebrated. Second, the blind man is sent to the pool of Siloam so that the faith of the blind man might be exercised by the long journey."[39]

Musculus argues that the miracle should be interpreted in two ways: both literally (*quod attinet ad rei gestae literam*) and figuratively (*quod facti huius mysterium concernit*). In his literal interpretation, he explains the significance of the "means" used by Jesus similarly to Brenz: the strangeness of the miracle contributed to its publication and ultimately to the glorification of the miracle's author. Certainly, Jesus could have healed the man by a "naked word" (*nudo verbo*), but he purposefully chose a particular method that would defy the expectations of reason. Who would believe, Musculus asks, that Jesus was about to heal a deaf man if he stopped up his ears with mud? Similarly, mud smeared on the eyes of a blind man would seem in the judgment of reason to compound rather than alleviate blindness. A surgical knife rather than a poultice of spit and clay would be much more agreeable to human reason. But by choosing means that appear "more harmful than helpful" (*noxia magis quam conducibilis*), Christ more firmly makes his power known. He shows that his word is efficacious no matter what means he should choose to use.[40]

More interesting, however, is the manner in which Musculus interprets the mystical significance of the miracle, an interpretation that distinguishes his commentary from the Lutheran expositions. Musculus here concedes the speculative nature of his ideas and claims no finality for his interpretation: "Without prejudging anyone, I say how it appears to me."[41] First, he suggests that the spit and clay smeared on the eyes of the blind man may symbolize earthly wisdom which prevents unbelievers from seeing divine truths. Accordingly, the water of Siloam represents the grace of the Holy Spirit, embodied in Christ sent by the Father. Therefore, "by this mystical deed" (*mystico hoc facto*) Jesus teaches that the truths of God cannot be discerned until the eyes of the mind are cleansed from the "clay of human wisdom" (*humanae sapientiae lutum*) by the waters of Christ's grace. The blind man thus bears the image of those like the scribes and Pharisees who blind themselves by accumulating earthly wisdom:

> Therefore, how insane are those who accumulate to themselves with the greatest zeal this earthly clay and smear it on the eyes of the mind, as if from that they will be more sharp-sighted for knowing the truth of Christ? They search for this clay with great expense from the writings of the philosophers from which they are blinded more than

illuminated. May the Lord grant that they should go to the pool of Siloam and there wash away the eyes of the mind and be recleansed from the clay of earthly wisdom.[42]

Second, Musculus interprets the spit and clay as an allegorical representation of the incarnation of Christ, an interpretation rooted in Augustine's commentary and well represented throughout the exegetical tradition. Here, the spit symbolizes the Word of God, while the clay symbolizes the human flesh assumed by that Word in the incarnation of Christ. The smearing of spit and clay on the eyes of the blind man represents, according to Musculus, the offense that the incarnation of Christ presents to unbelievers. The humility and abasement of the incarnate Word is such an offense to human reason that it blinds until reason is washed by the water of Siloam—that is, by the grace of the Holy Spirit.

Musculus sees no difficulty in asserting the validity of both allegorical interpretations, but he recognizes that some may prefer one to the other: "Neither exposition is impious, but I leave to your judgment, reader, which one you should accept."[43] While he seems to acknowledge the inconclusiveness of such allegories, he nevertheless presents this kind of exegesis throughout his interpretation of this miracle to an extent unparalleled by the Lutheran commentators. Indeed, very early in his comments on the story, Musculus indicates that the illumination of the blind man represents an allegory of salvation. There are some glimmers of this understanding of the miracle in the comments of Sarcerius, who argues that the story shows that salvation is not by human merits but by the grace and mercy of Christ.[44] But Musculus elaborates this way of reading the story in much fuller detail, seizing upon details that contribute to an overall picture of the miracle as an image of human salvation.

Thus, for Musculus, the blind man does not simply represent a needy individual but images the blindness that has stricken all of the descendants of Adam:

What is that birth that produces blind people? The birth of the flesh, which is from Adam, does not produce seeing but blind people. The birth of the spirit does not produce blind ones but seeing people. There are certain living beings that are in fact born blind but after the space of a few days open their eyes so that they see. But the posterity of Adam is born blind in such a way that unless it is regenerated by the spirit, it does not see the light of truth at all.[45]

Since the blind man represents the spiritual blindness of fallen humanity, the miracle demonstrates the manner in which spiritual illumination occurs. No intercession precedes the miracle, either from the blind man himself or from his friends. Rather, Jesus takes the initiative himself in conferring the benefit of sight; by doing so, he shows that spiritual illumination can occur only "by his prevenient grace" (*ipsius gratia praeveniente*).

Although Jesus could have healed the blind man on the spot, he sent him to the pool of Siloam to wash his eyes. This command is significant, according to Musculus, because it demonstrates the way "divine providence usually expends its grace to mortals." Christ is able to accomplish the works of the Father without any human effort, but he chooses to make human beings "co-operators with God" (*cooperatores Dei*) in order to strengthen faith and the knowledge of divine power.[46] Furthermore, the blind man was not sent to any pool, but specifically to the pool that is interpreted "sent," an interpretation that the Evangelist gives, according to Musculus, "in order to remind the reader of the mystical deed" (*ut lectorem mystici facti admoneat*).[47] Like Sarcerius, Musculus argues that the pool presents an image of Christian baptism. But unlike Sarcerius, he discusses baptism here in terms suggested by the story—namely, as a form of spiritual illumination: "Therefore to have washed in the waters of Siloam, that is, in the the streams of the baptism of Christ, is the same as to have been illuminated." Those who are baptized in Christ regain their spiritual vision, lost in the fall. This is why, Musculus argues, the ancient Greeks termed baptism φώτισμον (an enlightening).[48]

Turning now to the last component of the miracle of illumination, the obedience of the blind man to the command of Christ, we find that each of our commentators commends his response as an example to all believers. Sarcerius simply states that he gives an example of the obedience of faith.[49] Brenz argues that the man teaches us to seize the promises of God by faith and an eager obedience even when the things that are promised are nowhere evident. When the commands of God are faithfully executed, our faith will not be disappointed.[50] Musculus also praises the man's response as worthy of emulation, magnifying the greatness of his obedience by probing the psychology of the situation. The blind man might have turned away when he felt his eyes smeared with mud, thinking perhaps that he was being ridiculed. He might have laughed outright when ordered to wash in the pool, scorning such a command as absurd. But in fact he committed himself to Christ and "promptly obeyed the command even though all these things seemed ridiculous to human reason."[51]

Although the man's obedience serves as a general admonition to all believers, Musculus directs this admonition more specifically to certain heretics who dismiss the sacraments of baptism and the Lord's Supper as observances that proffer no spiritual benefit. These heretics see only the earthly elements in the sacraments, and hence they ridicule those who observe these dominical commands: "Thus they now croak, 'What power will water, bread, and wine have?'"[52] If they had stood in the blind man's shoes, they would have refused Jesus' command, responding indignantly that neither the clay nor the water of Siloam could possibly illumine blind eyes. If they had heard Peter's command to be baptized (Acts 2:38) they would have retorted that water is not able to wash away sins. If they had been among the Israelites bitten by venomous serpents (Nm 21:6–9), they would have refused as absurd the prescribed remedy of viewing Moses' bronze serpent. They are fools who "do not understand that neither water, nor bread, nor wine, nor a bronze serpent is able by itself to confer anything, but that the power of healing is in the Word of God seized by faith."[53] The obedient response of the blind man thus serves as a fitting rejoinder to these heretics: "Let the heretics of our times note that obedience of the blind man" who did not refuse the "earthly elements" (*elementa terrena*) prescribed by Christ but eagerly seized them by faith in Christ's word.[54]

CONCLUSION

Viewing Musculus's comments on John 9:1–7 in the context of Lutheran interpretations brings into relief a distinctive characteristic of his method of exposition: the tendency toward an exhaustive exegetical treatment of the scriptural text. At the most basic level of exposition, Musculus and the Lutherans focus on the same exegetical questions and offer similar interpretations. But Musculus consistently shows himself willing to probe these questions more deeply, to test differing possible interpretations, and to suggest more moral applications than one finds in the Lutheran expositions.

Thus, in his treatment of the disciples' question, Musculus gives a much fuller treatment of the context, suggesting not one but two different and equally valid ways of understanding the query. Furthermore, while the Lutherans find in the question no occasion for tropology, Musculus develops his interpretation into a moral admonition against two dangerous vices: prurient curiosity (if the question was asked "simply") and shameless temerity (if the question was asked "argumentatively"). In his interpretation of Jesus' response, Musculus, like the Lutherans, treats the basic and obvious question of how God is glorified when the suffering are miraculously liberated. But Musculus alone examines the related question of *why* such miracles are needed when God's glory is (or should be) apparent in the works of creation. Similarly, Musculus is not content with a simple approbation of the blind man's obedient response, such as one finds in the Lutheran interpretations, but magnifies the virtue of this response with a discussion of other ways in which he could have responded less faithfully to Jesus' strange deed.

At almost every turn, we find that Musculus simply has more to say than the Lutheran commentators. Although he assumes the same basic menu of exegetical questions, Musculus consistently educes further nuances, related questions, and moral applications. Yet there are two other ways in which Musculus protracts his treatment of the story of the blind man's illumination. First, Musculus makes use of the words and phrases of the gospel text as a springboard for logical and systematic discussions of certain doctrines and truths, which are (at best) only tangentially related to the text itself. This feature, seen throughout Musculus's interpretation of John 9 in his extended treatments of various topics, such as the causes of affliction, excommunication, the ways God is glorified, and various kinds of knowledge, finds no analogue in the Lutheran commentaries. Second, Musculus gives much fuller voice to the allegorical "images" in the miracle story than any of the Lutheran commentators. The spit and clay thus represent the incarnation of Christ or the blinding of earthly wisdom; the pool of Siloam represents baptism or the grace of the Holy Spirit; and the healing miracle represents an allegory of spiritual illumination, that is the salvation of the soul. Among the Lutheran commentators, Sarcerius alone points to the baptismal imagery of the pool and briefly suggests that the miracle portrays an image of salvation by grace apart from human merit. Melanchthon and Brenz, however, present no "mystical" reading of the healing story, a remarkable fact given how easily the elements of the story lend themselves to a Protestant understanding of salvation. It is certainly not the case that the Lutheran commentators dismiss allegorical interpretation altogether, for like Musculus, all three assume at least two basic levels of meaning in the text: literal and allegorical, or to use other terms, historical and mystical. But our comparative exegetical study suggests that Musculus gives more weight to allegorical modes of expression than do his Lutheran counterparts.[55]

In the attempt to provide a comprehensive commentary that takes full account of different interpretive possibilities, related doctrinal and theological topics, and the allegorical level of meaning, Musculus's exegesis reveals a different approach and follows a different model in the task of commenting than that seen in the Lutheran expositions. For the Lutherans, brevity is a virtue; the assembling of a diffuse, prolix, and ostentatious exegetical apparatus that eclipses the biblical text itself is avoided. For Musculus, however, it is not brevity but thoroughness that defines the great virtue of the biblical commentator. These two competing models were recognized by John Calvin in a prefatory letter to his commentary on Romans. On the one hand, he notes that Melanchthon's method of only treating relevant *loci* leaves too much unsaid; the reader always wishes for more. On the other hand, he argues that Bucer's exhaustive method of exegesis also has its shortcomings: "Bucer is too prolix to keep the interest of busy people. . . . Whenever he deals with any subject . . . [he] brings up so many things that he does not know how to take his hand off the paper."[56] Calvin's description of Bucer's method would certainly characterize Musculus's method as well. Perhaps, then, this comprehensive approach to exegesis characterizes a larger "school" of Reformed commentators that includes Bucer and Musculus. We examine this question in the next chapter by comparing Musculus and the Reformed commentators on the final Johannine sign, the raising of Lazarus.

SEVEN

Musculus and the Reformed Commentators on the Raising of Lazarus

We now examine Musculus's exegesis in the context of commentaries authored by theologians who shared an allegiance to the reform movements in southern Germany and Switzerland, centered in the cities of Zurich, Basel, Geneva, and Strasbourg. This southern wing of the Protestant Reformation, represented in its early stages by the central figures of Zwingli, Calvin, and Bucer, spawned a theological tradition that may be distinguished from the Wittenberg-oriented wing of the Reformation and later became known as the Reformed tradition.

Although the writings of Luther precipitated Musculus's break with Rome, it was this Reformed wing of Protestantism that defined his theological development. The first steps of his career as a Reformer came under the guiding influence of the Strasbourg luminaries Bucer and Capito, and in Augsburg Musculus guided a reform movement that was theologically oriented toward Zurich. When Musculus was exiled, his first inclination was to look to the south, where his natural theological compatriots were active, and he resided for brief periods in Zurich, Basel, and St. Gallen before receiving his call to Bern.

By examining Musculus's work on John in the context of other Reformed commentaries, we seek to learn whether the characteristic features of his exegesis may be explained, at least partially, in reference to the exegetical works of his theological allies. We have yet to find any interpreter on John who matches the remarkably thorough and exhaustive approach that Musculus takes in the exegetical task. His comments swell to such proportions that they consistently overwhelm the interpretations of his Lutheran, Catholic, and humanist peers. Does Musculus find a model for this approach among the Reformed expositors? Does his affinity for tropological exegesis—the extraction of moral analogies and observations from practically every detail of the biblical text—find any counterpart among his fellow reformers? Does his penchant for developing allegorical images from the miracle stories remain distinctive in a Reformed exegetical context?[1] The answers to these questions emerge in this final exegetical comparison, contributing to the characterization of Musculus's exegesis that has developed in the course of this study.

REFORMED COMMENTATORS ON JOHN

Four Reformed theologians authored works on John that appeared in print prior to Musculus's commentary: Ulrich Zwingli (1484–1531), the outstanding leader of the reform movement in Zurich; the Basel reformer, Johannes Œcolampadius (1482–1531); Heinrich Bullinger (1504–1575), Zwingli's successor in the post of people's priest at the Grossmünster; and the great Strasbourg reformer Martin Bucer (1491–1551). These men were accomplished exegetes who devoted much of their scholarly work to the exposition of Scripture. Bucer was universally admired as a first-rate commentator, whose exegetical magnum opus, the commentary on Romans (1536), is justly famous. Œcolampadius distinguished himself as a Hebraist who made use of the targums and Jewish exegesis in his exposition of prophetic literature of the Hebrew Bible; his Isaiah commentary (1525) was widely regarded as the sine qua non of any serious consideration of the prophet. Bullinger, also trained in humanist methods of biblical scholarship, produced commentaries on all of the New Testament writings; they were published first individually and then as a complete set in 1561. From the lecture halls of Zurich comes the great bulk of Zwingli's exegetical legacy. While Zwingli himself arranged for the publication of his Isaiah and Jeremiah commentaries, the majority of his biblical commentaries were published on the basis of student notes. All of his New Testament commentaries appeared after his death, edited by Leo Jud, who in 1539 published all known exegetical works of Zwingli.

The first Reformed John commentary to appear in print is the *Enarratio in Evangelium Iohannis* of Bucer, published in Strasbourg in 1528.[2] The commentary was reworked by Bucer himself, and new versions were produced for publication in 1530 and again in 1536.[3] Second, we have the *Annotationes piae ac doctae in Evangelium Ioannis* of Œcolampadius, published posthumously in 1533 in the form of 102 lectures on the gospel.[4] The work is based on a transcript of Johann Gast, who heard the lectures delivered in Basel sometime between the fall of 1529 and the fall of 1530.[5] Third, we have the *Annotationes* of Zwingli, delivered in lecture form some time in the year 1525 and published in 1539 on the basis of Leo Jud's recension of student notes.[6] Finally in 1543, just two years before the publication of Musculus's work on John, the commentary of Bullinger was released for publication; it went through two additional printings in 1548 and 1556 and was reissued as part of the complete set of his New Testament commentaries in 1554 and 1561.[7]

Although Musculus cites none of these Reformed commentators by name, he certainly makes use of Bucer's John commentary. If one examines Musculus's references to the opinions of "quidam" or "recentiores," there are several places where he possibly has Bucer's comments in mind. In most of these places, however, it is impossible to disprove the influence of another source that expresses the same opinion as Bucer.[8] But at Musculus's comments on John 10:10, there is a reference to an interpretation of "recent authorities" that is in fact a verbatim citation of Bucer's commentary: "Ex recentioribus quidam sic exponunt. Ut credentes vitam habent, & abundantius habeant: *hoc est, ut vitam aeternam fide percipiant, quae per spiritum eius semper incrementum accipiat, donec plene perfecta beataque reddatur*" (Bucer's words in italics).[9] Yet having given Bucer's opinion (along with the opinions of Augustine, Cyril, Chrysostom, and Theophylact), Musculus politely but firmly withholds his endorsement, preferring to offer his own interpretation, which accords better (he argues) with the simple meaning of the text. In fact, at several of the places where Musculus possibly cites the views of Bucer, he does so merely to show an exegetical opinion with which he does not fully concur.[10]

Yet one cannot conclude that Musculus only uses Bucer negatively, for the numerous general similarities of interpretation may owe a great deal to Bucer's work on John. Indeed, even in his method of presentation, Musculus's commentary almost certainly betrays the influence of his former teacher. Bucer divided the sections of his commentary into *paraphrasis, annotationes*, and *observationes*, and Musculus— although he omits the titles "paraphrase" and "annotation"—follows this basic division. In particular, by his use of observations for moral and dogmatic reflections on the text, Musculus adopted an organizational method that was particularly Bucerian.

Concerning the other three Reformed John commentaries, I have found no clear evidence to suggest a direct influence. However, given the close friendship of Musculus and Bullinger, it would be surprising if Musculus had not consulted Bullinger's commentary.[11] A thorough and systematic comparison of the two commentaries might turn up evidence of Musculus's knowledge of Bullinger's exegesis. One might also suspect the influence of Œcolampadius simply because Musculus, in his Isaiah commentary, makes extensive use of Œcolampadius's exegesis. Indeed, at the front of his Isaiah commentary, Musculus provides a table of the names of exegetes whose works he has consulted. Although many of his contemporary sources are hidden under the designation "recentiores" in this table, he singles out four contemporaries whom he mentions by name: Bucer, Calvin, Luther, and Œcolampadius.[12] Clearly, Musculus considered Œcolampadius an exegete worthy of serious consideration, and therefore it would not be surprising to find evidence of the influence of Œcolampadius's John commentary on Musculus.

THE RAISING OF LAZARUS (JN 11:1–46)

Musculus's interpretation of the Lazarus narrative (running to twenty-nine folio-sized pages) far exceeds the comments of his Reformed counterparts. Bullinger and

Œcolampadius come closest to matching the length of Musculus's treatment, while the comments of Bucer and Zwingli are dwarfed by comparison.[13] This basic discrepancy points to an important feature of Musculus's work as a commentator (as I have repeatedly argued), and some effort must be made to determine what accounts for the vastness of Musculus's exegesis. But in order to produce a manageable pool of exegetical data, it has been necessary to limit this study to selected portions of the Lazarus story.

In this comparative study, we will first examine the interpretations of the first four verses of the story (11:1–4), which describe Lazarus's illness and the message sent to Jesus by the sisters. Second, we move directly to the dialogues between Jesus, Martha, and Mary (11:20–32), focusing our attention exclusively on the interpretive portraits of the two sisters. Third, we examine the exegetical explanations of Jesus' emotive response (11:33–35). And finally, the study concludes with a consideration of the interpretations of the miraculous revivification of Lazarus (11:38–44).

Setting the Scene: News of Lazarus's Sickness (Jn 11:1–4)

The first two verses of the Lazarus narrative provide the background information for the unfolding of the drama. A man named Lazarus, who resided in Bethany, became ill. The Evangelist further relates that Lazarus's sister Mary was the same person who anointed Jesus with ointment and wiped his feet with her hair. With the exception of Musculus, none of the Reformed exegetes comment significantly on these opening verses, preferring to begin their interpretations with the message sent by the sisters to Jesus regarding Lazarus's illness (11:3).

From the background information of the first two verses, Musculus produces a lengthy treatment of various extraneous topics. First and most significant is a general discussion of human sickness. He examines the question of why human beings often become ill before death, concluding that such illnesses serve as harbingers of the future life, allowing the sick to put their human affairs in order and to prepare their souls for the life to come. Musculus also offers an explanation for the providentially arranged sickness of Lazarus, arguing that his illness, no less than his death, served to illustrate the glory of God. Second, prompted only by the mention in the text that Lazarus, Martha, and Mary lived in the same village, Musculus discusses the ideal love that should exist among siblings. He bemoans the fact that fraternal and sisterly love is so rare in his own day, arguing that the extraordinary harmony and love between Lazarus and his sisters was the chief reason Jesus especially loved this household. Finally, Musculus generates a grand allegory from the names Bethany, Lazarus, Martha, and Mary, whose meanings serve to establish an image of the redemptive work of Christ in the world.[14] Thus, at the very outset of his commentary on the Lazarus narrative, Musculus's interpretation distinguishes itself from the other Reformed commentaries simply by the scope of its investigation.

The first common topic of exegesis among our commentators centers on the third verse of the Lazarus narrative. The Evangelist relates that the sisters send word to Jesus regarding Lazarus's illness and that Jesus responds: "This sickness is not unto death, but for the glory of God so that the son of God might be glorified by it" (11:4). Although Zwingli and Bucer write nothing about the sisters' message, Œcolampadius, Bullinger, and Musculus each offer similar interpretations of the message as an example of pious prayer. Unlike Bullinger and Musculus, however, Œcolampadius interprets their petition according to a menu of allegorical correspondences: the house of Mary and Martha prefigures the Church; Lazarus represents those who have died in their sins; the messenger represents the prayers of the faithful. The sisters therefore intercede for their brother, just as the Church prays for fellow Christians who have fallen into sin or ignorance. They express a humanity and compassion worthy of emulation: "If we see an ass wandering astray, we lead it back according to the law. How much more if we see the soul of a brother going astray? Love requires that we beseech the Lord for his salvation."[15]

Although neither Bullinger nor Musculus interpret the sisters' message as an allegorical image of the prayers of the Church, they both make a prayer analogy similar to the interpretation of Œcolampadius. Bullinger notes that the sisters do not request any particular response of Jesus; they simply tell him that his friend is ill. Thus, they not only demonstrate an example of compassion for the sick but also show the proper way to seek aid from Christ. Nothing should be prescribed to him, for he knows when and how he will bring assistance. Similarly, Musculus observes that the sisters did not ask Jesus to come to Bethany but simply informed him of his sickness. Since they knew Lazarus was loved by Jesus, they rightfully prescribed no particular course of action but simply declared his need. For any human father, Musculus argues, it would be enough to hear "your son has fallen down a well." No one would think it necessary to prescribe anything further, because love would dictate the obvious course of action. Therefore, the sisters exhibit a commendable example of praying "with few words" (*paucis verbis*).[16]

Musculus argues that the sisters demonstrate another principle of prayer by the fact that they remind Jesus of his love for Lazarus. Rightly expecting no special prerogative on the basis of their blood relationship to Lazarus, they do not say, "Lord, our brother is sick," but, "Lord, he whom you love is sick." Their words thus present a model for the prayers of the faithful:

> Let us also follow this example so that when praying for the brethren let us make much of the fact that they were received in the grace of the Lord. And let us say, "Lord, behold he for whom you died is sick." Or if a brother is in the midst of temptations, let us say, "Lord, behold he whom you redeemed by your blood is being attacked by Satan." . . . Thus nowadays when praying for the Church let us say: "Lord, behold your bride, whom you singularly love, is being oppressed and ravaged by the tyranny of Antichrist."[17]

Therefore, for Musculus it is not merely that the economy of the sisters' words is commendable, but the words themselves have a "wonderful emphasis" (*mira emphasis*) that should be emulated in prayer.

In his interpretation of the sisters' message, Musculus also raises a question that is not explored by either Œcolampadius or Bullinger. Namely, why did the sisters send a message to Jesus instead of traveling to petition him in person? By sending a messenger, they seem to have shown disrespect for the dignity and honor of their lord. Yet there are three reasons, according to Musculus, why the sisters rightfully sent an envoy to Jesus. First, "it was not fitting to the female sex" (*muliebri sexui non conveniebat*) for Mary and Martha to set out on such a journey, leaving behind the domestic duties of their home. Second, they properly chose to remain with their sick brother, who sorely needed their attendance and aid. Third, because the sisters knew Jesus well, they were certain of his love and mercy. Being well acquainted with his "holy and admirable modesty" (*sancta & admirabilis modestia*), they knew he would not take offense at their message but would respond with kindness to whatever they asked simply and sincerely. For Musculus, the crucial point is that the sisters sent word to Jesus because they ardently longed for their brother's health. Their love and diligence contrasts vividly, Musculus argues, with the sad state of affairs in his own day, when sisters rarely "pray against" (*deprecentur*) the death of a brother, or brothers against the death of a sister, especially when some earthly gain may be expected from that death.[18]

Concerning Jesus' response to the sisters' message—"This sickness is not unto death but for the glory of God, that the son of God might be glorified by it" (11:4)—we find a common core of exegetical opinion in the Reformed commentaries. By his words, Jesus expresses two basic ideas. First, he does not deny that Lazarus will die but denies only that Lazarus will remain dead. Knowing that he would resurrect Lazarus, Jesus speaks these words in anticipation of the impending miracle. Second, Jesus discloses that his miracles confer glory equally on God the Father and God the Son; when the Father is glorified, so is the Son, and vice versa.[19] These very traditional and rather obvious exegetical ideas are also expressed in Musculus's commentary. But Musculus, who is rarely content with a simple gloss of the biblical text, discusses Jesus' response much more thoroughly in order to extract several moral observations.

First, Musculus notes that Jesus responded to the news of Lazarus's sickness with words of consolation in order to comfort the grieving sisters. Jesus thus bequeaths an example of the proper response to those in mourning: the faithful should offer comfort "with words producing a hope of better things" (*verbis rerum meliorum spem facientibus*). Although some people think they display their piety by a phony and dour pessimism in human affairs, they only succeed in demonstrating their lack of humanity. Hearing someone grieve for a sick loved one, "they do not say . . . 'Be of good cheer, God is able to raise him up' . . . but with a stern countenance they say: 'What use is mourning? He must die.'" This "absurd Christianity" (*praeposterus Christianismus*) not only violates the apostolic dictum to weep with those who weep but also flies in the face of the humanity and compassion expressed by Christ himself.[20]

Second, Musculus argues that Jesus' statement serves as a reminder that not every sickness leads to death but that illness is often inflicted by God as a divine corrective aimed at spiritual reformation. The infirmities of the body thus serve to protect human beings "from the infirmity and death of the soul" (*ab animae infirmitate & morte*). Not only do such infirmities work ultimately to our benefit, but they also work to the glory of God's son. Therefore we are taught, Musculus argues, to glory in our infirmities. Bucer makes the same argument, asserting that an eagerness for God's glory allows us to endure afflictions with equanimity, knowing that adversities "will work for the illustration of his glory . . . and also for our salvation."[21] Yet while Bucer briefly mentions this point, Musculus produces an extended discussion of *how* infirmities lead to the glory of God. If the question is viewed superficially, Musculus argues, one might conclude that such infirmities subtract from the glory of God's creative work: "What glory is able to overflow to him, through whom we were created, from an infirmity of our mortal bodies? Would not more glory return to him if we were strong as the angels of God than from the fact that we are prone to many infirmities? Surely, not the infirmity but the strength of a work is the glory of a creator."[22] Musculus responds that Jesus' words refer not to how we were created in the beginning but to how "in being reformed we are made" (*reformando reddimur*). Thus, it is not infirmities in themselves that bring glory to God but the divine process of transforming infirmities into strength. The glory of a physician, Musculus notes, comes not from making the healthy sick but from making the sick well.

Third, Musculus argues that Jesus' response also indicates by analogy that not every infirmity of the soul—namely, sin—leads to the death of the soul. There is a sin unto death and a sin not unto death (1 Jn 5:16–17). Although every violation of God's law is in fact worthy of death, the sins of those who are partners of Christ's grace will not lead to the destruction of their souls. Only those who sin without repentance "to the very end" (*finaliter*) commit sin unto death.[23] Musculus's interpretation here is in keeping with his general understanding of Lazarus as a type or image of the sinner, an understanding that becomes more apparent in the later stages of his commentary on the story. Œcolampadius, who also stresses this symbolic interpretation of Lazarus, offers a similar interpretation (which he explicitly terms allegory) of Jesus' response. Only those who sin against the Holy Spirit— that is, those who are unwilling to repent—sin unto death. The sins of those "preordained to life" (*praeordinati ad vitam*) will not lead to their perdition but to the ultimate strengthening of their spiritual life: "After a lapse, the sons of God are much more fervent and so order their life that God is more glorified through them." When they repent, like Lazarus, "they rise again, ordering their life in greater fear."[24]

Martha and Mary (Jn 11:20–32)

As Jesus approaches Bethany, he is greeted by Martha, who, having heard of his impending arrival, has run out to meet him. Mary, the Evangelist writes, remained at home. Initiating a dialogue (or perhaps a quarrel) with Jesus, Martha states: "Lord, if you had been here, my brother would not have died. But even now I know that whatever you ask of God, God will give you." Jesus' response leads her first to confess a belief in the general resurrection of the dead and finally to confess a belief in Jesus as the Christ, the son of God. Martha then informs her sister "secretly" (*silentio*) that Jesus is present and calling for her. Followed by an entourage of fellow mourners, Mary goes out to meet Jesus, falling at his feet and greeting him with the same words used previously by Martha: "Lord, if you had been here, my brother would not have died."

Here we focus on two central questions regarding the Reformed interpretations of this part of the Lazarus narrative. First, how do the commentators characterize the responses of the two sisters to Jesus' arrival? And second, how do the commentators develop their characterizations of Martha and Mary into moral or allegorical exegesis? Once again, we find that while Œcolampadius, Bullinger, and Musculus devote considerable attention to developing an exegetical portrait of the sisters, Zwingli and Bucer have very little to say.

Both Œcolampadius and Bullinger regard Martha's running to greet Jesus as a commendable act, demonstrating her zeal for Christ. According to Œcolampadius, Martha was not annoyed that Jesus had delayed his coming to Bethany but eagerly ran out to meet him, showing her "sedulity" (*sedulitatem*) both for Christ and for her brother. Bullinger believes Martha had been pacing to and fro, caring for domestic matters, when she heard that Jesus had arrived at the outskirts of Bethany. She then "by virtue of a sedulity natural to her" (*pro sedulitate sibi ingenita*) ran out to meet him, displaying not only zeal for her lord, whom she receives "with religion and reverence" (*cum religione & reverentia*), but also true piety, expressed in her humanity and love for Lazarus. Bullinger argues that Martha thus presents "a salutary example" (*exemplum salubre*) to be imitated by the faithful, who should also run to meet Christ "by a pure faith, sincere repentance, and ardent prayers" (*fide pura, poenitentia syncera & precibus ardentibus*).[25]

Like Œcolampadius and Bullinger, Musculus praises Martha's running to Christ, for by doing so, she displayed "a courteous and proper reverence" (*officiosam & honestam reverentiam*) for her lord. What distinguishes Musculus's exegesis, however, is its stress upon Martha's reception of Jesus as a multifaceted moral *exemplum*. First, Martha demonstrates the virtue of aggressive hospitality. Just as Abraham and Lot ran to meet their guests (Gn 18:2, 19:1), so Martha demonstrates the proper welcome that a host owes to visiting friends and guests. Yet Martha does not merely run to Jesus as her guest, but also as her lord; she thus demonstrates the appropriate reverence due to lords and masters by their subjects. Furthermore, like Bullinger,

Musculus spiritualizes Martha's running to Jesus as an image of the interior reception of Christ by the believer:

> And especially in respect to Christ let us imitate this example of Martha that we also
> should run to meet him coming to us. You say: where and how? Who would be
> unwilling to run to Christ coming to us? But how does he come to us? How may I
> run to him? He comes to us through his gospel, through the ministers of his Word,
> through his members. At the end of the world he will come visibly with glory. While
> you are in this life, run to meet him with a soul eager for truth, reverent, and grate-
> ful. Welcome him in his Word, ministry, and members so that at the end of the world
> you might be carried off to meet him and thus reign with him in heaven forever.[26]

Therefore, those who imitate Martha in welcoming Christ take part in a "most
happy exchange" (*foelicissima commutatio*): receiving Christ in the guest room of
their hearts in this present age, they are in turn welcomed by Christ to an eternal
heavenly guest room in the age to come.

If Martha is to be commended for running to Jesus, is Mary to be condemned
for remaining at home? Neither Œcolampadius nor Bullinger find fault with Mary,
defending her, however, for different reasons. Œcolampadius claims that Mary was
not expressing indifference, for she simply had not received the news of Jesus'
arrival. Otherwise, she would have joined Martha in running to her lord. Bullinger
argues that Mary remained at home to fulfill the purposes of divine providence: it
was more suitable to the glory of the future miracle that she remain at home to
receive her guests, who would later follow her to Jesus, witnessing ultimately the
miraculous raising of Lazarus. Although Musculus at a later point in his commentary argues for the work of divine providence in the assembly of Mary's attendants
as unwitting witnesses to the miracle, here he repeats Œcolampadius's explanation: if Mary had known that Jesus was in the suburbs of Bethany, she would have
run to him.[27]

In medieval exegesis, Mary is frequently interpreted as a representative of the
contemplative life and Martha as a representative of the active life. By remaining
at home, Mary thus images the meditative and contemplative soul, in contrast to
Martha who, by running to Christ, portrays the soul devoted to works of charity.[28]
Of the Reformed commentators, only Œcolampadius and Musculus echo this
traditional interpretation, arguing, however, against the tendency of monastic
theologians to elevate the contemplative over the active life. Thus, although
Œcolampadius sees the sisters as symbols of a twofold life in the Church, "contemplative and practical" (*contemplativam & practicam*), he argues against the sepa-
ration of these lives: "It is necessary that every one should take possession of each
life" (*Necesse est, ut utranque vitam quisque complectatur*). The illumination of the
mind amounts to very little if works of charity are abandoned, and conversely those
who actively give themselves in service to the neighbor must "make time for
contemplation"(*vacant contemplationi*) in order to establish themselves in God.[29]

Similarly, Musculus argues that by sitting at home Mary produces an image of a calm and restful mind that should be imitated by the faithful: "There is certainly a great benefit in tranquillity and rest, whereby the mind of a human being is withdrawn from the troublesome cares and business of this world." Yet Musculus quickly denounces the monks who sing the praises of the contemplative life merely to excuse their own laziness and gluttony; they have an active life, to be sure, but it is one of oppressing and exploiting the Church. In no respect do they reflect the true spiritual life, which engages actively in works of love for the neighbor while finding occasion periodically for times of rest and meditation.[30]

When Martha greets Jesus with the statement, "Lord, if you had been here, my brother would not have died," her words could certainly be read as an accusatory complaint, spoken in bitterness and frustration. Surprisingly, however, none of the Reformed commentators focus on this possibility, choosing to interpret her opening statement as an expression of faith, although perhaps a faith not perfectly strong or informed. Bucer states simply that Martha demonstrates the nature of true faith: she shows her love for Jesus, by whom she knows she is loved. Zwingli argues that Martha would not have made the statement if she did not believe in Christ, and thus she exhibits faith, although a faith that is weak and imperfect. Similarly, Œcolampadius states that Martha demonstrates a faith that was not entirely worthy of Christ; she believed in him and held him in high esteem "but not as much as was fitting" (*sed non quantum oportebat*). Her faith, unlike that of the centurion (Lk 7; Mt 8), was not informed by a proper understanding of Jesus' divine power; she should have realized that the salvation of her brother did not depend on the physical presence of Jesus.[31] Likewise, Bullinger argues that Martha's faith was weaker than the centurion's because she did not realize that Jesus could have banished Lazarus's sickness by a word. Yet Bullinger especially commends the moderation and self-control evident in Martha's statement: "She does nothing from weakness of soul: she does not grumble; she does not curse; she does not scold him for delaying at the first message; she does not wail in a womanly fashion and fall down and roll about in the dirt, as one unable to bear the grief; she does not tear out her hair and mutilate her cheeks; but with amazing moderation and endurance she laments her lot before Jesus, her most faithful master."[32]

In his interpretation of Martha's first statement, Musculus, unlike most of the Reformed commentators, finds no occasion to censure the deficiencies of her faith or understanding. Her words in fact express three commendable acts that serve as moral examples for the faithful. First, returning to his theme of hospitality, Musculus notes that she initiates the conversation with Jesus; by doing so, she demonstrates the proper reception of a guest. The host bears the social obligation of initiating conversation with a guest by friendly words of greeting and welcome. Second, Martha demonstrates the correct manner of expressing grief by pouring out her heart to the Lord. And third, her statement indicates her firm confidence and trust in Christ.[33]

In Martha's second statement—"But even now I know that whatever you ask of God, God will give you"—Musculus finds the first indication of a weak faith. Here, Musculus repeats the same argument made by Œcolampadius and Bullinger regarding the deficiency: her words betray her failure to understand Jesus' divine power. Thinking of Jesus as a holy and pious man of God, whose prayers had special efficacy with God, she urges him to intercede on Lazarus's behalf.[34] Yet unlike any of the Reformed commentators, Musculus takes pains even here to enumerate several commendable features of Martha's faith. First, her statement indicates at the very least her belief in God's existence. Second, she recognizes that God is sufficiently powerful to revive the dead. Third, she believes that God loves the righteous and pious. Fourth, she believes that God indulgently hears the prayers that the righteous make, both for themselves and for others. Fifth, she knows that Jesus is so loved by God the Father that nothing is denied him. Therefore, Martha's faith—although not perfectly heroic—must not be absolutely "disapproved" (*improbanda*), for she believed in Christ far differently than those who were saying, "We know this man is a sinner" (Jn 9:24). In fact, Martha images those among the faithful who confess and believe in Christ yet with a faith and understanding still deficient. Just as Jesus did not reject Martha's feeble faith but promoted and strengthened it, so also we are taught, argues Musculus, to embrace and support weaker Christians with patient and gentle instruction.[35]

Martha's third statement—"I know that he will rise again in the resurrection at the last day"—comes in response to Jesus' promise, "Your brother will rise again." According to Zwingli, Œcolampadius, and Bullinger, her confession—although prompted by a misunderstanding of Jesus' words—demonstrates that she had been instructed and firmly believed in the teaching of the future general resurrection of the dead. Bullinger argues that Martha did not dare to hope that Jesus was speaking of Lazarus's restoration in the present because she did not perfectly understand Jesus' power and glory. But her statement proves that the Jews had always believed in the resurrection of the flesh, and thus the heresiarchs who deny this doctrine are shown to be impure spirits and instruments of the devil. Œcolampadius notes that although Martha believed in the doctrine of the future resurrection, she did not understand "what sort it was" (*qualis esset*), nor that it would be accomplished by Christ himself. Furthermore, although she had been taught and confessed this doctrine of consolation, her sorrow was not entirely mitigated by her belief. Yet Œcolampadius does not condemn Martha's sorrow: "Even those who know the future resurrection are not able to repress the force of nature so as not to weep."[36]

Musculus focuses his comments squarely on the positive features of Martha's faith as indicated by her confession. In a manner unparalleled by any of the Reformed commentators, he extracts and analyzes five distinct features of the confession that serve as moral *imitanda* for Christians. First, her confession implies a belief in the end of the world and a rejection of the pagan doctrine of the world's eternity. Second, she rightly affirms a belief in the future resurrection of the dead, a doctrine the Sadducees ridiculed as contrary to reason. Third, she does not affirm simply a general belief in the future resurrection but a specific belief in the future resurrection of Lazarus. She thus demonstrates the true nature of Christian faith, which always moves from the general to the personal and specific: "Let us also make inferences in this way: all will rise again, therefore I also will rise again. Those who believe in Christ will rise again to eternal life, therefore I also etc. On account of Christ, God pardons and has mercy on the penitent and believing, therefore, he will have mercy also on me. God does not desert those who hope in him, therefore, he will not desert me."[37] Fourth, Martha expresses a remarkable certitude of faith because she does not say, "I believe," but "I know he will rise again." Her knowledge was not based on any natural arguments or proofs of the doctrine but solely on a faith and hope in God that is produced in the hearts of believers. Her confession was therefore superior to that of Nicodemus, who says, "We know that you are a teacher come from God" (Jn 3:2), and superior to that of the apostles, who declare, "We have believed and come to know that you are Christ, the son of the living God" (Jn 6:69).[38] Nicodemus and the apostles had witnessed distinct proofs and signs that supported the certitude of their confessions. Martha, on the other hand, expresses a certitude of faith in a matter entirely indistinct and unproved. Fifth, although Martha firmly believes that her brother will be resurrected, she nevertheless takes "little comfort" (*parum consolationis*) from this faith, longing for his immediate restoration in this life. Here, Musculus reiterates the interpretation of Œcolampadius, noting that Martha's continuing grief in no way belies her confession of faith: "This is an infirmity of the saints that Christ tolerates in them. And thus we also must guard against condemning anyone on account of this."[39]

The dialogue between Martha and Jesus ends with a further confession of faith, prompted by Jesus' direct question: "I am the resurrection and the life. He who believes in me, even if he should die, will live, and all who live and believe in me will never die. Do you believe this?" (11:25–26). Martha responds immediately: "Yes, Lord. I have believed that you are Christ, the son of God, who was to come into the world" (11:27). We find widely divergent assessments of Martha's final confession in the interpretations of Œcolampadius and Bullinger. Their disagreement stems partly from their use of different Latin translations for the text. Following Erasmus, Bullinger reads Martha's words as, "I believe" (*ego credo*), while Œcolampadius retains the traditional reading of the Vulgate, "I have believed" (*ego credidi*).[40] Zwingli and Bucer also comment on the content of Martha's words but voice no opinion regarding the adequacy of her faith as indicated by the confession.

Œcolampadius argues that Martha's faith has not suddenly become robust, absent the deficiencies her earlier statements exposed. Rather, in making this confession "she boasts about her faith" (*gloriatur de fide sua*), unwilling to acknowledge the true inadequacy of her belief in Christ. In effect she was saying: "Certainly I have long since believed great things of you, that you are the son of God, concerning whom the prophets have spoken." Nevertheless, she still did not understand the divine power of Christ. Martha says the right words, but the "spark of faith was shining too little" (*scintilla fidei parum lucebat*).[41]

Like Œcolampadius, Zwingli and Bucer both note that Martha uses the past tense to voice her confession. Clearly, they argue, Martha thinks that she has previously believed what she now confesses. But whether Martha is correct in this assumption, neither Zwingli nor Bucer say. Zwingli, however, in a rather strange interpretive move, seizes the occasion to attack his opponents on eucharistic doctrine: "She does not say, 'I believe that I eat you bodily in bread, but I believe that you are the Christ.'"[42]

Bullinger's characterization of Martha's confession contrasts vividly with that of Œcolampadius. Arguing that Martha was "now better established in faith" (*iam melius in fide instituta*), he describes her words as the "most complete example of a sincere confession of faith" (*absolutissimum exemplum syncerae confessionis fidei*). There is no boasting here, for Bullinger does not consider the implications of her use of the past tense (in the Greek and the Vulgate). Rather, she voices in complete sincerity "a catholic confession of orthodox faith" (*catholica orthodoxae fidei confessio*), saying in effect:

> "Yes indeed, Lord," that is, "I believe very much and most firmly in your words, that you, who save the souls of the faithful and revive the bodies of the dead, are life and resurrection." To this she now adds the basis of resurrection and the chief point of the whole Christian faith: "I believe," she says, "that you are Messiah, the son of the living God, who . . . comes into the world," that is, "I believe that you are true God and man, the savior and vivifier of the whole world."[43]

In his discussion of Martha's confession, Musculus takes a middle course between the interpretations of Œcolampadius and Bullinger, neither fully condemning nor extolling the adequacy of her faith. He notes that she seems not to have understood Jesus' words, for if she had, she would have more appropriately confessed, "I believe you are resurrection and life." However, Musculus believes that Martha implicitly confessed this by saying, "Yes, Lord," as though to say, "I absolutely believe what you say is true" (*Prorsus credo verum esse quod dicis*). Schooled in the prophetic writings concerning the Messiah, Martha adds a further eloquent and firm confession of her faith in Jesus as the Christ promised by God, a faith she shared with all the elect of the Old Testament.

Although Musculus follows Erasmus in translating Martha's words in the present tense (*ego credo*), he notes that the Greek literally reads, "I have believed" (ἐγὼ πεπίστευκα), not "I now believe" (ἐγὼ ἤδη πιστεύω). She thinks that she has always believed what she now confesses, but clearly, Musculus argues, her faith and knowledge of Christ was imperfect, as her earlier statements show. Musculus does not characterize her statement as harshly as Œcolampadius (i.e., as a boast), but he does argue that she portrays an image of those who cannot bear to acknowledge that they have not had a full and perfect knowledge and faith in Christ. Such people, Musculus argues, are found all too frequently in his own day. Hearing the evangelical doctrine of salvation by faith alone, these "simpletons" (*simpliciores*) readily give their assent, arguing that this doctrine is nothing new but something they have always believed. They simply are not intelligent enough (*tantum intelligentiae non habent*) to recognize that the things they did and believed "in papaldom" (*in papatu*) do not square with the faith required by the gospel.[44]

The verses following Martha's confession, which describe the summoning of Mary and her subsequent encounter with Jesus, are passed over in silence by Zwingli and Bucer. Œcolampadius, Bullinger, and Musculus, however, each develop further insights in their exegetical portraits of the sisters from this section of the narrative. Following her confession, Martha leaves Jesus in order to summon her sister, saying: "The master is present and is calling you" (11:28). Hearing this news, Mary immediately goes out to meet Jesus, followed by an entourage of comforters. When she finds Jesus, she falls at his feet and repeats the same words used by Martha: "Lord, if you had been here, my brother would not have died" (Jn 11:32).

Œcolampadius and Bullinger both regard Martha's summoning of Mary as an image of the effects or workings of faith, which always seeks to draw others into the same joy and salvation found in Christ. Never content with their own salvation, the truly faithful, like Martha, spread the joyous news: "The master is here and is calling you." At the literal level of interpretation, Œcolampadius notes that the Evangelist does not indicate that Jesus ordered Martha to summon Mary. But certainly, he believes, "she understood the mind of Christ" (*intellexit mentem Christi*), who wanted Mary and her attendants to be witnesses of the impending miracle.[45]

Musculus argues that Martha must have summoned Mary by a direct dominical command, for otherwise her sudden departure would have been thoughtless and rude. Martha would have preferred to accompany Jesus into the village, but having received Jesus' directive, she promptly and eagerly leapt to the task. Yet unlike Œcolampadius and Bullinger, Musculus is unwilling here to characterize Martha's behavior as an ideal image of obedience or the effects of faith. Although she summoned her sister at Jesus' command, she decided "at her own initiative" (*proprio instinctu*) to summon her "secretly" (*clanculum*), hoping to avoid the malice of the Jews who were seated with Mary in the house. She obeyed Jesus, but she did so cautiously, hoping to insulate Jesus from his enemies. Yet all of Martha's devices were for nothing because the Jews followed Mary—as divine providence had arranged—when she hurried out to meet Jesus. Thus, for Musculus, Martha represents not an ideal to be imitated but a vice to be avoided: "Therefore, we have here an example of human reason which thinks that the commands of God . . . must be performed secretly and cautiously in order to avoid the knowledge of the impious."[46]

In one respect, however, Musculus sees a positive moral example in Martha's summoning of Mary. Referring to Jesus simply as "διδάσκαλον," she knows without a doubt that Mary will understand whom she means. Although this title could have indicated any rabbi, Martha and Mary had reserved the title for Jesus alone, their one and only true master. Having devoted themselves completely to the teachings of Jesus, they could not bear to hear any other teacher. For Musculus, the moral is clear: "Therefore, we are reminded by this example that we ourselves should recognize no other master than this Christ, the son of God."[47]

Œcolampadius, Bullinger, and Musculus each interpret Mary's response to the summons as a commendable example of the response of faith and devotion to Christ. Faithful Christians respond like Mary, argues Œcolampadius; they do not delay, but as soon as they are called by Christ by the movement of the Holy Spirit in their hearts, they quickly rise and follow. Bullinger argues that Mary leapt for joy when she heard the news, producing an image of sincere piety and of eager and ardent faith in God. True faith never contrives long delays when it hears the calling of God "but makes haste, and in fact, joyfully" (*sed festinat, & laete quidem*). Similarly, Musculus describes Mary's avid response as an example "of quick and prompt obedience" (*alacris & promptae obedientiae*) and an image "of a mind eagerly embracing the heavenly teacher" (*animique coelestem* διδάσκαλον *avide complectentis*). Musculus also interprets Mary's response as a dramatic image of the restitution of the gospel occurring in his own age. Hearing the call of Christ, many people have imitated Mary by turning away from vacuous human doctrines (represented by the Jews consoling Mary) and by running to Christ.[48]

Bullinger and Œcolampadius have surprisingly little to say about Mary's encounter with Jesus. Bullinger simply states that she performed an act of worship by falling at Jesus' feet and notes that she repeats the same words used earlier by Martha. Œcolampadius argues that Mary confers "a little more honor" (*aliquanto plus honoris*) on Jesus by her act of adoration but maintains that she, like her sister, fails to recognize that Jesus was no less powerful when absent than when present. She had no more expectation of a miraculous restoration of Lazarus than did her sister.[49]

Musculus's commentary distinguishes itself once again, both by its breadth of analysis and by its attention to the moral lessons below the surface of the text. For Musculus, the great virtue of Mary's act of worship is its complete lack of inhibition. Followed by the Jews who she knew were hostile to Jesus, she nevertheless performed a dramatic act of devotion, demonstrating an example of her singular love for Christ. Without any dissimulation, she completely disregarded their opinion and openly revealed her true affection for her lord. Again, Musculus makes a pointed moral observation: "If we also were of this mind toward Christ, we would cling to his word as true disciples without any shame and with no fear of adversaries." Furthermore, Musculus argues that Mary reveals her deep love for her brother and for Christ by repeating the words used earlier by Martha—"Lord, if you had been here. . . ." It should come as no surprise that they use the same words, for the sisters felt the same longing for Christ and the same affection for their brother and no doubt frequently discussed their feelings with each other. Therefore, in Mary's statement (as in Martha's), Musculus sees a positive example of pious devotion to God and of faithful service to the neighbor. Only in one respect does Musculus propose a gentle criticism of Mary's statement: she shows that even the pious "from time to time" (*subinde*) fail to comprehend the "judgments and councils of divine providence" (*iudicia & consilia divinae providentia*).[50]

The Emotive Response of Jesus (Jn 11:33–35)

One of the most powerful moments in the Lazarus narrative describes Jesus' own emotional response to the tragic scene of Mary and her attendants weeping over Lazarus's death. This moment has generated a number of exegetical difficulties throughout the history of its interpretation because the language used to describe Jesus' affections is, at best, somewhat murky in meaning. This is no less true in the Greek than it is in the Latin of the Vulgate, which translates ἐνεβριμήσατο τῷ πνεύματι καὶ ἐτάραξεν ἑαυτὸν (Jn 11:33) as "infremuit spiritu et turbavit seipsum" (he groaned in spirit and troubled himself). For centuries, commentators have struggled to discern precisely what emotion(s) this phrase expresses, whether simply sadness or anger or some mixture thereof. The Latin verb *infremere* certainly conveys a sense of anger, meaning literally "to growl," but the story gives no definite clues to indicate a reason for anger at this point in the story. And while it is certainly understandable that Jesus could have been troubled by the appearance of those mourning Lazarus, it is far less clear how he could be said to have "troubled himself." The statement at John 11:33 that "Jesus wept" (*lacrimatus est Iesus*) is perfectly clear, but it poses other sorts of interpretive challenges. Namely, for whom or what was Jesus weeping? Lazarus? Mary? The human condition? And how was it in keeping with Jesus' superior character to weep? Does it not bespeak a lack of control or weakness of temperament that he should give such public vent to his emotions?

Among the Reformed commentators, Zwingli alone seems uninterested in pursuing these questions. He does, however, repeat an exegetical commonplace in asserting that the emotive response of Jesus gives evidence of his true human nature and of his deep love for human beings.[51] Œcolampadius makes the same point, arguing that Jesus wanted to demonstrate the truth of his human nature by revealing himself to possess a human soul "that could feel pain and be moved by affections" (*quae potuit dolere & tangi affectionibus*). Jesus was not indifferent to the sisters' grief, and because of his ardent love for them, he felt their sorrow and pain in his soul. Those who deny that Jesus had a soul similar to ours, Œcolampadius notes, succeed only in diminishing our consolation. For it is a great comfort to know that he who came for the salvation of the world also feels the pain of our ills. Regarding the anger implied by the verb *infremere*, Œcolampadius states that some think that Jesus was angry either at the "evil spirit" (*maligno spiritui*) or at human sin, through which death had entered the world.[52]

Bullinger also notes that some have argued that Jesus was angry either at the evil spirit, human sin, or the unbelief of the Jews, but he prefers to understand Jesus' emotive response simply as an expression of grief and condolence: "I think there is no other reason for the groaning, distress, and tears of the Lord than that expressed by John, namely that he especially loved Lazarus and the whole family, and when he saw [this family] oppressed by grave sorrow, and all the Jews condoling with it and weeping profusely, the Lord's heart was also moved."[53] Bullinger expends considerable effort in analysis of the Greek at John 11:33 and of the meaning of the Latin term *fremitus*, which he defines as "a vigorous, loud, and tumultuous movement of water" (*vehemens & sonora ac tumultuans aquae commotio*). He provides lexicographical data from Lorenzo Valla and offers several attempts at German paraphrase in order to elucidate the difficult expressions. These words, he argues, indicate that Jesus "was so moved and shaken in his entire innermost being, that he was unable to bring forth any sound at the time."[54] This powerful affection of the soul is frequently followed by weeping; tears flow from the heart as blood from a wound.

Bullinger argues that Christ's dignity was in no way harmed by his public display of tears, for by weeping over the misfortunes of his friends, he is in the company of other *amici dei* such as Abraham, Israel, Joseph, and others, who also mourned the calamities of friends. By weeping with Mary, Jesus not only demonstrates his true humanity, as the Church Fathers were so eager to point out, but also gives an example of true commiseration and sympathy.[55] Just as the apostle Paul does not absolutely forbid mourning and grief for the dead (at 1 Thes 4:13) but only a pagan sort of mourning, "lacking all hope and moderation" (*omni spe & modo carentem*), so Jesus gives a beautiful example of proper Christian commiseration, "for the Christian religion does not make human beings into stones or tree trunks."[56] Furthermore, Christ also teaches that we should groan over our sins so that we might learn true penitential sorrow.[57]

Like Œcolampadius and Bullinger, Bucer interprets the phrase "infremuit spiritu" as an expression of deep sorrow, not of divine anger. When Jesus saw the multitude of weeping people, "his bowels of compassion were moved" (*commota viscera eius fuere*) and he demonstrated the pain of his soul with a groan (*fremitu*) and tears. He wept because he truly and especially loved Mary, Martha, and Lazarus; he felt their loss as his own, their grief as his own. By this ardent love for the family of Lazarus and by his open expression of grief, Jesus demonstrated that he possessed a real human nature and thus refuted the future Marcionite heresy.[58]

For Bucer, the scene of the mourners and Jesus openly weeping over Lazarus's death paints a portrait of the kind of love required by God, a love that is not "senseless" (*stupentem*) but "living and ardent, which stirs up the heart and shows itself in the whole body."[59] Bucer develops this portrait of Christian love and compassion into an extended discussion of the proper Christian response to the death or misfortunes of others. Christian love, he argues, is unable *not* to grieve over the loss or death of a neighbor. Christians rightly grieve over the death of others, even though they know that all things work for the good of the elect (Rom 8:28), and that for believers "death is the door to life" (*mors ianua vitae*). Therefore the sisters were not scolded or rebuked by their lord when he saw them weeping over Lazarus's death but rather were joined in their grief by Jesus himself. Certainly, believers should not mourn "as the heathen, destitute of the hope of a future and better life" (*sicut ethnici, spe futurae et melioris vitae destituti*; 1 Thes 4:13) because the Holy Spirit offers consolation that soothes the sorrow of the heart. But "as long as a true brotherly love lives in the hearts of the saints, they are not able not to grieve and mourn the dead, or other afflicted ones."[60]

Bucer has in mind here the Anabaptists (or "Catabaptists" as he calls them), who interpret Paul's injunction at 1 Thessalonians 4:13 as an absolute prohibition of mourning for the dead.[61] To see the foolishness of their position, they need only look to the example of Christ, who wept not only over Lazarus's death but also over the destruction of Jerusalem (Lk 13:34). Certainly, no one can be imagined more "spiritual and constant" (*spirituale et constans*) than Christ, and yet in the face of human tragedy, "he was unable to contain himself" (*continere se non potuit*), giving way to tears. "Therefore," Bucer concludes, "some of our Catabaptists are Stoics more than Christians, who permit no mourning, no tears for the dead or for brothers afflicted in other ways."[62]

Each of the themes we have seen expressed by the Reformed commentators is reiterated by Musculus. Unlike Bucer, Bullinger, and Œcolampadius, however, Musculus fully endorses the view that the expressions "infremuit spiritu" and "turbavit seipsum" imply anger on Jesus' part. He was angry at Satan, whose malicious works allowed death to enter the world. Although Musculus concedes his inability to fully explain what the strange expressions mean—particularly what it means for Jesus to have "disturbed himself"—he is confident that Jesus was in some sense angry and that this anger was expressed as a moral example for all believers. When we consider the causes of our own mortality, Musculus suggests, we too should be disturbed in spirit and angry at the works of Satan. Just as this indignation was not unbecoming "to the mildness of the spirit of Christ" (*mansuetudini spiritus Christi*), so also it is fitting for a pious soul to groan over matters pertaining to God's glory—although it is not fitting to groan over "personal and trivial matters" (*rebus privatis ac levibus*).[63]

For Musculus, however, Jesus' emotive response is not a simple feeling of anger but a complex emotion encompassing both anger and grief. When Jesus saw Mary and her attendants weeping, he groaned in spirit and was deeply moved, partly by a feeling of anger at Satan and partly by feelings of sympathy and sorrow for those who were mourning. His feelings of commiseration ultimately manifested themselves in tears, proving not only his true humanity but also his merciful disposition toward human beings.[64] This is the same argument made by all of the Reformed expositors. Yet when Musculus comes to the subject of weeping, he develops a nuanced treatment of the topic quite different from anything found in the other Reformed commentaries. Musculus in fact examines the topic in three distinct contexts, each of which has a different significance or moral application: the weeping of Mary, the weeping of the Jews, and the weeping of Christ.

By her weeping, Mary gives an example of proper Christian mourning for the dead. Musculus argues that no one could possibly consider Mary as reprobate, lacking a faith in the resurrection. Yet despite her faith and despite the fact that her brother had been dead now for four days, she was not only weeping but also "wailing" (*plorasse*); and she was not wailing "in private places" (*in latebris*) but in full view of Christ and the multitude of onlookers. Therefore, like Bucer, Musculus concludes that it is not required of the elect to be "unfeeling and heartless" (*saxei & ἀστοργοί*) in the face of the death of others. For the apostle does not forbid the mourning of the dead at 1 Thessalonians 4:13 but only an excessive or immoderate mourning similar to those who have no hope. Yet while mourning is not forbidden, a public exhibition of grief is not always required. Therefore, Musculus argues that while Mary should not be condemned for her mourning, neither should Martha be condemned because she did not make a public display of her grief.[65]

The Jews who visited Mary in her home, followed her to the tomb, and joined her in her weeping demonstrate a model of proper Christian commiseration. These pious Jews were the same ones, Musculus argues, who began to believe in the Lord because of the raising of Lazarus. Certainly, they embody the Pauline admonition to weep with those who weep (Rom 12:15), and thus they exhibit an example that Christians should imitate.[66]

At first glance, according to Musculus, the weeping of Christ may appear as something of an embarrassment. For it is not seemly "if an eminent, mature, honorable, wise, and courageous man, should weep, even though bitterly moved."[67] The Evangelist almost seems to have been unconcerned about the glory of Christ by noting "so conspicuously" (*tam insigni*) the tears of his lord. Why then did the Evangelist record this event? First, Musculus argues, it was fitting to demonstrate not only that Christ was a real human being but also that he was a partaker of all human infirmities save sin alone. Faith is strengthened when the Christian recognizes Christ as a merciful priest, able to sympathize and condole with human miseries. Second, Musculus understands the weeping of Christ as an important part of the effectiveness of the miracle he was about to perform. The bald demonstration of divine power and majesty in the raising of Lazarus might have "scared away" (*absterreret*) people from Christ. Therefore, by weeping he joins an infirmity of the flesh to the work of divine power in order to attract people to himself. On the other hand, those who were offended by the "infirmity of weeping" (*lachrymantis infirmitate*) would be moved to faith in Christ as the son of God by the "power of revivification" (*resuscitantis virtute*).[68]

This understanding of the weeping of Jesus as a strategic ploy aimed at the effective reception of the miracle is found in none of the other Reformed commentaries. Musculus, however, does not argue that the weeping was dissimulation; Jesus wept because he truly loved Lazarus and his sisters and because he sincerely commiserated with their suffering. Here, Musculus argues in a similar vein to Bullinger and Bucer by praising the weeping of Jesus as an example of Christian commiseration that the faithful should imitate. Like Bucer, Musculus takes the occasion to criticize the teachings of the Anabaptists: "That Stoic ἀπάθεια, which the Anabaptists are once again attempting to introduce into the Church, is entirely foreign to the saints." No one would have been impressed if Jesus had expressed stony indifference to the death of Lazarus. But when Jesus weeps, the Jews are struck with admiration for the spirit of true love and humanity in Jesus. The Jews do not say, "Behold, a womanly soul" (*Ecce animum muliebrem*), but "Behold, how he loved him" (*Ecce quomodo amabat eum*). Therefore, Musculus argues (using almost the same words as Bucer), the religion of the Anabaptists "ought to be called Stoicism more than Christianity" (*magis Stoicismus quam Christianismus dici debet*).[69]

The Miraculous Revivification (Jn 11:38–44)

The most astonishing sign of Jesus' ministry is described by the Evangelist in short order. Jesus approaches the tomb, is again deeply moved, and orders the stone to be removed from the cave. Martha, who interrupts Jesus with concern about the offensive odor of the corpse, is reminded by Jesus that she will see God's glory if only she believes. With the stone removed, Jesus offers a prayer of thanksgiving and commands Lazarus to come out of the tomb. Appearing with his hands, feet, and face wrapped in burial cloths, Lazarus is unbound and released at Jesus' command.

Only three of our commentators—Œcolampadius, Bullinger, and Musculus—have anything to say about the description of the tomb. And at the literal level, these three commentators express a similar idea: by his burial in a cave closed by a heavy stone, the truth of Lazarus's death is made undeniable in order to highlight the truth of the future miracle. Œcolampadius notes that the miracle was arranged in such a way as to diminish the suspicion of a "deception" (*fraus*). By Lazarus's burial in a cave fortified by a large boulder, the spectators would be less likely to conclude that Lazarus had not been truly dead or that some kind of swapping of bodies had taken place.[70] Bullinger argues that the stone was so large and heavy that it could not be removed except by strong crowbars. Therefore, by the way in which Lazarus was buried, the "suspicion of a trick" (*suspitionem praestigii*) would be removed and any future calumnies would be disproved.[71]

Musculus echoes this same idea, noting that the Evangelist purposefully described the tomb and stone so that no one would suspect that the miracle occurred "by some deception" (*fraude aliqua*). But unlike Œcolampadius and Bullinger, Musculus pauses to consider how and why the bodies of human beings are buried. He notes that the dead bodies of humans are not simply "cast aside like beasts" (*instar bestiarum abjiciantur*) without a second thought but are carefully and lovingly buried so as to be protected from wild animals. This manner of burying the dead points to a "residual hope" (*spem residuam*) among humankind that the dead will be restored in the future. Insofar as burial custom hints at this hope in the future resurrection of the body, it is appropriate to treat human corpses with care. But nothing commendable is found, Musculus argues, in "superstitious, haughty, and expensive burials" (*superstitiosas, superbas, & sumptuosas sepulturas*).[72]

The order to remove the stone raises two basic interpretive questions: Why did Jesus order others to remove the stone, and to whom did he issue the command? Both Bullinger and Musculus note that Jesus certainly could have removed the stone himself by an act of divine power. Jesus chose not to do so, according to Bullinger, in order to avoid a pompous and extravagant display of power; his miracles occurred "within measure" (*intra modum*). Musculus, however, argues that Jesus frequently made use of human effort in order to heighten the psychological impact of his miracles. By their hands-on participation in the event, the witnesses would experience more vividly the truth of the miracle.[73] Œcolampadius argues in a similar vein when he states that Jesus gave the command in order to make everything "conspicuous" (*conspicua*) to the spectators. As to the identity of the recipients of the command, we find a basic disagreement between Œcolampadius, who thinks Jesus commanded the disciples, and Bullinger, who states forcefully that Jesus ordered "not his disciples, but undoubtedly relatives of Lazarus" (*non discipulos suos, sed haud dubie cognatos Lazari*). Musculus hazards no explicit guess, but he probably agrees with Bullinger that the disciples did not receive the command; Jesus ordered, he states, some of those who were standing by.[74]

For Œcolampadius and Musculus, the stone and its removal may also be interpreted figuratively to express allegorical and moral truths. Œcolampadius suggests that the stone represents the burden of unbelief that is placed upon the sinner dead in sins. By removing the stone, the disciples represent the work of the ministry in teaching and encouraging "external works" (*externa opera*). But the internal work, the raising of the sinner to life, is accomplished by Christ alone.[75] Musculus, on the other hand, argues that the removal of the stone produces an image of how God operates in the world. The removal of the stone was not necessary for Jesus to accomplish his purpose. But he elicited human cooperation in the accomplishment of the miracle in order to instruct them in the knowledge of divine power. Similarly, the world has been so arranged by the council of God that human beings are made copartners in matters that are beyond their capacity. Human beings participate actively in fulfilling the divine commands to procreate, to feed and care for their young, and to instruct others in the knowledge of God. Although all of these things are easily accomplished by God alone without human effort, it was pleasing to God "to make us co-operators of his wonderful and divine works, so that we might be exercised in knowledge and faith in his providence."[76]

According to Œcolampadius, Bullinger, and Musculus, when Martha interrupts Jesus with her concern about the stench of the corpse, she unwittingly contributes a further proof that Lazarus was truly dead and thus truly resurrected. Furthermore, her objection also served to emphasize the greatness of the miracle because she indicates that Lazarus was not recently dead but—to use the graphic description of Bullinger—that "the blood in his veins and in his entire body was dissolved into pus, the internal organs and especially vital parts were spoiled, and to such an extent as if they had rotted. For a stench arises from rottenness and spoilage." That Jesus by a word alone revives not simply a dead man but a stinking, rotten corpse serves to highlight, in Bullinger's view, the greatness of divine power in Christ. Musculus makes the same point, arguing that the Evangelist purposefully recorded Martha's objection in order to impress upon the reader the greatness of Christ's power in resurrecting a decaying dead body.[77] But Musculus also presents a moral interpretation of Martha's words found in none of the other Reformed commentators, an interpretation based upon the identification of Lazarus as a type or image of the sinner dead in sins. Mary's objection about his stench reminds us, argues Musculus, that "we ought to despise no sinner, however spoiled and fetid with the putridity of sins, that we should doubt him able to be restored by the grace of Christ to repentance and life."[78]

Although Martha's words may have contributed to the ultimate glory of the miracle, none of the Reformed commentators see her objection as laudable in itself. According to Œcolampadius her words betray her unbelief; earlier she said she believed, but here she expresses despair, attempting to dissuade her lord, just as the carnal disciples tried to dissuade him from returning to Judea. Bullinger characterizes her as "somewhat forgetful and vacillating in faith" (*nonnihil obliviosae & in fide vacillanti*). She did not truly believe that Jesus could revive her dead brother. Bucer is more forgiving, explaining her words as a simple misunderstanding. Martha believed that Jesus could raise Lazarus from the dead, but she did not realize that he actually intended to do so; she believed that Lazarus would be resurrected but only at the end of time. Musculus also carefully softens his criticism of Martha, describing her as "an example of a soul not wicked, but partly anxious and partly unsteady in faith." Her anxiety reminds Musculus of Jesus' words elsewhere: "Martha, Martha, you are anxious and troubled about many things" (Lk 10:41). Predictably, Musculus then proceeds to draw the moral lesson that "the more we lack faith in God's providence, the more we are vexed by superfluous cares and anxieties." Only a firm faith in divine providence will liberate us from such cares.[79]

According to Bullinger, Martha was anxious because she feared the awful smell would drive everyone away from the tomb. Œcolampadius, however, argues that Martha believed Jesus wanted to view the body and therefore warned him of the smell. In effect, she was saying: "We do not want to sadden you when you see him, for he will be a pitiable sight."[80] Musculus echoes this idea, stating that Martha believed Jesus ordered the stone's removal so that he could enter the tomb to view the corpse. This understanding of Martha's anxiety corresponds with Jesus' earlier query, "Where have you laid him?," to which Martha responds, "Lord, come and see" (11:34). But even though Jesus did not intend to view the body, Musculus, unlike any of the other Reformed commentators, develops a moral interpretation regarding the viewing of the dead. However much the faithful may sympathize and feel sorrow for a family experiencing the death of a loved one, they will not effectively commiserate with their neighbor unless they view the dead body. This active form of commiseration applies also to those experiencing other types of loss; when the misfortune is seen "in person" (*coram*), there is an increase in "compassion" (εὐσπλαγχνίαν) and the pain of those grieving their loss is soothed. The pious, Musculus argues, should exercise and foster this kind of commiseration by the habitual visitation of the neighbor in distress.[81]

While Zwingli and Bucer offer no commentary on Jesus' response to Martha, Œcolampadius, Bullinger, and Musculus each propose explanations for Jesus' words: "Did I not tell you that if you would believe you would see the glory of God?" (11:40). For Œcolampadius this rhetorical question was intended primarily to expose Martha's lack of faith. With or without faith she would in fact see the miracle, but she would not see God's glory in the miracle unless she believed. Jesus rebukes Martha by telling her in effect that her role is not to interrupt or obstruct his work but simply to believe.[82] Bullinger characterizes Jesus' words as a "little scolding" (*obiurgatiuncula*), by which he rebukes her forgetfulness. In Bullinger's view Jesus was really saying: "Do you remember my words, Martha, or perhaps you have forgotten what I just told you: if you would believe, the glory of God would be illustrated by your brother's future death? Perhaps you have forgotten that I promised you: your brother will rise again?" Yet in Bullinger's interpretation, Martha has not merely forgotten the word of promise but has also succumbed to the objections of the flesh and human reason, which tell her that the belief in bodily resurrection is completely absurd; she cannot believe that Jesus will really revive a stinking corpse. Therefore by his question Jesus not only reminds Martha of his promise but also encourages her to reject the reasonings of the flesh, saying in effect: "A stench, a purulent and rotten corpse will in no way impede the power of God. Just believe and you will discover that God is truthful and powerful."[83]

For Bullinger, the moral interpretation of Jesus' response is clear. His words represent an admonition and encouragement to Christians of all ages to cling to their faith in the bodily resurrection "against philosophers" (*contra philosophos*) who ridicule such faith as absurd. The pseudo-wisdom of these philosophers is rooted in the reasonings of the flesh, which is always at war with God. When they argue that it is impossible for decayed bodies to rise whole again, the faithful should remember and believe the word and promises of the omnipotent God, who created the whole world from nothing and the first man from the mud of the earth and by that same creative power reconstitutes dead human bodies.[84]

In Musculus's interpretation of Jesus' response, we find him repeating the themes expressed by Œcolampadius and Bullinger. Like Bullinger, Musculus understands Jesus' words as a rebuke of Martha's forgetfulness. Jesus did not simply encourage Martha to believe but also reminded her of his promise by saying, "Did I not tell you?" (*Nonne dixi tibi*). Unlike Bullinger, however, Musculus makes a moral observation regarding Martha's forgetfulness. The fact that she could hardly remember for one hour the word of promise she had heard from the mouth of Christ himself warns us *a fortiori* how likely we are to forget God's Word in times of trials. Like Œcolampadius, Musculus states that Jesus encourages Martha's faith not because the miracle was in any way dependent on her belief but only so that she would see the glory of God in the miracle. Jesus did not tell her that Lazarus would be resurrected if she believed but that the risen Lazarus would reveal God's glory only to the eyes of faith. The faithful are thus admonished not simply to see the works of God—for these are everywhere apparent in nature—but also to see these works with faith in God's goodness and power. If endowed with such faith, the Christian will see even the sky as a marvelous work of God's glory.[85]

Regarding Jesus' prayer of thanksgiving, we find a general similarity of interpretation among the Reformed commentators. They each assert that Jesus prays not for himself but for the sake of the audience that has gathered around the tomb. By the prayer, Jesus intends to show that he works miracles by the Father's power (Bullinger, Bucer), that he is loved by the Father (Zwingli, Œcolampadius), and that he shares the same will with the Father (Bullinger, Bucer). The ultimate purpose of the prayer was to instill the saving and life-giving faith that Jesus was sent by God the Father (Œcolampadius, Bullinger). Morally, the prayer may be interpreted as teaching Christians to recognize Christ as their advocate (Zwingli, Œcolampadius), to acknowledge God as the author of all good things (Bullinger), and to understand the absolute necessity of faith (Œcolampadius, Bullinger).[86]

Musculus repeats many of these same ideas in his interpretation of Jesus' prayer. Jesus intended to show that he shared the same will with God the Father and that he did his miracles not by satanic power but by the power of God. He referred the glory of the impending miracle to the Father in order to instill in the spectators saving faith—namely, the belief that he had been sent into the world by the Father. Like Œcolampadius and Zwingli, Musculus also sees the prayer as an image of Christ's role as eternal advocate, although he argues (unlike any of the Reformed commentators) that Jesus prays not as one "equal to the Father in divinity" (*divinitate patri aequalis*) but as the son of man, priest, and mediator between God and humankind.[87] The theme that most distinguishes Musculus's interpretation, however, is his understanding of Jesus' prayer as an *exemplum* or model of Christian prayer. While the Reformed commentators interpret the prayer exclusively for its christological significance, Musculus stresses above all the moral lessons that may be inferred from the manner in which Christ expressed his prayer.

First, Musculus notes that in raising his eyes Jesus reveals "a mind dependent on God and elevated to God" (*animi a Deo pendentis & ad Deum erecti*). This physical gesture thus represents the appropriate disposition of the heart in one praying to God, for "the heart is in the eyes" (*cor esse in oculis*). Yet Musculus argues that this gesture does not dictate a prescribed bodily posture for prayer, and he ridicules those who pray by stretching forth their hands and eyes "to images" (*ad simulachra*). Second, Musculus notes that Jesus gives thanks to God for hearing his prayer, even though no explicit petition is mentioned by the Evangelist. He concludes that the petition was expressed by the groaning, disturbance, and weeping of Jesus; his emotive response was a type of prayer that God heard. Therefore, Musculus concludes that an effective petition is not necessarily dependent on the use of words. Finally, Musculus observes that Jesus prays with great confidence, saying, "I knew you always hear me." The faithful should follow this example by praying with a firm confidence that they will acquire what they seek from God, as long as they seek things that pertain to the glory of God and the salvation of humankind. One must always distinguish, Musculus argues, between prayers that arise from the personal longings of the flesh and prayers that are prompted by the longing of the spirit for the glory of God. When Jesus prayed in the garden, "Let this cup pass from me," his prayer was of the flesh, not of the spirit. Such petitions of the flesh may indeed be brought before God, but not with a firm certitude that the petitions will be granted. And thus it was fitting that Jesus expressed his prayer in the garden not with the confidence he expressed before raising Lazarus but with the proviso, "Not my will, but your will be done."[88]

Having finished his prayer, Jesus "cried out with a loud voice, 'Lazarus, come forth'" (Jn 11:43), a command that is interpreted both for its literal and its allegorical significance by Reformed commentators. Bullinger and Bucer, however, concentrate solely on the literal purpose of Jesus' exclamation, arguing that Jesus wanted the spectators to know that he was raising Lazarus by his voice alone (Bucer) and that he alone by his own power was accomplishing the miraculous deed (Bullinger). Œcolampadius and Bullinger both note that the loud voice was not necessary for the revivification of Lazarus, for Jesus could have raised him silently at his mere pleasure; but the loud exclamation was needed so that the bystanders would understand what was taking place. Musculus likewise argues that as far as Lazarus was concerned, it made no difference whether Jesus commanded silently, in a whisper, or in a loud exclamation. But since Jesus was considering the "integrity and glory of the miracle" (*integritati & gloriae miraculi*), he cried out with a loud voice so that the onlookers would recognize his great confidence and authority and so that they would clearly hear that Jesus did not make use of magical incantations in restoring Lazarus to life.[89]

Regarding the allegorical meaning of Jesus' exclamation, we find two traditional interpretations. The first is expressed by Zwingli, who argues that the loud voice symbolizes the trumpet blast at the final resurrection of the dead.[90] The second is expressed by Œcolampadius, who sees the shout as a symbol of the spiritual call to repentance by Christ: "We also will be saved by Christ as he cries out to our hearts and mortifies our members and commands us to depart from those bodily things, leading us to spiritual things."[91] Rarely to be outdone by his fellow reformers in the area of spiritual exegesis, Musculus argues that Jesus' exclamation represents both the loud "shout" (*clamor*) that precedes the future awakening of the dead and the general call to repentance that takes place in the hearts of those who have fallen asleep in sin. Musculus especially stresses the latter idea, noting that the metaphor of "crying out" is used repeatedly in the Bible to convey the call to repentance. John the Baptist was a voice "crying out" in the wilderness (Jn 1:23), and Isaiah was commanded by God: "Do not stop your voice crying out like a raised trumpet and declare to my people their sins" (Is 58:1). In a similar fashion, by the crying out of Jesus, an image is "sketched" (*delineatum*) of the call to repentance. Such a call must be vigorous and loud, because for those who are dead in their sins, a gentle word simply will not suffice. Musculus notes that this forceful "crying out" is especially needed "nowadays" in the "preaching of repentance to this age, dead in sins not for just four days, but for many years."[92]

This understanding of Lazarus as an image of a sinner restored by Christ also dominates Musculus's interpretation of the emergence of Lazarus from the tomb. Here, his comments go well beyond the interpretations of the Reformed commentators, who explain solely the literal significance of the appearance of Lazarus in grave clothes. Zwingli argues that Lazarus appeared wrapped in burial garb so that no one would suspect trickery or that they were seeing a mere phantasm. The fact that Lazarus was able to emerge from the tomb was a miracle in itself, for normally the bindings would have immobilized his body. Bullinger, Œcolampadius, and Bucer echo this traditional understanding of Lazarus's emergence as a secondary miracle that contributed to the glory of the primary miracle of Lazarus's revivification.[93] Musculus, however, makes no such claim for an ancillary miraculous event; Lazarus emerged in burial clothes so that everyone would see that it was Lazarus himself who came out of the tomb, appearing in the same form in which he was buried. Jesus could have called him out nude, but it was more fitting for the "proof of the miracle" (*evidentiam miraculi*) that he should emerge wrapped in his "sepulchral bindings" (*fasciis sepulchralibus*).[94] But more important for Musculus's interpretation is the value of this scene as an image or allegorical portrait of the paradigmatic sinner: "Those who are dead in sins also have hands and feet bound by the habit of sins as by certain bindings, so that they are able neither to work nor to walk in the way of God, and a face so bound up by stubbornness that they can neither hear nor see." A further image is revealed by the advance of Lazarus from the tomb: "Those who are dead in sins are thus aroused that they not only come back to life but also show themselves vivified by the power of Christ by the conduct of life, as by a certain advance."[95]

Musculus continues with this basic allegory in his interpretation of Jesus' command to unbind Lazarus and let him go. But here Musculus treads on perilous ground, for the overwhelming majority of medieval commentators interpret the command to loosen (*solvere*) Lazarus as a command directed to the disciples as representatives of the future sacramental ministry of the priesthood in absolving (*absolvere*) the penitent sinner.[96] This allegory was rooted in the interpretation of Augustine, who argues that Lazarus comes forth as a sinner confessing sins, whose guilt nevertheless remains. In order to remove his sins, Jesus commands his servants to loosen him, fulfilling his promise: "Whatever you shall loosen [*solveris*] on earth, will be loosened in heaven" (Mt 16:19).[97] In general, the Reformed commentators steer clear of this traditional exegesis, preferring to emphasize the unbinding of Lazarus as the completion of the miraculous event that points to the future resurrection of the faithful. Bucer explicitly rejects the traditional allegory, noting that "those who delight in uncertainties invent mystical meanings here." We should simply learn, Bucer argues, that Christ is the resurrection and the life, and we should "let others talk nonsense about the power of absolving."[98] Unlike Bucer, Bullinger, and Zwingli, Œcolampadius openly embraces an allegorical reading of the scene: "I do not reject what pertains to allegory" (*Ad allegoriam quod attinet non respuo*). However, Œcolampadius discusses not the general power of absolution in the sacramental ministry of the Church but rather the power of excommunication. No one is made dead by being wrapped in a human binding such as a decree of excommunication unless already dead to Christ in sin. Likewise, the removal of such a decree does not make a person alive in Christ unless the grace of God has already revived that person. Œcolampadius has thus taken the old allegory regarding absolution and shifted its meaning in order to mitigate the force of the traditional reading. The clear implication of his interpretation is that the power of absolution means nothing unless the sinner has already been absolved by God.[99]

Like Œcolampadius, Musculus presents an allegorical reading of the loosening of Lazarus, though he comes closer to the traditional interpretation of this act as an image of the release or absolution of the sinner's guilt by the ecclesiastical ministry. When the sinner is made alive by Christ, "the bindings which are in sins and death . . . are uncoiled and loosened. And thus in Christ there is liberty, in the kingdom of Satan bindings and captivity."[100] Although Musculus does not identify those who unwrapped Lazarus as the disciples, he argues nevertheless that they image the ministry of the Church: "He himself did not loosen the binding, but he orders him to be loosened by those who were standing by, witnesses of this resurrection. You have here an image of the ecclesiastical ministry, through which they, who are aroused to life by the voice of Christ, are loosened from sins."[101] Musculus adds, however, the same caveat as Œcolampadius: no one is able "to be absolved in the

Church" (*in ecclesia absolui*) who remains in sin and death. The power of Christ must first awaken the sinner to life, just as Jesus first revived Lazarus before his burial clothes were removed.

Musculus notes additionally that Jesus ordered Lazarus not only to be unbound but also to be let go (*sinite abire*), a command that contributes to the image of the sinner restored by Christ. Those who hear the voice of Christ's gospel, respond in repentance, and come to life out of the tomb of sins must be allowed to advance in the discipline of faith. Just as Lazarus was released to dwell once again among the living, so the repentant sinner must be welcomed by the communion of the faithful to enter "the house of those living in Christ" (*domum viventium in Christo*).[102]

CONCLUSION

This study shows that within the Reformed exegetical tradition on John, no distinct model exists that can fully account for the characteristic features of Musculus's exegesis. However, of all the commentators contemporary to Musculus, the greatest affinities in interpretation are seen in this Reformed exegetical context. Thus, Musculus's characteristic predilection for moral exegesis finds significant analogues in the Reformed commentaries, particularly in the interpretations of Bullinger, Œcolampadius, and Bucer. And of all of the sixteenth-century commentators we have examined, Œcolampadius alone matches Musculus's eagerness to embrace allegorical interpretations.

Yet none of the Reformed commentators mirror Musculus in the extensive weight given to moral exposition. By his use of moral "observations," Bucer may provide the inspiration for this basic approach in Musculus's exegesis, but Musculus expands his own sections of observations into such enormous proportions that they dominate his exposition of the gospel text in a manner unparalleled by Bucer. Bullinger, while offering no separate sections of observations, in fact comes closer than Bucer in matching this tropological emphasis of Musculus's commentary. This point is significant, for one could expect a more thoroughgoing influence of Bucer's work on Musculus. After all, Musculus heard Bucer lecture on theology and the Bible and even transcribed for publication Bucer's Psalms and Zephaniah commentaries. Yet Musculus's John commentary, while betraying the influence of Bucer, is clearly not a slavish imitation.

Nowhere does Musculus demonstrate his independence from Bucer more than in his fondness for allegorical exposition. Bucer mentions the interpretation of the removal of Lazarus's burial clothes as an allegory for the absolving ministry of the Church, but only for the purpose of ridiculing it as nonsense. Musculus, however, eagerly embraces this traditional allegorical reading as well as many others, which all depend on the central allegorical equation of Lazarus as an image of the sinner dead in sins. Although Zwingli allegorizes Jesus' shout as a symbol of the final trumpet blast, he makes no use of the penitential imagery. Bullinger also purpose-fully avoids any allegorical exposition of the story. But Œcolampadius and Musculus share a devotion to the symbolic potency of the story that distinguishes their interpretations from the other Reformed commentaries. Both give full weight to the penitential allegory, and both give voice to the traditional interpretation of Mary and Martha as symbols of the contemplative and active lives. In addition, Musculus alone develops an allegorical interpretation of the Lazarus story as an image of the redemption of the world. The evidence clearly suggests a disagree-ment among the Reformed commentators regarding the propriety of allegorical modes of interpretation.

The fact that Musculus combines the allegorical emphasis of Œcolampadius with the moral emphasis of Bucer and Bullinger partially explains the extraordi-nary length of his exegesis. But there are other factors as well. For one thing, the commentaries of Zwingli and Bucer practically defy comparative analysis with Musculus at significant points in the Lazarus narrative simply because they do not offer a verse-by-verse exposition of the text. Zwingli's exegesis of the story is really nothing more than brief notes and banal glosses of selected phrases from the text. Bucer also employs criteria of selection, limiting his discussion to portions of the story that provide exegetical data for the topics of concern to him. Hence, Zwingli and Bucer have frequently fallen by the wayside in the comparative analysis of the Reformed commentators. But Musculus's comments also greatly outdistance the running commentaries of Œcolampadius and Bullinger, who like Musculus, touch upon each verse of the Lazarus story. How, then, are we to explain the prodigious scale of his exegesis? Certainly, as I have argued, Musculus draws out more moral injunctions from the text, but he also develops two other kinds of commentary, closely related to moral interpretation, which are distinctive features of his work.

First, Musculus frequently interprets the events in the gospel text as dramatic images of events occurring in his own time. For example, by her confession of faith, Martha represents those who, hearing the restored gospel message of salvation by faith alone, confess their agreement too quickly, arguing that they have always so believed. Mary, by leaving her Jewish attendants and running to Jesus, represents those who are turning away from false doctrines to embrace the gospel preached by the Protestant reformers. Jesus, by calling out with a loud voice, reminds Musculus of the vigorous and forceful preaching that is necessary for a Church asleep for centuries under papal domination. These images function in Musculus's commentary not simply (or even primarily) as moral admonitions but as inter-pretive keys or examples that elucidate the meaning of the gospel text.

Second, Musculus frequently allows the words and events of the text to trigger discursive discussions of topics that are only tangentially related to the gospel nar-rative. This is not a totally unique feature of his commentary, for Bucer engages in similar kinds of digressions. But the extent to which Musculus allows the text to blossom into various topical essays is indeed an important and distinctive feature of his commentary. Thus, the Lazarus narrative occasions lengthy discussions of bodily illness, the mutual love of siblings, hospitality, burial customs, and the practice of viewing the dead. The words of the biblical text have an extraordinary suggestive power for Musculus, whose comments range over topics unexplored by his contemporaries in building a remarkably imaginative and thorough edifice of interpretation.

Conclusion

I began this book by making a case for the historical importance of Musculus, an importance that is no way reflected in modern scholarship on the Protestant reformation. Certainly Musculus deserves attention for his prominent role as a leader of the reformations in Augsburg and Bern, and the full story of his reformational activities has yet to be written. This study, however, has focused on the importance of Musculus as a theologian and in particular as a interpreter of Scripture. His ten biblical commentaries, written over a span of twenty years, are the principal literary legacy of Musculus, representing the work that earned him a reputation in the sixteenth century as a first-rate biblical scholar. By examining Musculus's commentary on John, this study has developed a portrait of the distinctive and traditional features of his work as a commentator that point to the exceptional skill he brought to the exegetical task. I conclude this study by summarizing these principal features of Musculus's commentary as reflected in his exegesis of the Johannine signs.

First, I have shown how important the exegetical tradition is in defining and shaping much of what Musculus writes in his commentary. This fact is demonstrated in the first three chapters, which prove that his commentary serves as a conduit for the expression of exegetical ideas rooted in the patristic and medieval periods. While Musculus sprinkles his exegesis with insights from the commentaries of Cyril, Chrysostom, Augustine, and Nonnus, my research strongly suggests that the patristic influence is more significant and far-reaching than his occasional citations would indicate. The direct citations frequently occur in places where the biblical text occasions serious interpretive difficulties and where the Fathers voice differing interpretive solutions. Musculus occasionally states his preference for one solution or the other, occasionally surrenders the decision to the reader, and occasionally offers his own solution, which differs from the patristic options. These citations alone, however, do not reflect the strong current of patristic influence that flows just beneath the surface of Musculus's commentary. By comparing his exegesis and that of the Fathers, one quickly discerns a more general appropriation and adaptation of patristic ideas, in particular, those of Chrysostom. This general influence should not come as a complete surprise since Musculus devoted much scholarship to the patristic literature and made strong arguments for the value of the patristic witness in the construction of theology and exegesis.

More surprising, however, are the similarities of interpretation between Musculus and the medieval commentators. Although Musculus criticizes medieval exegetes for darkening the meaning of the text by their "absurd eagerness for allegorizing," my research clearly shows the remarkable parallels between the interpretations of Musculus and the medievals on the feeding of the five thousand. Certainly, Musculus's explicit citations of medieval exegetes are rare; in the entire commentary, only the views of Lyra and Theophylact are mentioned in a handful of places. But my research has uncovered recurring echoes of medieval exegetical ideas in his interpretation, a fact that suggests a more comprehensive and complex relationship of Musculus to his medieval predecessors. Yet it is not merely the similarity of ideas that binds Musculus's commentary to the medieval exegetical tradition but also a similar understanding of the nature of the Bible; as a book dense in layers of signification, the meaning of the Bible is appropriately expounded according to a multiplicity of senses. Notwithstanding his warnings against the fanciful excesses of medieval exegesis, Musculus betrays not simply a tolerance but also an eagerness for "spiritual" modes of exposition, utilizing the three standard methods expressed by medieval hermeneutical theory: tropology, anagogy, and allegory.

Second, I have established that Musculus's commentary reveals an extensive reliance on humanist biblical scholarship as represented by Erasmus, who, significantly, is the only modern author cited by name in the entire work. Erasmus's translation provides the basic text for Musculus's exegesis, and much of the linguistic and textual-critical data of Erasmus's *Annotationes* on John finds its way into Musculus's commentary. Yet Musculus does not simply incorporate Erasmus's insights but critically evaluates the data on the basis of his own linguistic skills. Donning the hat of a humanist scholar, Musculus carefully compares Erasmus's translation to the Vulgate and the Greek, altering, correcting, and improving the text and reverting, at times, to the reading of the Vulgate when it presents, in his view, a superior rendering of the Greek. Therefore, although Musculus gives voice to the exegetical tradition, his commentary is clearly not that of a reactionary traditionalist but that of a progressive making use of the latest and best biblical scholarship and assuming the new priorities for critical scholarship promoted by the humanists.

However, in spite of the extensive influence of humanist studies on Musculus's commentary, I have shown the sharp contrast in the interpretations of Musculus, Erasmus, and Faber on the story of the sea miracle. Indeed, in no other context does Musculus's exegesis stand out in such bold relief as in the context of human-ist commentaries on John. The rich tones of Musculus's allegorical images and the incessant preoccupation with moral admonitions contrast vividly with the some-what barren commentaries of the two humanists, who scarcely offer anything be-yond a strictly literal explanation of the text. For Musculus, one basic allegorical image dictates the course of his interpretation: the stormy sea represents the satanic opposition that plagues followers of Christ, and in particular ministers of the Word, represented by the disciples. Accordingly, Musculus interprets all of the elements of the story—the wind, the waves, the darkness of the night, and the boat—as symbolic images of truths conforming to this basic allegory. Furthermore, on the basis of his allegorical reading of the story, Musculus draws out multiple moral lessons concerning fear, courage, haughtiness, obedience, and carnality. This "spiri-tual" reading of the story finds no counterpart in the matter-of-fact commentaries of the two humanists and suggests a different understanding of the nature and pur-pose of biblical commentary. Musculus appropriates the tools and methods of the humanists in order to establish a correct text, a faithful translation, and a proper understanding of the literal-grammatical meaning of the words of the text. But this is only the beginning, or rather, the foundation on which he constructs an inter-pretation that edifies faith and promotes piety. For Musculus, a commentary on the Bible is not the same thing as a commentary on Homer or Virgil but represents a theological genre with explicitly theological purposes.

Third, I have shown that Musculus's preoccupation with allegorical interpreta-tions distinguishes his exegesis not only from the commentaries of the humanists but also from the commentaries of all of his contemporaries, Catholic, Lutheran, and Reformed. This point, however, must be carefully nuanced since none of the sixteenth-century commentators I have read reject allegorical exegesis altogether. What differentiates Musculus's commentary is not his use of allegorical exegesis as a mode of interpretation but rather the degree to which he makes use of this mode, spinning out allegorical interpretations from the text at almost every turn. Only in the figure of Œcolampadius have I found a sixteenth-century interpreter who embraces allegory as enthusiastically as Musculus. In five of the seven sign passages, Musculus offers at least one, and usually multiple, allegorical images of the miracle. Only in his interpretation of the wedding at Cana and the healing of the ruler's son does Musculus omit any discussion of the symbolic quality of the signs. The latter story, however, does not easily lend itself to allegorical interpreta-tion, and even the patristic and medieval commentators rarely move their exposi-tions in an allegorical direction. But the lack of allegory in Musculus's commen-tary on the wine miracle is certainly puzzling, for the symbols of wine and marriage are rich in allegorical potential, and Musculus usually shows an eagerness to draw out the content of such latent symbolism.

I argued in chapter 2 that Musculus enunciates a cautious approach to the use of "mystical" exposition: allegorical interpretations are acceptable only when they conform to "evident necessity"—that is, when the literal meaning and the context of a passage suggest the appropriateness of an allegorical reading. Thus, Musculus justifies his allegorical interpretation of the bread in the feeding miracle as evidently necessary because Jesus himself suggests this interpretation: "I am the bread of life." In conformity with this hermeneutical rule, Musculus rejects number allegory—a favorite mode of exposition among the medieval commentators—as evidently unnecessary. The five loaves may be interpreted allegorically, but nothing is to be made of the numerical symbolism, just as nothing is to be made of the two fish, or of the six water pots, or of the five porticos at the pool of Bethesda. But Musculus's actual exegesis shows that this cautious approach frequently breaks down. How is the allegorical interpretation of the disciples' boat as a symbol of the Church evidently necessary? This same question could be asked regarding his interpretations of the rinsing in the pool of Bethesda as baptism, of the poultice of spit and clay as an image of both the incarnate Word and the blinding of human wisdom, of the stormy sea as a symbol of satanic tyranny, and of Mary as a symbol of the contemplative life. Clearly, another force is at work that dictates Musculus's approach to these symbols, and that, I suggest, is the force of the exegetical tradition. Musculus knows that past exegetes have interpreted these things as symbols of greater spiritual realities, and he is unwilling to forego these interpretations entirely, especially when they contribute to his goals of edification and admonition. Even his aversion to number allegory breaks down occasionally, as when he offers an interpretation of the four days of Lazarus' death as symbolic of the four ages of the world. One senses that Musculus may have felt some embarrassment at proposing this symbolism (rooted in Augustine), for he relegates it to the margin. But the clear impression is that Musculus finds it difficult to pass up the opportunity for a good allegory.

Fourth, I have established an overriding preoccupation with moral exegesis in Musculus's commentary on the Johannine signs. This is arguably the most distinctive feature of his exegesis, for it comes to the fore in each of the contexts we have examined. This ethical quality of his interpretation, which appears particularly characteristic of Reformed exegesis, is underscored by Musculus's general reliance on the homilies of Chrysostom, who shares a similar devotion to the moral lessons embedded in the text of Scripture. Yet no commentator included in this study comes close to Musculus in terms of the sheer quantity and scope of moral exposition. No rule of evident necessity restrains Musculus here, for he discovers latent ethical principles in even the most seemingly innocuous details of the text. And occasionally, his moral observations grow to such proportions—such as in his discussion of marriage (chapter 1) and thankfulness (chapter 3)—that they resemble separate moral treatises, complete with titles and subdivisions. A fundamental pastoral purpose controls Musculus's exegesis as he attempts to demonstrate not only what the gospel text meant then but also what it means now and how as a living text it continues to demand a living response in the lives, hearts, and minds of its readers.

Finally, this study has demonstrated that as an exegete, Musculus displays exceptional talent and creativity in crafting an interpretation that is explainable in reference to no one commentator or group of commentators. Although he borrows insights from his exegetical forebears, he is certainly not an epigone—a second-rate imitator—of anyone; and at no place in his commentary does Musculus descend to the level of obsequious parrotry. His work on John reveals the full complexity of the exegetical task, which involves not merely a dialogue with the text of Scripture but also a sensitive engagement with the stream of traditional interpretations, a careful and critical use of the best and most recent biblical scholarship, and the application of a skillful and imaginative reading of the text to produce a commentary that served, and indeed still can serve, the faith of those who call themselves Christian.

Notes

ABBREVIATIONS

CCSL	*Corpus Christianorum*, Series Latina (Turnhout: Brepols, 1954–).
Comm. I	Wolfgang Musculus, *Commentariorum in Evangelistam Ioannem, heptas prima* (Basel: Bartholomäus Westheimer, 1545).
Comm. II	Wolfgang Musculus, *Commentariorum in Evangelistam Ioannem, heptas altera, item tertia et postrema in eundem* (Basel: Johann Herwagen, 1548).
CR	*Corpus Reformatorum*. Vols. 1–28 comprise *Philippi Melanchthonis opera quae supersunt omnia*. Edited by C. G. Bretschneider. Halle: C. A. Schwetschke and Sons, 1834–1860. Vols. 29–87 comprise *Ioannis Calvini opera quae supersunt omnia*. Edited by G. Baum, E. Cunitz, E. Reuss. Brunswick and Berlin: C. A. Schwetschke and Sons, 1863–1900. Vols. 88–101 comprise *Huldreich Zwinglis sämtliche Werke*. Edited by E. Egli et al. Berlin-Leipzig-Zurich: C. A. Schwetschke and Sons, 1905– .
FC	*The Fathers of the Church* (New York and Washington, D.C.: 1947–).
LC (1560)	Wolfgang Musculus, *Loci communes in usus sacrae theologiae candidatorum parati* (Basel: Johann Herwagen, 1560).
LC (1563)	Wolfgang Musculus, *Loci communes sacrae theologiae, iam recens recogniti et emendati* (Basel: Johann Herwagen, 1563).
PG	J. -P. Migne, ed., *Patrologiae cursus completus*, Series Graece, 162 vols. (Paris: 1857–1866).
PL	J. -P. Migne, ed., *Patrologiae cursus completus*, Series Latina, 221 vols. (Paris: 1844–1864).
Synopsis	ΣΥΝΟΨΙΣ *festalium concionum, authore D. Wolfgango Musculo Dusano. Eiusdem vita, obitus, erudita carmina* (Basel: Conrad Waldkirch, 1595).

INTRODUCTION

1. For a bibliography of Musculus's works, including the various printings, see Paul Romane-Musculus, "Catalogue des œuvres imprimées du théologien Wolfgang Musculus," *Revue d'Histoire et de Philosophie Religieuses* 43 (1963): 260–278.

2. Although Musculus does not explain his reasons for changing publishers, it seems that Westheimer, who left Basel for Mülhausen in 1547, was no longer publishing at the time Musculus finished the second volume. In 1548 Westheimer sold his publishing house "zum Bären" to Michael Isengrin. See Josef Benzing, *Buchdruckerlexikon des 16. Jahrhunderts* (*Deutsches Sprachgebiet*) (Frankfurt: Vittorio Klostermann, 1952), pp. 25–26.

3. Richard Simon, *Histoire Critique du Vieux Testament* (Rotterdam, 1685; reprint, Frankfurt: Minerva, 1967), pp. 438–439: "On peut dire que cet Auteur a connu la veritable manière d'expliquer l'Écriture." In particular, Simon praises Musculus's Psalms commentary for its careful attention to patristic scholarship. Musculus, he claims, showed more respect for antiquity than most Protestant authors. He also praises Musculus's new Latin translation of the Psalms, which altered the ancient translation only when necessary.

4. Both letters exist in the collection of the Zofingen Stadtbibliothek (call no. PA 15A). The letter from Micron (I.172) is dated August 24, 1556, and the letter from Cruciger (I.158) is dated August 20, 1556. The letter from Micron is printed in J. H. Gerretsen, *Micronius. Zijn leven, zijn geschriften, zijn geestesrichting* (Nijmegen: H. Ten Hoet, 1895), pp. ix–xi of the appendix. Further evidence of Musculus's influence in Poland is seen in a letter (December 1561) to Bullinger from the Polish theologian Christoph Thretius, founder and rector of the Latin school in Cracow, who writes that his program of Scripture reading is conjoined with study of the *Decades* of Bullinger, the *Institutes* of Calvin, and the *Loci communes* of Musculus. The letter is quoted in Walter Hollweg, *Heinrich Bullingers Hausbuch*, Beiträge zur Geschichte und Lehre der Reformierten Kirche, vol. 8 (Neukirchen: Erziehungsverein, 1956), p. 187.

5. Duncan Shaw, "Zwinglianische Einflüsse in der Schottischen Reformation," *Zwingliana* 17 (1988): 375–400. See also Gottfried W. Locher, "Zwinglis Einfluß in England und Schottland—Daten und Probleme," *Zwingliana* 14 (1975): 165–209.

6. Farel to Haller, March 1551 (*CR* 42:80 [#1466]): "Saluta quaeso pium Musculum. Nondum audimus istius psalmos absolutos, quos non pauci optant."

7. Calvin, *In Librum Psalmorum commentarius* (*CR* 59:13): "Nec vero de Wolphgangi Musculi commentariis, si iam tunc in lucem prodiissent, tacere fas fuisset quando et hic sedulitate et industria non parum laudis bonorum iudicio meritus est."

8. Andrew Pettegree, *Foreign Protestant Communities in Sixteenth-Century London* (Oxford: Clarendon, 1986), p. 24.

9. The evidence for all of these calls has been collected in handwritten copies of the correspondence in the Bürgerbibliothek Bern, Cod. 689 (8°f. 97): "Vocationes aliquot, quae domino Wolfgango Musculo contigerunt, ex litteris ipsius collectae" (fol. 1r–31v).

10. See the letter (dated January 7, 1556) from Musculus to Ambrosius Blaurer in *Briefwechsel der Brüder Ambrosius und Thomas Blaurer 1509–1567*, vol. 3, ed. Traugott Schieß (Freiburg: Friedrich Ernst Fehsenfeld, 1912), no. 2039, pp. 349–350: "Lysmaninus hac transiit. Persuadere mihi conatus est, ut conferam me in Poloniam, si illo vocer, verum haudquaquam persuasit."

11. In rhetorical modesty, Musculus replied to Erastus that he did not see how he was a suitable candidate for the position in Heidelberg since he was "a man educated in a monastery and not distinguished with the degree of a Master, still less of a Doctor" (*homo in monasterio educatus, et ne Magisterii quidem, nedum Doctoratii gradu insignitus*). Bürgerbibliothek Bern, Cod. 689.

12. Paul Josiah Schwab, *The Attitude of Wolfgang Musculus toward Religious Tolerance*, Yale Studies in Religion no. 6 (New Haven: Yale University Press, 1933).

13. Richard Bäumlin, "Naturrecht und obrigkeitliches Kirchenregiment bei Wolfgang Musculus," in *Für Kirche und Recht: Festschrift für Johannes Heckel zum 70. Geburtstag*, ed. Siegfried Grundmann (Cologne: Böhlau, 1959), pp. 120–143.

14. Helmut Kreßner, "Die Weiterbildung des Zwinglischen Systems durch Wolfgang Musculus," in *Schweizer Ursprünge des anglikanischen Staatskirchentums*, Schriften des Vereins für Reformationsgeschichte no. 170 (Gütersloh: C. Bertelsmann, 1953), pp. 45–72. See also R. Pfister, "Zürich und das anglikanische Staatskirchentum," *Zwingliana* 10 (1955): 249–256.

15. Alexander Schweizer, *Die Glaubenslehre der evangelisch-reformierten Kirche dargestellt und aus den Quellen belegt*, 2 vols. (Zurich: Orell, Füssli & Comp., 1844–1847); Otto Ritschl, *Dogmengeschichte des Protestantismus*, 4 vols. (Göttingen: Vandenhoeck & Ruprecht, 1908–1927), esp. 2:244, 249–250, 404, 415, 417; Heinrich Heppe, *Reformed Dogmatics Set Out and Illustrated from the Sources*, ed. Ernst Bizer, trans. G. T. Thomson (London: George Allen, 1950), pp. 23–24, 303–304, 362–363; Richard A. Muller, *Christ and the Decree: Christology and Predestination in Reformed Theology from Calvin to Perkins*, Studies in Historical Theology no. 2 (Durham, N.C.: Labyrinth, 1986), pp. 47–57, 71–75, and *Post-Reformation Reformed Dogmatics*, vol. 1: *Prolegomena to Theology* (Grand Rapids: Baker, 1987), pp. 69–79, 179–181; vol. 2: *Holy Scripture: The Cognitive Foundation of Theology* (Grand Rapids: Baker, 1993), pp. 64–66, 188–191, 248, 320–321, 342, 352, 364–366, 393–394, 467, 471–472.

16. Wilhelm Gass, *Geschichte der protestantischen Dogmatik*, vol. 1 (Berlin: Georg Reimer, 1854), p. 132; Heinrich Heppe, *Geschichte des Pietismus und der Mystik in der reformierten Kirche, namentlich in der Niederlande* (Leiden: E. J. Brill, 1879), pp. 208–209; Gottlob Schrenk, *Gottesreich und Bund im Älteren Protestantismus: vornemlich bei Johannes Cocceius* (Gütersloh: C. Bertelsmann, 1923), pp. 50–51, 55, 59, 212–214; Lyle Dean Bierma, "The Covenant Theology of Caspar Olevian," Ph.D. diss., Duke University, 1980, pp. 68–76; J. Wayne Baker, *Heinrich Bullinger and the Covenant: The Other Reformed Tradition* (Athens: Ohio University Press, 1980), pp. 200–202; Stephen Strehle, *Calvinism, Federalism, and Scholasticism: A Study of the Reformed Doctrine of Covenant*, Basler und Berner Studien zur historischen und systematischen Theologie, vol. 58 (Berne: Peter Lang, 1988), pp. 157–158; David A. Weir, *The Origins of Federal Theology in Sixteenth-Century Reformation Thought* (New York: Oxford University Press, 1990), pp. 12, 44; Charles S. McCoy and J. Wayne Baker, *Fountainhead of Federalism: Heinrich Bullinger and the Covenantal Tradition* (Louisville, Ky: Westminster/John Knox, 1991), p. 22.

17. Ruth Wesel-Roth, *Thomas Erastus. Ein Beitrag zur Geschichte der reformierten Kirche und zur Lehre von der Staatssouveränität*. Veröffentlichungen des Vereins für Kirchengeschichte in der evang. Landeskirche Badens 15 (Lahr/Baden: Moritz Schauenburg, 1954), pp. 107–110, "Die Lehre vom christlichen Staat bei Wolfgang Musculus."

18. Gerretsen, *Micronius,* pp. 9, 92.

19. Wolfram Lohse, "Die Fußwaschung (Joh. 13, 1–20). Eine Geschichte ihrer Deutung," Ph.D. diss., University of Erlangen/Nuremberg, 1967, p. 68; William Rader, *The Church and Racial Hostility: A History of Interpretation of Ephesians 2:11–22,* Beiträge zur Geschichte der Biblischen Exegese 20 (Tübingen: J. C. B. Mohr, 1978), pp. 77–78, 88–91, 95–96; Johannes Bouterse, *De boom en zijn vruchten. Bergrede-christendom bij Reformatoren, Anabaptisten en Spiritualisten in de zestiende eeuw* (Kampen: J. H. Kok, 1987), pp. 240–255, "De Bergrede bij Musculus."

20. Elsie Anne McKee, *Elders and the Plural Ministry: The Role of Exegetical History in Illuminating John Calvin's Theology* (Geneva: Librairie Droz S. A., 1988); John Lee Thompson, *John Calvin and the Daughters of Sarah: Women in Regular and Exceptional Roles in the Exegesis of Calvin, His Predecessors, and His Contemporaries* (Geneva: Librairie Droz S. A., 1992), pp. 92–96, 124–125, 131–133, 146–149, 165–176, 217–219.

21. The volume brings together poems attributed to Musculus and a confession on the Lord's Supper, "Confessio Wolfgangi Musculi de sacramento corporis et sanguinis Domini." The biography by Abraham Musculus (*Synopsis,* pp. 1–55) is entitled "Historia vitae et obitus clarissimi theologi D. Wolfgangi Musculi Dusani, S. Litterarum apud Bernates professoris, per Abrahamum Musculum filium, pietatis ergo scripta."

22. Ludwig Grote, *Wolfgang Musculus, ein biographischer Versuch* (Hamburg: Rauhes Haus, 1855).

23. Musculus's authorship of many of the hymns attributed to him has been questioned by more recent studies: A. E. Cherbuliez, "Das Gesangbuch Ambrosius Blauerers und die Chronologie der in der Schweiz gedruckten reformierten Gesangbücher des 16. Jahrhunderts," *Zwingliana* 5 (1933): 417–454; Manfred Schuler, "Ist Wolfgang Musculus wirklich der Autor mehrerer Kirchenlieder?" *Jahrbuch für Liturgik und Hymnologie* 17 (1972): 217–221.

24. Wilhelm Theodor Streuber, "Wolfgang Musculus oder Müslin. Ein Lebensbild aus der Reformationszeit. Aus dem handschriftichen Nachlasse des verstorbenen Dr. Wilhelm Theodor Streuber," *Berner Taschenbuch auf das Jahr 1860* (Bern, 1860), pp. 1–79.

25. The autograph of the diary exists in the Bürgerbibliothek Bern: "Wolfgangi Musculi diarium itineris ad conventum Isenacensem anno 1536." Portions are published in Theodor Kolde, *Analecta Lutherana. Briefe und Aktenstücke zur Geschichte Luthers* (Gotha: Perthes, 1883), pp. 216–230. Grote complains in the preface to his work (*Wolfgang Musculus,* pp. ix–x) that he had not been able to utilize the diary since Streuber had taken possession of it.

26. Rudolf Dellsperger, "Wolfgang Musculus (1497–1563)," in *Die Augsburger Kirchenordnung von 1537 und ihr Umfeld,* ed. Reinhard Schwarz (Gütersloh: Gütersloher Verlaghaus Gerd Mohn, 1988), pp. 91–110. In the volume are included several other articles that treat aspects of Musculus's life. See especially Gottfried Seebaß, "Die Augsburger Kirchenordnung von 1537 in ihrem historischen und theologischen Zusammenhang," pp. 33–58, and Marijn de Kroon, "Die Augsburger Reformation in der Korrespondenz des Straßburger Reformators Martin Bucer unter besonderer Berücksichtigung des Briefwechsels Gereon Sailers," pp. 59–89.

27. Theodor Beza, *Les vrais portraits des hommes illustres en piété et doctrine . . .* (Paris: Jean de Laon, 1581; reprint, Geneva: Slatkine, 1986), pp. 59–61.

28. Friedrich Roth, *Augsburgs Reformationsgeschichte,* 4 vols. (Munich: Theodor Acker-

mann, 1901–1911), esp. 2:46–49, 55–56, 192–194, 256–258, 288–297, 324–327, 433–435, 451–454. See also Horst Jesse, *Die Geschichte der Evangelischen Kirche in Augsburg* (Pfaffenhofen: W. Ludwig, 1983), pp. 109, 120, 122, 125, 138–140; and Philip Broadhead, "Politics and Expediency in the Augsburg Reformation," in *Reformation Principle and Practice: Essays in Honour of Arthur Geoffrey Dickens*, ed. Peter Newman Brooks (London: Scolar, 1980), pp. 53–70.

29. Henri Vuilleumier, *Histoire de l'Église Réformée du Pays de Vaud sous le Régime Bernois*, 4 vols. (Lausanne: Éditions la Concorde, 1927–1933), 1:266–267, 629, 668–671, 715–716; Kurt Guggisberg, *Bernische Kirchengeschichte* (Bern: Paul Haupt, 1958), pp. 172–174, 195–196, 257–258. See also Rudolf Pfister, *Kirchengeschichte der Schweiz*, vol. 2: *Von der Reformation bis zum zweiten Villmerger Krieg* (Zurich: Theologischer Verlag, 1974), pp. 213, 215, 300–301.

30. Hastings Eells, *Martin Bucer* (New Haven: Yale University Press, 1931), pp. 120, 183–184, 187–188, 197; R. Emmet McLaughlin, *Caspar Schwenckfeld, Reluctant Radical: His Life to 1540* (New Haven: Yale University Press, 1986), pp. 147–148, 164–166; Horst Weigelt, "Die Beziehungen Schwenckfelds zu Augsburg im Umfeld der Kirchenordnung von 1537," in Schwarz, *Die Augsburger Kirchenordnung von 1537 und ihr Umfeld*, pp. 111–122.

31. The following sketch of Musculus's career is based upon my own reading of the *Synopsis* and the biographies by Grote, Streuber, and Dellsperger.

32. His German name was rendered in a number of various forms, such as Mäuslein, Meüßlin, Mäusli, Meuslin, and Moesel. In his later years in Bern, Musculus was known as Müslin.

33. Bucer recommended Musculus and Ambrose Blaurer, the reformer in Constance. When Blaurer refused the call, Bucer recommended his student Boniface Wolfhart (Lycostenes), who arrived in Augsburg shortly after Musculus to take the preaching post at St. Anne's, a post previously held by the Lutherans. Bucer also sent two other preachers to Augsburg: Theobald Schwarz (Nigri), who remained only a few months before returning to Strasbourg, and Sebastian Meyer. See Eells, *Martin Bucer*, pp. 119–120.

34. See Ulrich Im Hof, "Die reformierte Hohe Schule zu Berne," in *450 Jahre Berner Reformation. Beiträge zur Geschichte der Berner Reformation und zu Niklaus Manuel* (Bern: Historischer Verein des Kantons Bern, 1980), pp. 194–224.

35. His last male heir was the renowned David Müslin, preacher at the Münster in Bern, who died in 1821.

36. Robert M. Grant and David Tracy, *A Short History of the Interpretation of the Bible*, 2d ed. (Philadelphia: Fortress, 1984), p. 92.

CHAPTER ONE

1. A. Rivera, "Nota sobre el simbolismo del milagro de Caná en la interpretación patrística," *Estudios Marianos* 13 (1953): 62–72; M.-E. Boismard, *Du Baptême à Cana (Jean 1, 19–2, 11)* (Paris: Les Éditions du Cerf, 1956); Angelo Bresolin, "L'esegesi di Giov. 2, 4 nei Padri Latini," *Revue des Études Augustiniennes* 8 (1962): 243–273; Joseph Reuss, "Joh 2, 3–4 in Johannes Kommentaren der griechischen Kirche," in *Neutestamentliche Aufsätze: Festschrift für Josef Schmid zum 70. Geburtstag*, ed. J. Blinzler, O. Kuss, F. Mussner (Regens-

burg: Pustet, 1963); José Ramos-Regidor, "Signo y Poder: a proposito de la exegesis patristica de Jn 2, 1–11," *Salesianum* (1965): 499–562; Adolf Smitmans, *Das Weinwunder von Kana: Die Auslegung von Jo 2, 1–11 bei den Vätern und heute* (Tübingen: J. C. B. Mohr, 1966); Rolf Heine, "Zur patristischen Auslegung von Ioh. 2, 1–12," *Wiener Studien* 83 (1970): 189–195.

2. Wolfgang Musculus, *Comm.* I, pp. 61–62.

3. Ibid., p. 60.

4. John Chrysostom, *Commentary on Saint John the Apostle and Evangelist: Homilies 1–47*, FC 33:215, hereafter cited as *Homilies on John*.

5. Thomas Aquinas, *Commentary on the Gospel of St. John*, trans. James A. Weisheipl and Fabian R. Larcher (Albany: Magi, 1980), p. 156, hereafter cited as *Commentary on John*; Hugh of St. Cher, *Postilla super totam Bibliam*, 8 vols. (Venice: N. Pezzana, 1732), vol. 6: *In Evangelia secundum Matthaeum, Lucam, Marcum, & Joannem.* fol. 291r, hereafter cited as *Postilla super Joannem*; Desiderius Erasmus, *Paraphrasis in Evangelium secundum Ioannem* . . . (Basel: J. Froben, 1523) p. 34, hereafter cited as *Paraphrasis in Ioannem*.

6. Musculus, *Comm.* I, p. 59. The Athenian measure *metreta* (μετρητής) would correspond to approximately nine English gallons. Each pot would have been able to hold from eighteen to twenty-seven gallons.

7. Ibid., pp. 59–60.

8. Thomas, *Commentary on John*, p. 156.

9. Erasmus, *Paraphrasis in Ioannem*, p. 35.

10. Musculus, *Comm.* I, pp. 59–60.

11. Ibid., p. 60: "Servandus erat ordo, quo miraculum redderetur magis conspicuum."

12. Chrysostom, *Homilies on John*, FC 33:217; Thomas, *Commentary on John*, p. 157; Hugh, *Postilla super Joannem*, fol. 291r; Erasmus, *Paraphrasis in Ioannem*, p. 34.

13. Erasmus, *Paraphrasis in Ioannem*, p. 35.

14. Musculus, *Comm.* I, p. 60: "Verum ita constituit ut nos plantemus ac rigemus, ipse vero incrementum addat."

15. Ibid.

16. Chrysostom, *Homilies on John*, FC 33:216.

17. Ibid.

18. Thomas, *Commentary on John*, p. 157; Hugh, *Postilla super Joannem*, fol. 291r. See also Denis, *Enarratio in Evangelium secundum Joannem*, vol. 12: *(In Lucam (X–XXI), et Johannem)* of *Opera omnia*, 42 vols. in 44 (Monstrolii: S. M. De Pratis, 1901), p. 315, hereafter cited as *Enarratio in Joannem*.

19. Musculus, *Comm.* I, p. 60.

20. Ibid.

21. Augustine of Hippo, *Tractates on the Gospel of John 1–10*, FC 78:179, hereafter cited as *Tractates on John*.

22. Hugh, *Postilla super Joannem*, fol. 291r.

23. Musculus, *Comm.* I, p. 61. Many of the miracles of the Bible, Musculus argues, can be classified as simple accelerations of natural processes. As an example, he mentions the blossoming of Aaron's rod (Nm. 17:8): "It was not unusual that the rod of Aaron blossomed, for we see the blossoming of branches every year, but that it blossomed in an unusual method and time certainly made it suffice as a miracle."

24. Vulgate: "Quid mihi et tibi, mulier? Nondum venit hora mea." However, Musculus, Melanchthon, and Bucer all follow Erasmus in translating the phrase as, "Quid mihi tecum est mulier."

25. Augustine, *Tractates on John, FC* 78:183.

26. This anonymous prologue to John, which affirms that John was the groom at Cana, was mistakenly attributed to Jerome by Bonaventure, Albert the Great, Hugh of St. Cher, and Nicholas of Lyra. See the notes of the Quaracchi editors, *Doctoris Seraphici S. Bonaventurae opera omnia* (Quaracchi: Collegium S. Bonaventurae, 1882–1902), 6:243, n. 2, 245, n. 1.

27. Hugh, *Postilla super Joannem*, fol. 290r.

28. Ibid., fol. 278r.

29. Denis, *Enarratio in Joannem*, p. 313.

30. Martin Bucer, *Martini Buceri Opera Latina*, vol. 2: *Enarratio in Evangelion Iohannis*, ed. Irena Backus (Leiden: E. J. Brill, 1988), p. 111: "Ioannem tamen affirmare fuisse hunc sponsum frivolum est"; hereafter cited as *Enarratio in Iohannem*.

31. Erasmus, *Paraphrasis in Ioannem*, p. 34; Musculus, *Comm.* I, p. 55.

32. Musculus, *Comm.* I, p. 55.

33. Chrysostom, *Homilies on John, FC* 33:206–207.

34. The reluctance to accuse Mary of base motives seems to be particular to the Latin exegetical tradition. Reuss, "Joh 2, 3–4 in Johannes Kommentaren der griechischen Kirche," p. 213, shows that several of the Greek Fathers, like Chrysostom, accuse Mary of erroneous behavior. In a fragment of a John catena attributed to Origen, Mary is accused of seeking her own glory through her son's miracles. According to Theodor of Mopsuestia, Mary erroneously believes that Jesus' miraculous power is bound to certain times and emergencies. In fragments from a John catena, Ammonius of Alexandria accuses Mary of forgetting the divinity of her son; by informing Jesus of the situation, she presupposes his ignorance. See also Smitmans, *Das Weinwunder von Kana*, pp. 114–115.

35. Thomas, *Commentary on John*, pp. 151–152.

36. Hugh, *Postilla super Joannem*, fol. 290v.

37. Denis, *Enarratio in Joannem*, p. 313; "Docemur causam et indigentiam nostram, superioribus nostris simpliciter atque modeste insinuare, et in eorum potestate quid faciendum sit relinquere."

38. Erasmus, *Paraphrasis in Ioannem*, p. 34.

39. Bucer, *Enarratio in Iohannem*, p. 111.

40. Ibid., p. 113.

41. Musculus, *Comm.* I, p. 57.

42. Ibid., pp. 57–58: "Non dicit: Omne vinum ebiberunt, & intemperanter consumpserunt. Sed simpliciter & modeste. Vinum non habent."

43. Musculus, *Comm.* I, p. 59.

44. Hugh, *Postilla super Joannem*, fol. 291r.

45. Denis, *Enarratio in Joannem*, p. 314.

46. Erasmus, *Paraphrasis in Ioannem*, p. 34.

47. Philip Melanchthon, *Annotationes in Evangelium Ioannis, CR* 14:1077, hereafter cited as *Annotationes in Ioannem*.

48. Musculus, *Comm.* I, p. 59.

49. Hugh, *Postilla super Joannem*, fol. 290v.

50. Chrysostom, *Homilies on John*, FC 33:215

51. Bucer, *Enarratio in Iohannem*, p. 111.

52. Melanchthon, *Annotationes in Ioannem*, CR 14:1077–1078.

53. Musculus, *Comm.* I, p. 59: "Haec erat in Virgine constantia fidei, quae nubila irati dei sola penetrat, & contra spem sperat, sperandoque tandem vincit."

54. Musculus, *Comm.* I, p. 59.

55. Ibid., p. 58.

56. Thomas, *Commentary on John*, pp. 154–55; Hugh, *Postilla super Joannem*, fol. 290v; Denis, *Enarratio in Joannem*, pp. 313–314.

57. On the tendency of medieval commentators to offer multiple literal interpretations, see Ceslaus Spicq, *Esquisse d'une histoire de l'exégèse latine au moyen age* (Paris: Librairie Philosophie J. Vrin, 1944), p. 207.

58. Reuss, "Joh 2, 3–4 in Johannes Kommentaren der griechischen Kirche," p. 209, shows that this explanation actually antedates Augustine; it is found in fragments of a John catena attributed to Origen.

59. Augustine, *Tractates on John*, FC 78:188.

60. Ibid., pp. 184–187.

61. Ibid., pp. 190–192.

62. Chrysostom, *Homilies on John*, FC 33:208.

63. Cyril of Alexandria, *Commentary on the Gospel According to S. John*, vol. 1: *S. John I–VIII*, trans. P. E. Pusey (Oxford: James Parker, 1874), p. 156, hereafter cited as *Commentary on John*.

64. Chrysostom's interpretation of Jesus' "hour" as the time of his public ministry reflects a Greek exegetical tradition. See Reuss, "Joh 2, 3–4 in Johannes Kommentaren der griechischen Kirche," p. 213.

65. Chrysostom, *Homilies on John*, FC 33:214–215.

66. Cyril, *Commentary on John*, p. 156.

67. Melanchthon, *Annotationes in Ioannem*, CR 14:1077.

68. Bucer, *Enarratio in Iohannem*, p. 111.

69. Erasmus, *Paraphrasis in Ioannem*, p. 35.

70. Musculus, *Comm.* I, pp. 58–59.

71. Cyril, *Commentary on John*, p. 155.

72. Chrysostom, *Homilies on John*, FC 33:204.

73. Thomas, *Commentary on John*, p. 151.

74. Hugh, *Postilla super Joannem*, fol. 290v.

75. Musculus, *Comm.* I, p. 59.

76. According to Smitmans, *Das Weinwunder von Kana*, p. 144, the Fathers variously interpret the miraculous wine as symbolic of: 1) the eucharistic blood; 2) the gospel, which supercedes the law; 3) the prophetic fulfillment of history in Christ; 4) the spiritual sense of Scripture; 5) the gift of the Holy Spirit; 6) the new life of grace; 7) conversion; 8) joy. In general, the wine is seen as a symbol of salvation that has a multifaceted signification.

77. Chrysostom, *Homilies on John*, FC 33:219–221.

78. Augustine, *Tractates on John*, FC 78:197–199.

79. Cyril, *Commentary on John*, p. 158; Erasmus, *Paraphrasis in Ioannem*, p. 36; Melanchthon, *Annotationes in Ioannem*, CR 14:1078.

80. Thomas, *Commentary on John*, p. 153; Hugh, *Postilla super Joannem*, fol. 291r–291v; Denis, *Enarratio in Joannem*, pp. 316–317.

81. Bucer, *Enarratio in Iohannem*, p. 113: "Et, quod mireris, sobrietatis autor tantum vini convivis—inter quos indubie fuere qui largius quam necessitas posceret, biberunt—donavit—et quidem optimum quale"; "Catabaptistae indubie, si tum adfuissent, graviter Dominum increpuissent, si non etiam excommunicassent."

82. Musculus's text reads: "Omnis homo primo loco bonum vinum ponit, & cum inebriati fuerint, tunc id quod deterius est."

83. Musculus, *Comm.* I, p. 61.

84. Ibid., p. 55: "Usurpari solet hic locus ad matrimonii cohonestationem, propterea quod in his nuptiis Christus comparuit."

85. Of the commentators I am treating, only Chrysostom and Melanchthon omit this point. However, Chrysostom argues in a sermon on Isaiah 6 and in a sermon on Colossians 3 that Jesus' presence at the wedding at Cana indicates his approval of marriage. The John commentary of Caspar Cruciger (*CR* 15:63–65), which was based on Melanchthon's lecture notes, makes Jesus' approval of marriage the central theme of the Cana story. Adolf Smitmans, *Das Weinwunder von Kana*, pp. 194–207, demonstrates that John 2:1–11 was a pivotal text in the patristic period in Christian discussion of the place of marriage. For example, Tertullian (in *De monogamia*) and Jerome (in *Adversus Iovinianum*) both argue that Jesus attended only one wedding during his ministry to show that Christians may only marry once and that he does not give a blanket approval of the married state per se. The majority of Fathers, however, see the Cana story as an indication of the sanctity of marriage.

86. Augustine, *Tractates on John*, FC 78:183; Cyril, *Commentary on John*, p. 157.

87. Augustine, *Tractates on John*, FC 78:204.

88. Thomas, *Commentary on John*, p. 150.

89. Hugh, *Postilla super Joannem*, fol. 290v.

90. Denis, *Enarratio in Joannem*, p. 316: "Celebremus ergo spirituales nuptias in conscientia nostra, uniendo et intime copulando animas nostras Verbo . . . sponso animarum sanctarum . . . ut animae nostrae fecundentur et impraegnentur coelesti semine, id est lumine gratiae copiosae, quatenus indesinenter producant fructus spirituales, seu actus virtuosos."

91. Erasmus, *Paraphrasis in Ioannem*, p. 36; Melanchthon, *Annotationes in Ioannem*, *CR* 14:1078.

92. Bucer, *Enarratio in Iohannem*, p. 114: "Texuntur ex his allegoriae, sed nihil, tam Christus quam Evangelista allegoricos in his dixit. Historia aperta est qua memoratur."

93. Bucer, *Enarratio in Iohannem*, p. 115: "Solet hic tractari locus communis, coniugium . . . . Summa est: *Non est bonum homini esse soli.*"

94. Musculus, *Comm.* 1, pp. 55–57.

CHAPTER TWO

1. From the Greek Fathers, Musculus presents quotations from Chrysostom, Basil, Gregory of Nazianzus, Origen, Athanasius, Epiphanius of Salamis, Hesychius of Jerusalem, Ignatius, and Cyril of Alexandria. For many of these citations, Musculus gives the original Greek, but usually he offers a Latin translation. From the Latin Fathers, Musculus cites a

vast spectrum of Augustine's writings in addition to quotations from Jerome, Tertullian, Cyprian, Ambrose, Lactantius, and Hilary of Poitiers.

2. *Synopsis*, pp. 4–5.

3. Paul Adam, "L'Humanisme à Sélestat," in *Les lettres en Alsace* (Strasbourg: Société savante d'Alsace, 1962), pp. 89–104.

4. C. Reedijk, ed., *The Poems of Desiderius Erasmus* (Leiden: E. J. Brill, 1956). Poem 98, "Encomium Selestadii": "Illa tibi propria est, quod & una, & parva, tot aedis / Virtute insignes ingenioque viros."

5. Ludwig Grote, *Wolfgang Musculus, ein biographischer Versuch* (Hamburg: Rauhes Haus, 1855), p. 11. The same assertion is made by Rudolf Dellsperger, "Wolfgang Musculus (1497–1563)," in *Die Augsburger Kirchenordnung von 1537 und ihr Umfeld*, ed. Reinhard Schwarz (Gütersloh: Gütersloher Verlaghaus Gerd Mohn, 1988), p. 92, n. 2.

6. *Synopsis*, p. 5: "Hoc fuit initium, & hic cursus studiorum eius, usque ad annum aetatis suae 15. primum monasticum vitae genus ingressus est."

7. The Latin text is quoted in Charles Schmidt, *Histoire Littéraire de l'Alsace a la fin du XVe et au commencement du XVIe siècle* (Hildesheim: Georg Olms, 1966), 2:160, n. 4: "Scripsisti in tuis litteris ut tibi scriberem quid noster magister faceret. Scias quod de mane Alexandrum facit; hora nona aliqua carmina ex aliquibus autoribus, scilicet ex Horacio, Ovidio, etc.; post duodecimam in Mantuano; die lune ascribit aliqua carmina que probare debemus per quantitates sillabarum. Hora quarta recapitulamus que per totam diem habuimus." Autograph in Universitätsbibliothek Basel.

8. The *Doctrinale* is actually a poem consisting of 2,645 hexameter verses, with notes on noun declensions and gender, the various verbal forms, and syntax. It was a standard grammar for more than three centuries until it was gradually replaced by the humanists.

9. Schmidt, *Histoire Littéraire de l'Alsace*, p. 160.

10. *Synopsis*, p. 5: "Post illinc discedens Colmariam, inde Selestadium venit, ibique operam literis dedit. Tenebatur autem iam tum in illa puerili aetate poëtices amore, inque poëtarum lectione perquam assiduus erat."

11. Ibid.: "Et cum eius studii propositum esset a praeceptore certamen, ut recitandis memoriter carminibus pueri inter se certarent, factum est cum hoc exercitii genere impensius delectaretur, ut diligentior esset in ediscendis multis carminibus, & scribendorum quoque versuum rationem facilius assequeretur."

12. Ibid., pp. 5–7. The monastery no longer exists. One building of the monastery still remains, serving as a Protestant church in Lixheim.

13. Ibid., p. 7. Musculus also began to study organ. The prior purchased an organ for the monastery and arranged for private lessons (at the expense of the monastery) in the neighboring town of Neuweiler.

14. Ibid., pp. 8–9.

15. Ibid., pp. 10–12.

16. Ibid., pp. 15–17.

17. According to ibid., p. 24, Musculus also began to study "very obscure rabbinic commentaries" (*rabinorum obscurissimos commentarios*) and Aramaic. In his first published work, *Ain frydsams unnd Christlichs Gesprech* (Augsburg: Philip Ulhardt?, 1533), Musculus demonstrates his familiarity with the commentaries of Rashi. He also composed his own Hebrew dictionary, the manuscript of which still exists in the Bremen Library, according

to Grote in *Wolfgang Musculus*, pp. 55–56. Grote also argues that a manuscript of a Hebrew grammar, extant in the Bern Library, was written by Musculus. However, I did not find this source in my own examination of the Bern collection.

18. *Synopsis*, pp. 19–20. One of Musculus's poems is entitled "In Tzephaniam Buceri," published in ibid., pp. 67–68.

19. Ibid., p. 25: "Designatum igitur ei primum fuit templum S. Crucis; in quo docuit septem illis annis." While every biographer has followed the *Synopsis* here in designating the Church of the Holy Cross as Musculus's first preaching post in Augsburg, this desig-nation may be an anachronism. According to Detlef von Dobschütz, "Die Geschichte der Kirchengemeinde Heilig-Kreuz und ihrer Kirche," in *Die Evangelische Heilig-Kreuz-Kirche in Augsburg* (Augsburg: Evangelisch-Lutherisches Pfarramt, 1981), pp. 9–18, the Chapel of St. Ottmar (St. Ottmarskapelle) was renovated and renamed Kirche zum Heiligen Kreuz in 1561. In July 1537 Musculus was assigned to the cathedral church (Dom), where he served until he left the city in June 1548.

20. According to *Synopsis*, p. 30, Musculus was in his fortieth year when he began his studies in Greek. This would indicate the years 1536 or 1537. However, since Musculus published his translation of Chrysostom in 1536, he must have begun his studies in Greek at an earlier date. Betuleius (1501–1554) studied classical literature at Erfurt and Tübingen. In 1523 he continued his education in Basel, where in 1529 he assumed the direction of a newly established Latin school. In 1536 Betuleius assumed the rectorate of the St. Anna Latin school in Augsburg. He brought fame to the Augsburg school through the many textbooks he authored, among which were several Latin plays based on Old Testament stories and annotated editions of the works of Cicero and Lactantius. See Karl Köberlin, *Geschichte des humanitischen Gymnasiums bei St. Anna in Augsburg von 1531 bis 1931* (Augs-burg: Gymnasium bei St. Anna, 1931), pp. 16–41; Friedrich Roth, *Augsburgs Reforma-tionsgeschichte* (Munich: Theodor Ackermann, 1904), 2:209, n. 85; and *Welt im Umbruch: Augsburg zwischen Renaissance und Barock* (Augsburg: Augsburger Druck- und Verlag-shaus, 1980), 1:328–329.

21. *Synopsis*, pp. 29–30. Musculus also acquired some knowledge of Arabic during his tenure in Augsburg. A rudimentary Arabic-Hebrew dictionary in Musculus's own hand is extant in the Bürgerbibliothek Bern (Cod. 686). Further evidence that Musculus knew some Arabic is contained in a letter from Martin Frecht to Ambrose Blaurer in which Frecht reports that he has sent a coin with an Arabic inscription to Musculus for translation. Frecht reports, however, that Musculus could not decipher the writing. Letter no. 1117 in *Brief-wechsel der Brüder Ambrosius und Thomas Blaurer 1509–1567*, ed. Traugott Schieß (Freiburg: Friedrich Ernst Fehsenfeld, 1910), 2:287–288.

22. *Ioannis Chrysostomi in D. Pauli epistolas commentarii* (Basel: Johann Herwagen, 1536).

23. *Opera D. Basilii Magni Caesariae Cappadociae Episcopi omnia* (Basel: Johann Herwagen, 1540); *Operum Divi Cyrilli Alexandrini Episcopi tomi quatuor* (Basel: Johann Herwagen, 1546); *Divi Gregorii Theologi Episcopi Nazianzeni opera omnia e graeco in latinum conversa*, in collaboration with Bilibald Pirkneimer (Basel: Johann Herwagen, 1550); *Athanasii Magni Alexandrini Episcopi, graviss. scriptoris, et sanctiss. martyris, opera* (Basel: Jerome Froben & Nicolas Episcopius, 1556). For a study of Musculus's edition of Basil, see Irena Backus, *Lectures humanistes de Basile de Césarée (Traductions latines 1439–1618)* (Paris: Etudes Augustiniennes, 1990), pt. 1, chap. 4.

24. From Eusebius, he included 10 books of the *Historia ecclesiastica* and 5 books of the *Vita Constantini*. From other ecclesiastical histories, he included 7 books from Socrates Scholasticus, 9 from Sozomen, 2 from Theodoret of Cyrrhus, and 6 from Evagrius Scholasticus. Musculus's translations continued to be reissued well into the seventeenth century. For a summary of the different editions of his translations, see Paul Romane-Musculus, "Catalogue des œuvres imprimées du théologien Wolfgang Musculus," *Revue D'Histoire et de Philosophie Religieuses* 43 (1963): 261–263. Musculus's work as a translator is summarized in *Synopsis*, pp. 29–30.

25. *Polybii Megalopolitani Historiarum libri priores quinque Nicolao Perotto Sipontino interprete. Item, epitome sequentium librorum usque ad decimum-septimum Wolfgango Musculo interprete* (Basel: Johann Herwagen, 1549). Contrary to the title, the translation in fact includes book 18. He prefaces his translation with a letter to the reader in which he writes a Christian defense of the study of history. Musculus also considered working on a Josephus project, as indicated by a letter from the Basel printer Hieronymus Froben dated March 3, 1545. In the letter Froben asks Musculus to help in the production of a new edition of Chrysostom and Josephus. The autograph exists in the Zofingen Stadtbibliothek, call number PA 15A (Ep. 109).

26. The only source that indicates this commission is the chronicle of Achilles Pirminus Gasser, "Annales Augustani" (Augsburg, 1576) (2° Cod. Aug. 41 in the Augsburg Staats- und Stadtbibliothek), fols. 541v–542r. The monasteries of the city were abandoned in 1537 when the council forbade Catholic services of worship.

27. The purchase was a considerable expenditure considering the fact that the council had given Betuleius a yearly budget of 50 guilders for the new library. The collection was purchased from Antonius Eparchus, a man living in Venice who had recently fled Turkish rule. See Loenhard Lenk, *Augsburger Bürgertum im Späthumanismus und Frühbarock (1580–1700)* (Augsburg: H. Mühlberger, 1968), p. 154; Richard Schmidbauer, *Die Augsburger Stadtbibliothekare durch vier Jahrhunderte* (Augsburg: Die Brig, 1963), pp. 19–20; *450 Jahre Staats- und Stadtbibliothek Augsburg* (Augsburg: Staats- und Stadtbibliothek, 1987), p. 7.

28. John M. Moore has demonstrated in *The Manuscript Tradition of Polybius* (Cambridge: Cambridge University Press, 1965), pp. 16–17, that Musculus in fact utilized the Polybius manuscript from the Eparchus collection in his translation of 1549. Preserved in the Augsburg Staats- und Stadtbibliothek is a catalog compiled by Hieronymus Wolf of the manuscripts sold by Eparchus: *Catalogus graecorum librorum, manuscriptorum, augustanae bibliothecae* (Augsburg: Michael Manger, 1575) (4° Aug. 202). The catalog lists a codex containing works of Cyril and four codices of Gregory of Nazianzus. The Eparchus manuscripts were moved to the Bayerische Staatsbibliothek in Munich in 1806. A textual study (such as that of Moore) comparing the Musculus editions with the Eparchus collection is needed to establish Musculus's use of the Cyril and Nazianzus manuscripts.

29. *Vom Ampt der Oberkeit in sachen der Religion und Gottesdienst. Ain bericht ausz götlicher schrifft des hailigen alten lerers und Bischoffs Augustini an Bonifacium den Kayserlichen Kriegs Graven in Aphrica* (Augsburg: Philippe Ulhardt, 1535).

30. Roth, *Augsburgs Reformationsgeschichte*, 2:288–290.

31. *Opera D. Ioannis Chrysostomi archiepiscopi* (Basel: Johann Herwagen, 1539), 5 vols. His letter to the reader appears in the beginning of the fourth volume with the title "Wolfgangus Musculus Dusanus, ad lectorem," hereafter cited as *Ad lectorem*.

32. *Ad lectorem,* p. ii: "Plurimum mihi delinquere videntur, qui ad omnia aliorum obsurdescunt, sua tamen adorant, quasi in universum defuerit priscis omnis veritatis cognitio."

33. Ibid.: "Bonum quomodo tenebit qui nihil probat, sed omnia aliorum fastidit? Quomodo probabit, qui ne legere quidem dignatur? Quomodo leget, qui summo etiam cum contemptu quaevis exibilat?"

34. Ibid., pp. ii–iii: "Non consulo ut noctesque diesque superstitiose magis quam religiose versentur scripta Patrum. Nam hoc a legendis Canonicis scripturis avocabit plurimum, quibus prima & potior studiorum nostrorum portio consecranda est. Regia potius ingrediamur via, quam sancti viri & scriptis & proprio exemplo monstrarunt. Ut enim periculum est, ne si indiscriminatim omnia complectare, pro veritate mendacium, pro certitudine voluntatis, humanae opinionis fallaciam apprehendas, ita vicissim timendum, ne si quae aliorum sunt prorsus contemnas, tuasque duntaxat cogitationes exosculere, veritatem ipsam aliorum sententiis expressam rejicias, proque illa proprii cordis phantasiam adores. Utrobique periculum est fere idem. Quid enim interest, sive propriis, sive aliorum erratis neglecta veritate decipiare?"

35. Ibid., iii.

36. Ibid.

37. Ibid., p. iv: "Vigilate fratres, vigilate, veteres astus satanae recognoscite, sanctorum Patrum studia diligentius expendite, ex illis quanta diligentia, quibusque modis & armis inania haereticorum phantasmata eventilanda sint."

38. Ibid., pp. iv–v.

39. For a discussion of these issues in a highly charged polemical context, see Musculus's *Adversus libellum Iohannis Cochlaei de sacerdotio et sacrificio novae legis aeditum* (Augsburg: Philip Ulhardt, 1544). Musculus reissued the booklet one year later in a German translation, *Auff das Büchlin Johannis Cochlei welches er zur verthüdigung Bäpstlichs Priesterthumbs unnd Messopffers im Jahr 1544 wider die leer des Euangelions inn den Truck geben hat. Erste Antwort und Ablaynung* (Augsburg: Philip Ulhardt, 1545). In the treatise, Musculus responds to Cochlaeus's charge that the Bible does not contain everything that Christians must believe, such as, for example, the orthodox formulation of Trinitarian teaching.

40. Musculus, *LC* (1563), p. 286: "Inter libros Novi testamenti sunt nonnulli, de quibus etiam veterum sententiae variant: utpote Epistola posterior Petri, duae posteriores Ioannis, Epistola Iudae, Epistola ad Ebraeos, & Apocalypsis Ioannis, quae in Concilio Laodiceno cap. 59 & ultimo, inter Canonicas scripturas non recitatur: quibus etiam eam quae Iacobo inscribitur, quidam recentiores connumerant."

41. Ibid.: "Meae modestiae non est, ut de illis pronunciem . . . . Iudicia tamen veterum hoc efficiunt, ut minus sim illis quam caeteris scripturis astrictus: licet haud facile quaevis damnanda censeam, quae in illis leguntur."

42. Ibid., pp. 293–94: "Ubi vero ex scriptis patrum aliquid contra nos adferunt, palam dico, nolle me ad illorum authoritatem adstringi. Literas enim illorum, ut Augustini verbis utar, non ut canonicas habeo, sed eas ex canonicis considero, & si quid in eis authoritati canonicarum Scripturarum congruit, accipio: sin minus, cum pace illorum respuo." Augustine, *Contra Cresconium*, book 2, chap. 32.

43. Musculus, *LC* (1563), p. 290.

44. He produces citations from Chrysostom's homilies on Matthew (Expositione 2,

Homilia 49), from several writings of Augustine (Epistolae 3, 7, 19, 166; *De doctrina Christiana*, book 1, chap. 37; book 2, chap. 6; *Contra Cresconium*, book 2, chap. 31), and from Jerome's preface to Galatians.

45. The autograph is in the Zofingen Stadtbibliothek, call number PA 15A (Ep. 242), hereafter cited as Epistola 242.

46. Epistola 242.

47. The actual focus of the controversy was on how to characterize the prohibition against graven images. The Catholics argued that this prohibition was not a separate command but an explanatory adjunct to the first command against having other gods. The command against coveting was then broken into two distinct commands in order to yield ten commandments. The Lutherans actually joined the Catholics in this scheme of enumeration. The Reformed theologians, however, argued that the prohibition of graven images was a separate command, distinct from the command against having other gods. See Bo Reicke, *Die zehn Worte in Geschichte und Gegenwart*, Beiträge zur Geschichte der biblischen Exegese 13 (Tübingen: J. C. B. Mohr, 1973).

48. Epistola 242. Musculus also discusses the controversy at length in the *Loci communes* (1563) under the topic heading "Divisio Decalogi" (pp. 53–54). He also published a previously unknown booklet on the topic entitled *Von der zaal und außtheylung der zehen gebott auß den alten Lereren gezogen* (Bern: Matthew Apiarius, 1551). The booklet is bound and virtually hidden in a large volume of manuscripts in the Zurich Zentralbibliothek, call number Ms. S 76.

49. Epistola 242: "Ubi ex Augustino pro doctrina gratiae et justificationis aliquid citamus, in promptu est adversariis ex Chrÿsostomo citare diversum, id quod exempli gratia loquor. Nam ex omnibus Patribus non dabuntur duo, quorum scripta inter se consentiant per omnia, praesertim in iis, quae ad nostram causam citari possunt."

50. Musculus, *LC* (1563), p. 293: "Quis adeo stupidus est, ut ex obscuro de claro, & non magis ex claro de obscuro iudicandum esse sentiat? Quem dabunt nobis de numero patrum, cuius scripta tanquam lucem ad illustrandas sacras Scripturas sequamur? Si cunctos, quorum scripta extant, sequi voluerimus, fiet ut quod in Scripturis sacris clarum est, adhibitis illorum expositionibus obnubiletur, propter sententiarum & expositionum diversitatem. Si unum duntaxat delegerimus, nec constabit quis nam ex illis deligendus sit: nec unius sententia certas nostras conscientias reddere poterit, caeteris diversa sentientibus."

51. Ibid., p. 291; Augustine, *De doctrina Christiana*, book 2, chap. 6.

52. Musculus, *LC* (1563), p. 293; Augustine, Epistola 19.

53. Musculus, *LC* (1563), p. 293: "Partim negligentia antiquariorum, partim temeritate haereticorum, tot seculorum decursu sic scripta patrum ab origine sua degenerarunt, ut plane stolidissimus sit, vel studiose malignus in Ecclesiam Dei, quisquis illorum calculis conscientias fidelium obstringendas esse putaverit."

54. Ibid., p. 294.

55. Ibid., p. 293.

56. Ibid., p. 292: "Obsecro, ubi consisteret universa Romana sedes cum omnibus istis personatis Episcopis, Carnalibus, Praelatis, Monachis, Academicis, Sophistis, Scotistis, Thomistis, Occamistis, & aliis id genus hominibus, qui iam seculis aliquot moderamina Christianae religionis per fas ac nephas, prece, precio, vi & armis occuparunt, si sanctorum patrum ac veterum canonum concilorumque iudicio subjicerentur?" My translation does not reflect Musculus's pun on Cardinalibus/Carnalibus.

57. See the appendix "Commentaries on the Gospel of John, 1470–1555," in Timothy J. Wengert, *Philip Melanchthon's Annotationes in Johannem in Relation to Its Predecessors and Contemporaries* (Geneva: Librairie Droz S. A., 1987), pp. 235–254. Musculus also could have read the commentary of Arnobius the Younger, which was printed in Basel in 1543 with the title *Annotationes ad quaedam evangeliorum loca* (*PL* 53:569–580). The work is actually a collection of scholien on selected pericopes from John, Matthew, and Luke. Since Arnobius does not comment on John 4:46–54, I will not utilize his commentary. See Berthold Altaner and Alfred Stuiber, *Patrologie* (Freiburg: Herder, 1978), p. 459, and Otto Bardenhewer, *Geschichte der Altkirchlichen Literatur* (Darmstadt: Wissenschaftliche Buchgesellschaft, 1962), 4:603–606.

58. He explicitly cites Augustine's *Tractates* 29 times, Chrysostom's *Homilies* 27 times, Cyril's *Commentary* 18 times, and Nonnus's *Paraphrase* 5 times.

59. For example, in his comments on John 1:14 (*Comm.* I, p. 19), Musculus presents the interpretations of Cyril and Chrysostom on the phrase "et habitavit in nobis." He pronounces their interpretations valid, saying, "Si cui ista sententia placet, per me licebit eam amplectatur." But he proceeds to offer his own contrasting interpretation. In his comments on John 3:8 ("Spiritus ubi vult spirat"), Musculus presents Cyril's and Chrysostom's understanding of *spiritus* as the wind and Augustine's understanding of *spiritus* as the Holy Spirit; Musculus proclaims either interpretation acceptable (*Comm.* I, p. 78). In his interpretation of John 1:16 (*Comm.* I, p. 26), Musculus offers the opinions of Augustine, Chrysostom, Cyril, and "recentiores" on the meaning of the phrase "gratiam pro gratia." He respectfully rejects all of their interpretations and offers his own. In his comments on John 1:49 (*Comm.* I, p. 53), Musculus presents the contrasting interpretations of Augustine and Chrysostom on Nathanael's confession and sides with Augustine. Similarly, on John 13:6ff. (*Comm.* II, pp. 299–300), Musculus prefers Augustine's to Chrysostom's interpretation. But on John 7:28 (*Comm.* I, pp. 421–422), Musculus agrees with Chrysostom against Augustine. On the identity of the unknown disciple of John 18:15, Musculus sides with Chrysostom and Cyril against Augustine (*Comm.* II, p. 415).

60. Nonnus's paraphrase received new life in the Reformation through Melanchthon, who used it in his own commentary on John and who arranged for the publication of the Greek original and a Latin translation. See Wengert, *Philip Melanchthon's Annotationes in Johannen*, pp. 64–65. See also Johannes Quasten, *Patrology*, 3 vols. (Antwerp: Spectrum, 1960), 3:114–116.

61. Raymond E. Brown, *The Gospel According to John I–XII* (New York: Doubleday, 1966), pp. 194–195.

62. Musculus, *Comm.* I, p. 150.

63. Chrysostom, *Homilies on John*, FC 33:346.

64. Cyril, *Commentary on John*, p. 232.

65. Musculus, *Comm.* I, p. 150.

66. Both the Greek New Testament term ὁ βασιλικός and the Vulgate term "regulus" are ambiguous, meaning "petty king" or "princelet." See C. K. Barrett, *The Gospel According to St. John* (Philadelphia: Westminster, 1978), p. 247.

67. The synoptic comparison occurs as early as Irenaeus (*Adversus omnes haereses* II, 22:3). See Brown, *Gospel According to John I–XII*, pp. 192–193.

68. Augustine (*Tractates on John*, FC 79:102, 105) implies he was a Jew by contrasting his faith with the faith of the Samaritans, who believed without any miracles, and with the

faith of the "foreign centurion," who believed in the power of Jesus' spoken word. Cyril (*Commentary on John*, p. 235) argues that the story indicates "the extreme readiness of the aliens to obedience."

69. Nonnus, *Paraphrasis in Joannem, PG* 43:781.

70. Chrysostom, *Homilies on John, FC* 33:347.

71. Musculus, *Comm.* I, p. 150.

72. Ibid.

73. Augustine, *Tractates on John, FC* 79:102.

74. Nonnus, *Paraphrasis in Joannem, PG* 43:781: Καὶ γενέτης φιλότεκνος ἴσῳ μαστίζετο πυρσῷ / Παιδὸς ἱμασσομένοιο, τάχα πλέον.

75. Chrysostom, *Homilies on John, FC* 33:348.

76. Augustine, *Tractates on John, FC* 79:102.

77. Cyril, *Commentary on John*, p. 233.

78. Chrysostom, *Homilies on John, FC* 33:348–349.

79. Musculus, *Comm.* I, p. 150.

80. Here Musculus quotes Mt 16:14: "Some say John the Baptist; some, Elijah, and others Jeremiah, or one of the prophets."

81. Musculus, *Comm.* I, p. 151: "Nam pro sua bonitate linum fumigans non extinguit." A reference to Is 42:3: "Et linum fumigans non exstinguet" (Vulg.).

82. Nonnus, *Paraphrasis in Joannem, PG* 43:784.

83. Augustine, *Tractates on John, FC* 79:105.

84. Ibid., p. 104.

85. Cyril, *Commentary on John*, pp. 233–234.

86. Chrysostom, *Homilies on John, FC* 33:347–349.

87. Musculus, *Comm.* I, p. 151: "Non enim dicit: Nisi videris, sed: nisi videretis signa & prodigia non creditis."

88. Ibid.

89. Ibid.: "Oremus ergo dominum, ut det nobis simplici & syncero corde verbo & evangelio regni dei credere, ut nec cum Iudaeis signa, nec cum Graecis mundi quaeramus sapientiam, sed cum electis sensum nostrum in obsequium fidei captivemus, quo Christum crucifixum dei virtutem & sapientiam solida & indubitata fide appraehendamus."

90. Ibid.

91. Ibid., p. 152.

92. Here Musculus echoes the comments of Chrysostom (*Homilies on John, FC* 33:348), who argues that the ruler failed to recognize that miracles are intended for the soul, not the body.

93. Musculus, *Comm.* I, p. 152: "Quis unquam parens ad dominum venit, qui dixerit: Domine, filius meus nullo est timore dei praeditus, nullo afficitur pietatis studio, unde intelligo illum de animae salute periclitari, succurre quaes?"

94. Ibid.

95. Ibid.: "Poterat dicere: Credisne me etiam absentem posse curare? Quid opus est, ut tecum descendam? Deinde etiamsi moriatur filius, non credis me posse mortuum vitae restituere?"

96. Ibid., p. 153.

97. Ibid.

98. Cyril, *Commentary on John*, p. 234; Chrysostom, *Homilies on John*, FC 33:350.

99. Augustine, *Tractates on John*, FC 79:104.

100. Musculus, *Comm.* I, p. 153.

101. Ibid.

102. Chrysostom, *Homilies on John*, FC 33:350.

103. Musculus, *Comm.* I, p. 153.

CHAPTER THREE

1. See, for example, *LC* (1560), pp. 429, 565.

2. Ibid., pp. 39, 40, 190, 374, 430, 435, 667, 704, 706, 726.

3. Ibid., p. 286. Musculus lists the following disputed questions: "Dum disputant, sit ne Theologia de Deo, ut de subiecto, ratione infiniti, vel attributali: an Theologia sit scientia, sub alternata ne, vel in lumine medio, practica vel speculativa, vel affectiva? an in divinis sit aliqua productio intrinseca, utrum ens dicatur univoce de Deo & creatura, an habeat proprium conceptum, an sit analogum, an quidditas rei materialis sit primum obiectum intellectus ex natura potentiae, an oporteat ponere speciem in intellectu, an essentia divina generet vel generetur, utrum unitas divinarum personarum sit collectiva, an filius sit de substantia patris quasi de materia, an essentia divina generetur subiective: an productio filij sit ex voluntate patris, vel ex necessitate, & naturalis: utrum generatio divina sit univoca vel aequivoca, an in Deo sit compositio ex materia & forma, utrum spiritussanctus producatur per actum voluntatis, an pater & filius principient uniformiter spiritum sanctum, utrum personae divinae sint aequales secundum magnitudinem, an aequalitas in divinis sit relatio realis, an Deus potuerit facere mundum meliorem: & innumera alia, de quibus inter se cententiosissime & acerbe digladiantur."

4. Ibid., p. 198: "An sit incarnatio verbi res possibilis, quid addat persona vel suppositum supra naturam, an una persona possit incarnari sine alia, quae sit formalis ratio terminandi incarnationem, utrum tres personae possint assumere eandem naturam numero: an Deus incarnatus fuisset, si homo non peccasset, . . . an Deus possit assumere naturam rationalem, an corpus Christi fuerit subito ac in instanti formatum, utrum B. Virgo operata sit aliquid active in conceptione filii sui, utrum persona possit assumere personam, an in Christo sint plura esse, an in Christo sint duae filiationes reales, utrum Christus secundum quod homo sit, sit persona, an Deus potuerit aliunde assumere hominem quam de genere Adae, & licuerit ne Deo assumere hominem de sexu foemineo, & quae alia consimilis farinae etiam de anima Christi disputant."

5. Ibid., p. 198: "Inutilis & curiosa Scholasticorum ac Sophistarum argutiae."

6. Musculus quotes from sermons 33 and 67 of the *Super Cantica Canticorum* on pp. 465, 356 of the *LC* (1560), respectively. He quotes from *In quadragesima de Psalmo "Qui habitat"* in three places: pp. 383, 400, 657. There are two citations from both *In cena Domini* (pp. 405, 445) and *In annuntiatione dominica* (pp. 335, 355) and one reference to Epistola 77 (p. 445).

7. Musculus, *LC* (1560), pp. 490, 491, 497, 498, 499, 503, 506, 509–510, 515, 516.

8. I have counted at least twenty citations of Lombard in the *LC* (1560). Occasionally, when Musculus cites an opinion of the *scholastici*, he is actually quoting from Lombard (for

example, see pp. 322, 365). Sometimes, however, Musculus distinguishes Lombard from the opinions of "quidam scholastici" (see p. 724). For additional citations of Lombard, see pp. 320, 324, 363, 366, 404, 405, 407, 409, 422, 431, 443, 565–566, 572, 573, 591, 666, 708.

9. In the order listed above, the topics appear in the *LC* (1560) on pp. 324, 350, 363, 365, 572, 573, 591, 595.

10. See, for example, Musculus's treatment of the question "An semper sit malum, quod est novum" on p. 528 of the *LC* (1560).

11. Musculus, *LC* (1560), pp. 565–566.

12. Ibid., p. 324.

13. Musculus, *In epistolas apostoli Pauli ad Galatas et Ephesios commentarii* (Basel: Johann Herwagen, 1561), p. 153.

14. Musculus, *In Esaiam prophetam commentarii locupletissimi ac recens editi* (Basel: Johann Herwagen, 1557), p. 493: "Contempto historico sensu, recta ad mysteria regni Christi trahuntur."

15. Ibid.: "Quod illorum studium quamvis haud in se culpandum sit, plurimas tamen tenebras simplicitati historicae offundit, & valvas aperit Scripturarum sensus pro cuiusvis ingenii acumine in mille formas transformandi, id quod cordatis hominibus ludus magis quam recta & sincera Scripturarum expositio esse videtur. Plurimum in eo errant, quod putant hac ratione Christi servatoris mysteria explicari, regnumque illius illustrari. Sic enim dum subtiliter omnia transformant, omnem Scripturarum expositionem . . . suspectam reddunt."

16. Musculus, *In Davidis Psalterium Sacrosanctum commentarii* (Basel: Sebastian Henricpetri, 1599), p. 166.

17. Ibid.: "Haud enim temere confugiendum est ad allegorias in exponendis Scripturis . . . nisi evidens cogat necessitas."

18. Musculus, *Comm.* I, p. 208: "Quando ipsa scripturae verba ultra literae sensum penitius introspiciuntur, ut sensus spiritus eruatur, id quod in parabolis, allegoriis, metaphoris & figuris mysticis est faciendum."

19. Ibid.

20. In the preface to his Genesis commentary, *In Mosis Genesim plenissimi commentarii, in quibus veterum & recentiorum sententiae diligenter expenduntur* (Basel: Johann Herwagen, 1554), Musculus argues that "the greatest advantage of sacred reading" (*potissimum sacrae lectionis emolumentus)* lies in the moral exposition of the biblical text.

21. In his commentaries on Matthew, John, Genesis, and the Psalms, Musculus structures his comments according to this basic pattern. His Genesis commentary, however, also adds separate sections entitled "quaestiones" in which he addresses troublesome questions raised by the text. In his Psalms commentary, Musculus includes sections entitled "lectio" in which he offers Hebrew, Septuagint, Vulgate, and patristic renderings of selected lemmata. In his commentaries on 1 and 2 Corinthians and Galatians, the breaks for observations are much less frequent, and in his commentaries on Isaiah, Philippians, Colossians, 1 and 2 Thessalonians, and 1 Timothy, there are no separate sections of observations. The moral observations have simply been absorbed into the "explanatio" sections. Only the Genesis commentary corresponds to the description of Musculus's commentaries given by Basil Hall in *The Cambridge History of the Bible III: The West from the Reformation to the Present Day* (Cambridge: Cambridge University Press, 1963), p. 91.

22. Musculus, *In Esaiam,* p. 29: "In cortice illius haerebunt, & ad nuclei suavitatem pertingere non poterunt."

23. Possible choices include the *Glossa Ordinaria* and the commentaries of Alcuin, [pseudo-] Bede, Rupert of Deutz, Theophylact, Hugh of St. Cher, Thomas Aquinas, Alexander of Hales, Albertus Magnus, Nicholas of Gorran, Euthymius Zigabenus, Nicholas of Lyra, Simon (Fidati) of Cascia, Lorenzo Valla, and Denis the Carthusian. See the appendix "Commentaries on the Gospel of John, 1470–1555," in Timothy Wengert's *Philip Melanchthon's Annotationes in Johannem in Relation to Its Predecessors and Contemporaries* (Geneva: Librairie Droz S. A., 1987), pp. 236–254.

24. From 1470 to 1544, Lyra's postils were printed at least thirty-seven times, being translated into Low German in 1478 and French in 1480. Theophylact's commentary on the fourth gospel was first published in 1524 in a Latin translation by Œcolampadius. It was printed a total of fifteen times in the period 1524–1543.

25. I have counted four citations of Lyra in Musculus's commentary (*Comm.* 1, pp. 375, 380; *Comm.* II, pp. 142, 461). Five quotations of Theophylact were found (*Comm.* I, pp. 368, 376, 380, 422; *Comm.* II, p. 178). One of Musculus's quotations from Theophylact is given in Greek (*Comm.* I, p. 376), indicating that he may have used the Blado edition of 1542. Theophylact repeats much of the exegesis of Chrysostom, a fact that Musculus himself recognizes. See *Comm.* I, p. 422, where Musculus, after citing Chrysostom, remarks: "Hunc sequitur pro suo more Theophylactus."

26. The commentaries of Thomas and Hugh were both published at least eight times in the period 1470–1537. Robert E. Lerner has recently argued that Hugh's postils on the Bible were actually produced by a consortium of exegetes at St. Jacques and that "Hugh of St. Cher, the great Dominican commentator on Scripture, is a figment of bibliographers' imaginations." See "Poverty, Preaching, and Eschatology in the Revelation Commentaries of 'Hugh of St. Cher,'" in *The Bible in the Medieval World: Essays in Memory of Beryl Smalley,* ed. Katherine Walsh and Diana Wood (Oxford: Basil Blackwell, 1985), pp. 157–189.

27. First published in 1532, Denis's commentary was reissued in 1542 and 1543.

28. The only other early medieval John commentaries are those of [pseudo-] Bede and Alcuin, both of which are heavily dependent on Augustine's *Tractates.* While Musculus does not refer explicitly to Rupert's John commentary, he does quote Rupert's Matthew commentary on p. 318 of his *Comm.* II. He also refers to an opinion of the Gloss at *Comm.* II, p. 142.

29. Rupert of Deutz, *Commentaria in Evangelium Sancti Iohannis, CCSL* 9:300–301, hereafter cited as *Comm. in Evang. Iohannis.*

30. Hugh, *Postilla super Joannem,* fol. 322r.

31. Musculus, *Comm.* I, p. 218.

32. Ibid.; Rupert, *Comm. in Evang. Iohannis, CCSL* 9:301; Hugh, *Postilla super Joannem,* fol. 322r; Denis, *Enarratio in Joannem,* p. 382.

33. Musculus, *Comm.* I, p. 218; Denis, *Enarratio in Joannem,* p. 382.

34. Musculus, *Comm.* I, pp. 218–219; Denis, *Enarratio in Joannem,* p. 382; *Biblia sacra cum glossis, interlineari et ordinaria, Nicolai Lyrani postilla* (Venice, 1588), 5:203b, hereafter cited as *Postilla* for Lyra and *Glossa* for the *Glossa ordinaria;* Thomas, *Commentary on John,* p. 340; Hugh, *Postilla super Joannem,* fol. 322r; Theophylact, *Enarratio in Evangelion*

Joannis, PG 123:1284, hereafter cited as *Enar. in Evang. Joannis*; Chrysostom, *Homilies on John, FC* 33:424.

35. Musculus, *Comm.* I, p. 219: "Certa quadam ac destinata dispensatione sit exequutus."

36. Rupert, *Comm. in Evang. Iohannis, CCSL* 9:303.

37. Theophylact, *Enar. in Evang. Joannis, PG* 123:1284; Thomas, *Commentary on John,* p. 341. Chrysostom argues that their following of Jesus "was not an indication of a very stable mental attitude." They should have followed Jesus because of his teaching (*Homilies on John, FC* 33:424).

38. Musculus, *Comm.* I, p. 219.

39. Lyra, *Postilla,* p. 203b.

40. Hugh, *Postilla super Joannem,* fol. 322v; Denis, *Enarratio in Joannem,* p. 382: "Et quoniam Dominus Iesus etiam secundum corpus speciosus valde et eloquentissimus fuit . . . verisimile est quod multi sequenbantur eum delectati specie et eloquentia eius."

41. Lyra, *Postilla,* p. 203b.

42. Musculus, *Comm.* I, p. 220.

43. Ibid.: "Lupi ululatum intellexerit: & scapulam ovis in mensa loquentem sibi, ne se ederet, eo quod venenum haberet, audiverit: et quod noctu in coelum ascenderit: item quod orbem Lunae diviserit, & rursus integrarit." Musculus is in fact recounting authentic legends that developed in popular Islam. The disputations with Christians gave impetus to this tendency to apotheosize the Prophet. See Annemarie Schimmel, *Und Muhammed ist Sein Prophet: Die Verehrung des Propheten in der islamischen Frömmigkeit* (Düsseldorf: Eugen Diedrichs, 1981), pp. 51–85.

44. Lyra, *Postilla,* p. 203b; Theophylact, *Enar. in Evang. Joannis, PG* 123:1284; Denis, *Enarratio in Joannem,* p. 383; Thomas, *Commentary on John,* p. 341. According to Chrysostom, the mountain is a suitable place for solitude and prayer (*Homilies on John, FC* 33:425).

45. Theophylact, *Enar. in Evang. Joannis, PG* 123:1284.

46. Musculus, *Comm.* I, p. 221.

47. Ibid. Chrysostom also argues that when Christ sat with his disciples, it was for a lofty purpose, "perhaps to explain something to them, or to teach them, or to attract them to himself" (*Homilies on John, FC* 33:425).

48. Denis, *Enarratio in Joannem,* p. 383: "Nam, sicut saepe observavit legalia, ostendendo se hominem verum factum sub lege; sic interdum praetermisit ea, ostendens se verum Deum ac legislatorem supra legem."

49. Theophylact, *Enar. in Evang. Joannis, PG* 123:1284; Thomas, *Commentary on John,* p. 342; Hugh, *Postilla super Joannem,* fol. 322v. Perhaps these commentators take their cue from Chrysostom, who claims that Jesus avoided the Passover festival in order to show that "in future He would be gradually breaking away from the Law, taking occasion from the perversity of the Jews" (*Homilies on John, FC* 33:425).

50. Lyra, *Postilla,* p. 203b.

51. Musculus, *Comm.* I, p. 222: "Quomodo contra legem dei faciebant, & non magis hanc adimplebant, qui relicto paschate illo umbratili ac figurali verum pascha Christum sequebantur?"

52. Rupert, *Comm. in Evang. Iohannis, CCSL* 9:305; Theophylact, *Enar. in Evang. Joannis, PG* 123:1286; Hugh, *Postilla super Joannem,* fol. 323r; Thomas, *Commentary on John,* p. 343; Denis, *Enarratio in Joannem,* p. 383.

53. Rupert, *Comm. in Evang. Iohannis, CCSL* 9:305.

54. Theophylact, *Enar. in Evang. Joannis, PG* 123:1286; Hugh, *Postilla super Joannem,* fol. 323r; Thomas, *Commentary on John,* p. 343; Denis, *Enarratio in Joannem,* p. 383. These commentators are reiterating the basic interpretation of Chrysostom in *Homilies on John, FC* 33:426.

55. Denis, *Enarratio in Joannem,* p. 383.

56. Theophylact, *Enar. in Evang. Joannis, PG* 123:1286; Hugh, *Postilla super Joannem,* fol. 323r; Lyra, *Postilla,* p. 204a.

57. Musculus, *Comm.* I, pp. 224–225.

58. Ibid., p. 225.

59. See, for example, Hugh, *Postilla super Joannem,* fols. 323r–323v. The distinction between Philip and Andrew owes its inspiration to Chrysostom, who argues that Philip "most needed instruction" and that Andrew "had a more exalted view than Philip" (*Homilies on John, FC* 33:426–428).

60. Musculus, *Comm.* I, pp. 225–226.

61. Ibid., p. 226: "Ne putemus ingentes fuisse hos pisces, quales plerunque in mari capiuntur."

62. Ibid., p. 227: "Et ob eam causam aedita sunt miracula, ut humana ratio in stuporem & admirationem adducta divinae virtutis cognitioni ac fidei locum faciat."

63. Ibid.: "In credentibus non extinguat, sed inconcussum retineat, illoque hactenus utatur, ut admirationi operum dei serviat."

64. Theophylaet, *Enar. in Evang. Joannis, PG* 123:1288; Thomas, *Commentary on John,* p. 346; Lyra, *Postilla,* p. 204a; Denis, *Enarratio in Joannem,* p. 384.

65. Thomas, *Commentary on John,* p. 346.

66. Musculus, *Comm.* I, p. 229.

67. Hugh, *Postilla super Joannem,* fol. 324r; Chrysostom, *Homilies on John, FC* 33:429–430.

68. Thomas, *Commentary on John,* p. 347; Theophylact, *Enar. in Evang Joannis, PG* 123:1288.

69. Lyra, *Postilla,* p. 204a.

70. Musculus, *Comm.* I, p. 233: "Respondeo: Si solam divinam in Christo naturam inspicias, non invenies, qua ratione Christo convenerit patri gratias agere."

71. Ibid., pp. 233–234.

72. Thomas, *Commentary on John,* p. 347.

73. Theophylact, *Enar. in Evang. Joannis, PG* 123:1288. His version reads: ἔλαβε δὲ τοὺς ἄρτους ὁ Ἰησοῦς καὶ εὐχαριστήσας διέδωκε τοῖς μαθηταῖς οἱ δὲ μαθηταὶ τοῖς ἀνακειμένοις.

74. Musculus and Erasmus both translate verse 11 as: "Accepit autem panes Iesus, cumque gratias egisset, distribuit discipulis: discipulis vero discumbentibus." See Desiderius Erasmus, *Erasmus' Annotations on the New Testament: The Gospels,* ed. Anne Reeve (London: Duckworth, 1986), p. 240.

75. Theophylact, *Enar. in Evang. Joannis, PG* 123:1288; Hugh, *Postilla super Joannem,* fol. 324v; Thomas, *Commentary on John,* p. 347. Chrysostom writes that the excess "was not an empty display of power, but was intended that the miracle might not be thought an illusion" (*Homilies on John, FC* 33:430).

76. Rupert, *Comm. in Evang. Iohannis, CCSL* 9:309; Denis, *Enarratio in Joannem,* p. 385.

77. Lyra, *Postilla,* p. 204a.

78. Theophylact, *Enar. in Evang. Joannis*, PG 123:1288; Hugh, *Postilla super Joannem*, fol. 324v; Thomas, *Commentary on John*, p. 347; Lyra, *Postilla*, p. 204a. See also Chrysostom, *Homilies on John*, FC 33:431.

79. Musculus, *Comm.* I, p. 235.

80. *Glossa*, p. 204a.

81. Lyra, *Postilla*, p. 204a. Augustine makes the opposite point, arguing that because of their carnal understanding, they confessed Jesus to be a prophet without realizing that he was the special prophet foretold in Deuteronomy 18 (*Tractates on John*, FC 79:237). Chrysostom praises the confession itself but decries the fact that it was prompted by their full bellies (*Homilies on John*, FC 33:431–432).

82. Hugh, *Postilla super Joannem*, fol. 324v; Thomas, *Commentary on John*, p. 349; Denis, *Enarratio in Joannem*, p. 385.

83. Thomas, *Commentary on John*, pp. 348–349.

84. Denis, *Enarratio in Joannem*, pp. 385–386: "Quamvis vero intellectualis cognitio Christi fuit perfecta, non proprie prophetalis, tamen secundum notitiam imaginativae potentiae, habuit convenientiam cum Prophetis, quia in imaginatione animae Christi formari poterant formae sensibiles, per quas occulta atque futura repraesentabantur animae suae."

85. Musculus, *Comm.* I, p. 238.

86. Ibid., p. 239: "Diversis respectibus idem Christus & propheta est, & Dominus prophetarum, & rex, & sacerdos, & pastor, & doctor, & servus, & dominus, & homo, & Deus, & caro, & verbum, & filius Dei & apostolus, etc. Non ergo negatur dominus esse prophetarum, si quando propheta vocatur sicuti non negatur esse filius Dei, quando servus & minister, & apostolus, & sacerdos vocatur, neque Deus negatur, quando homo & filius hominis nominatur. In his appellationibus nemo errabit, nisi qui duas in Christo naturas, & rationem susceptae dispensationis non intelligit."

87. Ibid., pp. 239–242.

88. Rupert, *Comm. in Evang. Iohannis*, CCSL 9:312; Thomas, *Commentary on John*, p. 349; Lyra, *Postilla*, p. 204b; Chrysostom, *Homilies on John*, FC 33:432–433.

89. Musculus, *Comm.* I, pp. 242–243, 245.

90. Denis, *Enarratio in Joannem*, p. 386.

91. Thomas, *Commentary on John*, p. 344.

92. Denis, *Enarratio in Joannem*, p. 384: "Condemnata est ergo deliciositas, gulositas atque carnalitas nostra." See also Chrysostom, *Homilies on John*, FC 33:428.

93. Hugh, *Postilla super Joannem*, fol. 323v.

94. Musculus, *Comm.* I, p. 228: "Animos mortalium non satiant ingentes pecuniarum & opum cumuli."

95. Ibid.: "Stomachus modico cibo, necessario videlicet, assuetus, & facile satiatur & minus adfert molestiae, luxui vero deditus, & multa poscit, nec quiescit, nisi solitam adeptus abundantiam."

96. Ibid. In his discussion of this *via media*, Musculus recounts an interesting event that took place at the Colloquy of Worms (1540), which he attended as a delegate from Augsburg. A Catholic delegate, Musculus claims, publicly attacked Philip Melanchthon for neglecting the importance of fasting. Yet this same man (whose name Musculus does not mention) had only the day before feasted extravagantly and was "red and swollen by Bacchus" (*ruber atque inflatus Iacho*). Musculus defends Melanchthon as one who exhib-

ited temperance and frugality of life "by his very appearance and by his body, thinned in a wonderful way" (*ipso aspectu, & corpore mirum in modum extenuato*).

97. See, for example, Hugh's remark that "per hoc vult ostendere, quod qui comestionem incipiunt, gratias agere Deo oportet" (*Postilla super Joannem*, fol. 324r). Chrysostom also remarks that Jesus' prayer teaches "that those who are beginning to partake of food ought to give thanks to God" (*Homilies on John, FC* 33:430).

98. Musculus, *Comm.* I, p. 232: "Ut nec agnitio beneficii sine laude ac benedictione Dei, nec benedictio dei sine agnitione beneficii, gratiarum actionem constituat."

99. Ibid., pp. 232–233.

100. Ibid., pp. 233–234.

101. Rupert, *Comm. in Evang. Iohannis, CCSL* 9:309; Hugh, *Postilla super Joannem*, fol. 324v; Denis, *Enarratio in Joannem*, p. 385.

102. Musculus, *Comm.* I, p. 235.

103. Ibid., p. 236: "Quomodo miraculoso isto pastu, quasi in tabella quadam convivium spiritualis ac coelestis alimoniae depictum sit, quo non corpora sed animae, non temporaria sed sempiterna pascuntur alimonia."

104. Ibid.

105. Rupert, *Comm. in Evang. Iohannis, CCSL* 9:310; Theophylact, *Enar. in Evang. Joannis, PG* 123:1289; Denis, *Enarratio in Joannem*, p. 385.

106. *Glossa*, p. 204a; Rupert, *Comm. in Evang. Iohannis, CCSL* 9:306–307; Thomas, *Commentary on John*, pp. 344–345. The equation of the loaves with the five books of Moses owes its inspiration to Augustine, *Tractates on John, FC* 79:234.

107. Hugh, *Postilla super Joannem*, fol. 324r.

108. Ibid., fol. 323v.

109. Denis, *Enarratio in Joannem*, pp. 387–388.

110. Musculus, *Comm.* l, p. 236.

111. Hugh, *Postilla super Joannem*, fol. 323v.

112. Rupert, *Comm. in Evang. Iohannis, CCSL* 9:307: "At illae Scripturae secundum litteralem sensum non ualde magnae sunt."

113. Musculus, *Comm.* I, p. 236.

114. Ibid., pp. 236–237: "Negociosos ac tumultuantes animos non saginat haec mensa, sed discumbentes ac quietos."

115. *Glossa*, p. 204a; Rupert, *Comm. in Evang. Iohannis, CCSL* 9:308; Thomas, *Commentary on John*, p. 346; Hugh, *Postilla super Joannem*, fol. 323v; Denis, *Enarratio in Joannem*, p. 388. These commentators are following Augustine, who writes that "they were reclining in the grass; therefore they understood carnally and rested in carnal things. For all flesh is grass" (*Tractates on John, FC* 79:236).

116. Rupert, *Comm. in Evang. Iohannis, CCSL* 9:308; Hugh, *Postilla super Joannem*, fol. 324r.

117. Musculus, *Comm.* I, p. 237.

118. Ibid.: "Etiam in hoc anagogico sensu ratione non caret, quod dominus panes istos in manus suas accepit, gratias egit, fregit ac distribuit discipulis, & per discipulos turbis. Hac imagine delineatum est verbi ministerium."

119. Rupert, *Comm. in Evang. Iohannis, CCSL* 9:308–309.

120. Musculus, *Comm.* I, p. 237: "Potest sine verbo, & sine ministris abunde instruere & pascere mortalium mentes, verum & verbo & ministris utitur."

121. Ibid.: "Repudiata ministrandi humilitate, magisterii ac dominii fastigium tanquam veri antichristi ad se rapiunt."

122. Ibid.: "Nec philosophia, nec lex, famen mentium tollere potuerunt, sed hanc magis auxerunt, solus vero convivator iste Christus pabulo verbi sui, credentium mentes recreat, satiat, & pacificat."

123. Ibid.: "Praepostera securitas conscientiae, vel ex impietate, vel ex falsa fiducia meritorum propriorum vel alienorum, aut ex persuasione misericordiae dei, sine vera resipiscentia et renovatione mentis."

124. Ibid., pp. 237–238: "Saturis obrepat fastidium coelestis alimoniae, & irreverentia quaedam erga verbi Christi copiam & abundantiam."

125. *Glossa*, p. 204a; Theophylact, *Enar. in Evang. Joannis*, *PG* 123:1289; Denis, *Enarratio in Joannem*, p. 385; Augustine, *Tractates on John*, *FC* 79:236.

126. Musculus, *Comm.* I, p. 238: "Ne proteratur contemptim, nec altercandi libidine discerpatur, sed intactum & illibatum cum reverentia in promptuarium spiritus sancti, futuris usibus servandum reponatur."

127. Ibid.

128. Ibid., pp. 221–222: "Sedet cum suis dominus, quos ex humili hoc depressoque mundi huius deserto, ad verae fidei, pietatis, coelestisque conversationis sublimitatem elegit."

129. Rupert, *Comm. in Evang. Iohannis*, *CCSL* 9:302–303; Thomas, *Commentary on John*, p. 340; Denis, *Enarratio in Joannem*, p. 386.

130. Thomas, *Commentary on John*, p. 341.

131. Denis, *Enarratio in Joannem*, p. 382: "Christus enim propter sanctissimae vitae excellentiam, propter miraculorum eminentiam, propter contemplationis celsitudinem, propter caritatis omniumque virtutum incomparabilem sublimitatem, mons appellatur."

132. Musculus, *Comm.* I, p. 222: "In vanitatibus huius mundi, nec sedent, nec vivunt, sed in monte regni dei, in quo Christus sedet."

133. Ibid.: "Quae in hac vita orditur, in futura plenitudinem ac perfectionem suam acquiret, postquam ex hac miseriarum valle, ex omnibus huius vitae molestiis erepti mortis beneficio, & interventu ad coelestia migraverimus, ubi cum Christo in sempiternum sedebimus & quiescemus."

CHAPTER FOUR

1. In addition to his quotations of Church Fathers, Musculus quotes Plato, Plutarch, Pythagoras, Thales of Miletus, Menander, Euripides, Cato, Persius, Cicero, Virgil, Livy, and Valerius Maximus.

2. It is not my intention here to enter the longstanding debate regarding the nature and definition of Renaissancc humanism. I am using the terms "humanist" and "humanism" in their broadest sense to designate the movement that developed in Italy in the early fourteenth century and spread north of the Alps in the fifteenth century. I understand this movement generally in the way it has been described by Paul Oskar Kristeller as a broad cultural, literary, and educational movement devoted to a renewed study of classical literature, the *studia humanitatis*, and the ideal of eloquence (*Renaissance Thought: The Classic,*

Scholastic, and Humanist Strains [New York: Harper, 1961], pp. 3–22). By using this broad definition, I omit in this chapter other sixteenth-century exegetes who qualify as humanists. Melanchthon, for example, undoubtedly remained committed throughout his life to the humanist approach to the study of texts that emphasized history, rhetoric, and philology. However, the content of Melanchthon's commentary on John is shaped primarily by the Wittenberg theology. Timothy Wengert (*Philip Melanchthon's Annotationes in Johannem in Relation to Its Predecessors and Contemporaries* [Geneva: Librairie Droz S. A., 1987], pp. 139–141) has demonstrated that except for certain methodological concerns (i.e., his use of "loci communes"), Melanchthon's commentary is remarkably free of the influence of northern humanism. Therefore, I have treated Melanchthon together with other representatives of the Wittenberg theology in chapter 6.

3. The Complutensian Greek New Testament was printed in 1514 but was not bound and published until the editors received a papal license in 1520. The first edition of Erasmus's work is available in a modern facsimile edition: *Novum Instrumentum* (Stuttgart-Bad Cannstatt: Frommann-Holzboog, 1986).

4. Erasmus's *Annotationes* on the four gospels are available in a modern facsimile edition of the 1535 text, collated with all four earlier editions: Anne Reeve, ed., *Erasmus' Annotations on the New Testament: The Gospels* (London: Duckworth, 1986). References to the *Annotationes* are to Reeve's edition. For studies on the *Annotationes*, see especially Erika Rummel, *Erasmus' Annotations on the New Testament: From Philologist to Theologian* (Toronto: University of Toronto Press, 1986); Jerry H. Bentley, "Erasmus' *Annotationes in Novum Testamentum* and the Textual Criticism of the Gospels," *Archiv für Reformationsgeschichte* 67 (1976): 33–53; Albert Rabil, Jr., *Erasmus and the New Testament: The Mind of a Christian Humanist* (San Antonio: Trinity University Press, 1972).

5. For studies on the paraphrases, see Jacques Chomarat, "Grammar and Rhetoric in the Paraphrases of the Gospels by Erasmus," *Erasmus of Rotterdam Society Yearbook One* (1981), pp. 30–68; Albert Rabil, Jr., "Erasmus' Paraphrase of the Gospel of John," *Church History* 48 (1979): 142–155; Albert Rabil, Jr., "Erasmus' Paraphrases of the New Testament," in *Essays on the Works of Erasmus*, ed. Richard L. DeMolen (New Haven: Yale University Press, 1978), 145–161; Roland H. Bainton, "The Paraphrases of Erasmus," *Archiv für Reformationsgeschichte* 57 (1966): 67–75; Joseph Coppens, "Les idées réformistes d'Erasme dans les Préfaces aux Paraphrases du Nouveau Testament," in *Scrinium Lovaniense*, ed. Etienne van Cauwenbergh (Louvain: Editions J. Duculot, S. A. Gembloux, 1961), 344–371; Rudolf Padberg, "Glaubenstheologie und Glaubensverkündigung bei Erasmus von Rotterdam dargestellt auf der Grundlage der Paraphrase zum Römerbrief," in *Verkündigung und Glaube: Festgabe für Franz X. Arnold*, ed. T. Filthaut and J. A. Jungmann (Freiburg: Herder, 1958), pp. 58–75; and Hermann Schlingensiepen, "Erasmus als Exeget auf Grund seiner Schriften zu Matthäus," *Zeitschrift für Kirchengeschichte* 48 (1929): 16–57.

6. Four significant editions of the Greek New Testament were available to Musculus as he worked on his commentary: the 1516 and 1527 Erasmus editions, the 1522 Complutensian edition, and the 1534 edition of Colinaeus. T. H. L. Parker, *Calvin's New Testament Commentaries* (Grand Rapids: Eerdmans, 1971), pp. 93–123, gives a very helpful analysis of the different editions of the Greek New Testament that were published in the first half of the sixteenth century.

7. Analyzed on a verse-by-verse basis, Musculus's deviations from the Erasmus trans-

lation average about six verses per chapter. The range is quite high, with only one devia-
tion occurring in chapters 2 and 13 and eighteen deviations occurring in chapter 6. I have
collated Musculus's text with a 1520 printing of Erasmus's Latin text taken from the 1519
edition—*Novum Testamentum totum Erasmo interpraete per eum castigatis aliquot locis, in
quibus operatum incuria, fuerat erratum, adiecta et nova illius praefatione* (Antwerp: Michael
Hillenius, 1520)—and with a 1555 printing of Robert Estienne's Vulgate based on his 1540
edition—*Biblia* (Paris: Conrad Badius, 1555). References to Erasmus's Latin and to the
Vulgate in the analysis that follows will be based on these editions. Greek citations are from
Erasmus's *Novum Instrumentum omne* (Basel: J. Froben, 1516). In order to avoid a tedious
array of notes, I do not indicate the page numbers of citations from these editions, or from
the biblical citations of Musculus. The reader will easily find these citations *ad locum* indicated by the reference to chapter and verse.

8. Erasmus confesses his inability to decide on the best Latin equivalent of the Greek
phrase in his notes on John 16:23 in his *Annotationes*. The expression *in nomine meo*, he
argues, is precise but inelegant, while *nomine meo* is elegant but less precise. *Sub nomine
meo* is also possible, he suggests, but "it does not express exactly the same thing" (*non
prorsus idem exprimit*). At John 17:11 Erasmus translates ἐν τῷ ὀνόματί σου as *per nomen
tuum*. Musculus adopts this rendering in his own translation but argues that *in nomine
tuo*, as the Vulgate has it, "squares better with the mind of Christ, than that which Erasmus
translates, per nomen tuum" (*rectius ad mentem Christi quadrat, quam quod Erasmus vertit,
per nomen tuum*).

9. Musculus, *Comm.* I, p. 288: "Erasmus, magis Latini sermonis structurae consulturus,
quam mentem verborum domini expressurus."

10. Ibid.: "Non animarum tantum, sed & corporum, ut ne corpora quidem electorum,
quamvis morte absorpta & pulveri commissa, imo in pulverem conversa, peritura sint."

11. Ibid.: "Satius est ut simpliciter sicut verba habent, cum vulgata aeditione legamus."

12. Erasmus, *Annotationes*, on 2 Cor 11, n. 22. This is noted in Rummel, *Erasmus' Annotations on the New Testament*, pp. 91–92.

13. Musculus, *Comm.* II, p. 178: "Nemini praeiudicio, sed quid mihi videatur simpliciter
dico. Quoniam verba Domini non habent περισσότερον, id est abundantius, sed simpliciter
περισσόν, quae dictio abundantiam, copiam, & affluentiam significat: arbitror Dominum
loqui de omnis generis copia & abundantia coelestis gratiae & benedictionis, quam una
cum vita habeant in ipsum credentes, ita ut non vitam modo credentibus in se polliceatur,
sed & veram illam felicitatem & omnium bonorum exuberantiam, quae veram vitam in
regno Dei comitatur, ac si germanice dicat, ich aber bin komen daß sie leben und alles ubrig
gnug habend."

14. Ibid.

15. Ibid., p. 194.

16. Musculus, *Comm.* I, pp. 89–90.

17. Ibid., p. 351; cf. ibid., p. 350.

18. C. A. L. Joirrot, "Erasmus' *In Principio Erat Sermo*: A Controversial Translation,"
Studies in Philology 61 (1964): 35–40.

19. Musculus, *Comm.* I, p. 5: "Erasmi versio quae habet, Hic erat in principio apud
deum. Amphibola est, ut & de deo & de verbo eius exponi possit demonstratio, hic, & tam
intelligi quod deus in principio fuerit apud deum, quam sermo. Monui autem supra non

absque singulari cautione Evangelistam non dicere, & deus erat apud deum: sed & verbum erat apud deum. Proinde malo iuxta veterem versionem legere. In principio erat verbum."

20. See, for example, John 4:27, 5:45, 8:23. In each of these places, Musculus rejects the translation of Erasmus for another rendering given in the *Annotationes*.

21. See, for example, his comments on John 14:1, 14:2, 21:22.

22. See, for example, his argument concerning the meaning of the verb σώζεσθαι at John 10:9. Erasmus does not gloss the word in the *Annotationes*. Yet in Erasmian fashion, Musculus offers a lengthy explanation of the word's meaning, supported by a quotation from Virgil.

23. Musculus, *Comm.* I, p. 10: "Illud annotavit Erasmus, quod Graeca dictio ἀναμάρτητος non eum notet qui nihil peccarit, sed eum qui ne possit quidem peccare."

24. This would indicate that Musculus is using the 1535 edition of the *Annotationes* since Erasmus's definition does not occur in any of the earlier editions.

25. Musculus, *Comm.* I, pp. 21–22: "Duriusculum quidem est, quod non dicit plenem, ut ad gloriam, vel pleni, ut ad unigenitum referatur, sed plenum: quasi haec omnia, et vidimus gloriam eius gloriam tanquam unigeniti a patre, veluit parenthesis vice inserta sint, ut haud immerito Erasmus haec verba ad ea, quae de Ioanne sequuntur pertinere suspicetur. Verum sequamur receptam lectionem, ut non de Ioanne, sed de Christo Evangelistam hic loqui intelligamus."

26. Musculus, *Comm.* II, p. 50: "Illud τὴν ἀρχήν, quod Erasmus reddidit, in primis, nihil aliud significat, quam vel praecipue, vel ante omnia, vel in summa. . . . Arbitror itaque Evangelistam hunc sensum verborum Domini hac formula exprimere voluisse . . . id est, hoc sum ante omnia & in summa quod vobis iam toties esse me dico. Si quis alia desiderat, legat Erasmum."

27. Ibid.: "Loquutus est Dominus dubio procul non Graece, sed vel Ebraice, vel Syriace, ut verisimile sit illum dixisse vel ברשונה vel רבשית quod non solum in principio, ut ad ordinem & seriem rerum sit respiciendum, sed & in summa, & caput, significat." The suspicion that Jesus spoke Syriac was common in the sixteenth century. Erasmus himself, in the preface to his *Paraphrasis in Ioannem*, suggests that Hebrew or Syriac was Jesus' spoken tongue.

28. See, for example, his comments on John 1:17 (*Comm.* I, pp. 27–28), 2:11 (ibid., pp. 62–63); 6:50 (ibid., p. 304); 9:37 (*Comm.* II, p. 263); 15:9 (ibid., p. 350); 15:25 (ibid., p. 360), 20:1 (ibid., p. 443).

29. Erasmus farmed out the Hebrew studies of the *Annotationes* to his editorial assistant, Johannes Œcolampadius.

30. Bethany is in fact the reading of most manuscripts. Erasmus, however, follows the lead of Origen, who was unable to find a Bethany beyond the Jordan in his travels in Palestine. See C. C. Tarelli, "Erasmus' Manuscripts of the Gospels," *Journal of Theological Studies* 44 (1943): 157.

31. Musculus, *Comm.* I, p. 37: "Vetus translatio mendose habet Bethaniam. Quanquam iam corrigi coepit, etiam ab illis qui Erasmicam respuunt."

32. Ibid.: "Vicio impressoris, qui pro Bethabara mendosa metathesi reddidit Bethbaara."

33. Musculus, *Comm.* II, p. 283: "Formatus est hic sermo prophetae in praeterito, more Hebraeae linguae, legi tamen potest in futuro sic, Quis credet auditiui, id est, sermoni nostro? & brachium Domini cui revelabitur? Loquutus est enim propheta eo capite de passione ac morte Christi."

34. Ibid.: "Si puncta abijcias in Hebraeo, perinde legere poteris, Quis credet auditui eius, Christi videlicet: atque, Quis credet auditui nostro. Etenim articulus נו non modo nos, & nostrum, sed & eum, & eius significat: ut illud לשמועתנו aeque, si dages sit in litera, Num, auditiui eius, atque auditui nostro, legi queat."

35. Ibid.: "Certe lectio pulcherrime proposito Evangelistae quadraret."

36. Ibid., p. 284. Cf. Musculus, *In Esaiam Prophetam Commentarii* (Basel: J. Herwagen, 1557), p. 719.

37. Musculus, *Comm.* l, p. 373: "Chrysostomus omnino non legit οὐ γὰρ ἤθελεν, id est, non enim volebat, sed οὐ γὰρ εἶχε τὴν ἐξουσίαν περιπατεῖν ἐν τῇ Ἰουδαία, id est, non enim habebat potestam circueundi in Galilaea. Sed hac de re vide annot. Erasmi."

38. Musculus, *Comm.* II, p. 325: "Quam possint quadrifariam legi, annotatum est ab Erasmo."

39. Musculus uses language very similar to Erasmus's in describing the disagreement between the two Fathers. This similarity of language and the fact that Musculus in numerous places explicitly cites the *Annotationes* strongly suggests his reliance on Erasmus at this place. We also find Musculus repeating Erasmus's summaries of patristic opinion at John 1:16, 3:8.

40. John B. Payne, Albert Rabil, and Warren S. Smith, "The *Paraphrases* of Erasmus: Origen and Character," in *Collected Works of Erasmus*, vol. 42: *New Testament Scholarship: Paraphrases on Romans and Galatians*, ed. Robert D. Sider (Toronto: University of Toronto Press, 1984), pp. xv–xvi.

41. In *The Correspondence of Erasmus*, vol. 9: *Letters 1252 to 1355*, trans. R. A. B. Mynors (Toronto: University of Toronto Press, 1989), p. 243, no. 1333, "To Archduke Ferdinand."

42. Musculus also frequently offers German paraphrases introduced by the formula "et nos Germani dicimus" (and we Germans say).

43. Musculus, *Comm.* I, p. 288 (Jn 6:39); *Comm.* II, p. 444 (Jn 19:35).

44. Faber, *Commentarii initiatorii in quatuor Evangelia* (Basel: Andreas Cratander, 1523), fol. 324r, hereafter cited as *Comm. init.*; Musculus, *Comm.* I, p. 421. Timothy Wengert, *Philip Melanchthon's Annotationes in Johannem*, p. 135, argues that the interpretation of John 7:28 as an ironical statement originates with Faber's commentary.

45. Melanchthon, *Annotationes in Ioannem*, CR 14:1113: "Non puto ironiam esse sed simplicem sententiam."

46. Bucer, *Enarratio in Iohannem*, p. 300: "Respondit eis per ironiam qua significabat eos falli, neque id scire quod iactabant."

47. Erasmus, *Paraphrasis in Evangelium secundum Ioannem, ad illustrissimum principem Ferdinandum, per autorem recognita* (Basel: J. Froben, 1534), pp. 137–138, hereafter cited as *Paraphrasis*. Chrysostom argues that night had overtaken the disciples when they set out across the lake. The Evangelist purposefully relates the time to indicate the disciples' willingness to risk the dangers of a nighttime passage on the lake (*Homilies on John*, FC 33:436).

48. Faber, *Comm. init.*, fols. 313v–314r: "Nam indefinitum nonnunquam etiam pro praeterito imperfecto capi solet, maxime ubi materia id exigit, quod hic esse videtur."

49. Erasmus defends this translation in the *Annotationes*, p. 240.

50. Musculus, *Comm.* I, pp. 247–248: "Si vespera iam tum fuit, antequam de pascendis istis turbas consultaretur, quomodo hic noster discipulos ubi vespera facta esset navim abituros conscendisse dicit? Nam omnino aliquot horas pascendas turbis insumptas fuisse

credendum est." Chrysostom avoids these difficulties by arguing that the synoptic account relates a different miracle than the one related in John (*Homilies on John, FC* 33:437–438). Hugh of St. Cher repeats Chrysostom's argument but notes additionally that "tamen communiter dicitur ab aliis, quod idem fuit miraculum hic & ibi, sed quod ibi narratum est, non oportuit Evangelistam hic omnino totum ponere" (*Postilla super Joannem*, fol. 326r). Thomas Aquinas also notes Chrysostom's argument but argues for the "better opinion" that sees John and Matthew as describing the same miracle (*Commentary on John*, p. 353).

51. Musculus, *Comm.* I, p. 248: "Est autem vespera non unius tantum horae spacium, sed complectitur in se vulgariter omne illud tempus, quod a tertia promeridiana est ad noctis usque tenebras" (reading *pomeridiana* for *promeridiana*).

52. Erasmus, *Paraphrasis*, p. 137.

53. Faber, *Comm. init.*, fol. 314r: "Nam id verisimile non est, quod fuerint Capharnaum, & deinde redierint ad mare, remigantes iterum unde venerant. Nam si trans fretum fuissent, illic expectassent dominum."

54. Musculus, *Comm.* I, p. 248: "Si diligenter expendas nihil erit hic discrepantiae."

55. Thomas argues similarly (*Commentary on John*, p. 353) that Capernaum and Gennesaret are neighboring towns on the same side of the lake. The disciples landed somewhere in the vicinity of both towns, and therefore Matthew mentions Gennesaret, while John mentions Capernaum.

56. Musculus, *Comm.* I, p. 248: "Forsan commodior esset illac transitus, vel quod aliud quid, nobis incognitum, hoc mandato, intenderit."

57. Faber, *Comm. init.*, fol. 314v.

58. Erasmus, *Paraphrasis*, p. 138: "Ambulantem super indas lacus, perinde quasi solidam terram calcaret: ut se non terrae solum, sed omnium elementorum dominum declararet."

59. Musculus, *Comm.* I, p. 252: "Quod super mare dominus idque tempestuosum ambulavit, declarationem habet divinae illius virtutis ac potentiae, quam inanimata quoque agnoscere, imo ita vereri coguntur, ut illi etiam contra naturam suam serviant." This point is practically an exegetical commonplace, rooted in Chrysostom, who argues that Jesus wanted to show that he controlled the storm (*Homilies on John, FC* 33:437).

60. Musculus, *Comm.* I, p. 252: "Quid aliud hoc exemplo venti ac mare proclamant, quam Christum hunc filium esse dei ac conditorem suum?"

61. *Ibid.*: "Habet homo quoque in homines imperium, mari vero ac ventis nemo mortalium, utut potens imperabit, nisi unus hic omnium rex & dominus. Quanto ergo facilius est Christo imperare mortalibus, quos venti ac mare saepenumero subvertunt ac perdunt, cum ipsis istis indomitis elementis, mortalium domitoribus, tanta facilitate frenum imponat, illisque pro arbitrio suo, contra ipsorum quoque naturam, utatur?"

62. Erasmus, *Paraphrasis*, p. 139: "His argumentis miraculum hoc diligenter infixum est animis discipulorum, quorum credulitas omnibus modis erat formanda, confirmandaque."

63. Musculus, *Comm.* I, p. 249. Musculus's comments here seem indebted to Chrysostom, who mentions various causes for the disciples' fear—namely, the darkness, the rising sea, their distance from shore, and the unexpected appearance of Jesus (*Homilies on John, FC* 33:437). These four reasons are repeated in Hugh, *Postilla super Joannem*, fol. 325v.

64. Musculus, *Comm.* I, p. 247: "Quid igitur domino faciendum erat aliud, quam ut singulari & efficaci miraculo hanc cordium eorum obcaecationem excuteret, & virtutis suae sensum inderet?"

65. Ibid., p. 257: "Credebant eum esse Messiah, in prophetis promissum, & filium Davidis, sperabantque brevi regnum Israëlis occupaturum. Hac illum fide sequebantur, esse filium Dei, ne somniabant quidem. . . . Ergo hoc egit isto miraculo Christus, nec egit solum, sed & effecit, ut discipuli in fide erga se crescerent, seque vere Dei esse filium, ventorum, maris, & totius universi Dominum cognoscerent."

66. Faber, *Comm. init.*, fol. 314v.

67. Erasmus, *Paraphrasis*, p. 140.

68. Musculus, *Comm.* I, p. 257: "Inventumque quando illuc venisset, interrogarunt, qua certe interrogatione miraculi suspicionem quam ex praemissis conjecturis conceperant, significarunt." Musculus here follows a great number of commentators, including Augustine (*Tractates on John*, FC 79:246), Chrysostom (*Homilies on John*, FC 33:439), Hugh (*Postilla super Joannem*, fol. 326r), and Thomas (*Commentary on John*, p. 354), all of whom suggest that the multitude had some suspicion that Jesus had miraculously walked across the lake.

69. Musculus, *Comm.* I, p. 259: "Malebat, quod & se decebat, & saluti istorum hominum necessarium magis erat respondendo facere, quam & suae gloriae, & illorum curiositati servire."

70. Erasmus, *Paraphrasis*, p. 140.

71. Faber, *Comm. init.*, fol. 314v.

72. Ibid.: "Et ita seipsos respiciebant, & propter seipsos omnia faciebant."

73. Erasmus, *Paraphrasis*, pp. 140–141: "Caeterum affectum multitudinis, non solum inconstantem, sed etiam crassum minimeque dignum Evangelica doctrina, corrigit objurgatione severa, quod quum maiora vidissent miracula, divinam virtutem arguentia, tamen magis illos commoverit saturitas unius convivii, quam aeternae salutis desiderium."

74. Ibid., p. 141: "Fingit ac format ingenium rude, quibusdam elementis donec ad exactam artis cognitionem provexerit, ut iam rudimentis illis non sit opus."

75. Musculus, *Comm.* I, p. 259.

76. Ibid., pp. 249–250.

77. Ibid., p. 249: "Ut enim solis praesentia diem, absentia noctem, ita praesentia Christi, qui vera lux est, cordium illuminationem, absentia vero obscurationem inducit." For Augustine, the darkness represents the increase in sinfulness and brotherly hatred as the end of the world approaches (*Tractates on John*, FC 79:243), a theme repeated by Thomas, who suggests that darkness mystically signifies the absence of love (*Commentary on John*, p. 351). Hugh gives an extended discussion of how the darkness and the storm represent various spiritual dangers (*Postilla super Joannem*, fols. 325r–325v).

78. Erasmus, *Paraphrasis*, p. 138: "Habet autem etiam in tenebris oculos Evangelica charitas: & ibi nox non est, ubi adest Iesus: nec tempestas illic exitialis est, ubi in propinquo est is qui serenat omnia."

79. Musculus, *Comm.* I, p. 250.

80. Ibid., pp. 250–251: "Ad hunc plane modum comparati sunt tyranni huius mundi, contra doctrinam Christi saevientes. Captivi sunt Satanae, flatibus & impulsibus ipsius obnoxii. Suapte sponte nec excitantur ad saevitiam, nec demittuntur ad placiditatem . . . nec suum, sed Satanae negocium agunt."

81. Ibid., p. 251: "Quoties igitur sive in nobis sive in aliis, animi motus tumentes ac saevientes, velut elatos ac ferocientes excitati maris fluctus, viderimus, agnoscamus ventum

hunc adversarium, placiditatem & humilitatem animorum impulsu suo turbantem, excitantem, extollentem, & ad ferociam abripientem, oremusque dominum, qui & maris & cordium motus reprimere potest, ut ipse adversario hoc vento represso, sedataque tempestate, tranquillitatem & submissionem animorum restituat." Thomas writes that when Christ is present with the faithful, they suppress the swelling pride of the world and tread upon the waves of tribulation (*Commentary on John*, p. 353).

82. Musculus, *Comm.* I, p. 248: "Sola obedientia pios & fideles animos in eo conservat . . . etiam tum, cum plane consiliorum dei sunt ignari."

83. Ibid., p. 254: "Spectrum enim nihil est aliud, quam illusio, & falsa apparitio, unde & φάντασμα Graecis dicitur."

84. Ibid.: "Corporis aegritudo, terrenarum rerum penuria, contemptus in mundo, & mors ipsa, non sunt vere mala, sed malorum phantasmata. Qui per haec terrentur inanibus spectris terrentur. Rursus sanitas corporis, opes, gloria, vita diuturna, & caet. non sunt vera bona, sed bonorum spectra. Qui his delectatur, spectris delectatur."

85. Ibid., p. 251.

86. Ibid., p. 252. Thomas writes similarly that the Lord does not immediately rescue the faithful from their troubles but allows them to struggle for a while in order to test their virtue (*Commentary on John*, p. 352).

87. Musculus, *Comm.* I, p. 251: "Non solum scire Christum, & videre tentationes nostras . . . conservare ne pereamus, sed etiam opportuno tempore summa cum consolatione & gratia accurrere, & laborantes liberare."

88. Ibid., p. 253.

89. Erasmus, *Paraphrasis*, p. 139.

90. Augustine argues that the boat prefigures the Church of Christ (*Tractates on John*, *FC* 79:242), and this interpretation is repeated throughout the medieval exegetical tradition.

91. Musculus, *Comm.* I, p. 258: "Una est igitur Christi navicula, una est item vera illius ecclesia. Quae illa? In qua videlicet Christus cum suis vehitur, in qua sunt qui verbo Christi obsequuntur, & ad iussum illius navigant, in qua Christus verus dei filius agnoscitur, & adoratur. Quae Christo, verbo & apostolis caret, in qua Christus nec cognoscitur rite, nec ut par est adoratur, ecclesiae Christi nomine non censeri, sed inter mercenarias deputari debet."

92. Ibid.: "Videmus hic imaginem carnalium Christianorum, quibus princeps huius mundi nihil negocii facessit." For Thomas, the boats of the multitude represent various sects of heretics who are separated from the true Church of Christ (*Commentary on John*, p. 355).

93. Musculus, *Comm.* I, p. 260: "Probet ergo se quisque, quo animo, quove fine verbum & evangelion Christi audiat."

94. Faber, *Comm. init.*, fols. 314v–315r. Faber echoes Augustine' s remark that Jesus must be sought for his own sake, not for the sake of something else (*Tractates on John*, *FC* 79:247).

CHAPTER FIVE

1. *Evangelia cum commentariis* (Venice: L. A. Iuntae, 1530). My discussion of Cajetan is based upon the following works: J. F. Groner, *Kardinal Cajetan: Eine Gestalt aus der Reformationszeit* (Freiburg: Société Philosophique, 1951); Thomas Aquinas Collins, "Car-

dinal Cajetan's Fundamental Biblical Principles," *Catholic Biblical Quarterly* 17 (1955): 363–378; *Theologische Realenzyklopädie* VII, ed. Gerhard Krause and Gerhard Müller (Berlin: Walther de Gruyter, 1981), pp. 538–546; *Contemporaries of Erasmus: A Biographical Register of the Renaissance and Reformation*, ed. Peter G. Bietenholz (Toronto: University of Toronto Press, 1985), 1:239–242.

2. Cajetan's indebtedness to the humanists is seen in three main areas. First, he argued for exegesis based upon the original Greek and Hebrew. Although he lacked the necessary skills for independent linguistic analysis, Cajetan compensated for his deficiencies by employing assistants to help him understand the meaning of the original languages. Second, Cajetan purposefully limited himself to a strictly literal interpretation of the Bible. While he did not assert that the spiritual levels of meaning were entirely invalid, he believed that misguided interpretations of the Bible had often been introduced under the guise of spiritual exegesis. Third, Cajetan published opinions that were rooted in the textual and canon criticism of the humanists. Thus, he doubted the authenticity of passages lacking a strong textual witness (Mk 16:9ff., Jn 8:1–11), and he expressed suspicion concerning the canonicity of Hebrews, James, 1 and 2 John, and Jude. Cajetan also argued that the deuterocanonical books of the Old Testament should be placed on a level of secondary authority.

3. The controversy is treated in Josef Schweizer, *Ambrosius Catharinus Politus (1484–1553) ein Theologe des Reformationszeitalters* (Munster: Verlag der Aschendorffschen Buchhandlung, 1910), pp. 43–63; Thomas Aquinas Collins, "The Cajetan Controversy," *American Ecclesiastical Review* 128 (1953): 90–100; Ulrich Horst, "Der Streit um die hl. Schrift zwischen Kardinal Cajetan und Ambrosius Catharinus " in *Wahrheit und Verkündigung* I, ed. Leo Scheffczyk et al. (Munich: Ferdinand Schöningh, 1967), pp. 551–557.

4. Because of the controversy surrounding Cajetan, Luther ironically remarked around 1532 that "Cajetan has finally become a Lutheran" (*Cajetanus postremo factus est Lutheranus*) (*D. Martin Luthers Werke: Tischreden* [Weimar: Hermann Böhlaus Nachfolger, 1912–1921], 2.2668).

5. *In quatuor Evangelia expositiones luculentae et disquisitiones et disputationes contra haereticos plurimae, praemisso serie literarum indice, et additis ad finem operis quatuor quaestionibus non impertinentibus* (Paris: Josse Bade, 1529), hereafter cited as *In Evang. exposit.* The work was never reprinted.

6. The sources for this discussion of Major are John Major, *A History of Greater Britain*, trans. Archibald Constable, with a biography of Major by Aeneas J. G. Mackay (Edinburgh: Scottish History Society, 1892); John Durkan and James Kirk, *The University of Glasgow* (Glasgow: University of Glasgow Press, 1977), of which chap. 9 is a sketch of Major's life with a review of modern scholarship on Major; and James K. Farge, *Biographical Register of Paris Doctors of Theology, 1500–1536* (Toronto: Pontifical Institute of Medieval Studies, 1980).

7. For a bibliography of Major's writings, see Farge, *Biographical Register*, pp. 308–311, and John Durkan, "The School of John Major: Bibliography," *Innes Review* 1 (1950): 140–146.

8. Alexander Broadie, *The Circle of John Mair: Logic and Logicians in Pre-Reformation Scotland* (Oxford: Clarendon, 1985).

9. Scholars have speculated concerning the students Major may have influenced dur-

ing his second tenure in Paris, such as John Calvin, Ignatius Loyola, Reginald Pole, François Rabelais, and George Buchanan. Thomas F. Torrance, *The Hermeneutics of John Calvin* (Edinburgh: Scottish Academic Press, 1988), pp. 80–95, is the most recent attempt to prove a direct influence of Major upon Calvin's thought.

10. To what extent Major may be termed a nominalist is a subject of speculation. Some scholars call him a Scotist, others an Ockhamist. But a definitive study on Major's thought has yet to be written.

11. Francis Oakley, "Almain and Major: Conciliar Theory on the Eve of the Reformation," *American Historical Review* 70 (1965): 673–690; Francis Oakley, "From Constance to 1688: The Political Thought of John Major and George Buchanan," *Journal of British Studies* 1 (1962): 12–19.

12. Arguing for the permissibility of marital sexual pleasure, Major wrote: "Neither reason nor the Bible show me to be in error, and consequently even though the doctors and the saints may be opposed to this opinion, they are wrong on this point." Quoted in Farge, *Biographical Register*, p. 307. See also Louis Vereecke, "Mariage et sexualité au déclin du moyen-âge," *Supplément* 56, no. 14 (1961): 119–225.

13. The French humanist François Rabelais wrote ironically in his *Pantagruel* (chap. 7) that Major authored a treatise entitled *De modo faciendi boudinos* (How to make puddings). Farge, *Biographical Register*, p. 306.

14. *In quatuor Evangelia enarrationum, nunc primum ex ipso archetypo excerptarum, opus praeclarum, in duas partes divisum* (Cologne: P. Quentel, 1539), hereafter cited as *In Evang. enar.* Quentel published two different editions of the work: a deluxe single-volume folio printing and a more affordable two-volume octavo printing.

15. The debate is summarized in Benjamin De Troeyer, *Bio-bibliographia Franciscana Neerlandica Saeculi XVI*, 2 vols. (Nieuwkoop: B. De Graaf, 1969–1970), 1:107–117. This remains by far the best and most recent study of Broickwy's life and work. It is the basic source for the discussion that follows. But see also Wolfgang Schmitz, *Het Aandeel der Minderbroeders in Onze Middeleeuwse Literatuur: Inleiding tot een Bibliografie der Nederlandse Franciscanen* (Nijmegen: Dekker & Van de Vegt, 1936), pp. 96–97.

16. De Troeyer includes him in his survey of Dutch authors because he spent his last years in Nijmegen.

17. *Concordantiae breviores rerum optimarum, magisque memorabilium ex sacris bibliorum libris diligenter collectae et in ordinem redactae alphabeticum* (Cologne: P. Quentel, 1529). For a complete bibliography of Broickwy with all printings noted, see De Troeyer, *Bio-bibliographia*, 2:32–52.

18. In addition to his commentary on the gospels, Broickwy also published a commentary on Romans and on the Passion according to the four gospels.

19. *Elucidatio paraphrastica in sanctum Christi Evangelium secundum Ioannem, cum annotationibus in aliquot capita* (Antwerp: Simon Coquus, 1543), hereafter cited as *Elucid. paraphr. in Ioannem*. The commentary was issued again in 1556 and was printed with his Matthew commentary in seven printings from 1545 to 1556.

20. In addition to his paraphrastic commentary on John, he wrote commentaries on the apostolic epistles (1528), Psalms (1530), Ecclesiastes (1536), Matthew (1545), Job (1547), and the Song of Songs (1547). Titelmans also authored a work on Romans (1529), which is not strictly speaking a commentary but a polemical treatise directed against hu-

manist exegesis on the epistle. In similar fashion, Titelmans wrote a treatise on the Apocalypse in which he attempts to defend its authority and apostolic authorship against the doubts expressed by Erasmus. Titelmans's philosophical works were very popular in the sixteenth century. His *Libri duodecim de consideratione rerum naturalium* (1530) went through thirty-six printings in the sixteenth century alone. His book on Aristotle's logic (1533) was printed thirty-eight times. Among his theological works are an exposition of the Mass, a study on the Trinity, and a *Summa* of Christian mysteries. At least 197 different sixteenth-century editions are known of his works. By 1557 several of his books had found their way as far as the Jesuit mission in Japan (F. Verwilghen, "De werken van Frans Titelmans O.F.M. in Japan [1556])," *Franciscana* 16 [1961]: 113–119). For a complete bibliography of Titelmans, see De Troeyer, *Bio-Bibliographia*, 2:278–365. The discussion that follows is based largely on ibid., 1:87–100, and Jerry H. Bentley, "New Testament Scholarship at Louvain in the Early Sixteenth Century," *Studies in Medieval and Renaissance History*, n.s., ed. J. A. S. Evans (Vancouver: University of British Columbia, 1979), 2:53–79.

21. Antwerp: Willem Vorsterman, 1529. In the preface to the work, Titelmans denounces the textual emendations of the humanists, whose biblical scholarship serves to weaken the Catholic response to the errors of Protestantism. See Erika Rummel, *Erasmus and His Catholic Critics II (1523–1536)* (Nieuwkoop: De Graaf, 1989), p. 17.

22. John Major, *In Evang. exposit.*, dedicatory letter to James Beaton: "Quocirca Theophilacti Bulgarorum episcopi evangeliorum explanationes, ubi ab orthodoxorum sententia aberrare visae sunt, refellimus. Witclevistarum item & Hussitarum & eorum sequacium Lutheranorum pestiferas zizanias e bono dominici agri semine, quantum potuimus, evellimus."

23. See, for example, ibid., fols. 247r–247v, where Major rejects the views of "neoterici" who prefer "Bethabara" to "Bethany" at John 1:28. He rejects this modern reading because "receptissimus usus ecclesiae Bethaniam habet." See also ibid., fols. 312r–312v. However, on fols. 284r–284v, Major repeats without acknowledgment a view of Erasmus concerning John 7:38. This is the only place I have found where Major makes positive use of Erasmus's *Annotationes*. Therefore, I would concur with the judgment expressed by Thomas F. Torrance in *The Hermeneutics of John Calvin* (pp. 94–95) that "Major shows evidence of having studied it [humanist scholarship], but shows little evidence of having allowed it to influence his interpretation of the Gospels."

24. Major, *In Evang. exposit.*, fols. 274r–279v, 321v–323r, 337r–339v.

25. For example, ibid., fol. 256r: "Non impertinenter haeres, an infidelis, actus moraliter bonos elicere queat." The status of good works done in and outside a state of grace is a standard area of discussion in scholastic theology. The scholastic formal of Major's commentaries has led to a rather harsh judgment by the modern scholar Alexandre Ganoczy. He dismisses Major's commentary on Matthew as a worthless attempt at exegesis: "I must say that the book is more a collection of scholastic speculations in reference to passages from Matthew than a clearly exegetical work. . . . The reader who seeks primarily to understand the biblical text itself will not find it discussed." *The Young Calvin*, trans. David Foxgrover and Wade Provo (Philadelphia: Westminster, 1987), p. 176. Ganoczy's characterization of Major's Matthew commentary is, I suspect, unfair; it certainly does not reflect Major's work on John.

26. At various points, Major praises Aristotelian teaching as harmonious with Christian doctrine. He concedes that Aristotle was mistaken regarding the eternity of the world,

but this error, Major argues, does not detract from the overall usefulness of his philosophy. For example, see Major, *In Evang. exposit.*, fol. 294v: "Plus philosopho attribuendum quam mille nugis plutarchi & caeterorum gentilium in philosophia minus educatorum. Quare non miror si nostri prisci theologi Aristotelicam doctrinam sunt amplexi. Consonantissime enim ad veritatem docet."

27. Broickwy, *In Evang. enar.*, fols. 202r–202v, 226v, 227v, 228v–229r, 265v–267v, 281r.

28. It is possible, however, to interpret some of his refutations of classical heresies as synecdochial references to Protestant teachings.

29. Erasmus's name never appears in the commentary, but Broickwy was clearly familiar with the *Annotationes* because there are places where he repeats information (sometimes verbatim) from that source without acknowledgment. The information he borrows from Erasmus is always rather innocuous, usually dealing with questions of word etymologies or patristic interpretations. He never makes use of Erasmus regarding textual problems or the adequacy of the Vulgate. For examples of his borrowings from Erasmus, see *In Evang. enar.*, fols. 200r, 205r, 206v–207r, 210v, 227v, 239v, 261v.

30. De Troeyer, *Bio-Bibliographia*, 1:107.

31. Other favorites of Broickwy include Origen, Jerome, Gregory, Bede, Anselm, Bernard, and Bonaventure.

32. Jean Leclercq, *The Love of Learning and the Desire for God: A Study of Monastic Culture*, trans. Catharine Misrahi (New York: Fordham University Press, 1982), pp. 182–184.

33. Major, *In Evang. exposit.*, fol. 264r: "Erat lacus quidem quo oves ac pecora lavabantur. . . . Exenteratae oves ad sacrificium aptae illic purgabantur."

34. Broickwy, *In Evang. enar.*, fol. 220r; Titelmans, *Elucid. paraphr. in Ioannem*, fol. 37r.

35. Musculus, *Comm.* II, p. 154: "Simplicius est, ut intelligamus locum fuisse Hierosolymis, ovibus vel conservandis vel vendendis, vel lavandis destinatum, quem pro usu ipsius προβατικόν vocarint."

36. Major, *In Evang. exposit.*, fol. 264r. Major himself concedes the scholastic nature of this kind of question: "Haec obiectiuncula sorbonicum cavillum sonat."

37. Musculus, *Comm.* I, p. 155.

38. Ibid., pp. 155–156.

39. Tertullian and Chrysostom both suggested the baptismal symbolism of the pool; and in the early Church, the story served as one of the readings for preparing catechumens for baptism. Raymond E. Brown, *The Gospel According to John I–XII* (New York: Doubleday, 1966), p. 211; Chrysostom, *Homilies on John*, FC 33:352.

40. Titelmans, *Elucid. paraphr. in Ioannem*, fol. 37v: "Experientia enim antiqua certo edocti, aquam piscinae hostiarum caeremonialium sanguine permixtam, angelo operante, ab omni infirmitate intinctos curare, disponebantur ad credendum quod in baptismali lavacro, per aquam sanguine verae illius hostiae pro totius mundi salute immolandae commixtam, operante spiritusancto, omnium omnino peccatorum plena conferretur remissio, & perfecta ipsi animae sanitas redderetur."

41. Broickwy, *In Evang. enar.*, fol. 220r. Broickwy here clearly echoes Chrysostom's exegesis (*Homilies on John*, FC 33:353).

42. Broickwy, *In Evang. enar.*, fol 220v. A similar discussion of the various kinds of sins represented by those who were awaiting healing at the pool is offered by Thomas, *Commentary on John*, pp. 283–284. See also Hugh, *Postilla super Joannem*, fol. 312r.

43. Major, *In Evang. exposit.*, fol. 264r. Thomas also lists the differences between baptism and the pool in *Commentary on John*, p. 285.

44. Musculus, *Comm.* I, p. 155: "Quis enim ita insanit, ut elementum aquae, quo corpus tingitur, virtute sua animam quam tangere nequit, purgare ac renovare posse putet?"

45. Ibid.

46. Ibid., p. 156: "Quis enim aegrotus non cupit sanus fieri? Praesertim tam diuturno morbo adflictatus?"

47. Broickwy, *In Evang. enar.*, fol. 220v; Titelmans, *Elucid. paraphr. in Ioannem*, fol. 37v.

48. Musculus echoes here the comments of Augustine, who argues that the miracle was intended more for the salvation of souls than for the healing of the man's body (*Tractates on John*, FC 79:109).

49. Musculus, *Comm.* I, p. 156: "Libera dispensatione divinae providentiae administrari, sive id miraculo fiat, sive per artem medicam."

50. Major, *In Evang. exposit.*, fol. 264v; Broickwy, *In Evang. enar.*, fol 220r.

51. Musculus, *Comm.* I, p. 157: "Huiusmodi loquutiones affectum commiserationis resipiunt, ex intenta & singulari praesentis alicuius miseriae consideratione natum."

52. Broickwy, *In Evang. enar.*, fol. 220r.

53. Titelmans, *Elucid. paraphr. in Ioannem*, fols. 37v–38r. Chrysostom also lists the things the paralytic did not do and suggests that he was making a tacit request to be helped into the water (*Homilies on John*, FC 33:360).

54. Major *In Evang. exposit.*, fol. 264v.

55. Ibid.: "Quaeritur hic obiter an flagella nobis illata, utpote nephretis, cholica, & caetera id genus, sint pro nostris lapsibus satisfactoria. "

56. Major, *In Evang. exposit.*, fols. 264v–265r. Thomas also argues that by his patience the paralytic made himself worthy of being cured (*Commentary on John*, p. 286). Cf. Thomas Aquinas, *Summa Theologiae* I, 95, 4 ad 2: "Quod sit satisfactoria pro peccto."

57. Musculus, *Comm.* I, p. 157.

58. Ibid.: "Certa & conspicua verae & indubitate sanitatis illi praecipit indicia, quae ad divinae virtutis illustrationem in omnium erat oculis factura."

59. Major, *In Evang. exposit.*, fol. 264v; Broickwy, *In Evang. enar.*, fol. 220r; Titelmans, *Elucid. paraphr. in Ioannem*, fol. 38r.

60. Broickwy, *In Evang. enar.*, fol. 220v. My translation of his quotations is based on his own wording, which reflects the Vulgate. Medieval commentators frequently interpret the commands in this way. Thomas, for example, interprets the three commands as the three stages in the justification of the sinner—namely, repentance, satisfaction, and progress in virtue (*Commentary on John*, p. 288). See also Hugh, *Postilla super Joannem*, fol. 313v.

61. Musculus, *Comm.* I, p. 158: "Ubi per spiritum Christi mentibus nostris dicitur: dilige Deum, diligemus Deum, dilige proximum, diligemus proximum, time dominum, timebimus dominum."

62. Ibid.: "Si curati sumus a morbo interioris hominis per virtutem et spiritum Christi, non competit nobis, ut impossibilia nobis per verbum Christi praecipi dicamus. Neque hic aegrotus dicebat: praecipis mihi quae praestare nequeo, sed confestim virtute verbi Christi senatus surrexit, grabatum abstulit, & ambulavit, hoc est, verbo Christi obedivit eaque praestitit, quae ut sanorum tantum sunt, ita impossibilia paralyticis."

63. Ibid.: "Donec in hac corruptione & peccati servitute detinemur, impossibilia nobis sunt quae divinitus praecipiuntur."

64. Ibid., p. 159: "Non satis est a peccatis per poenitentiam surgere, & corpus circumferre rego peccati non amplius serviliter obnoxium, sed exigitur etiam, ut ambulemus, hoc est, ut iter ad coelestem patriam per studium verae pietatis solida fide & dilectione instituamus."

65. Ibid., pp. 159–160.

66. Ibid., p. 160: "Imaginem habet humani generis, in peccati servitute detenti, & opus Christi . . . imaginem redemptionis humanae expressit."

67. Ibid.

68. Major, *In Evang. exposit.*, fol. 265r; Broickwy, *In Evang. enar.*, fol. 220v; Titelmans, *Elucid. paraphr. in Ioannem*, fol. 38r.

69. Augustine makes the same point (*Tractates on John*, FC 79:118).

70. Musculus, *Comm.* I, pp. 160–161.

71. Titelmans, *Elucid. paraphr. in Ioannem*, fols. 38r–38v; Broickwy, *In Evang. enar.*, fols. 220v–221r; Major, *In Evang. exposit.*, fol. 265r.

72. Musculus, *Comm.* I, p. 161: "Qui me sanum fecit, imo qui me sanguine suo redemit, is mihi quod facio, praecepit."

73. Titelmans, *Elucid. paraphr. in Ioannem*, fol. 38v; Broickwy, *In Evang. enar.*, fol. 221r; Major, *In Evang. exposit.*, fol. 265r; Musculus, *Comm.* I, p. 162. In addition to these two explanations, Broickwy and Titelmans each offer a third reason for Jesus' departure: Jesus left the scene because he did not want to prejudice the testimony of the healed man. Since Jesus was absent, no one could suspect that the man was simply trying to please Jesus by his testimony. This third explanation is one of the reasons offered by Chrysostom for Jesus' disappearance (*Homilies on John*, FC 33:364).

74. The Vulgate reads: "Ecce sanus factus es; iam noli peccare, ne deterius tibi aliquid contingat."

75. Broickwy, *In Evang. enar.*, fol. 221r; Musculus, *Comm.* I, p. 263.

76. Titelmans, *Elucid. paraphr. in Ioannem*, fol. 39r.

77. Much of their discussion follows the general course of Chrysostom's exegesis, which distinguishes various causes for human sickness (*Homilies on John*, FC 33:293–294).

78. Broickwy, *In Evang. enar.*, fol. 221r.

79. Major, *In Evang. exposit.*, fol. 265v: "Secundo orthodoxam fidem non recipientes interdum temperanter vitam degunt minus fraudant proximum quam multi nos-tratium."

80. In his discussion of the relationship between sin and suffering, Chrysostom also argues that some sicknesses arise as a natural consequence of gluttony, drunkenness, and sloth (*Homilies on John*, FC 33:369).

81. Major, *In Evang. exposit.*, fol. 265r.

82. Musculus, *Comm.* I, p. 263.

83. Ibid., p. 264: "Neque enim credibile est, ob leve aliquod delictum, tam gravem ac diuturnum illi morbum fuisse divinitus inflictum."

84. Broickwy, *In Evang. enar.*, fol. 221r; Major, *In Evang. exposit.*, fol. 265v; Titelmans, *Elucid. paraphr. in Ioannem*, fol. 39r.

85. Musculus, *Comm.* I, p. 164: "Nunquam procliviores sumus ad peccandum, quam dum sani & extra adflictionem sumus."

CHAPTER SIX

1. The only exception I have found to this is a single citation of Osiander's *Harmoniae Evangelicae* (*Comm.* II, p. 323).

2. Musculus, *Comm.* I, "Wolfgangus Musculus Lectori S. in Domino," n.p.: "Quibus quisque secundum gratiam quam a Domino accepit veritatis sensum aliis placide sine ullo stomacho criminosaque ac proterva aliorum ingeniorum insectatione tradit." Musculus concedes that there may be "some use" for contentious writings but only "if moderation is added."

3. It is, of course, anachronistic to speak of a commentary written in the 1520s as "Lutheran." The term is used loosely to refer to those commentators who clearly saw themselves aligned with Martin Luther and the reform movement in Wittenberg.

4. The work was published eleven times in 1523 alone, three times in 1524, and once in both 1541 and 1542. See Timothy J. Wengert, *Philip Melanchthon's Annotationes in Johannem in Relation to Its Predecessors and Contemporaries* (Geneva: Librairie Droz S. A., 1987), pp. 43–54.

5. Musculus, *Comm.* I, p. 26: "Recentiores quidam priorem gratiam eam intelligunt, quae patris est erga filium, posteriorem vero qua nos filii gratia patri grati facti sumus & accepti."

6. Melanchthon, *Annotationes in Ioannem, CR* 14:1065: "Gratiam pro gratia nos consecutos esse; gratiam, id est remissionem peccatorum; pro gratia, quia pater Christum amat. . . . Gratiam pro gratia, i.e. ut filius diligitur, ita diligimur et nos, qui in filio sumus per fidem." Brenz, *In D. Iohannis Evangelion, Iohannis Brentii exegesis, per authorem iam primum diligenter reuisa, ac multis in locis locupletata* (Haguenau: J. Setzer, 1530), fol. 14v: "Accepimus gratiam, id est, Deus pater nobis favet. Pro gratia, id est, propterea quod Christo filio suo, cuius nos fratres sumus, & in quem credimus, faveat"; hereafter cited as *Exegesis in Ioh. Evang.*

7. Sarcerius, *In Ioannem Evangelistam iusta scholia summa diligentia, ad perpetuae textus cohaerentiae filium, per Erasmum Sarcerium Annemontanum conscripta* (Basel: Bartholomäus Westheimer, 1541), pp. 381–382, hereafter cited as *Scholia in Ioannem.* Cf. Brenz, *Exegesis in Ioh. Evang.*, fols. 171v–172r; Melanchthon, *Annotationes in Ioannem, CR* 14:1129.

8. Melanchthon, *Annotationes in Ioannem, CR* 14:1129: "Ratio sic colligit: hic affligitur, ergo peccator est et a Deo reiectus; hic fortunatus est, ergo pius est, et Deo charus."

9. Brenz, *Exegesis in Ioh. Evang.*, fols. 171v–172r; 171v: "Nam propter peccatum introiverunt in mundum, maledictiones, infirmitates, plagae, calamitates, adeoque ipsa mors."

10. Sarcerius, *Scholia in Ioannem*, pp. 381–382: "In impiis perpetuo verum est, eos adfligi propter peccata sua. In piis non semper verum est."

11. Brenz, *Exegesis in Ioh. Evang.*, fols. 172r–172v.

12. Musculus, *Comm.* II, p. 126: "Si huiusmodi erumnae sunt divinae ultiones propter peccata inflictae, quid de caeco hoc dicemus, qui caecus natus est antequam peccarit? Cuius nam peccatis tribuemus hanc caecitatem? Caeci ne? At hoc videtur absurdum. Quomodo nanque peccasset nondum natus? Sed qua aequitate puniretur infans propter peccata parentum, cum scriptum sit, filium non portare delicta parentum?"

13. Musculus does not cite the source, claiming simply that "Augustine says somewhere."

14. Musculus, *Comm.* II, pp. 126–127. In addition to Romans 9:20, Musculus also quotes Job 25:4 ("How can a man be justified to God or to appear clean, born of a woman?") and Job 14:4 ("Who can make those conceived of unclean seed clean?").

15. Melanchthon, *Annotationes in Ioannem, CR* 14:1130; Brenz, *Exegesis in Ioh. Evang.*, fol. 172v; Sarcerius, *Scholia in Ioannem*, p. 384.

16. Musculus, *Comm.* II, p. 127. Musculus presents a variant reading of Chrysostom, which adds "that he should be born blind" to the words "neither this man nor his parents sinned." In fact, Chrysostom merely states that Jesus added the words "by implication." It is Theophylact, not Chrysostom, who proffers the variant reading (*Enar. in Evang. Joannis, PG* 124 *ad locum*).

17. Melanchthon *Annotationes in Ioannem, CR* 14:1130.

18. Sarcerius, *Scholia in Ioannem*, p. 384.

19. Brenz *Exegesis in Ioh. Evang.*, fol. 173r: "Cum enim eos deijciat in extremam miseriam, & postea eripiat, hunc titulum refert, quod sit DEUS LIBERATOR, ET ADIVTOR IN NECESSITATIBUS (eyn nothelffer) qui est titulus magnificentissimus, & omnes homines ad Deum invocandum invitans."

20. Ibid., fols. 173r–173v.

21. Musculus, *Comm.* II, pp. 128–129: "Ad hunc modum itaque modum infirmitatibus nostris gloriae Dei servimus, quam dum sani sumus, magis obscuramus."

22. Melanchthon, *Annotationes in Ioannem, CR* 14:1130; Brenz, *Exegesis in Ioh. Evang.*, fol. 171v; Sarcerius, *Scholia in Ioannem*, p. 382.

23. Musculus, *Comm.* II, p. 128. Musculus cites Psalms 89:32 and the examples of the paralytics in Matthew 5 and John 5.

24. Ibid.: "Fides in tribulationibus augescit, oratio redditur ferventior, animus humiliatur, vivitur sobrie: & in summa mortificatur vetus homo, & novus grandescit."

25. Ibid., pp. 141–143.

26. Ibid., pp. 144–146.

27. Ibid., pp. 157–158.

28. Brenz argues that there is a twofold communion and a twofold excommunication— namely, internal and external (*Exegesis in Ioh. Evang.*, fol. 177r).

29. In a sermon on John 9, Brenz gives an extended discussion of the "causae calamitatum" similar to that of Musculus. But the significant fact is that Brenz omits such a discussion in his formal commentary on the chapter. See *Operum . . . D. Ioannis Brentii* (Tübingen: George Gruppenbach, 1576–1590), vol. 6: *In Evangelion Ioannis Homiliae*, p. 397.

30. Melanchthon, *Annotationes in Ioannem, CR* 14:1131: "Damnatur igitur quicquid ratio potest non illuminata verbo Dei."

31. Sarcerius, *Scholia in Ioannem*, p. 386: "Christus esse mundo lucem, quandiu eum fide retinet: ubi vero cessat fides in Christum ibi non est amplius Christus lux mundi."

32. Brenz, *Exegesis in Ioh. Evang.*, fols. 173v–174r: "Me veram esse lucem mundi, quam-quam nihil minus in cruce, ministerio meo cessante & potestate tenebrarum praevalente, videbitur."

33. The view is expressed by Bucer, *Enarratio in Iohannem* p. 329: "Ea nox Iudaeis venit cum et ab ipso et apostolis deserti fuere."

34. Musculus, *Comm.* II, p. 128: "Similitudines Christi simplici sensu capiendae sunt, nec trahendae ultra propositum."

35. Ibid., pp. 127–128.

36. Sarcerius, *Scholia in Ioannem*, p. 387: "Commendatur etiam nobis hic obiter medicinae studium, quod Deus de coelo creavit, & quod vir sapiens [non] spernet."

37. Ibid., p. 388.

38. Brenz, *Exegesis in Ioh. Evang.*, fol. 174v: "Deus enim non vult nobis sua bona distribuere, his mediis, quae nos elegimus, sed quae ipse elegit."

39. Ibid., fols. 174v–175r: "Ita & hoc loco Christus sanat caecum, malagmate ex luto & sputo facto, primum, ut huius malagmatis novitate, miraculum & Verbi sui potentia celebriora fierent. Dein mittitur caecus ad piscinam Siloë, ut longiore via, caeci fides interim exerceretur." Brenz here clearly echoes Chrysostom, who writes: "Christ first of all made certain by the long journey to Siloe that there would be many witnesses, and by the strangeness of the sight He made those who witnessed it keenly attentive." *Homilies*, *FC* 41:97.

40. Musculus, *Comm.* II, pp, 130–131.

41. Ibid., p. 131: "Quod mysterium concernit, dicam sine cuiuspiam praejudicio quid mihi videatur."

42. Ibid.: "Quam sunt ergo insani, qui sibiipsis terrestre hoc lutum summo studio cumulant, & mentis oculis illinunt, quasi inde sint futuri perspicaciores ad cognoscendam Christi veritatem? Hoc lutum magnis sumptibus ex scriptis philosophorum petunt, unde magis excaecantur quam illuminantur. Det Dominus ut ad piscinam Siloae vadant, ibique mentis oculos lavent, & a luto terrestris sapientiae repurgent."

43. Ibid.: "Neutra expositio impia est, utram vero accipias, tuo lector judicio committo."

44. Sarcerius, *Scholia in Ioannem*, pp. 380–381: "Locus hic est de causis salutis nostrae, quae non sunt haec aut illa merita, sed gratia & misericordia Christi, quae causae omnia nostra merita praecedunt." The fact that Jesus, without even being asked, takes the initiative in healing the blind man demonstrates the nature of prevenient grace in accomplishing human salvation.

45. Musculus, *Comm.* II, p. 126: "Quae nativitas illa est, quae caecos gignit? Carnis nativitas, quae ex Adam est, non producit videntes, sed caecos. Nativitas spiritus non caecos, sed videntes generat. Sunt animantia quaedam quae caeca quidem nascuntur, sed post aliquot dierum spacium oculos aperiunt, ut videant: at posteritas Adae ita caeca nascitur, ut nisi regeneretur spiritu, lucem veritatis haudquaquam videat."

46. Ibid., p. 131.

47. Ibid., p. 130.

48. Ibid., p. 132: "Est ergo lavari in aquis Siloae, hoc est, baptismatis Christi fluentis, idem quod illuminari."

49. Sarcerius, *Scholia in Ioannem*, p. 388.

50. Brenz, *Exegesis in Ioh. Evang.*, fol. 175r.

51. Musculus, *Comm.* II, p. 131: "Jussui illius prompte obedivit, etiamsi cuncta haec rationi humanae viderentur ridicula."

52. Ibid.: "Sic iam occinunt, quid poterit aqua, quid panis, quid vinum?"

53. Ibid., p. 132: "Stulti non intelligunt, nec aquam, nec panem, nec vinum, nec aeneum serpentem quicquam per se conferre posse, sed vim sanationis esse verbi Dei fide apprehendendi."

54. Ibid., p. 131: "Notent istam obedientiam caeci nostrorum temporum haeretici."

55. This is an especially noteworthy fact since the rejection of allegory has been seen as characteristic of the Reformed tradition. Wengert, *Philip Melanchthon's Annotationes in Johannem*, p. 110, argues that this rejection of allegory "in many ways becomes the hallmark of Reformed, but not Lutheran or Roman Catholic, exegesis."

56. John Calvin, *Calvin: Commentaries*, trans. and ed. by Joseph Haroutunian and Louis P. Smith, Library of Christian Classics 23 (Philadelphia: Westminster, 1958), p. 75.

CHAPTER SEVEN

1. It has in fact been suggested by Bernard Roussel (*Le temps des Réformes et la Bible*, ed. Guy Bedouelle and Bernard Roussel, La Collection Bible de Tous les Temps [Paris: Beauchesne, 1989], 5:215–252) that Musculus should be considered a late representative of a "Rhenish school" of exegesis (in distinction to the "Wittenberg group") that was centered in Strasbourg, Basel, and Zurich, and flourished around 1525–1540. Although most of the biblical scholars in this "school" are Reformed theologians (C. Pellikan, S. Münster, J. Œcolampadius, U. Zwingli, W. Capito, M. Bucer, H. Bullinger, J. Calvin, and others), Roussel also includes the Lutheran J. Brenz, whose exegesis represents the emphases of the Rhenish school. Some of the common features of the school are the influence of humanist linguistic studies, an emphasis on Old Testament studies that make use of Jewish exegesis, a predilection for typological exegesis, avoidance of allegories, and a propensity to search the Scriptures for ethical, disciplinary, and liturgical rules. Roussel has developed an interesting hypothesis, but his use of the term "school" is, I believe, misleading since it suggests a common, explicit, and programmatic approach to biblical interpretation. Roussel himself uses the term loosely to describe "a dense network of relationships [and] of analogous activities" (ibid., p. 215), but the fact that some of these scholars were friends who read each other's works is not enough evidence to prove a school of exegesis. Certainly, there are similarities of approach and emphasis, as Roussel admirably demonstrates. But even here, generalizations often break down. Roussel admits, for example, that Zwingli may not share the aversion of the school to allegorical interpretation (p. 226). My research shows that Musculus and Œcolampadius (unlike Bucer) do not systematically oppose allegorical exegesis.

2. Bucer offered private lectures on John in 1523, but it remains impossible to ascertain to what degree he incorporated these into his formal commentary since no manuscript of the lectures has survived. See Irena Backus's "Introduction" to her modern critical edition of Bucer's *Enarratio in Evangelion Iohannis* (Leiden: E. J. Brill, 1988), p. xii.

3. For a description of the major alterations between the three versions, see Backus, "Introduction," pp. xxxiii–xlii. The commentary was printed once more (Geneva, 1553) as part of Robert Estienne's edition of Bucer's commentaries.

4. Johannis Œcolampadius, *Annotationes piae ac doctae in Evangelium Ioannis* (Basel: Andreas Cratander and Johann Bebel, 1533). My citations are based on the second and final printing of the book in 1535, hereafter cited as *Annot. in Evang. Ioannis.*

5. Ernst Staehelin, *Das theologische Lebenswerk Johannes Oekolampads* (Leipzig: M. Heinsius Nachfolger, 1939), p. 574.

6. *In evangelicam historiam de Domino nostro Iesv Christo, per Matthaevm, Marcvm, Lucam, & Ioannem conscriptam, Epistolasque aliquot Pauli, annotationes D. Hvldrychi Zvinglii per Leonem Iudae exceptae & aeditae* (Zurich: C. Froschauer, 1539). The commentary appears in the sixth volume (part 1) of *Huldrici Zuinglii Opera*, ed. M. Schuler and J. Schulthess (Zurich: F. Schulthess, 1836), pp. 682–766. My citations, however, are based on the pagi-

nation of the 1539 printing, hereafter cited as *Annot. in Evang. hist.* Walter Meyer, "Die Entstehung von Huldrych Zwinglis neutestamentlichen Kommentaren und Predigtnachschriften," *Zwingliana* 14 (1976): 288–331, argues that the lectures occurred from July through December of 1528. Timothy J. Wengert, "The Dating of Huldrych Zwingli's Lectures on John," *Zwingliana* 24 (1986): 6–10, has argued convincingly for the earlier dating on the basis of his own inspection of the manuscript materials.

7. My citations are from the 1543 printing: *In Divinum Iesu Christi Domini nostri Euangelium secundum Ioannem, commentariorum libri X* (Zurich: C. Froschauer, 1543), hereafter cited as *In Evang. comm.* Froschauer also published the 1548 and 1556 printings with the same title. See *Heinrich Bullinger Werke*, part 1, vol. 1: *Bibliographie*, ed. Joachim Staedtke (Zurich: Theologischer Verlag, 1972), bib. nos. 153–155, 274, 275.

8. For places where I suspect an influence, see, for example, Musculus and Bucer on the meaning of John 13:20, 16:12, 20:8, 20:19 (*Comm.* II, pp. 308, 371, 445, 454; *Enarratio in Iohannem*, pp. 407, 464–465, 541, 544).

9. Musculus, *Comm.* II, p. 178. Cf. Bucer, *Enarratio in Iohannem*, p. 343.

10. For examples, see Musculus and Bucer on the meaning of "night" at John 9:4 and on the meaning of "propterea" at John 10:17 (*Comm.* II, pp. 127–128, 196; *Enarratio in Iohannem*, pp. 330, 345).

11. Over a hundred letters from Musculus to Bullinger and several from Bullinger to Musculus are extant in autograph or handwritten copies in the Zurich Zentralbibliothek. See Ernst Gagliardi and Ludwig Forrer, *Katalog der Handschriften der Zentralbibliothek Zürich II: Neuere Handschriften seit 1500* (Zurich: Zentralbibliothek Zürich, 1982). After the Interim, Musculus fled to Zurich, where he was received by Bullinger, who helped him acquire his post in Bern. Bullinger wrote letters of recommendation to Bern, attempting to appease the fears of some who suspected Musculus of being a crypto-Lutheran. See Rudolf Dellsperger, "Wolfgang Musculus (1497–1563)," in *Die Augsburger Kirchenordnung von 1537 und ihr Umfeld*, ed. Reinhard Schwarz (Gütersloh: Gütersloher Verlaghaus Gerd Mohn, 1988), p. 104, n. 58.

12. Musculus, *In Esaiam prophetam commentarii locupletissimi . . .* (Basel: Johann Herwagen, 1557). The table immediately follows the dedicatory letter to the Strasbourg city council.

13. Bullinger's comments run to eight folio-sized pages and Œcolampadius's to thirty octavo-sized pages. The comments of Bucer fill five folio-sized pages in the 1536 edition and those of Zwingli fill two folio-sized pages.

14. Musculus, *Comm.* II, pp. 223–224. Later in the commentary (p. 235), Musculus returns to this allegory, noting in a marginal comment that Lazarus had been dead and entombed for four days, which symbolize the four ages of the world: the age before the flood, the age after the flood before Moses, the age from Moses to Christ, and the age from Christ to the end of the world. Just as Lazarus was raised on the fourth day, so Adam's posterity, entombed for four ages, is redeemed in the fourth age.

15. Œcolampadius, *Annot. in Evang. Ioannis*, fols. 211v–212r: "Si videmus asinum errantem, reducimus juxta legem: quanto magis si anima fratris? Et charitas requirit, ut dominum pro illius salute imploremus."

16. Bullinger, *In Evang. comm.*, fol. 127v; Musculus, *Comm.* II, pp. 224–225.

17. Musculus, *Comm.* II, p. 225: "Sequamur hoc exemplum & nos, ut pro fratribus

orantes, plurimi faciamus quod in gratiam Domini sunt assumpti: dicamusque, Domine, ecce pro quo mortuus es, aegrotat: vel, si in tentationibus sit frater, Domine ecce quem sanguine tuo redemisti, infestatur a Satana. . . . Sic dicamus hodie pro Ecclesia orantes: Domine, ecce sponsa tua, quam unice diligis, premitur, & Antichristi tyrannide vastatur."

18. Ibid.

19. Zwingli, *Annot. in Evang. hist.*, p. 325; Œcolampadius, *Annot. in Evang. Ioannis*, fol. 212v; Bullinger, *In Evang. comm.*, fol. 127v. Bucer does not comment on the verse.

20. Musculus, *Comm.* II, pp. 225–226: "Non dicunt . . . Bono animo sitis, potest hunc Deus erigere . . . sed austero vulto, Quid attinet, inquiunt, lugere? moriendum est."

21. Bucer, *Enarratio in Iohannem*, p. 358: "Ad illustrationem gloriae eius facient . . . ad nostram quoque salutem."

22. Musculus, *Comm.* II, p. 226: "Quae poterit gloria ex mortalium nostrorum corporum infirmitate ad eum redundare, per quem sumus conditi? An non maior gloria ad eum rediret, si firmi essemus sicut angeli Dei, quam ex eo quod multis sumus infirmitatibus obnoxii? Utique operis non infirmitas, sed fermitudo opificis est gloria."

23. Ibid.

24. Œcolampadius, *Annot. in Evang. Ioannis*, fol. 213r: "Filii Dei post lapsum multo ferventiores sunt, & vitam ita instituunt, ut Deus magis per illos glorificetur." Fol. 212v: "Qui vero filii Dei, postea resurgent, maiori timore vitam instituentes."

25. Œcolampadius, *Annot. in Evang. Ioannis*, fol. 217v; Bullinger, *In Evang. comm.*, fols. 129r–129v.

26. Musculus, *Comm.* II, pp. 236–237: "Et praecipue quod Christum attinet, imitemur exemplum hoc Marthae, ut & ipsi venienti illi ad nos occurramus. Dicis, Quo & quomodo? Quis nollet Christo ad nos venienti occurrere? Sed quomodo ad nos venit? Quomodo illi occurram? Venit ad nos per evangelium suum, per ministros verbi sui, per membra sua. Venturus est in fine mundi visibiliter cum gloria. Occurre illi animo veritatis avido, reverenti, grato, dum es in hac vita. Excipe illum in verbo, in ministro, & in membris eius: ut olim in fine mundi obviam ei rapiaris, ac sic semper cum eo regnes in coelis."

27. Œcolampadius, *Annot. in Evang. Ioannis*, fol. 218r; Bullinger, *In Evang. comm.*, fol. 129r; Musculus, *Comm.* II, p. 236. Œcolampadius and Musculus here follow the lead of Chrysostom, who argues that by running to Jesus Martha did not express a more fervent love than Mary, who had not heard the news of Jesus' arrival (*Homilies on John*, FC 41:171).

28. For example, Thomas Aquinas, *Commentum in Matthaeum et Joannem Evangelistas*, vol. 10 of *Opera Omnia* (Parma: P. Fiaccadore, 1852–1873; reprint, New York: Musurgia, 1948–1950), p. 493: "Mystice autem signantur per haec vita activa quae signatur per Martham, quae occurrit Christo ad exhibendum obsequii beneficium membris eius; et vita contemplativa, quae per Mariam signatur: quae domi sedet quieti contemplationis et puritati conscientiae vacans." See also Denis, *Enarratio in Joannem*, p. 481: "Martha vitam signat activam, Maria contemplativam."

29. Œcolampadius, *Annot. in Evang. Ioannis*, fols. 211v, 218r.

30. Musculus, *Comm.* II, p. 237: "Est quidem magna commoditas tranquillitatis & quietis, qua mens hominis a turbulentis curis ac negociis huius seculi avocatur."

31. Bucer, *Enarratio in Iohannem*, p. 359; Zwingli, *Annot. in Evang. hist.*, p. 325; Œcolampadius, *Annot. in Evang. Ioannis*, fol. 218v.

32. Bullinger, *In Evang. comm.*, fol. 129v: "Nihil agit ex animi impotentia, non

obmurmurat, non execratur, non obiurgat quod ad primum nuncium venire distulisset, non eiulat muliebriter, & prae doloris impatientia decidit & volutat se in pulvere, non crines evellit & laniat genas, sed mira cum modestia & tolerantia sortem suam deplorat apud Iesum magistrum fidelissimum." Bullinger's comments here closely follow Chrysostom's diatribe against the mourning customs of women who "make a show of their mourning and lamentation: baring their arms, tearing their hair, making scratches down their cheeks." (*Homilies on John, FC* 41:174).

33. Musculus, *Comm.* II, p. 237.

34. Œolampadius, *Annot. in Evang. Ioannis*, fol. 218v; Bullinger, *In Evang. comm.*, fol. 129v; Musculus, *Comm.* II, p. 237.

35. Musculus, *Comm.* II, pp. 237–238.

36. Zwingli, *Annot. in Evang. hist.*, p. 325; Bullinger, *In Evang. comm.*, fols. 129v–130f.; Œcolampadius, *Annot. in Evang. Ioannis*, fol. 219r: "Etiam qui sciunt futuram resurrectionem, non possunt impetum naturae reprimere, quin lachrymentur." Bucer does not comment on Martha's confession.

37. Musculus, *Comm.* II, p. 239: "Ad hunc modum colligamus & nos: Resurgent omnes, resurgam ergo & ego. Resurgent ad vitam aeternam qui credunt in Christum, igitur & ego, &c. Parcit Deus propter Christum, & ignoscit poenitentibus & credentibus: parcet igitur & mihi. Non deserit Deus sperantes in se, ergo nec me deseret."

38. I translate John 6:69 here as Musculus renders it. Although Musculus here refers to this confession as one made jointly by the apostles, the statement at 6:69 is made solely by Peter.

39. Musculus, *Comm.* II, pp. 239–240: "Haec est sanctorum infirmitas, quam Christus in illis tolerat. Cavendum itaque & nobis, ne propter hanc quempiam damnemus."

40. Erasmus defends his translation in the *Annotationes* (p. 252) as a case where the Greek perfect is used for present time.

41. Œcolampadius, *Annot. in Evang. Ioannis*, fol. 220r: "Plane credidi iampridem magna de te, quod sis filius dei, de quo prophetae locuti sunt."

42. Bucer follows Erasmus's translation of "ego credo" but directs the reader's attention to the sense of the underlying Greek, which literally means "I have believed" (*Enarratio in Iohannem*, p. 359). Zwingli, *Annot. in Evang. hist.*, p. 325: "Non ergo dicit, Ego credo quod te in pane edam corporaliter, sed quod tu sis ille Christus."

43. Bullinger, *In Evang. comm.*, fol. 130v: "Etiam domine, ait, id est maxime & firmissime credo verbis tuis, quod sis vita & resurrectio, qui animas fidelium serves & corpora resuscites mortuorum. Huic addit iam fundamentum resurrectionis & caput totius fidei Christianae, Ego credo, inquit, te esse Messiam illum filium dei vivi, qui ... veneris in mundum: id est, credo te esse verum deum & hominem salvatorem & vivificatorem totius mundi."

44. Musculus, *Comm.* II, pp. 239, 241.

45. Œcolampadius, *Annot. in Evang. Ioannis*, fol. 220v; Bullinger, *In Evang. comm.*, fols. 130v–131r.

46. Musculus, *Comm.* II, pp. 241–242: "Ergo exemplum hic habemus humanae rationis, quae mandata Dei ... clanculum & caute obeunda putat, ut impiorum conscientia fugiatur."

47. Ibid., p. 242: "Admonemur igitur hoc exemplo, ut nec ipsi alium magistrum agnoscamus quam Christum hunc filium Dei."

48. Œcolampadius, *Annot. in Evang. Ioannis*, fol. 220v; Bullinger, *In Evang. comm.*, fol. 131r; Musculus, *Comm.* II, p. 242.

49. Bullinger, *In Evang. comm.*, fol. 131r; Œcolampadius, *Annot. in Evang. Ioannis*, fol. 221r.

50. Musculus, *Comm.* II, p. 243: "Si hoc animo essemus erga Christum & nos, utique absque ullo pudore, & omni adversariorum metu rejecto, tanquam germani discipuli verbo illius adhaereremus."

51. Zwingli, *Annot. in Evang. hist.*, pp. 325–326.

52. Œcolampadius, *Annot. in Evang. Ioannis*, fol. 221v.

53. Bullinger, *In Evang. comm.*, fols. 131r–131v: "Non aliam puto caussam fremitus, conturbationis & lachrymarum domini quam expressam illam a Ioanne, quod videlicet singulariter amarit Lazarum totamque familiam, quam cum gravi luctu videret oppressam ac condolere ei Iudaeos omnes & flere largissime, commota fuerint & domini viscera."

54. Ibid., fol. 131v: "Ipsum totis visceribus ita esse commotum atque concussum, ut vocem ullam ad tempus aedere nequiverit."

55. Bullinger quotes statements of Gregory of Nyssa, Athanasius, and Basil that interpret Jesus' weeping as a proof of his true humanity (ibid., fol. 131v).

56. Ibid.: "Neque enim ex hominibus lapides aut truncos facit religio Christiana."

57. Ibid., fols. 131v–132r. Bullinger cites Augustine's commentary on John for this tropological interpretation of Jesus' tears.

58. Bucer, *Enarratio in Iohannem*, p. 361. In her editorial notes on this passage, Irena Backus notes that by "Marcionites," Bucer here means the *novi Marcionitae*—that is, the Lutherans ("Introduction," p. 361, n. 41). She suggests that Bucer particularly has in mind the exegesis of Brenz, who interprets *infremuit spiritu* as an expression of divine indignation. See also ibid., pp. xxiii–xxiv.

59. Bucer, *Enarratio in Iohannem*, p. 359: "Neque enim stupentem a nobis, sed vivam et ardentem, quae viscera exagitet totoque se corpore prodat, dilectionem Deus requirit."

60. Ibid., p. 360: "Dumque verus vivit in cordibus sanctorum amor fratrum, non possunt non dolere et lugere mortuos, aut alios afflictos."

61. Backus, "Introduction," p. 360, n. 31, argues that Bucer's remarks are directed against Karlstadt's treatise *Ein Sermon vom Stand der Christglaubigen seelen und fegfeuer*, in which Karlstadt interprets Paul's dictum as an interdiction of mourning.

62. Bucer, *Enarratio in Iohannem*, p. 360: "Stoici igitur, magis quam Christiani, sunt nostri Catabaptistae quidam, qui nullum luctum, nullas lachrymas pro mortuis vel alias afflictis fratribus ferunt."

63. Musculus, *Comm.* II, p. 244.

64. Ibid.

65. Ibid. Musculus adds the marginal annotation: "Tam non est damnanda Maria quod plorasse, quam Martham nemo condemnat quod non plorasse legitur."

66. Ibid.

67. Ibid., p. 245: "Parum decoris habere videtur, si vir gravis, maturus, honestus, sapiens, ac fortis, quamvis acerbe affectus, illachrymetur."

68. Ibid.

69. Ibid.: "Est enim omnino aliena a sanctis Stoica illa ἀπάθεια, quam Anabaptistae rursus in ecclesiam inducere conantur."

70. Œcolampadius, *Annot. in Evang. Ioannis,* fol. 223r.

71. Bullinger, *In Evang. comm.,* fol. 132r.

72. Musculus, *Comm.* II, p. 246.

73. This idea is rooted in Chrysostom's commentary on the passage (*Homilies on John, FC* 41:183–184) and appears with frequency throughout the medieval exegetical tradition. Cf. Thomas Aquinas, *Catena aurea in quatuor Evangelia,* vol. 12 of *Opera omnia* (Parma: Fiaccadori, 1852–1873; reprint, New York: Musurgia, 1948–1950), p. 382.

74. Bullinger, *In Evang. comm.,* fol. 132r; Œcolampadius, *Annot. in Evang. Ioannis,* fols. 223r–223v; Musculus, *Comm.* II, p. 246.

75. Œcolampadius here presents an interesting variation on the allegory first proposed by Augustine and appearing throughout the exegetical tradition. For Augustine, the stone represents the burden of the law (which was inscribed in stone), and the command to remove the stone represents the command to preach the gospel of grace (*Tractates on John, FC* 88:255–256). See Jacob Kremer, *Lazarus: Die Geschichte einer Auferstehung* (Stuttgart: Katholisches Bibelwerk, 1985), p. 132.

76. Musculus, *Comm.* II, pp. 246–247: "Ut nos cooperarios operum suorum mirabilium ac divinorum constituat, quo in cognitione ac fide providentiae ipsius exerceamur."

77. Œcolampadius, *Annot. in Evang. Ioannis,* fol. 223r; Bullinger, *In Evang. comm.,* fols. 132r–132v: "Sanguinem in venis & toto corpore in pus esse resolutum, exta item corrupta, adeoque & vitalia maxime membra quasi computruisse. Foetor enim e putredine & corruptione exoritur." Musculus, *Comm.* II, p. 246.

78. Musculus, *Comm.* II, p. 247: "Per anagogiam admonemur, quam nullam debeamus peccatorem, quantumvis putredine peccatorum corruptum & foetidum, sic aspernari, ut dubitemus eum posse gratia Christi ad resipiscentiam & vitam restitui."

79. Œcolampadius, *Annot. in Evang. Ioannis,* fol. 223r; Bullinger, *In Evang. comm.,* fol. 132v; Bucer, *Enarratio in Iohannem,* p. 362; Musculus, *Comm.* II, p. 247: "Principio observemus hic exemplum animi non mali quidem, sed interim partim solliciti, partim in fide non admodum constantis"; "Ergo quantum in fide providentiae Dei deficimus, tantum curis ac solicitudinibus superfluis divexamur."

80. Bullinger, *In Evang. comm.,* fol. 132v; Œcolampadius, *Annot. in Evang. Ioannis,* fol. 223v: "Nolumus te contristare ut hunc videas: erit enim spectaculum miserum."

81. Musculus, *Comm.* II, pp. 245–246.

82. Œcolampadius, *Annot. in Evang. Ioannis,* fol. 224r.

83. Bullinger, *In Evang. comm.,* fol. 132v: "Memineris ergo Martha verborum meorum, An excidit quod tibi modo dixi, Si credideris, futurum ut per fratris tui mortem illustretur gloria dei? An excidit quod tibi promisi, Resurget frater tuus"; "Nihil ergo impediet dei potentiam foetor, nihil purulentia & cadaveris putredo. Crede modo & experieris deum esse & veracem & potentem."

84. Ibid.

85. Musculus, *Comm.* II, p. 247.

86. Zwingli, *Annot. in Evang. hist.,* p. 326; Œcolampadius, *Annot. in Evang. Ioannis,* fol. 224r; Bullinger, *In Evang. comm.,* fols. 132v–133r; Bucer, *Enarratio in Iohannem,* pp. 362–363.

87. Musculus, *Comm.* II, pp. 248–249.

88. Ibid., pp. 248–250.

89. Bullinger, *In Evang. comm.*, fol. 133v; Bucer, *Enarratio in Iohannem*, p. 363; Œcolampadius, *Annot. in Evang. Ioannis*, fols. 224v–225r; Musculus, *Comm.* II, p. 248.

90. Zwingli, *Annot. in Evang. hist.*, p. 326: "Quod enim Lazarum voce magna suscitat, praefigurat nobis tubam illam ultimam, quae personabit in generali ista resurrectione, ad cuius clangorem omnes mortui excitabuntur."

91. Œcolampadius, *Annot. in Evang. Ioannis*, fol. 225r: "Nos quoque per Christum salvabimur, ut ille inclamaverit cordibus nostris, & mortificaverit nostra membra, & iusserit a corporalibus istis abire, ducens ad spiritualia."

92. Musculus, *Comm.* II, p. 250: "Hodie quoque reipsa experimur, quantum clamoris requirat ad praedicandum resipiscentiam seculo huic, non quatuor tantum dies, sed multos annos in peccatis mortuo."

93. Zwingli, *Annot. in Evang. hist.*, p. 326; Bullinger, *In Evang. comm.*, fol. 133v; Œcolampadius, *Annot. in Evang. Ioannis*, fol. 225r; Bucer, *Enarratio in Iohannem*, p. 363.

94. Musculus, *Comm.* II, p. 248.

95. Ibid., p. 251: "Qui in peccatis sunt mortui, & ipsi manus ac pedes habent peccatorum consuetudine veluti fasciis quibusdam revinctos, ut nec operari, nec ambulare in via Dei: et faciem ita obvinctam obstinatione, ut nec audire nec videre queant." P. 250: "Ad hanc imaginem etiam illi qui in peccatis sunt mortui, sic excitantur, ut non solum reviviscant, sed & vitae conversatione veluti progressu quodam, Christi se virtute vivificatos esse declarent."

96. Kremer, *Lazarus*, p. 229.

97. Augustine, *Tractates on John*, FC 88:257.

98. Bucer, *Enarratio in Iohannem*, p. 363: "Mysticos intellectus fingant hic qui incertis delectantur"; "Nugentur alii de virtute absolvendi." These polemical statements appear in the 1528 and 1530 editions but were suppressed by Bucer in the 1536 edition. Backus argues that Bucer's attack is directed against the exegesis of Brenz, who interprets the *fasciae sepulchrales* as the remnants of original sin. See Backus, "Introduction," p. xxiv. Bucer frequently attacks allegorical interpretations throughout his commentary, and at 14:26 introduces a critique of those who continue to be enamored by allegorical modes of exposition. In the margin he adds the title: "Contra eos qui alegoriis, anagogiis et mysteriis ex Scripturis eruendis intenti sunt, necessaria admonitio" (*Enarratio in Iohannem*, p. 432). Bullinger, although not rejecting allegorical interpretation altogether, seems to have considered it inappropriate in the exposition of the gospels. See T. H. L. Parker, *Calvin's New Testament Commentaries* (Grand Rapids: Eerdmans, 1971), p. 38.

99. Œcolampadius, *Annot. in Evang. Ioannis*, fol. 225v.

100. Musculus, *Comm.* II, p. 251: "Vincula quae sunt in peccatis & morte . . . explicantur ac soluunter. Itaque in Christo est libertas, in regno satanae vincula & captivitas."

101. Ibid.: "Non soluit ipse vinctum, sed jubet ut solvatur per eos qui testes resurrectionis huius adstabant. Imaginem hic habes ministerii ecclesiastici, per quod a peccatis soluuntur, qui voce Christi ad vitam excitantur."

102. Ibid.

Selected Bibliography

PRIMARY SOURCES

Augustine of Hippo. *Tractatus CXXIV in Joannem.* Vol. 36 of *Corpus Christianorum.* Turnholt: Brepols, 1954.
———. *On the Gospel of John.* Translated by John W. Rettig. Vols. 78, 79, and 88 of *The Fathers of the Church.* Washington, D.C.: Catholic University of America Press, 1988.
Bible. Latin. *Biblia sacra cum glossis, interlineari et ordinaria, Nicolai Lyrani postilla, ac moralitatibus, Burgensis additionibus, & Thoringi replicis.* 6 vols. in 5. Venice, 1588.
———. *Biblia.* Edited by Robert Estienne. Paris: Conrad Badius, 1555.
Bonaventure. *Opera omnia.* 10 vols. Quaracchi: Collegium S. Bonaventurae, 1882–1902.
Brenz, Johannes. *In D. Iohannis Evangelion, Iohannis Brentii exegesis, per authorem iam primum diligenter reuisa, ac multis in locis locupletata.* Haguenau: J. Setzer, 1530.
Briefwechsel der Brüder Ambrosius und Thomas Blaurer, 1509–1567. Edited by Traugott Schieß. 3 vols. Freiburg: Friedrich Ernst Fehsenfeld, 1908–1912.
Broickwy von Königstein, Antonius. *In quatuor Evangelia enarrationum, nunc primum ex ipso archetypo excerptarum, opus praeclarum, in duas partes divisum.* Cologne: P. Quentel, 1539.
Bucer, Martin. *Enarratio in Evangelion Iohannis.* Vol. 2 of *Martini Buceri Opera Latina.* Edited by Irena Backus. Leiden: E. J. Brill, 1988.
Bullinger, Heinrich. *In Divinum Iesu Christi Dominis nostri Euangelium secundum Ioannem commentariorum libri X.* Zurich: C. Froschauer, 1543.
Bürgerbibliothek Bern. Cod. 689.
Cajetan, Tommaso de Vio. *Evangelia cum commentariis.* Paris: J. Badius Ascensian, J. Parvum & J. Roigny, 1532.
Catalogus graecorum librorum, manuscriptorum, augustanae bibliothecae. Compiled by Hieronymus Wolf. Augsburg: Michael Manger, 1575.
Corpus Christianorum. Series Latina. Turnholt: Brepols, 1954– .

Cyril of Alexandria. *Commentary on the Gospel According to S. John.* 2 vols. Vol. 1: *S. John I–VIII.* Translated by P. E. Pusey. Oxford: James Parker, 1874. Vol. 2: *S. John IX–XXI.* Translated by Thomas Randell. London: Walter Smith, 1885.

Denis the Carthusian. *Enarratio in Evangelium secundum Joannem.* Vol. 12 of *Opera omnia*, 42 vols. in 44. Monstrolii: S. M. De Pratis, 1901.

Erasmus of Rotterdam. *Des. Erasmi Roterodami in Novum Testamentum ab eodem tertio recognitum, annotationes item ab ipso recognitae, & auctario neutiquam poenitendo locupletatae.* Basel: J. Froben, 1522.

———. *Erasmus' Annotations on the New Testament: The Gospels.* Facsimile of the final Latin text (1535) with all earlier variants. Edited by Anne Reeve. London: Duckworth, 1986.

———. *Novum Instrumentum omne.* Basel: J. Froben, 1516. Facsimile. Stuttgart-Bad Cannstatt: Frommann-Holzboog, 1986.

———. *Paraphrase on John.* Translated by Jane E. Phillips. Vol. 46 of *Collected Works of Erasmus.* Toronto: University of Toronto Press, 1991.

———. *Paraphrasis in Evangelium secundum Ioannem.* Basel: J. Froben, 1523.

———. *Paraphrasis in Evangelium secundum Ioannem, ad illustrissimum principem Ferdinandum, per autorem recognita.* Basel: J. Froben, 1534.

Faber Stapulensis, Jacobus. *Commentarii initiatorii in quatuor Evangelia.* Basel: Andreas Cratander, 1523.

Hugh of St. Cher. *Postilla super totam Bibliam.* Vol. 6: *In Evangelia secundum Matthaeum, Marcum, Lucam, & Joannem.* Venice: N. Pezzana, 1732.

John Chrysostom. *Commentary on Saint John the Apostle and Evangelist.* Vols. 33 and 41 of *The Fathers of the Church.* Translated by Sister Thomas Aquinas Goggin. New York: Fathers of the Church, 1957–1959.

———. *Opera D. Ioannis Chrysostomi archiepiscopi constantinopolitani.* Basel: Johann Herwagen, 1539.

John Major. *In quatuor Euangelia expositiones luculentae et disquisitiones et disputationes contra haereticos plurime, praemisso serie literarum indice, et additis ad finem operis quatuor quaestionibus non impertinentibus.* Paris: Josse Bade, 1529.

Melanchthon, Philip. *Philippi Melanchthonis opera quae supersunt omnia.* Edited by C. G. Bretschneider and H. E. Bindseil. Vol. 14 of the *Corpus Reformatorum.* Halle and Brunswick: C. A. Schwetschke and Sons, 1847.

Migne, Jacques Paul, general editor. *Patrologiae cursus completus.* Series Graece. 161 vols. in 166. Paris, 1857–1866.

———. *Patrologiae cursus completus.* Series Latina. 221 vols. Paris, 1844–1890.

Musculus, Wolfgang. *Adversus libellum Iohannis Cochlaei de sacerdotio et sacrificio novae legis aeditum.* Augsburg: Philip Ulhardt, 1544.

———. *Ain frydsams unnd Christlichs Gesprech ains Evangelischen auff ainer und ains Widerteuffers auff der andern seyten so sy des Aydschwürs halben mitainander thünd.* Augsburg: Philip Ulhardt?, 1533.

———. *Auff das Büchlin Johannis Cochlei welche er zur verthüdigung Bäpstlichs Priesterthumbs unnd Messopffers im Jahr 1544 wider die leer des Euangelions inn den Truck geben hat. Erste Antwort und Ablaynung.* Augsburg: Philip Ulhardt, 1545.

———. *In Mosis Genesim plenissimi commentarii, in quibus veterum & recentiorum sententiae diligenter expenduntur.* Basel: Johann Herwagen, 1554.

————. *Commentariorum in Evangelistam Ioannem, heptas prima.* Basel: Bartholomäus Westheimer, 1545. *Heptas altera, item tertia et postrema in eundem.* Basel: Johann Herwagen, 1548.

————. *In Davidis Psalterium Sacrosanctum commentarii: In quibus et reliqua catholicae religionis nostrae capita passim, non praetermissis orthodoxorum etiam Patrum sententiis, ita tractantur, ut Christianus lector nihil desiderare amplius possit.* Basel: Sebastian Henricpetri, 1599.

————. *In epistolas apostoli Pauli, ad Galatas et Ephesios commentarii.* Basel: Johann Herwagen, 1561.

————. *In Esaiam prophetam commentarii locupletissimi ac recens editi.* Basel: Johann Herwagen, 1557.

————. *Loci communes in usus sacrae theologiae candidatorum parati.* Basel: Johann Herwagen, 1560.

————. *Loci communes sacrae theologiae, iam recens recogniti et emendati.* Basel: Johann Herwagen, 1563.

————. *Von der zaal und außtheylung der zehen gebott auß den alten Lereren gezogen.* Bern: Matthew Apiarius, 1551.

New Testament. Latin. *Novum Testamentum totum Erasmo interpraete per eum castigatis aliquot locis, in quibus operatum incuria, fuerat erratum, adiecta et nova illius praefatione.* Antwerp: Michael Hillenius, 1520.

Nicholas of Lyra. *Postilla super totam Bibliam.* 4 vols. Strasbourg, 1492. Reprint. Frankfurt: Minerva, 1971.

Nonnus of Panopolis. *Paraphrasis in Joannem.* Vol. 43 of Migne, *Patrologiae.* Series Graece.

Œcolampadius, Johannis. *Annotationes piae ac doctae in Evangelium Ioannis.* Basel: Andreas Cratander and Johannes Bebel, 1535.

Rupert of Deutz. *Commentaria in Evangelium Sancti Iohannis.* Vol. 9 of *Corpus Christianorum.* Edited by Rhabanus Haacke. Turnholt: Brepols, 1969.

Sarcerius, Erasmus. *In Ioannem Evangelistam iusta scholia summa diligentia, ad perpetuae textus cohaerentiae filium, per Erasmum Sarcerium Annemontanum conscripta.* Basel: Bartholomäus Westheimer, 1541.

Theophylact. *Enarratio in Evangelion Joannis.* Vol. 123 of Migne, *Patrologiae.* Series Graece.

Titelmans, Francis. *Elucidatio paraphrastica in sanctum Christi Evangelium secundum Ioannem, cum annotationibus in aliquot capita.* Antwerp: Simon Coquus, 1543.

Thomas Aquinas. *Commentary on the Gospel of St. John.* Vol. 4 of Aquinas Scripture Series. Translated by James A. Weisheipl and Fabian R. Larcher. Albany: Magi, 1980.

————. *Sancti Thomae Aquinatis Doctoris Angelici Ordinis Praedicatorum opera omnia.* Vol. 10: *Commentum in Matthaeum et Joannem Evangelistas.* Vol. 12: *Catena aurea in quatuor Evangelia.* Parma: P. Fiaccadori, 1852–1873. Reprint. New York: Musurgia, 1948–1950.

Zofingen. Stadtbibliothek. MS, PA 15A.

Zwingli, Ulrich. *In evangelicam historiam de Domino nostro Iesv Christo, per Matthaevm, Marcvm, Lucam, & Ioannem conscriptam, Epistolasque aliquot Pauli, annotationes D. Hvldrychi Zvinglii per Leonem Iudae exceptae & aeditae.* Edited by Leo Jud. Zurich: C. Froschauer, 1539.

SECONDARY SOURCES

General Studies

Adam, Paul. "L'Humanisme à Sélestat." In *Les lettres en Alsace*. Strasbourg: Société savante d'Alsace, 1962.

Altaner, Berthold, and Alfred Stuiber. *Patrologie*. Freiburg: Herder, 1978.

Backus, Irena. *Lectures humanistes de Basile de Césarée (Traductions latines 1439–1618)*. Paris: Etudes Augustiniennes, 1990.

Baker, J. Wayne. *Heinrich Bullinger and the Covenant: The Other Reformed Tradition*. Athens: Ohio University Press, 1980.

Bardenhewer, Otto. *Geschichte der Altkirchlichen Literatur*. 4 vols. Darmstadt: Wissenschaftliche Buchgesellschaft, 1962.

Barrett, C. K. *The Gospel According to St. John*. Philadelphia: Westminster, 1978.

Benzing, Josef von. *Buchdruckerlexikon des 16. Jahrhunderts (Deutsches Sprachgebiet)*. Frankfurt: Vittorio Klostermann, 1952.

Bierma, Lyle Dean. "The Covenant Theology of Caspar Olevian." Ph.D. diss., Duke University, 1980.

Broadhead, Philip. "Politics and Expediency in the Augsburg Reformation." In *Reformation Principle and Practice: Essays in Honour of Arthur Geoffrey Dickens*. Edited by Peter Newman Brooks. London: Scolar, 1980.

Broadie, Alexander. *The Circle of John Mair: Logic and Logicians in Pre-Reformation Scotland*. Oxford: Clarendon, 1985.

Brown, Raymond E. *The Gospel According to John I–XII*. New York: Doubleday, 1966.

Cappelli, Adriano. *The Elements of Abbreviation in Medieval Latin Paleography*. Translated by David Heimann and Richard Kay. Lawrence: University of Kansas Libraries, 1982.

Coppens, Joseph. "Les idées réformistes d'Erasme dans les Préfaces aux Paraphrases du Nouveau Testament." In *Scrinium Lovaniense*. Edited by Etienne van Cauwenbergh. Louvain: Editions J. Duculot, S. A. Gembloux, 1961.

De Troeyer, Benjamin. *Bio-bibliographia Franciscana Neerlandica Saeculi XVI*. 2 vols. Nieuwkoop: B. De Graaf, 1969–1970.

Dobschütz, Detlef von. "Die Geschichte der Kirchengemeinde Heilig-Kreuz und ihrer Kirche." In *Die Evangelische Heilig-Kreuz-Kirche in Augsburg*. Augsburg: Evangelisch-Lutherisches Pfarramt, 1981.

Durkan, John. "The School of John Major: Bibliography." *Innes Review* 1 (1950): 140–146.

Eells, Hastings. *Martin Bucer*. New Haven: Yale University Press, 1931.

Farge, James K. *Biographical Register of Paris Doctors of Theology, 1500–1536*. Toronto: Pontifical Institute of Medieval Studies, 1980.

Gerretsen, J. H. *Micronius. Zijn leven, zijn geschriften, zijn geestesrichting*. Nijmegen: H. Ten Hoet, 1895.

Groner, J. F. *Kardinal Cajetan: Eine Gestalt aus der Reformationszeit*. Freiburg: Société Philosophique, 1951.

Guggisberg, Kurt. *Bernische Kirchengeschichte*. Bern: Paul Haupt, 1958.

Harbison, E. Harris. *The Christian Scholar in the Age of the Reformation.* New York: Scribner, 1956.

Heppe, Heinrich. *Geschichte des Pietismus und der Mystik in der reformierten Kirche, namentlich in der Niederlande.* Leiden: E. J. Brill, 1879.

———. *Reformed Dogmatics Set Out and Illustrated from the Sources.* Edited by Ernst Bizer. Translated by G. T. Thomson. London: George Allen, 1950.

Im Hof, Ulrich. "Die reformierte Hohe Schule zu Bern. Vom Gründungsjahr 1528 bis in die zweite Hälfte des 16. Jahrhunderts." In *450 Jahre Berner Reformation. Beiträge zur Geschichte der Berner Reformation und zu Niklaus Manuel.* Bern: Historischer Verein des Kantons Bern, 1980.

Jesse, Horst. *Die Geschichte der Evangelischen Kirche in Augsburg.* Pfaffenhofen: W. Ludwig, 1983.

Köberlin, Karl. *Geschichte des humanistischen Gymnasiums bei St. Anna in Augsburg von 1531 bis 1931.* Augsburg: Gymnasium bei St. Anna, 1931.

Kristeller, Paul Oskar. *Renaissance Thought: The Classic, Scholastic, and Humanist Strains.* New York: Harper, 1961.

Leclercq, Jean. *The Love of Learning and the Desire for God: A Study of Monastic Culture.* Translated by Catharine Misrahi. New York: Fordham University Press, 1982.

Lenk, Loenhard. *Augsburger Bürgertum in Späthumanismus und Frühbarock (1580–1700).* Augsburg: H. Mühlberger, 1968.

Locher, Gottfried W. *Die Zwinglische Reformation im Rahmen der europäischen Kirchengeschichte.* Göttingen: Vandenhoeck & Ruprecht, 1979.

———. "Zwinglis Einfluß in England und Schottland—Daten und Probleme." *Zwingliana* 14 (1975): 165–209.

McCoy, Charles S., and J. Wayne Baker. *Fountainhead of Federalism: Heinrich Bullinger and the Covenantal Tradition.* Louisville, Ky.: Westminster/John Knox, 1991.

McLaughlin, R. Emmet. *Caspar Schwenckfeld, Reluctant Radical: His Life to 1540.* New Haven: Yale University Press, 1986.

Muller, Richard A. *Christ and the Decree: Christology and Predestination in Reformed Theology from Calvin to Perkins.* Studies in Historical Theology no. 2. Durham, N.C.: Labyrinth, 1986.

———. *Dictionary of Latin and Greek Theological Terms.* Grand Rapids: Baker, 1985.

———. *Post-Reformation Reformed Dogmatics.* Vol. 1: *Prolegomena to Theology.* Grand Rapids: Baker, 1987. Vol. 2: *Holy Scripture: The Cognitive Foundation of Theology.* Grand Rapids: Baker, 1993.

Oakley, Francis. "Almain and Major: Conciliar Theory on the Eve of the Reformation." *American Historical Review* 70 (1965): 673–690.

———. "From Constance to 1688: The Political Thought of John Major and George Buchanan." *Journal of British Studies* 1 (1962): 12–19.

Pettegree, Andrew. *Foreign Protestant Communities in Sixteenth-Century London.* Oxford: Clarendon, 1986.

Pfister, Rudolf. *Kirchengeschichte der Schweiz.* Vol. 2: *Von der Reformation bis zum zweiten Villmerger Krieg.* Zurich: Theologischer Verlag, 1974.

Quasten, Johannes. *Patrology.* 3 vols. Antwerp: Spectrum, 1960.

Ritschl, Otto. *Dogmengeschichte des Protestantismus.* 4 vols. Göttingen: Vandenhoeck & Ruprecht, 1908–1927.

Roth, Friedrich. *Augsburgs Reformationsgeschichte.* 4 vols. Munich: Theodor Ackermann, 1901–1911.

Rummel, Erika. *Erasmus and His Catholic Critics II. 1523–1536.* Nieuwkoop: De Graaf, 1989.

Schmidt, Charles. *Histoire Littéraire de l'Alsace a la fin du XVe et au commencement du XVIe siècle.* Hildesheim: Georg Olms, 1966.

Schmitz, Wolfgang. *Het Aandeel der Minderbroeders in Onze Middeleeuwse Literatur: Inleidung tot een Bibliografie der Nederlandse Franciscanen.* Nijmegen: Dekker & Van de Vegt, 1936.

Schrenk, Gottlob. *Gottesreich und Bund im Älteren Protestantismus: vornemlich bei Johannes Cocceius.* Gütersloh: C. Bertelsmann, 1923.

Schwarz, W. *Principles and Problems of Biblical Translation: Some Reformation Controversies and Their Background.* Cambridge: Cambridge University Press, 1955.

Schweizer, Alexander. *Die Glaubenslehre der evangelish-reformierten Kirche dargestellt und aus den Quellen belegt.* 2 vols. Zurich: Orell, Füssli & Comp., 1844–1847.

Schweizer, Josef. *Ambrosius Catharinus Politus (1484–1553) ein Theologe des Reformationszeitalters.* Münster: Verlag der Aschendorffschen Buchhandlung, 1910.

Shaw, Duncan. "Zwinglianische Einflüsse in der Schottischen Reformation." *Zwingliana* 17 (1988): 375–400.

Staehelin, Ernst. *Das theologische Lebenswerk Johannes Oekolampads.* Leipzig: M. Heinsius Nachfolger, 1939.

Strehle, Stephen. *Calvinism, Federalism, and Scholasticism: A Study of the Reformed Doctrine of Covenant.* Basler und Berner Studien zur historischen und systematischen Theologie 58. Bern: Peter Lang, 1988.

Stupperich, Robert. *Reformatorenlexikon.* Gütersloh: Gerd Mohn, 1984.

Vuilleumier, Henri. *Histoire de l'Église Réformée du Pays de Vaud sous le Régime Bernois.* 4 vols. Lausanne: Éditions la Concorde, 1927–1933.

Weir, David A. *The Origins of Federal Theology in Sixteenth-Century Reformation Thought.* New York: Oxford, 1990.

Wesel-Roth, Ruth. *Thomas Erastus. Ein Beitrag zur Geschichte der reformierten Kirche und zur Lehre von der Staatssouveränität.* Veröffentlichungen des Vereins für Kirchengeschichte in der evang. Landeskirche Badens 15. Lahr/Baden: Moritz Schauenburg, 1954.

On Wolfgang Musculus

Bäumlin, Richard. "Naturrecht und obrigkeitliches Kirchenregiment bei Wolfgang Musculus." In *Für Kirche und Recht: Festschrift für Johannes Heckel zum 70. Geburtstag.* Edited by Siegfried Grundmann. Cologne: Böhlau, 1959.

Beza, Theodor. *Les vrais portraits des hommes illustres en piété et doctrine.* Paris: Jean de Laon, 1581. Reprint, Geneva: Slatkine, 1986.

Dellsperger, Rudolf. "Wolfgang Musculus (1497–1563)." In *Die Augsburger Kirchenordnung von 1537 und ihr Umfeld.* Edited by Reinhard Schwarz. Schriften des Vereins für Reformationsgeschichte 196. Gütersloh: Gütersloher Verlaghaus Gerd Mohn, 1988.

Farmer, Craig S. "Wolfgang Musculus and the Allegory of Malchus's Ear." *Westminster Theological Journal* 56 (1994): 285–301.

————. "Wolfgang Musculus's Commentary on John: Tradition and Innovation in the Story of the Woman Taken in Adultery." In *Biblical Interpretation in the Era of the Reformation*, ed. Richard A. Muller and John L. Thompson. Grand Rapids: Eerdmans, 1996.

Ford, James Thomas. "The Shaping of a Reformer: An Introduction to the Life and Thought of Wolfgang Musculus." M.A. thesis, University of Wisconsin-Madison, 1992.

Grimme, F. "Wolfgang Musculus. Vortrag gehalten in der Sitzung vom 23. Januar, 1894." *Jahr-Buch der Gesellschaft für lothringische Geschichte und Altertumskunde* 5 (1893): 1–20.

Grote, Ludwig. *Wolfgang Musculus, ein biographischer Versuch.* Hamburg: Rauhes Haus, 1855.

Kreßner, Helmut. "Die Weiterbildung des Zwinglischen Systems durch Wolfgang Musculus." In *Schweizer Ursprünge des anglikanischen Staatskirchentums.* Schriften des Vereins für Reformationsgeschichte no. 170. Gütersloh: C. Bertelsmann, 1953.

Lenoir, S. "Wolfgang Musculus—Biographie, 1497–1563." In *Le Chrétien Évangélique revue religieuse de la suisse romande.* Lausanne, 1883.

Musculus, Abraham. "Historia vitae et obitus clarissimi theologi D. Wolfgangi Musculus Dusani, S. Litterarum apud Bernates professoris." In *ΣΥΝΟΨΙΣ festalium concionum, authore D. Wolfgango Musculo Dusano. Eiusdem vita, obitus, erudita carmina.* Basel: Conrad Waldkirch, 1595.

Romane-Musculus, Paul. "Catalogue des oeuvres imprimées du théologien Wolfgang Musculus." *Revue D'Histoire et de Philosophie Religieuses* 43 (1963): 260–278.

————. "Wolfgang Musculus en Lorraine et en Alsace." *Société de l'Histoire du Protestantisme français*, Oct.–Dec. 1931, 487–501.

Schuler, Manfred. "Ist Wolfgang Musculus wirklich der Autor mehrerer Kirchenlieder?" *Jahrbuch für Liturgik und Hymnologie* 17 (1972): 217–221.

Schwab, Paul J. *The Attitude of Wolfgang Musculus toward Religious Tolerance.* Yale Studies in Religion no. 6. New Haven: Yale University Press, 1933.

Streuber, Wilhelm T. "Wolfgang Musculus oder Müslin. Ein Lebensbild aus der Reformationszeit. Aus dem handschriftichen Nachlasse des verstorbenen Dr. Wilhelm Theodor Streuber." In *Berner Taschenbuch auf das Jahr 1860.* Bern, 1860.

Weber, Rudolf. "Wolfgang und Abraham Musculus. Die Sammler der Zofinger Humanistenbriefe." *Zofinger Neujahrsblatt* 69 (1984): 5–19.

History of Exegesis

Aldridge, J. W. *The Hermeneutic of Erasmus.* Zurich, 1966.

Anderson, Marvin. "Erasmus the Exegete." *Concordia Theological Monthly* 40 (1969): 722–733.

Bainton, Roland H. "The Paraphrases of Erasmus." *Archiv für Reformationsgeschichte* 57 (1966): 67–75.

Bedouelle, Guy. *Lefèvre d'Etaples et l'Intelligence des Ecritures.* Geneva: Librairie Droz S. A., 1976.

Bedouelle, Guy, and Bernard Roussel, eds. *Le temps des Réformes et la Bible.* La Collection Bible de Tous les Temps 5. Paris: Beauchesne, 1989.

Bentley, Jerry H. "Erasmus' *Annotationes in Novum Testamentum* and the Textual Criticism of the Gospels." *Archiv für Reformationsgeschichte* 67 (1976): 33–53.

———. *Humanists and Holy Writ: New Testament Scholarship in the Renaissance.* Princeton: Princeton University Press, 1983.

———. "New Testament Scholarship at Louvain in the Early Sixteenth Century." In *Studies in Medieval and Renaissance History.* New series, vol. 2. Edited by J. A. S. Evans. Vancouver: University of British Columbia, 1979.

Bouterse, Johannes. *De boom en zijn vruchten. Bergrede-christendom bij Reformatoren, Anabaptisten en Spiritualisten in de zestiende eeuw.* Kampen: J. H. Kok, 1987.

Cambridge History of the Bible. Vol. 1: *From Beginnings to Jerome.* Edited by P. R. Ackroyd and C. F. Evans. Vol. 2: *The West from the Fathers to the Reformation.* Edited by G. W. H. Lampe. Vol. 3: *The West from the Reformation to the Present Day.* Edited by S. L. Greenslade. Cambridge: Cambridge University Press, 1963–1970.

Childs, Brevard S. "The *Sensus Literalis* of Scripture: An Ancient and Modern Problem." In *Beiträge zur alttestamentlichen Theologie. Festschrift für Walther Zimmerli zum 70. Geburtstag.* Edited by Herbert Donner et al. Göttingen: Vandenhoeck und Ruprecht, 1977.

Chomarat, Jacques. "Grammar and Rhetoric in the Paraphrases of the Gospels by Erasmus." *Erasmus of Rotterdam Society Yearbook One* (1981): 30–68.

Collins, Thomas Aquinas. "Cardinal Cajetan's Fundamental Biblical Principles." *Catholic Biblical Quarterly* 17 (1955): 363–378.

———. "The Cajetan Controversy." *American Ecclesiastical Review* 128 (1953): 90–100.

Ebeling, Gerhard. "Die Anfänge von Luthers Hermeneutik." *Zeitschrift für Theologie und Kirche* 48 (1961): 172–230.

———. *Evangelische Evangelienauslegung: Eine Untersuchung zu Luthers Hermeneutik.* Munich: Christian Kaiser, 1942.

Evans, G. R. *The Language and Logic of the Bible: The Earlier Middle Ages.* Cambridge: Cambridge University Press, 1984.

———. *The Language and Logic of the Bible: The Road to Reformation.* Cambridge: Cambridge University Press, 1985.

Fatio, Oliver, and Pierre Fraenkel, comps. *Histoire de l'exégèse au XVIe siécle: Textes du colloque international tenu à Genève en 1976.* Geneva: Librairie Droz S. A., 1978.

Froehlich, Karlfried. "'Always to Keep the Literal Sense in Holy Scripture Means to Kill One's Soul': The State of Biblical Hermeneutics at the Beginning of the Fifteenth Century." In *Literary Uses of Typology from the Late Middle Ages to the Present.* Edited by Earl Miller. Princeton: Princeton University Press, 1977.

Grant, Robert M., and David Tracy. *A Short History of the Interpretation of the Bible.* 2d ed. Philadelphia: Fortress, 1984.

Hendrix, Scott H. "Luther against the Background of the History of Biblical Interpretation." *Interpretation* 37 (1983): 229–239.

Horst, Ulrich. "Der Streit um die hl. Schrift zwischen Kardinal Cajetan und Ambrosius Catharinus." In *Wahrheit und Verkündigung* I. Edited by Leo Scheffczyk et al. Munich: Ferdinand Schöningh, 1967.

Kümmel, Friedrich. *The New Testament: The History of the Investigation of Its Problems.* Translated by S. M. Gilmour and H. C. Kee. Nashville: Abingdon, 1972.

Lerner, Robert E. "Poverty, Preaching, and Eschatology in the Revelation Commentaries of 'Hugh of St. Cher.'" In *The Bible in the Medieval World: Essays in Memory of Beryl Smalley.* Edited by Katherine Walsh and Diana Wood. Oxford: Basil Blackwell, 1985.

Lubac, Henri de. *Exégèse médiévale: Les quatre sens de l'Écriture.* 4 vols. Paris: Aubier, 1959–1964.

McKee, Elsie Anne. *Elders and the Plural Ministry: The Role of Exegetical History in Illuminating John Calvin's Theology.* Geneva: Librairie Droz S. A., 1988.

Margerie, Betrand de. *The Greek Fathers.* Translated by Leonard Maluf. Vol. 1 of *An Introduction to the History of Exegesis.* Petersham, Mass.: Saint Bede's Publications, 1993.

————. *Saint Augustine.* Translated by Pierre de Fontnouvelle. Vol. 3 of *An Introduction to the History of Exegesis.* Petersham, Mass.: Saint Bede's Publications, 1991.

Meyer, Walter E. "Die Entstehung von Huldrych Zwinglis neutestamentlichen Kommentaren und Predigtnachschriften." *Zwingliana* 14 (1976): 288–331.

Müller, Johannes. *Martin Bucers Hermeneutik.* Quellen und Forschungen zur Reformationsgeschichte 32. Gütersloh: Gütersloher Verlaghaus Gerd Mohn, 1965.

Muller, Richard A., and John L. Thompson, eds. *Biblical Interpretation in the Era of the Reformation.* Grand Rapids: Eerdmans, 1996.

Payne, John B., Albert Rabil, and Warren S. Smith. "The *Paraphrases* of Erasmus: Origen and Character." In *Collected Works of Erasmus.* Vol. 42: *New Testament Scholarship: Paraphrases on Romans and Galatians.* Edited by Robert D. Sider. Toronto: University of Toronto Press, 1984.

Parker, T. H. L. *Calvin's New Testament Commentaries.* Grand Rapids: Eerdmans, 1971.

Preus, James S. *From Shadow to Promise: Old Testament Interpretations from Augustine to the Young Luther.* Cambridge: Harvard University Press, 1969.

Quinn, Dennis B. "Erasmus as Exegete." *Proceedings of the Patristic, Medieval and Renaissance Conference* 3 (1978): 59–66.

Rabil, Albert. *Erasmus and the New Testament: The Mind of a Christian Humanist.* San Antonio: Trinity University Press, 1972.

————. "Erasmus' Paraphrases of the New Testament." In *Essays on the Works of Erasmus.* Edited by Richard L. DeMolen. New Haven: Yale University Press, 1978.

Rader, William. *The Church and Racial Hostility: A History of Interpretation of Ephesians 2:11–22.* Beiträge zur Geschichte der Biblischen Exegese 20. Tübingen: J. C. B. Mohr, 1978.

Rogerson, John, Christopher Rowland, and Barnabas Lindars. *The Study and Use of the Bible.* Vol. 2 of *The History of Christian Theology.* Edited by Paul Avis. Grand Rapids: Eerdmans, 1988.

Roussel, Bernard. "De Strasbourg a Bâle et Zurich: une 'École Rhénane' d'Exégèse (ca. 1525–1540)." *Revue d'Histoire et de Philosophie Religieuses* 68 (1988): 19–39.

Rummel, Erika. *Erasmus' Annotations on the New Testament: From Philologist to Theologian.* Toronto: University of Toronto Press, 1986.

Schlingensiepen, Hermann. "Erasmus als Exeget auf Grund seiner Schriften zu Matthäus." *Zeitschrift für Kirchengeschichte* 48 (1929): 16–57.

Simon, Richard. *Histoire Critique du Vieux Testament.* Rotterdam, 1685. Reprint. Frankfurt: Minerva, 1967.

Smalley, Beryl. *The Study of the Bible in the Middle Ages.* 1952. Notre Dame: University of Notre Dame Press, 1964.

Spicq, Ceslaus. *Esquisse d'une histoire de l'exégèse latine au moyen âge.* Paris: Libraire philosophie J. Vrin, 1944.

Steinmetz, David C. "The Superiority of Pre-Critical Exegesis." *Theology Today* 37 (1980): 27–38.

―――, ed. *The Bible in the Sixteenth Century.* Duke Monographs in Medieval and Renaissance Studies 11. Durham, NC: Duke University Press, 1990.

Stierle, Beate. "Schriftauslegung der Reformationszeit." *Verkündigung und Forschung* 16 (1971): 55–88.

Thompson, John Lee. *John Calvin and the Daughters of Sarah: Women in Regular and Exceptional Roles in the Exegesis of Calvin, His Predecessors, and His Contemporaries.* Geneva: Librairie Droz S.A., 1992.

Torrance, Thomas F. *The Hermeneutics of John Calvin.* Edinburgh: Scottish Academic Press, 1988.

Walsh, Katherine, and Diana Wood, eds. *The Bible in the Medieval World: Essays in Memory of Beryl Smalley.* Oxford: Basil Blackwell, 1985.

History of Exegesis of the Gospel of John

Boismard, M.-E. *Du Baptême à Cana (Jean 1, 19–2, 11).* Paris: Les Éditions du Cerf, 1956.

Bresolin, Angelo. "L'esegesi di Giov. 2, 4 nei Padri Latini." *Revue des Etudes Augustiniennes* 8 (1962): 243–273.

Cavallera, Ferdinand. "L'interprétation du chapitre VI de saint Jean: Une controverse exégétique au Concile de Trente." *Revue d'Histoire Ecclésiastique* 10 (1909): 687–709.

du Manoir, H. "La scène de Cana commentée par Cyrille d'Alexandrie." In *De primordiis cultus Mariani. Acta Congressus Mariologici-Mariani* III. Rome, 1970.

Ellwein, Eduard. *Summus Evangelista: Die Botschaft des Johannesevangelium in der Auslegung Luther.* Munich: Christian Kaiser, 1960.

Farmer, Craig S. "Changing Images of the Samaritan Woman in Early Reformed Commentaries on John." *Church History* 65 (1996): 365–375.

Gäbler, Ulrich. "Bullingers Vorlesung über das Johannesevangelium aus dem Jahre 1523." In *Heinrich Bullinger 1504–1575: Gesammelte Aufsätze zum 400. Todestag.* Edited by U. Gäbler and E. Herkenrath. Zurich: Theologischer Verlag, 1975.

Heine, Rolf. "Zur patristischen Auslegung von Ioh. 2, 1–12." *Wiener Studien* 83 (1970): 189–195.

Joirrot, C. A. L. "Erasmus' *In Principio Erat Sermo* : A Controversial Translation." *Studies in Philology* 61 (1964): 35–40.

Kremer, Jacob. *Lazarus: Die Geschichte einer Auferstehung.* Stuttgart: Katholisches Bibelwerk, 1985.

Lohse, Wolfram. "Die Fußwaschung (Joh. 13, 1–20). Eine Geschichte ihrer Deutung." Ph.D. diss., University of Erlangen/Nuremberg, 1967.

Löwenich, Walther von. *Die Eigenart von Luthers Auslegung des Johannes-Prologs.* Munich: Verlag der Bayerischen Akademie der Wissenschaften, 1960.

Rabil, Albert. "Erasmus' Paraphrase of the Gospel of John." *Church History* 48 (1979): 142–155.

Ramos-Regidor, José. "Signo y Poder: a proposito de la exegesis patristica de Jn 2, 1–11." *Salesianum* (1965): 499–562.

Reuss, Joseph. "Joh 2, 3–4 in Johannes Kommentaren der griechischen Kirche." In *Neutestamentliche Aufsätze: Festschrift für Josef Schmid zum 70. Geburtstag.* Edited by J. Blinzler, O. Kuss, and F. Mussner. Regensburg: Pustet, 1963.

Rivera, A. "Nota sobre el simbolismo del milagro de Caná en la interpretación patrística." *Estudios Marianos* 13 (1953): 62–72.

Sanders, J. N. *The Fourth Gospel in the Early Church.* Cambridge: Cambridge University Press, 1943.

Smitmans, Adolf. *Das Weinwunder von Kana: Die Auslegung von Jo 2, 1–11 bei den Vätern und heute.* Tübingen: J. C. B. Mohr, 1966.

Weisheipl, J. A. "The Johannine Commentary of Friar Thomas." *Church History* 45 (1976): 185–195.

Wengert, Timothy J. *Philip Melanchthon's Annotationes in Johannem in Relation to its Predecessors and Contemporaries.* Geneva: Librairie Droz S. A., 1987.

———. "The Dating of Huldrych Zwingli's Lectures on John." *Zwingliana* 24 (1986): 6–10.

Wiles, M. F. *The Spiritual Gospel: The Interpretation of the Fourth Gospel in the Early Church.* Cambridge: Cambridge University Press, 1960.

Index

Abraham, 155, 164
Active/contemplative life, 156–157
Albertists, 49
Albert the Great, 189n26, 201n23
Alcuin, 201nn23, 28
Alexander of Hales, 201n23
Alexander of Villa Dei, 31
Allegory, 9, 26–28, 50–53, 62, 67–68, 77,
  107–108, 131, 146, 148, 155, 175–
  176, 179–181, 222n55, 223n1,
  229n98
  boat, 106, 181, 213nn90, 92
  darkness, 101–102
  grass, 73
  healing of man born blind, 143–144,
    147
  healing of paralytic, 121–123, 130–131
  loaves and fish, 71–72, 181
  marriage, 24–26
  ministry of Word, 71, 180
  mountain, 57, 75–77
  pool of Bethesda, 117–118, 181
  pool of Siloam, 143, 145, 147
  raising of Lazarus, 151–152, 154, 173–
    176, 181, 224n14
  shout of Jesus, 172–173, 175–176
  spit and clay, 143–144, 146–147, 181
  stone on Lazarus's tomb, 168, 228n75
  storm at sea, 101–105, 180, 212n77
  water into wine, 14, 23, 180, 190n76
Alsace, 30

Ambrose, 34, 36, 192n1
Amerbach, Boniface, 31
Ammonius of Alexandria, 189n34
Anabaptists, 7, 23, 132, 165, 167
Anagogy, 51–53, 67, 70–75, 77, 179
  disciples, 74
  food, 70–71, 75
  leftovers, 75
  satiety, 74–75
  wedding feast, 77
Anger. See Jesus Christ; anger of; Moral
  interpretation: anger
Anselm of Canterbury, 217n31
Aquinas, Thomas, 12–14, 17, 19–20, 22–
  23, 53, 55–59, 62–68, 71, 73, 76,
  201n23, 211n50, 212nn68, 77,
  213nn81, 86, 92, 217n42, 218nn43,
  56, 60
Aristotle, 110, 113, 216n26
Arnobius the Younger, 197n57
Astrology, 20
Athanasius, 32, 36, 227n55
Augsburg, 3–4, 6–7, 32–33, 148, 178,
  187n33, 193n20
Augustine, 8, 12, 15, 20–21, 23–24, 27, 29,
  33–34, 36–42, 45, 47, 63, 75, 84,
  92, 113, 132–133, 150, 174, 178,
  181, 192n1, 197n59, 212nn68, 77,
  213nn90, 94, 218n48, 219n69,
  228n75
Authority, spheres of, 21

243

Backus, Irena, 227nn58, 61, 229n98
Baptism, 117–118, 130, 142, 145, 147,
    217n39
Baptist of Mantua, 31
Barth, Margaretha, 6
Basel, 7, 148–149, 184n2, 193n20, 223n1
Basil of Caesarea, 32–34, 191n1, 227n55
Bäumlin, Richard, 5
Beaton, James, 112
Bede, 201nn23, 28, 217n31
Bern, 3, 5–7, 148, 178, 187n35, 224n11
Bernard of Clairvaux, 48, 217n31
Betuleius, Xystus, 32–33, 78, 193n20,
    194n27
Beza, Theodor, 6
Biel, Gabriel, 49
Birk, Sixt. *See* Betuleius, Xystus
Blaurer, Ambrose, 184n10, 187n33,
    193n21
Blindness, spiritual, 144–145
Bonaventure, 8, 189n26, 217n31
Bondage of will, 123, 131
Brenz, Johannes, 132–135, 137–143, 147,
    221nn28, 29, 223n1, 227n58,
    229n98
Brethren of the Common Life, 30
Broickwy von Königstein, Antonius,
    109–113, 115, 117–122, 124–130,
    215nn15, 18, 217n29, 219n73
Brühl, 111
Bucer, Martin, 4, 6–7, 12, 15–17, 19, 21,
    23–24, 26, 30, 32–33, 86, 93–94,
    132, 147–152, 154–155, 159–161,
    164–167, 169–176, 223nn1, 2
Buchanan, George, 215n9
Bullinger, Heinrich, 7, 149–150, 152–153,
    155–162, 164–165, 167–176,
    184n3, 223n1, 224n11, 229n98
Bürgerbibliothek Bern, 184n9, 186n25,
    193n21
Burial of dead. *See* Moral interpretation:
    burial of dead

Cajetan, Tommaso de Vio, 109, 214nn2, 4
Calvin, John, 4–5, 7, 49, 86, 147–148,
    184n4, 215n9, 223n1
Cambridge, 4, 110
Canterbury, 4
Capito, Wolfgang, 7, 32, 78, 148, 223n1

Capuchins, 112
Catharinus, Ambrosius, 109
Cato, 206n1
Celibacy, 25–26
Chrysostom, John, 8, 12–17, 19–23, 27,
    29, 33–36, 38–43, 45–47, 55, 61,
    63, 67, 84, 91–92, 113, 126–127,
    132–133, 150, 178–179, 181,
    189n34, 191nn1, 85, 193n20,
    194n25, 197n59, 210n47, 211nn50,
    59, 63, 212n68, 217nn39, 41,
    218n53, 219nn73, 77, 80, 221n16,
    222n39, 225n27, 226n32, 228n73
Church of the Holy Cross, 7, 32, 193n19
Cicero, 31, 193n20
Cochlaeus, Johann, 46, 195n39
Colmar, 30–31
Cologne, 111
Compassion. *See* Mary: compassion of;
    Moral interpretation: compassion
Confession, auricular, 112
Constance, 7
Contemplative/active life, 156–157
Conversion, process of, 122–123, 131
Cranmer, Thomas, 4
Creation, *ex nihilo*, 14–15, 27
Cruciger, Caspar, 191n85
Cruciger, Felix, 4, 184n4
Curiosity, 56, 99–100, 136–137, 146
Cyprian, 34, 192n1
Cyril of Alexandria, 12, 20–24, 29, 32–34,
    38–42, 45, 55, 84, 113, 119, 132–
    133, 150, 178, 191n1, 194n28,
    197n59

Decalogue, division of, 36, 196nn47, 48
Dellsperger, Rudolf, 6
Denis of Leeuwen. *See* Denis the
    Carthusian
Denis the Carthusian, 12, 16–20, 23–25,
    53, 55–59, 62, 64–66, 68, 70–73,
    75–76, 201n23
De Troeyer, Benjamin, 111
Dieuz, 6, 30–31
Donauwörth, 7
Dorlitzheim, 6
Dringenberg, Ludwig, 30
Drunkenness. *See* Moral interpretation:
    drunkenness

East Frisia, 4
Elijah, 66
Elisha, 41, 61, 66, 142–143
Eparchus, Antonius, 194nn27, 28
Epiphanius of Salamis, 191n1
Episcopius, Eusebius, 3
Erasmus, Desiderius, 12–18, 21, 23, 26,
    30, 64, 78–102, 105, 107, 111–114,
    132, 159–160, 179, 208n8
  annotations of, 64, 79, 86–92, 107, 113,
    179, 216n23, 217n29
  paraphrases of, 79, 82, 93
  translation of New Testament of. *See*
    New Testament, Latin: Erasmus's
    translation of
Erastus, Thomas, 4, 5, 185n11
Estienne, Robert, 208n7, 223n3
Eucharist. *See* Lord's Supper
Euripides, 206n1
Eusebius, 34, 89, 194n24
Evagrius Scholasticus, 194n24
Excommunication, 139, 146, 174, 221n28
Exegesis. *See also* Tradition, exegetical
  history of, 5, 8–9, 11–12
  Jewish, 149
  loci method of, 133, 147
  Rhenish school of, 223n1
Exorcism, 118

Faber Stapulensis, Jacobus, 78, 92–102,
    106–107, 112
Faith, 19, 39, 61, 157, 160, 162, 166, 171
  certitude of, 159
  confession of, 65–66, 158–160, 176
  effects of, 161
  as goal of miracles, 13, 39, 46, 64, 98,
    143
  in miracles, 43, 45
  mysteries of, 75
  and obedience, 145
  and prayer, 17, 19
  in providence, 169
  and reason, 47, 62
  as result of miracles, 39, 45
  as result of suffering, 139
  without signs, 39, 42–43
  weakness of, 40–44, 65, 97–98, 157–
    161, 169–170
Farel, Guillaume, 4

Fate, 20–21
Fear. *See* Moral interpretation: fear
Florilegium, 113–114
Franciscans, 111–112
Frankfurt-am-Main, 111
Frecht, Martin, 193n21
Friars Minor, Order of. *See* Franciscans
Froben, Hieronymus, 194n25

Ganoczy, Alexandre, 216n25
Gasser, Achilles Pirminus, 194n26
Gast, Johann, 149
Gebwiler, Hieronymus, 30
Gemuseus, Hieronymus, 30
Geneva, 148
Glasgow, University of, 110
Glossa ordinaria, 53, 65, 71–73, 75,
    201nn23, 28
Gospel, 43, 140
  as *philosophia Christi*, 79
  restitution of, 162
  as spiritual food, 73
  supersedes law, 23
Gregory of Nazianzus, 32–34, 191n1,
    194n28
Gregory of Nyssa, 227n55
Grief. *See* Jesus Christ: sorrow of; Moral
    interpretation: grief
Grossmünster, 149
Grote, Ludwig, 5–6, 30, 186n25, 193n17
Guggisberg, Kurt, 6
Guilt, inherited, 135–137

Heidelberg, University of, 4, 185n11
Henricpetri, Sebastian, 3
Heresy
  and the Fathers, 36
  Manichaean, 14, 20
  Marcionite, 164
  resurrection of body, 158
  sacramental, 142, 145–146
  trinitarian, 35
Hermeneutics, medieval, 50–52, 179
Herod, 40, 55
Herwagen, Johann, 3–4, 7
Hesychius of Jerusalem, 191n1
Hilary of Poitiers, 34, 192n1
History, salvation, 76, 123, 131
Höchstetten, 5

Hofmann, Crato, 30
Horace, 31
Hospitality. *See* Moral interpretation: hospitality
Hugh of St. Cher, 12–20, 22–25, 53–56, 58–60, 63–65, 68, 70, 72–73, 189n26, 201nn23, 26, 211nn50, 63, 212nn68, 77
Humanism, definition of, 206n2
Humanists, biblical scholarship of, 8, 10, 78–79, 88, 92, 107–114, 130, 179–180, 214n2, 216n21, 223n1
Humility
   of the disciples, 74
   of Jesus, 22, 100
Hussites, 112

Ignatius of Antioch, 191n1
Illumination, spiritual, 145, 147
Interim, Augsburg, 4, 7, 224n11
Interpretation, christological, 52
Irenaeus, 34, 197n67
Irony, 93–94, 210n44
Isengrin, Michael, 184n2
Islam, 66–67, 202n43
   and polemics against Christianity, 66
Israel, 164

Jerome, 15, 34, 36, 90, 115, 130, 189n26, 191n85, 192n1, 217n31
Jerusalem, 54, 58, 114, 116
Jesus Christ
   as advocate, 171
   anger of, 163–165
   as bread of life, 70–71, 181
   divine power of, 13, 41, 45, 63, 97–98, 157, 160
   as fulfillment of law, 59
   human nature of, 20, 163–166, 227n55
   incarnation of, 24–25, 144, 146
   as king, 65, 67
   as light of world, 139–141
   as lord of nature, 14–15, 96–98
   as Passover, 59
   poverty of, 22, 68–69
   as priest, 166, 171
   as prophet, 41, 43, 45, 65–66
   sorrow of, 163–165
   two natures of, 20, 63, 66

Job, 127, 135, 139
John the Baptist, 55, 88, 90, 173
John the Evangelist, 16, 189n26
Joseph, 138, 164
Josephus, 194n25
Joshua, 90
Jud, Leo, 30, 149
Judaism: and polemics against Christianity, 66

Karlstadt, Andreas Bodenstein von, 227n61
Knowledge, prophetic, 65–66
Koblenz, 111
Königstein-am-Taunus, 111
Kreßner, Helmut, 5
Kristeller, Paul Oskar, 206n2

Lactantius, 192n1, 193n20
Latomus, Jacobus, 111
Lauterburg, Ludwig, 5
Law, 74, 134–136
   Mosaic, 71, 118
   natural, 5
   and Passover observance, 58–59
   and Sabbath observance, 124–125
Lefèvre d'Étaples. *See* Faber Stapulensis, Jacobus
Lerner, Robert E., 201n26
Livy, 206n1
Lixheim, 6, 31–32, 192n12
Lombard, Peter, 49–50, 110, 199n8
London, 4
Lord's Supper, 7, 69, 71, 75, 114, 145, 160
Lorraine, 6, 30
Lot, 155
Louvain, 111–112
Loyola, Ignatius, 215n9
Luther, Martin, 6, 31–32, 35, 49, 148
Lutherans, Lutheranism, 7, 112, 132, 187n33, 220n3, 227n58

Magic, 56, 99, 118
   suspicion of, 15, 63, 172
Major, John, 109–113, 115–116, 118–121, 124–130, 214n9, 215nn10, 12, 216nn23, 25, 26
Manlius, 137

Marburg, 4
Mariology, 17, 19
Marriage. *See* Allegory: marriage; Moral interpretation: marriage
Mary, 12, 15–21, 24, 27, 62, 189n34
    compassion of, 17
    faith of, 19
    as mediatrix, 17–19
    and prayer, 19
Mass, 7, 49
Medicine, study of, 142
Melanchthon, Philip, 8, 12, 15, 18–19, 21, 23, 26, 93, 133–135, 137–141, 147, 191n85, 204n96, 207n2
Memory, 69
Menander, 206n1
Merit, 74, 121, 131
Meyer, Sebastian, 187n33
Micron, Martin, 4–5, 184n4
Milan, 112
Ministry of Word. *See* Allegory: ministry of Word; Moral interpretation: ministry of Word
Miracles
    and divinity of Christ, 13, 20, 98, 100
    method of, 12–15, 20–21, 27, 97, 116, 141–145, 168
    and nature, 15, 188n23
    proof of, 13–14, 27, 44–45, 61, 64, 167, 169, 173
    purpose of, 13–14, 21, 39, 42–43, 46, 57, 62, 64, 70–71, 96–98, 100, 117, 119, 143
    suspicion of, 99
Monasticism, 22, 25, 156–157
Montaigu, Collège de, 110
Moore, John M., 194n28
Moral interpretation, 9, 18, 28, 46–47, 51–53, 62, 68, 76–77, 93, 101, 103, 106–108, 126, 130, 136, 148, 158, 162–163, 171, 175–176, 179–181
    anger, 165
    burial of dead, 167–168, 177
    carnality, 106
    compassion, 18, 152–154, 164–167, 170
    confession of sin, 18
    conversion of rulers, 40, 46–47
    corruption of human nature, 39, 46

curiosity, 136–137, 146. *See also* Curiosity
drunkenness, 23–24, 27
faith, 19, 43, 155, 159, 169–171. *See also* Faith
fear, 104–105
feasting on Word, 73–75
fleeing honor, 67, 126
forbearance, 158–159
grief, 157
hospitality, 155, 157, 177
marriage, 12, 22–27, 181, 191n85
meals, 69
merriment, 22–23
ministry of Word, 72–75, 102
mourning, 166. *See also* Mourning
obedience, 73, 103, 126, 145–146, 162. *See also* Obedience
parental love, 44, 47. *See also* Parents: love for children
prayer, 18–19, 22, 152–153, 171–172. *See also* Prayer
reason, judgment of, 72, 103–104, 137, 161. *See also* Reason, judgment of
repentance, 173. *See also* Repentance
rest, 157
sacraments, 145–146
satanic opposition, 103
siblings, love among, 151, 153, 177
sickness, 154, 177. *See also* Sickness
sinners, 169
sorrow for sins, 164
stewardship, 70
suffering, 22, 101, 129, 139. *See also* Suffering
thankfulness, 68–69, 70, 181
tribulation, 104–105, 139
unbelief, 43–44, 47. *See also* Unbelief
viewing the dead, 170, 177
wastefulness, 68, 70, 75
wealth, 68–69, 104
welcoming Christ, 156
Moses, 62, 65–67, 71, 145
Mourning, 164–166, 227n61
Muhammad, 57, 67
Mülhausen, 184n2
Münster, Sebastian, 223n1
Musculus, Abraham, 5–6, 30–31
Musculus, Wolfgang (1556–1625), 5

Musculus, Wolfgang (1497–1563)
  on authority of canon, 35–36
  on authority of Fathers, 33–38, 46,
      91–92, 179
  as authority on Fathers, 29, 46
  as Benedictine monk, 6, 31, 32
  biography of, 6–8
  commentaries (biblical)
    Colossians, 3, 200n21
    1 & 2 Corinthians, 3, 200n21
    Decalogue, 3
    Galatians, 3, 51, 200n21
    Genesis, 3, 29, 200nn20,
        21
    Isaiah, 3, 51, 200n21
    Matthew, 3
    Philippians, 3, 200n21
    Psalms, 3, 4, 29, 184n3, 200n21
    Romans, 3
    1 & 2 Thessalonians, 3, 200n21
    1 Timothy, 3, 7, 200n21
  education of, 6, 30–33, 78
  fame of, 3–4
  heirs of, 7–8
  influence of, 4
  and medieval hermeneutics, 50–
      52
  and medieval theology, 49–50
  modern studies of, 4–6
  and poetry, 5, 31
  study of Arabic, 193n21
  study of Greek, 32, 193n20
  study of Hebrew, 7, 32, 192n17
  study of organ, 192n13
  as translator of classics, 29, 32–33, 78,
      193n20
  works
    letter to Protestant clergy of
        Hungary, 36
    Loci communes, 3, 5, 29, 35–38,
        49–50, 184n4
    introduction to translation of
        Chrysostom, 33–35
Müslin, David, 187n35

Naaman, 41, 142–143
Navarre, 110
Neuburg an der Donau, 4
Neuweiler, 192n13

New Testament, Greek
  Colinaeus's edition of, 207n6
  Complutensian edition of, 207nn3,
      6
  Erasmus's edition of, 78–79
New Testament, Latin
  Erasmus's translation of, 64, 79–87, 89,
      92, 95, 107, 159–160, 179
  Vulgate, 64, 79–87, 89, 94–95, 107, 112,
      114, 159–160, 163, 179, 200n21,
      208nn7, 8
Nicholas of Gorran, 201n23
Nicholas of Lyra, 53, 55–58, 60, 62–65, 67,
      179, 189n26, 201nn23, 24
Nicodemus, 159
Nijmegan, 111, 215n16
Nonnus of Panopolis, 38, 40, 42, 178,
      197n60

Obedience. *See also* Moral interpretation:
      obedience
  to Christ, 19, 73, 103, 122, 125–126,
      130, 145–146, 161–162
  to the law, 58–59
  modeled by Mary, 17
  monastic, 17, 25
Ochino, Bernardino, 4
Ockham, William, 110
Ockhamists, 38, 49, 215n9
Œcolampadius, Johannes, 149–165,
      167–176, 201n24, 209n29, 223n1
Old Testament, 71, 73, 116, 160
Origen, 34, 36, 189n34, 190n58, 191n1,
      209n30, 217n31
Osiander, Andreas, 220n1
Otto Henry, Elector, 4
Ovid, 31–32

Papacy, 114
Paraphrase, 38, 114, 150, 164, 210n42
  compared to commentary, 93
Parents
  love for children, 40, 44, 47, 152
  obedience to, 16, 20, 21
Paris, 110
Passover, 53–55, 58, 59
Patience, 120–121
Pellikan, Conrad, 223n1
Penance, 25, 50

Pentecost, 53–54
Persius, 206n1
Pharaoh, 138
Pharisees, 56, 69, 143
Phrygio, Paulus Constantinus, 30
Plato, 206n1
Plutarch, 206n1
Poland, 4, 184n4
Pole, Reginald, 215n9
Polybius, 32–33
Prayer, 17–19, 22, 27, 62–63, 69, 139, 152–
    153, 158, 171, 172
  modeled by Martha and Mary, 152–153
  modeled by Mary, 17–18, 27
Providence, 45, 98, 103–104, 117, 119,
    135, 144–145, 156, 163, 168–169
Purgatory, 113
Purification, Jewish ceremonial, 13, 58,
    203
Pythagoras, 206n1

Rabelais, François, 215nn9, 13
Rappoltsweiler. *See* Ribeauvillé
Rashi, 192n17
Reason, judgment of, 43, 47, 61–62, 72,
    103–104, 134, 136–137, 140, 142–
    145, 161, 170
Regensburg, conference at, 7
Repentance, 122–123, 173, 175, 218n60
Resurrection, doctrine of, 155, 158–160,
    169–170, 173
Rhenanus, Beatus, 30
Ribeauvillé, 30
Roman Catholics, Roman Catholicism, 7,
    33, 36–38, 48, 109, 111
Rome, 112
Roth, Friedrich, 6
Roussel, Bernard, 223n1
Rupert of Deutz, 53–55, 59, 64, 70–74, 76,
    201nn23, 28

Sabbath
  controversy over, 114, 124–126, 130
  purpose of, 123–125
Sadducees, 159
St. Andrews University, 110
St. Gallen, 7, 148
Saints, worship of, 19, 112, 117
Samaritans, 39, 42–43, 197n68

Samaritan woman, 41
Sapidus, Johannes, 30
Sarah, 62
Sarcerius, Erasmus, 133–135, 137–142,
    145, 147
Schmalkald League, 7
Scholastics, scholasticism, 38, 49–50,
    113, 116, 199n8, 216n25,
    217n36
Schwab, Paul Josiah, 5
Schwäbisch Hall, 133
Schwarz, Theobald, 187n33
Schwenckfeld, Caspar, 6
Scipio, 137
Scotists, 38, 49, 215n10
Scotland, 4, 110
Scotus, Duns, 110
Secymin, 4
Sélestat, 30–31, 78
Selfishness, 100–101, 106
Septuagint, 90–91, 200n21
Siblings. *See* Moral interpretation:
    siblings, love among
Sickness
  corrective, 127–129, 154
  glorifies God, 151, 154
  reasons for, 127–128, 151
Signs, 8, 13, 40, 42–43, 55–57, 66, 99–100,
    137, 159
Simon, Richard, 4, 184n3
Sin
  confession of, 18
  and impotence of will, 122–123
  mortal/nonmortal, 154
  relationship to suffering, 127–130,
    134–141, 219n80
Smitmans, Adolf, 190n76, 191n85
Socrates Scholasticus, 194n24
Sorbonne, 109–110
Sorrow. *See* Jesus Christ: sorrow of; Moral
    interpretation: sorrow
    for sins
Soul sleep, 113
Sozomen, Salaminius Hermias,
    194n24
Stewardship. *See* Moral interpretation:
    stewardship
Strasbourg, 4, 6, 32, 148–149, 223n1
Streuber, Wilhelm T., 5–6, 186n25

Sturm, Jacob, 6
Suffering, 120–121
  as corrective, 127, 129, 154
  and glory of God, 60, 137–138, 146,
    151, 154
  and piety, 139
  and thankfulness, 22
Sulzer, Simon, 7

Tertullian, 191n85, 192n1, 217n39
Testing, 59–60, 104–105
Thales of Miletus, 206n1
Thankfulness. *See* Moral interpretation:
  thankfulness
Theodoret of Cyrrhus, 194n24
Theodor of Mopsuestia, 189n34
Theology
  federal, 5
  medieval, 48–50
Theophylact, 53, 55–60, 62–64, 71, 75, 84,
    112, 150, 179, 201nn23, 24, 25,
    221n16
Thomas Aquinas. *See* Aquinas, Thomas
Thomists, 38, 49
Thretius, Christoph, 184n4
Titelmans, Francis, 109–112, 114–115,
    117–121, 124–126, 129–130,
    215n20, 216n21, 219n73
Titelmans, Pieter, 111
Tobit, 127
Torrance, Thomas F., 216n23
Tradition. *See also* Exegesis: history of
  authority of, 35–38, 112, 114
  exegetical, 8–9, 11, 26–27, 55, 113, 130,
    178–179, 181–182
Transubstantiation, 113
Tropology. *See* Moral interpretation

Ulrich, Duke of Württemburg, 133
Unbelief, 41, 43–45, 47, 60, 97–99.
  See also Faith: weakness of

Valerius Maximus, 206n1
Valla, Lorenzo, 111, 164, 201n23
Virgil, 206n1, 209n22
Virginity, 16
Vows, monastic, 25–26
Vuilleumier, Henri, 6
Vulgate. *See* New Testament, Latin:
  Vulgate

Wastefulness. *See* Moral interpretation:
  wastefulness
Wealth. *See* Jesus Christ: poverty of;
  Moral interpretation: wealth
Wengert, Timothy J., 207n2, 210n44,
    222n55, 224n6
Westheimer, Bartholomäus, 3, 184n2
Whitgift, John, 5
Wilhelm von Nassau, Landgrave,
    133
Wimpfeling, Jakob, 30
Witcliffites, 112
Wittenberg Concord, 5, 7
Wolfhart, Boniface, 187n33
Worms, Colloquy of, 204n96

Zacharias, 62
Zell, Matthäus, 6
Zigabenus, Euthymius, 201n23
Zofingen Stadtbibliothek, 196n45
Zurich, 7, 148–149, 223n1, 224n11
Zwingli, Ulrich, 8, 86, 148–149, 151–152,
    155, 157–161, 163, 170–171,
    173–176, 223n1
Zwinglians, 7